RETHINKING LEADERSHIP FOR A GREEN WORLD

First James Lovelock, and recently Prince William and David Attenborough believe that we have reached a tipping point in the process of climate change. Whether they are right or not, it is certainly true that the impact of humankind upon the ecology of the earth has reached a point where real changes in human behaviour are required. If managers are to be enablers of planetary survival then we need to develop a new approach to risk, which explicitly includes ecological limits upon economic behaviour. This implies a fundamental reorientation of their role in allocating resources to minimise risk and maximise reward.

This book brings together some of the brightest contemporary thinkers on leadership, complexity and sustainability to consider the big ideas that we will need to make the changes required, and to outline the major themes that can inform a new approach to constructing a green world. It looks at how to ensure that local models of sustainability are able to flourish in the context of global networks and presents specific case studies of markets and organisations that offer insights into the development integrated solutions and the leadership lessons we can learn.

Combining both theory and practice, this book serves to guide business managers and provides deeper insight and critical perspectives on some of the key issues facing leaders moving towards the green economy. It also provides useful supplementary reading for students in business and environmental studies.

Andrew Taylor has won global awards for projects bringing street children and managers together, diversity and environmental policy. He leads Connect CEE and the NGO Transilvania Executive Education. Andrew has a PhD in environmental politics from Cardiff University and has published two co-authored books.

RETHINKING LEADERSHIP FOR A GREEN WORLD

Edited by Andrew Taylor

LONDON AND NEW YORK

Cover image: Bogdan Stefan

First published 2022
by Routledge
4 Park Square, Milton Park, Abingdon, Oxon OX14 4RN

and by Routledge
605 Third Avenue, New York, NY 10158

Routledge is an imprint of the Taylor & Francis Group, an informa business

© 2022 selection and editorial matter, Andrew Taylor; individual chapters, the contributors

The right of Andrew Taylor to be identified as the author of the editorial material, and of the authors for their individual chapters, has been asserted in accordance with sections 77 and 78 of the Copyright, Designs and Patents Act 1988.

All rights reserved. No part of this book may be reprinted or reproduced or utilised in any form or by any electronic, mechanical, or other means, now known or hereafter invented, including photocopying and recording, or in any information storage or retrieval system, without permission in writing from the publishers.

Trademark notice: Product or corporate names may be trademarks or registered trademarks, and are used only for identification and explanation without intent to infringe.

British Library Cataloguing-in-Publication Data
A catalogue record for this book is available from the British Library

Library of Congress Cataloging-in-Publication Data
Names: Taylor, Andrew, 1972- editor.
Title: Rethinking leadership for a green world/edited by Andrew Taylor.
Description: Milton Park, Abingdon, Oxon; New York, NY: Routledge, 2022. |
Includes bibliographical references and index. |
Identifiers: LCCN 2021048654 (print) | LCCN 2021048655 (ebook) |
ISBN 9781032041834 (hardback) | ISBN 9781032041841 (paperback) |
ISBN 9781003190820 (ebook)
Subjects: LCSH: Leadership. | Climatic changes–Social aspects. |
Climatic changes–Political aspects.
Classification: LCC HM1261 .R48 2022 (print) | LCC HM1261 (ebook) |
DDC 303.3/4–dc23/eng/20211012
LC record available at https://lccn.loc.gov/2021048654
LC ebook record available at https://lccn.loc.gov/2021048655

ISBN: 9781032041834 (hbk)
ISBN: 9781032041841 (pbk)
ISBN: 9781003190820 (ebk)

DOI: 10.4324/9781003190820

Typeset in Joanna
by Deanta Global Publishing Services, Chennai, India

I would like to dedicate this book to my daughter, Elena, in the hope that her generation does a better job of looking after the world than mine has.

CONTENTS

	List of contributors	x
	Acknowledgements	xiv
1	**Introduction** Andrew Taylor	1
PART I	**Shaping the leadership challenge**	**11**
2	**Speaking truth to power: the perils of (scientific) leadership in the green economy** David Collins	13
3	**Values and leadership in the Anthropocene** Chris Rose and Pat Dade	40
4	**What can young social entrepreneurs tell us about environmental leadership? Perspectives from Brazil and India** Bharati Singh	69
5	**Frontiers of freedom: US environmental leadership** Heather Crawford and Adam Bronstone	92

viii CONTENTS

6 **The weaponisation of climate change: environmental leadership in the age of Trump** 120
Elesa Zehndorfer

PART II Systems and complexity 143

7 **Complex systems literacy: social dilemmas – the setup for managerial decision-making in a complex world** 145
Ligia Cremene

8 **Green shoots: emergent systemic leadership and critical systems practice** 176
Amanda J. Gregory and Jonathan P. Atkins

9 **Complexity and networks** 190
Yasmin Merali

PART III Looking forward 209

10 **Stewardship and strategy in turbulent times** 211
Andrew Taylor

11 **The 'Undergrowth Movement' and the virtues of leadership** 235
Sr Margaret Atkins

12 **The 'interesting' case of EU Commission leadership and the emission trading scheme** 261
Vanessa Oakes and Adam Bronstone

13 **Reshaping green retail supply chains in a new world order** 282
David B. Grant, Dan-Cristian Dabija and Virva Tuomala

14 **Climate risk and adaptation in Wales: leadership for future generations?** 310
Alan Netherwood and Andrew Flynn

CONTENTS ix

PART IV   Further reading **341**

15 **Bibliometric analysis of management and leadership in the sustainability agenda** **343**
Dr Ashish Dwivedi

16 **Conclusion** **395**

Index 405

CONTRIBUTORS

Jonathan P. Atkins is an economist in the Hull University Business School, UK, with expertise in applied microeconomics, especially in the field of environmental economics of marine and terrestrial environments.

Sr Margaret Atkins is a member of the Community of Augustinian Sisters at Boarbank Hall in Cumbria and a visiting Research Fellow of Blackfriars, Oxford. She studied classics and theology and was Senior lecturer in theology at Trinity and All Saints College, Leeds.

Adam Bronstone works in the non-profit sector in Nashville (USA). He holds a doctorate from the University of Hull in political science and has taught at several universities in the areas of international and domestic politics, including comparative politics.

David Collins is Professor in management at the Newcastle Business School, Northumbria University, and Visiting Professor at the University of the Faroe Islands. A graduate of the Universities of Glasgow, Strathclyde and Essex, David is British by birth and Scottish by the Grace of God.

Heather Crawford has over 30 years' experience in outdoor and experiential learning in the UK. She has lectured in leadership, people development and the history of outdoor education. Her interests include using the outdoors as a development tool for individuals and teams, sustainability, and the psychology of performance.

Ligia Cremene is Tenured Associate Professor at The Technical University of Cluj-Napoca, Romania. She teaches cognitive communications, systems thinking, and academic ethics and integrity. She was awarded the Ericsson Telecommunications Excellence Award in 2006, and the Romanian Academy Award in 2012.

Dan-Cristian Dabija is Professor in the Department of Marketing, Faculty of Economics and Business Administration, Babeș-Bolyai University, Romania. He was awarded first prize in 2017 by the Romanian Association of Economic Faculties and also received the Victor Slăvescu Prize from the Romanian Academy of Science in 2019.

Pat Dade is one of the world's leading experts on psycho-social cultural change. He is a founding director of Cultural Dynamics Strategy and Marketing Ltd. He has been central to running the longest running survey of British values, currently known as The British Values Survey.

Ashish Dwivedi is a member of the Centre for Systems Studies at Hull University Business School, UK. He was the principal investigator for a string of recent funded research projects on Sustainability, Social Enterprise and Agricultural Supply Chains from the British Council and UK–India Education and Research Initiative (UKIERI).

Andrew Flynn is Professor of environmental policy and planning at the University of Cardiff, UK. His research has focused on the changing nature of the local state, the governance of sustainability and standard setting. He has led ESRC-funded research into eco-developments in China and Europe and analysis of well-being, funded by the Office of Future Generations. With a background in policy analysis and environmental geography, his principal research interests are the making and delivery of policy on sustainable development, the implementation of policy and its evaluation.

David B. Grant is Dean of Research and Societal Impact, Hanken School of Economics, Finland, and Bualuang ASEAN Chair Professor, Thammasat University, Thailand. Grant's PhD won the UK's Chartered Institute of

Logistics and Transport James Cooper Memorial Cup PhD Award. He was ranked first in Industrial Economics and Logistics and fifth in Economics, Business and Management in a 2019 study evaluating Finnish professorial research impact and productivity.

Amanda J. Gregory is a senior lecturer in the Hull University Business School, UK. She is the Editor-in-Chief of Systems Research and Behavioral Science, the official journal of the International Federation for Systems Research (IFSR). She has published in a number of high-ranking journals, and her most recent research has focused on stakeholder engagement, citizen science and leadership.

Yasmin Merali is Director of the Centre for Systems Studies at the University of Hull, UK. Her research transcends the natural and human sciences, by drawing on complex systems science to study the resilience of socio-economic systems in the networked world. She is an expert evaluator for the EU, and has received two BT Fellowships and an IBM Faculty Award for her work.

Alan Netherwood is a sustainable development consultant and an Honorary Research Fellow at the School of Geography and Planning in Cardiff University, UK. His work includes advising the UK Climate Change Committee on Welsh perspectives and providing support to public bodies on regional and local climate adaptation and implementation of the Wellbeing of Future Generations Act.

Vanessa Oakes is Course Director for leadership and professional programmes at Staffordshire University, UK. Her research interests lie in leadership and management and leadership development programmes. She is also involved in helping SMEs to implement good leadership practices during challenging times, through the funded projects delivered by Staffordshire Business School.

Chris Rose has directed campaigns for groups such as Greenpeace, WWF International and Friends of the Earth. He is author of *What Makes People Tick: The Three Hidden Worlds of Settlers, Prospectors and Pioneers* (Matador) and *How to Win Campaigns: Communications for Change* (Routledge). He created the first free campaigning help website, www.campaignstrategy.org.

Bharati Singh is a Senior Lecturer with Staffordshire Business School at Staffordshire University, UK. She is also the award leader for the School's MBA and Undergraduate Business Awards. Prior to this, she has worked in corporate, investment and global banking with multinational banks, and in corporate and banking finance with a leading Indian company for 16 years.

Andrew Taylor is the founder of the consulting firm Connect CEE, and leads the not-for-profit foundation Transylvania Executive Education. He has co-authored two books: *Taking Care of Business: Innovation, Ethics & Sustainability* (with W. Krouwel; published by RoPrint) and *People Place & Global Order: Foundations of a Networked Political Economy* (with A. Bronstone; published by Routledge).

Virva Tuomala is a researcher in supply chain management and social responsibility at Hanken School of Economics in Helsinki. Tuomala holds BSc and MSc degrees in logistics from University of Turku, an MSc in environment and development from University College London and a PhD from Hanken. She previously worked for an IT consulting company in Manila, Philippines.

Elesa Zehndorfer is a Research Officer for British Mensa and Visiting Lecturer at the University of Roehampton Business School. She is author of *Leadership: Performance Beyond Expectations* (Routledge); *Evolution, Politics & Charisma: Why do Populists Win?* (Routledge); *Charismatic Leadership* (Routledge); *Emotional & Irrational Investing: Causes & Solutions* (Routledge) and *Leadership: A Critical Introduction* (Routledge).

ACKNOWLEDGEMENTS

My interest in environmental issues was first stirred by my sixth form geography teacher, Mr Parish, and subsequently developed into a lifetime's passion by a university lecturer, who became my PhD supervisor and friend, Professor Andrew Flynn. I am profoundly grateful for their encouragement, support and mentoring. Most importantly for this book, I am grateful to all of the contributors for both believing in the project and taking the time to produce their chapters. Particular thanks must go to both Professor David Collins for his endless encouragement and to Dr Adam Bronstone for helping me out, mocking my failings and giving far more than could be expected from a friend. Thanks also to Bogdan Stefan for his cover design. On behalf of all of the authors, I would like to thank our families for giving us the time to produce this book. Finally, I would like to thank my proofreader, Nancy Rice, without whom my writing would make far less sense!

1

INTRODUCTION

Andrew Taylor

As foreseen by Creswick and Williams (1979) and others, complexity and uncertainty are rising both in our daily lives and in business. In business, many of those accorded guru status, such as Charles Handy (1990, 2002), Henry Mintzberg (1989) and more recently Dave Snowden (2007), are discussing a future with less order and structure, whilst the scientists Jared Diamond (2005) and James Lovelock (2007) have both made strong and well-researched cases for this being a tipping point in human history. As Tett (2016) puts it:

> if you look around the world today, our twenty-first-century society is marked by a striking paradox. In some senses, we live in an age where the globe is more interlinked, as a common system, than ever before. The forces of globalization and technological change mean that news can flash across the planet at lightning speed. Digital supply chains link companies, consumers, and economies across the globe. Ideas— good and bad—spread easily. So do people, pandemics, and panics. When trades turn sour in a tiny corner of the financial markets, the

DOI: 10.4324/9781003190820-1

> global banking system can go topsy-turvy. We live, in short, in a world plagued by what the economist Ian Goldin has dubbed the 'Butterfly Defect': a system that is so tightly integrated that there is an ever-present threat of contagion. 'The world has become a hum of inter-connected voices and a hive of interlinked lives,' as Christine Lagarde, head of the International Monetary Fund, observes. '[This is a] break-neck pattern of integration and interconnectedness that defines our time'.
>
> (Tett 2016, p. 2)

Diamond (2005) concludes that if we, as a species, are to avoid ecological collapse, we must change our way of thinking and challenge our cultural and economic assumptions about life.

The Covid-19 pandemic is an unpleasant, if timely, reminder that we remain a biological component of the earth's ecology and certainly not its master. It is increasingly clear that the Covid-19 pandemic is merely the breaking of a wave of related diseases. SARS, swine flu, Middle East Respiratory Syndrome (MERS), bird flu and Ebola have all emerged as ecological push-back against the treatment of nature as little more than a unit of production (Shiva 2020). It is, of course, not only the rapid spread of disease that indicates that our species is overshooting its resource base (Meadows, Meadows & Jorgen 1992). Climate change, first suggested by James Lovelock (1979, 1988), is now causing changes in weather patterns and events that are materially affecting the way that we live and organ-ise. From warming British summers, which make holidaying at home so much more fun for Londoners, to floods in Europe, melting glaciers in the Himalayas, fires across Australia and California and sinking islands in the Pacific, the evidence is stacking up and becoming tangible to everyone. Plastic pollution of our seas has caused the formation of a dead area in the Pacific covered by a floating plastic island that in 2018 was three times the size of France (ABC News 2018; Liu 2018). Air pollution is a chronic problem across most urban areas. Even in developed countries such as the UK, 70 years after the introduction of legislation to end the great smogs that hung over cities, *The Times* has, throughout 2020, run a '*Clean Air for All*' campaign to do something about the causes and fatal consequences of air pollution in the UK. Even as we continue to discover new forms of life in the deep jungles and oceans, species decline continues at a catastrophic pace (Lewis 2020). The breadth and scale of environmental impact 'signal

INTRODUCTION 3

a fundamentally broken relationship between humans and the natural world' (WWF 2020). Whilst we are busy arguing over the rules of trade that increasingly define power in the world, the environmental foundation of that power is being eroded; and we cannot argue that this is taking place unconsciously. We are like passengers on the Titanic struggling and bickering over access to the first-class deck whilst the ship is sinking. If it were not so serious it would be laughable.

Our attempts to organise the world along nice, neat lines of cause and effect have been over-simplistic, reductionist and naive. The world is far more complex than economists' minds and, as Oliver James (2007) notes, so are people. Whilst business process re-engineering, with its neat flow diagrams and cost-cutting, may deliver economic efficiency, it has done so at the expense of ecological resilience. Trying to stuff all of the world's ecology into the concept of economics has simply failed (McBurney 1990). The world will function perfectly well without economics, but economics cannot function without ecology. In fact, as Lovelock (1979, 1988) has pointed out, Gaia (the name he gave to the earth's self-adjusting ecology) is indifferent about whether humans walk the earth at all. It is the consequences of their actions that leave scars on the earth that are far more damaging and concerning than their presence (1988).

If managers, as the controllers of much of the world's resources (Senge et al. 2008; Doppelt 2008), are to be enablers of planetary survival then we need to develop a new approach to risk and value creation, one which explicitly includes ecological limits upon economic behaviour. This implies a fundamental reorientation of their role in defining risk and reward. One of the arguments of this book is that we need to shift away from the simplistic cause-and-effect view of the world that has grown out of utilitarian modernism and its focus upon economics as the basis of value. It requires no less than a shift away from the anthropocentric world view that has characterised the post-enlightenment era (Dobson 1990), to a more eco-centric model of organisation that roots humans within ecological systems and embraces their complexity, not just as metaphors, but as models of organisational design. As Diamond (2005) puts it 'a lower impact society is the most impossible scenario for our future except for all other conceivable scenarios'.

This book seeks to look at the challenges of providing leadership at a time when ecological feedback loops, such as climate change, species decline, extreme weather and virus pandemics are conflating globally and being experienced increasingly directly. This book uses case studies to explore the challenges of addressing environmental change individually in terms of values, systems and practicalities and it brings together some of the brightest contemporary thinkers on leadership, systems thinking, complexity and sustainability in order to:

- First, consider the big ideas that have informed the discussion of environmental leadership;
- Second, think about the relationships between people and values and the ideas and practice that have got us to where we are today;
- Third, define and explore those relationships as complex systems and as a key component of going beyond a best practices approach to leadership;
- Fourth, consider whether local models of sustainability are able to flourish in the context of global networks and specific case studies of markets and organisations that offer insights into the development of integrated solutions and the leadership lessons we can learn.

Chapter 2: David Collins reveals the importance of narratives and sense-making that flows from storytelling for leaders of all types. Specifically, he reveals, through case studies, the parallels between counter narratives told by big tobacco and climate change deniers. Both are shown, for example, to fund sympathetic research and to demand, on the grounds of balance, that their counter narrative is heard. The impact upon the debate, the individual scientists and the organisations that they work for is captured through the case studies which not only reveal the risks that must be taken to reputations, but also underlines the importance of controlling the narrative and its presentation, which is as important to the leadership of environmental challenges as the facts themselves.

    Chapter 3: Chris Rose and Pat Dade use their model of motivational states to provide a structured approach to understanding how, why and when different groups of people are motivated to engage with issues. In so doing they reveal how and why Brexit leaders outmanoeuvred their opponents and, after reading David Collins and Elesa Zehndorfer's chapters, it is not hard to see how effective use of this knowledge has enabled Trump and other climate change deniers to ensure their continued relevance.

Furthermore, they reveal the importance of leaders understanding which group they are talking to, when to do so and how to engage if environmental change is to be delivered and with the guidelines for doing so.

Chapter 4: Bharati Singh defines environmental leadership as distinct from both leadership and activism. This is key if we are to develop models and practices that go beyond both business as usual and describing problems rather than developing solutions. Importantly, such a model explicitly makes space for a profit motive, but it positions commercial behaviour as valuable to the extent that it is able to reduce environmental impact and create positive ecological feedback loops. Discussion of two young leaders endeavouring to sustain and drive forward business organisations provides both insights and practical substance to the chapter and the wider issues raised within this volume.

Chapter 5: Heather Crawford and Adam Bronstone explore the tensions between economics and environment in America that define the iconic idea of the West (and the wilderness that it represents), which lies at the heart of American culture. They show, through specific examples, the conflict between a political system driven by money that is often constrained by business and the global thought leadership that has emerged through writers, musicians and protest groups. The chapter seeks to capture both how united America is in its attachment to its natural environment as a cultural icon and how, simultaneously, it is so divided on ideas of how to engage with it socially and economically. It is pulled between populations on the coasts which seek to protect and those in the middle that seek jobs, the artists who seek inspiration and business that seeks to exploit. America's status as both a global power and as the leading emitter of greenhouse gases positions these debates on the global stage, with consequences for us all.

Chapter 6: Elesa Zehndorfer explores how climate change denial, which formed a cornerstone of President Donald Trump's term in office, was combined with development of charismatic authority (Weber, 1968) as a form of leadership. The case study allows a closer look at the phenomenon of how, and why, charismatic populist political leaders tend to rely on the denigration and demonisation of climate change scientists and other intellectuals as a central part of their political strategy. In so doing, the author provides clear insights into how the leadership of climate change denial has connected with its base to form an almost cult-like devotion.

Chapter 7: Ligia Cremene introduces the reader to systems thinking complexity and the relationship to feedback loops and the externalities that they drive. She shows how a continued reliance upon linear deterministic systems is wreaking ecological havoc and how it is increasingly irrelevant economically in a networked digital world. The author demonstrates how effective leadership of both contemporary economic and ecological change requires us to learn new tools to identify and channel emergence, rather than apply predictable best practice. In so doing she provides a toolkit for leaders to focus upon feedback loops as the source of both future sustainability and value creation.

Chapter 8: Personified by Greta Thunberg, Amanda Gregory and Jonathan Atkins explore the explosion of interest in climate change by young people. The emergence of these young leaders and the issues that they are addressing are not easily explained by traditional theories of leadership. The nature of complex problems is that they are systemic in nature and, as we see with the pandemic, do not respond in predictable, linear ways to robust action. Complex systems require leadership that is defined in systemic terms. Traditional theories do not adequately differentiate between leadership and authority, thus the authors propose Critical Systems Practice as a way to enable emergent leaders to structure their instinctive systemic response to wicked problems.

Chapter 9: Yasmin Merali adopts an interdisciplinary approach to understanding complex ecosystems outlining what makes them resilient and sustainable as well as the extent to which their stability is threatened by climate change and human activity. Drawing upon the science of Complex Adaptive Systems, she highlights the intersectionality of social, economic and environmental networks, and how, if we are to develop more ecocentric ways of being, we need to reset cognitive constructs by using a model of network-based organisation.

Chapter 10: Andrew Taylor argues that, for leadership to make a meaningful contribution to questions of sustainability, leaders need to rediscover a sense of duty and not only entitlements. For too long capitalism has been rooted in a twisted version of utilitarianism that is destroying the planet and leaving ever more people behind. The amoral algorithms of the digital economy are, through the global search for lowest cost, only multiplying such problems. He claims that it needs to be replaced by a contemporary stewardship that is grounded in virtue ethics. Examples of using global networks to invest in and to support and sustain social and ecological capital within local networks are shown to both offer a different future and to be grounded in a philanthropic past that has always defined capitalism as a means and not an end.

Chapter 11: Margaret Atkins seeks to question distant and centralised models of technocratic power and control, which are outcome-oriented. She argues that such logic has caused us to forget the connected nature of people and planet. Loss of connection flowing from economies of scale not only separates people from the consequences of their actions, but it also denies them any sense of agency to do anything about problems that seem to be beyond their control. She positions people and organisations that are challenging modernist logic as drawing upon an ethic of virtue in what she calls the Undergrowth Movement. She emphasises the importance of small, but systemic, local actions, such as the Transition Towns Movement, and describes how governance and leadership should look less like a jelly mould, constraining us, but act more like a trellis, enabling us to grow from the bottom up.

Chapter 12: Vanessa Oakes and Adam Bronstone examine the emergence of the EU Emission Trading System (EU ETS), the factors that motivated its formation and the wider role of the EU in providing environmental leadership. This is interesting for at least three reasons. First, the EU is a major global lawmaker and, as such, has a significant impact upon how human relations with environmental resources are constructed. EU ETS remains a pioneering use of market mechanisms to embrace the underlying complexity of feedback loops between economic decisions and environmental outcomes. Second, as a large bureaucracy, the EU embodies both the opportunities and challenges facing many multinational organisations. Third, the relationships between individual leaders and European citizens provides wider insights into the leadership questions facing other individuals, organisations and societies.

Chapter 13: David Grant, Dan-Cristian Dabija and Virva Tuomala argue that neo-liberal efficiency-driven supply chains are increasingly unsustainable, both economically and ecologically. The waste produced by single-use plastics, fast fashion and the carbon cost of global supply chains are clearly unsustainable from any environmental perspective. The social cost of global networks' ability to seek out the lowest possible costs on the planet is clearly leaving many behind and driving inequality within and between societies. The rise of e-commerce has both globalised consumption and its associated externalities and continues to fail to address growing demand for greener consumption. Increasingly consumers are looking beyond products to think about the total impact of production and supply. And whilst technology hubs, like Amazon and eBay, have proven highly capable of delivering efficient robustness, they have a poor record of developing either internal resilience or aiding the resilience of people and place. The authors show how their model of reducing purchasing to a purely transactional experience looks increasingly out of touch with both shifts in consumer demand and the social and ecological needs of people and planet.

Chapter 14: Whilst much of the work on leadership is concentrated on business organisations, Alan Netherwood and Andrew Flynn examine the challenges of climate risk and adaptation to public administrations in Wales. Through examination of a series of case studies, they reveal how climate change planning is focused upon problems of the here and now. Presenting a model for identifying risks for different people according to their generational needs and informed by identifying the need for more systemic and self-critical leadership, they show why managing risks and adaptation have been largely absent from debates and how a more reflexive style of leadership is likely to deliver superior outcomes.

Chapter 15: Ashish Dwivedi uses bibliographic analysis to explore and map the growth of research interest in questions of business sustainability, the most-cited authors and the journals that have the most impact. In so doing we hope to reveal the remarkable interest in what are quickly becoming the defining questions of contemporary leadership. Furthermore, we hope that this will provide a useful academic foundation to aid the reader in identifying further reading.

References

ABC News (2018), 'Great Pacific Garbage Patch' is massive floating island of plastic, now three times the size of France'. 23 March 2018.

Creswick C. and Williams R. (1979), *Using the Outdoors for Management Development and Team Building*. Gloucester: Food, Drink and Tobacco Industrial Training Board.

Diamond J. (2005), *Collapse: How Societies Choose to Fail or Survive*. London: Penguin.

Dobson A. (1990), *Green Political Thought*. London: HarperCollins.

Doppelt B. (2008), *The Power of Sustainable Thinking*. London: Earthscan.

Handy C. (1990), *The Age of Unreason*. London: Arrow.

Handy C. (2002), *The Elephant and The Flea: New Thinking for A New World*. New York: Random House.

James O. (2007), *Affluenza*. London: Vermillion.

Lewis S. (2020), 'Animal populations worldwide have declined nearly 70% in just 50 years, new report says'. CBSNews, Sept. 10th, posted at 9.00 pm.

Liu M. (2018), 'Great Pacific Garbage Patch now three times the size of France'. *CNN*, 23 March.

Lovelock J. (1979), *Gaia: A New Look at Life on Earth*. Oxford: Oxford University Press.

Lovelock J. (1988), *The Ages of Gaia: A Biography of our Living Earth*. Oxford: Oxford University Press.

Lovelock J. (2007), *The Revenge of Gaia*. London: Penguin.

McBurney S. (1990), *Ecology into Economics Won't Go: Or Life is Not a Concept*. Bideford Devon, UK: Green Books.

Meadows D. H., Meadows D. L., and Jorgen R. (1992), *Beyond the Limits: Global Collapse or a Sustainable Future*. London: Earthscan.

Mintzberg, H. (1989), *Mintzberg on Management: Inside Our Strange World of Organizations*. New York: The Free Press.

Senge P., Smith B., Kruschwitz N., Laur J., and Schley S. (2008), *The Necessary Revolution: How Individuals and Organizations Are Working Together to Create a Sustainable World*. New York: Doubleday.

Shiva V. (2020), 'One planet: One health'. *Resurgence & Ecologist*, Issue 321, May/June.

Snowden D. and Boone M. E. (2007), 'A leader's framework for decision making', *Harvard Business Review*, November 2007.

Tett G. (2016), *The Silo Effect: The Peril of Expertise and the Promise of Breaking Down Barriers*. London: Simon & Schuster.

WWF (2020), *Living Planet Report 2020*. (Available at: https://livingplanet .panda.org/en-us/ and accessed 28 February 2021.)

Part I

SHAPING THE LEADERSHIP CHALLENGE

2

SPEAKING TRUTH TO POWER

THE PERILS OF (SCIENTIFIC) LEADERSHIP IN THE GREEN ECONOMY

David Collins

Introduction

This chapter offers a case study on the perils that await those who would shape our understanding of two scientific facts:

1. The earth's climate is changing;
2. The climate change which has been recorded and which we are now experiencing is anthropogenic in nature.

Contemporary understanding of the problems of management and the processes of leadership has been shaped by analyses which suggest that 'leaders' are 'world builders' (Latour, 1987); architects of 'moral economies' (Watson, 2001) who must build upon the skills of the storyteller in order to secure their strategic aspirations (see Fairhurst and Sarr, 1996; Collins, 2018). Such narrative accounts of leadership, while broadly persuasive, however, remain truncated and potentially misleading because, too often, they reduce storytelling to the simple transfer of information

DOI: 10.4324/9781003190820-3

within contexts which are assumed to be politically benign. Challenging this account of leadership, I offer an alternative account of organisational storytelling, designed to reveal, so that we might pursue, the political agendas that mark our organised existence.

To this end I offer a case study of a scandal. This scandal, as we shall see, developed in November 2009 following the disclosure of information from the Climatic Research Unit (CRU) based at the University of East Anglia (UEA). Framing this sad tale[1] within a historical context, I will argue that this controversy is but the latest in a long line of manufactured scandals. Indeed, I will argue that the processes at work in 'Climategate'[2] (Pearce, 2010) are similar to those previously invoked to allow corporations first to deny scientific knowledge and later to delay action in the face of the developing scientific consensus on the harm caused by tobacco smoke.

I will show that 'Climategate' is, in effect, a re-run of what has come to be known as 'the tobacco strategy' (Oreskes and Conway, 2010), albeit with new and troubling refinements. Thus I will argue that while the 'Climategate' scandal has its roots in the tobacco strategy, it differs from this in two key respects: firstly, Climategate commenced with a criminal act. And it was, secondly, built upon a brazen attempt to crush the professional reputation and, indeed, the social standing of leading and highly respected members of the scientific academy. These developments within the tobacco strategy, I will suggest, prompt further reflection on the narrative processes that shape social organisation and, what is more, demand a deeper appreciation of the perils that await those who would offer (scientific) leadership in the green economy.

Narratives, stories and leadership

Grant et al. (2004: 1) note that the business of management and the processes of leadership have, increasingly, been rendered in discursive terms. They concede, however, that this growing interest in all things narrative 'appears to have been achieved through the widespread use of broad, non-specific definitions [of discourse] and a bewildering array of methods, approaches and perspectives'. In an attempt to bring some structure to this arena, Grant et al. suggest that the field might be subdivided to acknowledge the overlapping, yet nonetheless distinctive, contributions of those who have analysed organisation discursively. Thus the authors observe that students of organisational discourse may pursue their concerns by exploring:

- Conversation and dialogue;
- Narratives and stories;
- Rhetorics;
- Tropes.

This chapter, while noting the potential for overlap, will focus upon narratives and stories.

Reflecting upon the roots of the current interest in narratives and stories, Gabriel (1995; 1998; 2000; 2004) reminds us that contemporary interest in storytelling derives from earlier attempts to harvest and to catalogue folklore, and yet departs from this tradition insofar as it insists that organisational stories have meaning and significance only when they are acknowledged to be, in any sense, vital constituents of social organisation. In this respect the interpretative studies of organisational storytelling, preferred by Gabriel and by contemporaries such as Boje (1991; 2001) and Czarniawska (1997; 1999), represent attempts to redeem stories from those traditions of modernist scholarship which suggest that such narratives are secondary to social organisation and subordinate to social facts.

Yet a review of the literature on organisational storytelling quickly reveals that a shared interest in interpretative methods of inquiry seems to be about all that unites the key commentaries in this arena. Indeed, the literature on stories in, at and of work appears to have grown in the absence of any meaningful consensus as to the essential nature of these tales (see Collins, 2007; 2018; 2021a; 2021b).

Sensegiving stories and sensemaking tales

The debate on the problems and practices of organisational storytelling might be articulated in a number of different ways. Here I will explore the (unacknowledged) politics of storytelling through an analysis of the distinction that may be drawn between sensegiving (Gioia and Chittepeddi, 1991) and sensemaking perspectives (Weick, 1995).

The sensegiving side of this debate reveals itself within the 'popular management' texts prepared, for example, by Tom Peters (Peters and

Waterman, 1982; Peters and Austin, 1985) and his contemporaries (see, for example, Deal and Kennedy, 1982; 1999; Pascale and Athos, [1981] 1986). These texts exhibit, and are often defined in terms of, their common lexical and grammatical characteristics (see Pagel and Westerfelhaus, 1999; 2005; Rüling, 2005). It is, of course, accurate to suggest that popular management texts trade in imperatives and utilise simple sentences and a limited vocabulary. Yet this grammatical focus can obscure the extent to which the snappy sentences of popular management actually depend upon the articulation of core rhetorics (see Huczynski, 1993; Kieser, 1997; Collins 2021a), which suggest that management is a force for good and that leaders are heroic individuals, uniquely charged with the destiny of others.

Sensegiving accounts of organisational storytelling build upon this rhetorical formulation. They suggest that leaders *should* use stories to communicate their heightened understanding of organisational problems to others who lack the benefit of this world-view. This act of sensegiving *for and in the name of others*, it is assumed, involves a transfer of information between those who know and understand 'the issues' and those who struggle under either an information deficit or the psychological inability to face reality (see Collins, 1998).

Yet this *Olympian* presumption tends to obscure the extent to which sensegiving accounts straddle or, perhaps more truthfully, lurch between contrasting and somewhat contradictory perspectives (Collins, 1998). Thus the sensegiving approach assumes the operation of a simplistic unitary account of social organisation (Fox, 1985) – which asserts that organisations are naturally united, harmonious and so driven by a common purpose – *and yet must call upon* a benignly pluralistic reading of management (Clegg, 1975; Fox, 1985) – which concedes that active and on-going managerial intervention will be required to manufacture the natural consensus that is elsewhere assumed to be the organisation's normal state. Viewed from a sensegiving perspective, therefore, stories are informational resources; supplements to an otherwise technical world that managers use *on others* to secure the emotional commitment to change agendas which they, uniquely, know to be necessary. Yet, despite the desire to portray management and managers as *Masters of the Universe* (Wolfe, 1987), it is clear that our 'leaders' are 'satisficers'; *Bargained Olympians* who are obliged to call upon emotional projections and the techniques of seduction in order to achieve what would be, in a wholly rational world, the simple transfer of facts and information.

SPEAKING TRUTH TO POWER 17

Over the border, on the sensemaking side of this debate, things look rather different. Here contributors such as Boje (1991) and Gabriel (2000) insist that it would be foolhardy to regard stories as simple tools for the advancement of technically necessary goals. Instead those inclined to a sensemaking perspective utilise a more political reading of management and of the dynamics of social organisation. Thus Gabriel and Boje protest that organisational stories are, in truth, products of organisational difference, division and, indeed, dissent. Where advocates for 'sensegiving' view stories as a means to transfer information to those denied 'the bigger picture', supporters of 'sensemaking' suggest that the tales we tell others, and indeed ourselves (see Sims, 2003; Taylor, 2019: 9)[3] reflect and express the enduring material differences which shape our consciousness. On the sensemaking side of the storytelling debate, therefore, organisational tales are viewed as narrative resources that individuals use to bring shape and meaning to their own lives. In this regard the function of stories is not so much to enable top-down change as to allow individuals to enact (Weick, 1995) scenarios that can explain and account for the ambiguities and conflicts that make daily life a series of dilemmas. Challenging the narrowly managerialist agenda advanced by the sensegiving account of storytelling, therefore, a sensemaking perspective would tend to suggest that, at the organisational apex, stories represent an attempt to reduce (often through simple obfuscation and/or misdirection) the enduring tensions that shape social organisation whereas, from the bottom up, organisational stories offer counter-cultural strategies of opposition; 'weapons of the weak' (Scott, 1990) in an on-going struggle for meaning and identity.

The sensegiving narratives developed in and through 'popular management', of course, claim utility through their 'practical' orientation – that is why they, so often, disavow 'theory' (Collins, 1998). Yet this claimed, practical application is bogus because the narratives developed in and through popular management fail to address, in any meaningful sense, the contexts, conflicts and controversies that managerial leaders might expect to encounter in their daily lives (Collins, 1998; 2000). Conversely, sensemaking accounts of organisational storytelling are clearly 'political' *and* 'theoretical' insofar as they seek to account for the tensions that shape social organisation. Yet these organisational (counter)narratives often remain aloof from the problems of managing; refusing fully to address the terms of the compromise necessary for the regulation of conflict and, indeed, for the maintenance of employment concerns. From time to time, however, the worlds that are separated by the sensegiving and sensemaking accounts of storytelling do collide. For example, Collins and Rainwater (2005) offer a review of the 'turnaround of Sears Roebuck and Company' which, in demonstrating the fragmentary nature of organised narratives, is designed to challenge the accounts of this organisation that have been popularised by *Harvard Business Review* and by *Sloan Management Review*. In a similar fashion, Boje (1998) has attempted to challenge the tales that *Nike* tells of itself. Noting that *Nike* has attempted to portray itself as the bringer of opportunity and economic development, Boje offers an alternative tale of *Nike*'s conduct which casts the corporation as a predator, systematically despoiling the planet. Boje's re-storying initiative is, of course, interesting and well-intentioned, yet it remains limited as an expression of corporate politics because it represents but a single turn in a game in which corporate interests have chosen, simply, to 'play on through'.[4] Recent accounts of *Amazon* offer a clear example of this process and approach.

Calling Amazon to account

Over the past few years a number of journalists (see Bonazzo, 2018; Sainato, 2019a; 2019b) have drawn our attention to the insecure employment practices which many of the employees of *Amazon* must now endure. These practices, it is claimed, force employees to present themselves for work even when they are seriously unwell or otherwise unfit. Indeed, it has been suggested that ambulances are now routinely called to *Amazon*'s British warehouses to address, for example, the needs of pregnant women who feel pressured to continue to work, literally, until the birth of their newborn infants.

These narratives of the realities of working for *Amazon* are alarming and have rightly led to public outcry. *Amazon* has, perhaps unsurprisingly, felt obliged to respond. Yet rather than address their critics directly, the corporation has embarked upon a Public Relations campaign, which includes television advertising. This advertising campaign encourages the general public to take a tour of *Amazon*'s facilities while constructing a new storyworld designed to account for the corporation's employment policies. This storyworld, we should note, is populated by happy workers who, on camera at least, confide that they (a) like working for *Amazon* because they (b) value the personal flexibility that accompanies their (precarious) employment. In short, *Amazon* has, in effect, shifted the story and re-defined the core issue, simply, by refusing a direct engagement with critics and opponents.

As clever and privileged people we may choose to mock the rhetoric that enables *Amazon*'s PR,[5] but pause for a minute to imagine a world where corporations choose to respond to critical voices by launching counter-narratives which target both the message and the messenger. Imagine a world where the projection of your sensemaking leads to attacks on your character and identity. Imagine a world, for example, wherein your own painstaking attempts to construct a narrative of anthropogenic climate change leads to the development and widespread circulation of an entirely bogus counter-narrative which suggests that you are professionally incompetent; a liar who has no legitimate place in 'the academy'; a fraud who deserves to be dismissed from their employment.[6]

This imagined world is, of course, hateful, hate-filled and contrary to any reasonable or reasoned engagement. That is probably why *Amazon* has chosen the 'high ground' in its re-storying endeavour. The bad news, however, is that this is the storyworld of 'Climategate'; this is the narrative strategy that underpins climate change denial. And it is this narrative strategy which demonstrates that our understanding of the dynamics of leadership in the green economy is naïve and in need of urgent revision. Yet to understand the storyworld of the climate contrarians, and, to a lesser extent, the climate change sceptics,[7] we must first consider the tobacco strategy.

Climategate and tobacco strategy
The tobacco strategy

In 2006 US District Judge, Gladys Kessler ruled that the tobacco industry had breached the Racketeer Influenced and Corrupt Organizations (RICO) Act. The tobacco industry, Judge Kessler ruled, had been aware of the dangers of smoking as early as 1953 but had 'developed and executed a scheme to defraud consumers and potential consumers about the hazards of cigarettes' (Oreskes and Conway, 2010: 32).

How has this long-term fraud been achieved? Oreskes and Conway tell us that it is, at root, a narrative achievement; a story. The tobacco industry, Oreskes and Conway (2010: 33) observe, cultivated a narrative strategy designed 'to merchandise doubt' on the emerging medical-scientific consensus on the hazards posed by cigarette smoke. This strategy, Oreskes and Conway (2010: 14) observe, developed and was successful over a 50-year period. Indeed they note that, between 1954 and 1979, the US courts had considered 117 cases against the tobacco industry, yet 'no plaintiff … ever collected a penny from any tobacco company in lawsuits claiming that smoking causes lung cancer or cardiovascular illness'.

Exploring the general processes associated with what has come to be known as the tobacco strategy, Oreskes and Conway (2010) suggest that the tobacco industry developed a strategy of 'defence in depth'[8] designed to maintain the pretence that the science which had developed to consider the harm associated with cigarette smoke remained incomplete *and* unconfirmed. This strategy, which built upon a number of adaptive, tactical endeavours, included:

- Challenging the statistical linkage which had been demonstrated between smoking and lung cancer, in part by suggesting alternative hypotheses. For example, scientists have observed that only some smokers contract lung cancer. Given this, the tobacco industry developed a tactic designed to popularise alternative hypotheses. The industry promoted, for example, C. C. Little's work on genetics to suggest that lung cancer *might* be caused by a genetic weakness which would simply predispose some individuals to this disease (Oreskes and Conway 2010: 17).
- Using the ethics of good scientific practice to place 'negative salients' (Latour, 1987) in the knowledge claims advanced by science. To understand the potency of this defensive strategy it is, of course, important that we understand that science does not 'prove' things. Rather, science proceeds on the basis of 'falsification'. In other words, scientists work, primarily, to disprove things, and since our knowledge is always by definition incomplete (*we cannot know what we do not know*) no good scientist would ever claim, definitively, to have proved something. Instead scientists will suggest that they are, for example, '90% confident' that the link observed between x and y is statistically significant and could not have emerged by chance. Yet this observation is, for the lay-person and for the opportunistic legal counsel alike, something that may be spun as a failure to prove a link between x and y. So whenever a new scientific study suggested a link between exposure to tobacco and hazards

to health, the industry would simply respond that no causative link had been definitively established. *Not guilty, your honour!*

- Funding research which it was hoped would advance the suggestion that cancer had either (a) a single root cause other than tobacco smoke, or (b) simply too many environmental causes to allow tobacco to be singled out as the primary problem. Between the mid-1950s (when industry insiders accepted, in private, that there was a clear link between tobacco smoke and hazards to health) and 1979 the tobacco industry distributed grants to the value of $43.4 million to conduct scientific research. These grants were, publicly at least, targeted at those forms of inquiry that promised innovative forms of research. For example, the tobacco industry-funded research designed to explore links between ill-health and state-of-mind. Research in this vein is, of course, innovative and may someday prove worthwhile. However, the fact that the industry had privately conceded the link between cancer and ill-health, and the fact that the individual in charge of grant allocation was obliged to work closely with the legal counsel retained by the tobacco industry, and had to approve all press releases with the legal department (Oreskes and Conway, 2010: 29), suggests that there was something at stake here beyond the pursuit of knowledge. That something was, of course, the manufacture of doubt as regards the hazard to health posed by tobacco smoke!

- Demanding that broadcasters honour their statutory commitment to 'balanced coverage' by allowing industry representatives the right to challenge the scientists and to speak for tobacco on their programmes. These engagements, we should note, allowed spokesmen for the tobacco industry to pose rhetorical questions designed to suggest that the science associated with the harm caused by tobacco smoke remained ill-formed and incomplete. Oreskes and Conway (2010) do concede that many of the questions which were raised by the industry representatives — *why is the lung cancer rate among women lower than that experienced by men?* — were legitimate subjects for inquiry (that is in part why they were effective as rhetorical projections). But the scientists had already addressed these questions: male lung cancers had been, until the 1930s, rare because lung cancers tend to occur some time after the habit of smoking has been acquired. The lung cancers diagnosed among men in the 1930s had developed in response to the widespread distribution of cigarettes to troops during World War I. Women began smoking *en masse* later than men. Lung cancers in women would (and did) emerge in time. The scientists knew this, as did the tobacco industry. But raising this question and others like it (see Oreskes and Conway, 2010: 18 for a list of smokescreen questions) was sufficient to manufacture and to maintain, in the minds of the public, a bogus complacency on the hazards present in tobacco smoke.[9]

- Funding polling organisations to conduct social research that might allow the tobacco industry to understand more fully the sentiments of their consumers and their understanding of the scientific controversy which they were stage-managing. This polling, of course, enabled the industry to target and to refine those communication channels that would merchandise doubt more successfully.

- Disseminating the results of their sponsored scientific and PR endeavours to a broad public and in a fashion that would continue to suggest that there remained no clear link between smoking and ill-health. This activity we should note included newspaper articles; advertisements aimed at the general public and publications prepared for medical physicians and dentists.

- Seeking to suggest common cause with other business endeavours, such as the alcohol and gambling industries which were fearful of increased regulation in the hope that a broad coalition of opposition might be developed.

- Conflating issues so that regulation designed to limit smoking in particular places – within aeroplanes, for example – might be portrayed as a constitutional infringement on individual liberty; the first step on a slippery slope to state control. And if this sounds just a little strong it might be useful to remind ourselves that, in Britain, the grass-roots,[10] but industry-funded pro-tobacco lobby was known as FOREST: the 'freedom organization for the right to enjoy smoking tobacco'!

The tobacco strategy, Oreskes and Conway (2010) note, has proved to be effective over the long term. Indeed, this strategy continues to work, albeit in a modified form today,[11] and has been adopted by those who would challenge the scientific research that has been developed to explore damage to the ozone layer; the risks posed by acid rain; the climatic perils posed by nuclear war; and the anthropogenic causes of our warming climate. Yet as we reflect upon 'Climategate', we shall see that the tobacco strategy has developed new and alarming innovations which now make scientific leadership in the green economy a very risky endeavour indeed.

The origins of Climategate

The Climategate story broke on 17 Friday November 2009, when more than 1,000 email messages, a range of documents and a number of data sets were leaked by hackers. We could begin our Climategate narrative at this point. This moment plainly offers a very dramatic opening for a narrative endeavour. It is, after all, the event which precipitated no fewer than eight inquiries (conducted on both sides of the Atlantic) plus a police investigation in the UK.

The inquiries

The University of East Anglia commissioned two internal inquiries to address the issues raised by Climategate. The first of these, chaired by Muir Russell, set aside scientific considerations to examine the 'integrity' of the CRU.[12] The second internal review, led by Lord Oxburgh, however, took a different tack and was convened to reappraise the scientific work undertaken by Jones and his colleagues (see Pearce, 2010). In addition a parliamentary inquiry (House of Commons Science and Technology Committee, 2010) was convened to consider the leak and the claims that had emerged in its aftermath. This inquiry, we should note, considered the reviews undertaken on behalf of UEA. In addition it took evidence from Jones and from other leading scientists. The parliamentary inquiry, it is worth observing, also took testimony[13] from a range of climate change sceptics and contrarians. Britain's Information Commissioner also convened an inquiry to establish the extent to which UEA had upheld its obligations under the Freedom of Information Act.

A number of parallel inquiries also commenced in the US around this time (see Pearce, 2010). Penn State University, for example, launched an inquiry into the activities of Professor Mike Mann (whose work had featured prominently in the IPCC) and who had been a regular correspondent of Jones. The Office of the Inspector General of the National Science Foundation, we should note, also convened an investigation into the conduct of Professor Mann.

Responding to concerns raised by Senator Infhoe (a renowned climate change contrarian), the Inspector General of the US Department of Commerce launched its own inquiry. In addition, the Environmental Protection Agency – responding to petitions lodged by the Chambers of Commerce (amongst other business lobbies) – launched its own review.

Setting aside this avalanche of inquiries, it is worth pointing out that 17 November 2019 has an additional claim to represent a useful starting point for our cautionary tale on scientific leadership in the green economy because this is the moment at which Professor Phil Jones, Head of the Climate Research Unit (and to a lesser extent his colleague from Penn State, Professor Michael Mann), surrendered his private life and, soon after, began to contemplate suicide (see Pearce, 2010: 3).

Yet there are good reasons to reject this date as our 'once upon a time' moment. The choice as to the opening moment of a tale is always in some sense arbitrary (Collins, 2018). We retain some discretion therefore as to the point at which we introduce our tale to the world. Indeed, we should concede that, in the stories we tell, the openings we choose are, in truth, always moments in *the middle of something else* (see Collins, 2021b) and will depend upon some level of contextualisation to secure an appropriate conclusion (and narrative effect).

Dickens [1841] (1922: 2–3) captures this rather well. He observes, for example, that Shakespeare's *Hamlet* works as a narrative only if we understand that we are about to enter a storyworld that is populated by spirits and ghostly apparitions. Indeed, Dickens himself concedes that the failure to achieve this literary contextualisation would make *Hamlet*'s tale bland and mundane:

> If we were not perfectly convinced that Hamlet's father died before the play began, there would be nothing more remarkable in his taking a stroll at night, in an easterly wind, upon his own ramparts than there would be in any middle-aged man rashly turning out after dark in a breezy spot – say Saint Paul's Churchyard for instance – literally to astonish his son's weak mind.

Our tale of Climategate does not deal with a spirit-world nor does it contain ghostly apparitions. It does, however, deal with fantastical notions and it will require significant contextualisation if we are to understand the perils of scientific leadership. Thus while our rendering of the Climategate *could* begin in late 2009 we choose to begin our story at an earlier point in history. But how far back beyond 2009 do we have to reach in order to tell our tale?

Once upon a time: Climategate

We *could* announce our 'once upon a time' in 1990 because it was at this date that the Intergovernmental Panel on Climate Change (IPCC) produced its first assessment of the science of climate change. Equally, we *could* commence our tale in 1995 because it was in this year that the second IPCC assessment deemed that, on the balance of evidence, human impact upon the climate was 'discernible' (see Oreskes and Conway, 2010: 205). Of course, some might suggest that we *should* begin the tale of Climategate in 2001 because it was in this year that the IPCC's third assessment report observed that the evidence to support anthropogenic climate change was strong and getting stronger. Although some might suggest that the roots of Climategate and the real fight against science are to be found in 2007, because it was in this year that the IPCC's fourth assessment directly challenged the climate contrarians when it announced that the evidence for (hu)man-made climate change was unequivocal.

Each of these points on the calendar has a legitimate claim to represent our 'once upon a time moment'. But we will choose another point in time. We choose 1982 and the report of the Acid Rain Peer Review Panel, for it is at this moment that we can truly discern (a) clear political interference in the scientific peer review process, and (b) the introduction to the official transcript (Scott, 1990) of expertise from beyond the natural science community.

Acid rain

Scientists have long been aware of 'acid rain'. Prior to its observation in the North Eastern US, for example, it had been observed in 'industrial' areas such as the Ruhr valley of Germany and in England's North West.

In 1963 Herbert Bormann and his colleagues identified acid rain falling in parts of the US which were unlike the Ruhr valley, for example, some distance from 'industrial areas'. In 1974 a follow-up study revealed that acid rain, causing damage to buildings and wildlife (including a reduction in fish stocks); the acidification of rivers and lakes; and the leaching of nutrients from the soil was falling on most of the North Eastern US. By 1979 further scientific study had established – unequivocally – that the cause of acid rain was due to the release of sulphur and nitrogen into the upper atmosphere and that the principal cause was the burning of fossil fuels. In response President Carter's administration took steps to assess, further, the impact of this pollutant while developing institutional arrangements to manage its cross-border effects. In 1982, therefore, the US Government convened a panel drawn largely from the National Academy of Sciences and from the National Academy of Engineering to review the work undertaken by those working to forge a US–Canada bilateral agreement on acid rain. The panel agreed that acid rain was a problem. It conceded that some additional details needed to be worked out but argued that policy action was now warranted.

Fred Singer, alumnus of the Manhattan Project and advocate for the tobacco industry (see Oreskes and Conway, 2010: 5–6; 8–9; 85; 238), had been appointed to this panel by the White House. By the time the Peer Review Panel convened for the first time in 1983 Singer had already made it clear that he was far from convinced of the case for regulation designed to address the acid rain problem. Science, of course, proceeds and depends upon the free and frank consideration of evidence. The Peer Review Panel agreed, therefore, that its report would be jointly authored and that dissenting opinion would be aired within the main body of the text.

The first draft report requested by the White House in 1984 was hard-hitting: 'Lakes were acidifying, fish were dying, forests were being damaged, and the time had come to act' (Oreskes and Conway, 2010: 87). Yet when the report was returned to the panel chair (Bill Nierenberg), he found that key paragraphs (those which suggested the prospect of far-reaching damage and irreversible change) had been struck out. In addition Nierenberg learned that White House staff members had suggested revisions to the structure and lay-out of the text. These revisions altered substantially the report. Where the Peer Review Panel had arrived at a consensus position that demonstrated the need for policy action, the narrative preferred by the White House asserted that the scientific knowledge on acid rain remained incomplete and unstable.

Despite this political intervention the Peer Review Panel struggled on with its endeavours. Pulled in different directions by the White House and by Singer's determination to undermine the emerging scientific consensus it settled upon an unusual compromise: the bulk of the report would be jointly authored as previously agreed. Singer, working alone, however, would be allowed to author a chapter (which later became a separate appendix), designed to consider the economic consequences (the cost/benefit trade-off) of the regulation designed to address the problem of acid rain.

In 1979 the White House Council on Environmental Quality had valued improvements in air quality subsequent to the passage of the Clean Air Act at $21.4 billion per annum (Oreskes and Conway, 2010: 92). Singer's appendix, however, ignored this. He simply asserted that the costs of taking no action on acid rain could be calculated at zero. In addition, Singer asserted that the control technologies suggested to tackle pollution were unreliable and, since it was claimed that inaction cost nothing, uneconomic.

Oreskes and Conway (2010) observe that the popular press (as opposed to the scientific-technical press) soon began to run accounts of the Peer Review Panel's deliberations which focused narrowly upon Singer's appendix. Furthermore, they observed that the White House suggested and drafted an Executive Summary, with Nierenberg's help but without the knowledge of the other panel members. This 'summary' was, in fact, no such thing, since it contradicted the thrust of the main report by suggesting that there was, as yet, no consensus on the problem of acid rain or on the need for action.

In response, key scientists, who had been members of the Peer Review Panel, published scientific papers which took issue with the position spun by the White House: acid rain, they argued, was a major threat and action was necessary and was certainly not uneconomic. But who was reading these papers?

Who among the lay-population would understand that *Fortune* and *Business Week* were simply wrong when they counselled that the jury was still out on climate change?

And who was countermanding the outrageous suggestion voiced by Singer in *Regulation* that avoiding the rush to unnecessary regulation on acid rain had already saved the US $10 billion per year (Oreskes and Conway, 2010: 103)?

The answer of course is almost no one. The problem of acid rain had been 'kicked into the long grass'. It was 'business as usual'. The tobacco strategy had triumphed again.

Yet the game which Singer and the White House had played, while political, was at least still sporting. Singer had suggested that the science was incomplete. He had not suggested that the scientists were incompetent or worse, corrupt. That narrative ploy was still to come and would receive its fullest elaboration to date, I suggest, in the Climategate scandal.

Climategate: science versus 'experts'

The third climate assessment report published by the IPCC in 2001 placed a depiction of Mike Mann's now infamous 'hockey stick' diagram in its 'summary'. This model, which had for some time been the subject of debate within the climate science community, estimates average global temperature over a 1,000-year period. It suggests that for over 900 years there was little variation in global temperature but reports a sharp rise during the last century. This observation (in conjunction with related studies) allowed the IPCC to suggest that the evidence for an anthropogenic account of climate change was strong and becoming stronger. Climate change contrarians, and to a lesser extent sceptics, were far from convinced. They responded not with questions on 'the science' but with attacks on the scientists themselves. For example, the Republican Senator for Oklahoma, James Inhofe told the Senate in July 2003 that global warming was a 'hoax'. Indeed, Inhofe asserted that Mann had deliberately erased evidence of the medieval warming period and a more recent little ice age (see Pearce, 2010: 90).

Commenting upon the so-called contradictory 'evidence' that Mann is said to 'have erased', Pearce (2010: 45–46) provides a useful counterpoint. Quoting, Mike Hulme, a Professor of climate science based at UEA, he observes:

> Put simply and loudly, we don't know whether there was a global medieval warm period or not. It is not the case that prior to the hockey stick there was good evidence for it. There just wasn't. What we had was Hubert Lamb's sketch on the back of an envelope, which was endlessly repeated ... The hockey stick may be rubbish, too, but it was not over-turning a well-established orthodoxy. It was replacing a rather dodgy bit of hand-waving from the 1970s and 1980s.

Undeterred, Steve McIntrye (a mathematician and former mining engineer) and Ross McKittrick published a paper in *Energy and Environment* which called

Mann's statistical methods into question. Mann was, apparently, livid. His work, as a leading member of the academy, was being challenged by outsiders. Furthermore, and in a breach of normal protocol, he had not been invited to review the paper prior to its publication. A follow-up paper prepared for (but rejected by *Nature*) was subsequently published in *Geophysical Research Letters* in 2005. This paper, we should note, emerged against a backdrop of correspondence between McIntyre and Jones, which although it had started cordially had soon degenerated as McIntyre's requests for data became, in the eyes of the CRU, more and more intrusive.

Thanks to the efforts of McKittrick, who had launched a PR campaign designed to ensure that the attacks on Mann's work featured prominently in *The Wall Street Journal* and other national newspapers (see Pearce, 2010: 96), McIntyre quickly became the poster boy for climate contrarians and, as we shall see, a rallying point for their increasingly bold attacks.

Hacking the CRU

The police investigation into hacking at the CRU closed in 2012. The identity of the individual who leaked the emails and documents in 2009 (and the later leak of some 5,000 more emails in November 2011) remains a mystery. Nonetheless Pearce (2010: 13) suggests that:

> Climategate would not have happened without ... Steve McIntyre. Whether you see him as a hero or villain his [persistent requests for information often pursued through Freedom of Information (FOI) requests] helped create [a] siege mentality among the scientists and set them on a path of opposition to freedom of information. By drawing in scores of data liberationists [who submitted FOI requests on his behalf, McIntyre] ... almost certainly inspired whoever stole and released the emails.

Commenting upon the leak, Pearce (2010: 11) observes 'when the Climatic Research Unit's emails were subjected to public gaze they revealed that the climate scientists seemed traumatised by a long-term assault from critics'. Indeed, he adds that reading the leaked emails 'gives the impression that they were huddling together in the storm' (12). And, frankly who could blame them? They had been subjected to a decade of abuse, which had publicly questioned their capabilities and their ethics. Yet Pearce suggests that this feeling of victimisation may have prevented Jones and Mann from discerning the crucial difference between the contrarians and the sceptics; obliging McIntyre, who has always focused upon 'the science' and who has never descended into *ad hominem* attacks to make common purpose with those who demonstrate no such scruples.

Noting that climate science has been conducted on a landscape scarred by the activities of climate change deniers, Pearce observes that the leaks seemed to provide 'the smoking gun' that would establish beyond doubt what contrarians knew to be true:

1. Anthropogenic climate change was a hoax; a fraud perpetrated upon the world by Jones, Mann and others involved within the IPCC.

    Central to this claim we should note was the email written by Jones to Mann which suggested using 'Mike's *Nature* trick' to 'hide the decline' in temperatures evident within certain data sets (Pearce, 2010: 174). Reflecting upon the conspiracy necessary to effect this 'trick' the inquiries conducted in the UK observed that, while Jones undoubtedly regretted using this short-hand expression, the 'trick' was in fact a statistical technique developed to deal with a data set that had proven unreliable. Furthermore it was noted that the utility (and limitations) of this 'trick' had been discussed openly within the scientific community and had been acknowledged within the papers that had been published within the leading journals. The 'trick' was, in short, anything but a clandestine cover-up.

2. Jones, Mann and others had abused their position within the scientific community to subvert the peer review system and had intervened to block or to suppress the publication of analyses which questioned their work.

    'Evidence' for this claim, the contrarians suggested, was to be found in emails which demonstrated that leading scientists had (a) questioned editorial decisions, (b) advised that papers hostile to their views and methods should be rejected by journal editors and (c) sought to arrange the boycott of journals which refused to toe the line.

    It is of course plain from the emails released that Jones, Mann and others had actively questioned editorial decisions taken by certain journals. The correspondence does not, however, suggest that such interventions were inappropriate. Indeed, Pearce (2010: 125–141) makes it plain that the editorial board of *Climate Research* resigned *en masse* when a complaint launched by Mann revealed that the editor, Chris de Freitas of the University of Auckland had chosen to publish a paper against the advice of four reviewers who had each, independently, recommended rejection of a paper, questioning Mann's 'hockey stick analysis'. Indeed, if the emails prove anything on this issue it is that Mann, Jones and others intervened to protect the peer review process from an individual who had abused his position to publish work that was substandard.

The presence of clear evidence that Mann and others had acted to uphold the peer review process did not, however, prevent those called before the parliamentary inquiry such as Lord Lawson (speaking for the think tank; the Global Policy Warming Foundation) from claiming that the scientific claims of the CRU were largely fraudulent. The tobacco strategy, of course, teaches us that in the absence of good, searching, journalism (see Delingpole, 2009, for an example of this absence) one 'expert' is just as good as another. Quite what Lord Lawson (one-time financial journalist and former Chancellor of the Exchequer) and his free-market foundation really understood about climate science was, therefore, never adequately considered by the inquiry or the press who reported its proceedings.

Turning to the issue of the suggested academic boycott of key journals, we should note that this strategy was never brought to fruition and does not seem to have diverted the inquiries. This issue, however, does bear further reflection because it is, surely, strange that the free-market 'think tanks' and 'lobby organisations' who have chosen to intervene in the debates on climate science to prevent regulation should set their faces against what is, after all, an expression of consumer sovereignty!

3. Jones, Mann and others had sought to evade legitimate FOI requests that, if honoured, would have (a) revealed the fraud that is at the heart of the climate science practiced at CRU and at Penn State, and which had (b) allowed the IPCC to label climate change as anthropogenic.

The inquiry undertaken by the Information Commissioner regretted that UEA and the CRU had not been more amenable to FOI requests and had been inclined towards an obstructive mind-set. Acknowledging the context that had enabled this posture, the Information Commissioner chose not to pursue an action against UEA on procedural grounds: any offence that might have occurred fell beyond the statute of limitations.

The contrarians, of course, called foul at this technicality. And they may have had a point. The CRU had been pretty obstructive. Nonetheless it is plain that at least some of McIntyre's FOI requests (for example) were mischievous and were indeed unnecessary since he was already in possession of the data that he was requesting from CRU. Furthermore, it is worth pointing out that many of those who have demanded openness from the scientific community and who have cried foul when FOI requests are refused do not, themselves, act reciprocally. Challenged by MPs to reveal the source(s) of funding that enable the work of the Global Warming Policy Foundation, for example, Lord Lawson was simply allowed to bat away the question insisting that this might cause embarrassment to some of those who had donated to his foundation!

But none of this should come as a surprise: the tobacco strategy never did let facts get in the way of a good story so it was, perhaps, only a question of when, not if, the climate change contrarians would part company with manners and with the reciprocal obligations that *should be* the hallmarks of responsible debate and the foundation of reasoned policymaking.

In my concluding comments I will offer reflections on Climategate; on narrative strategy; and on scientific leadership in a world of smears and outright criminality.

Concluding comments

This chapter has offered reflections on the challenges, the snake-pits and bear-traps which now await those who would intervene to provide (scientific) leadership in the green economy. Noting that leadership is, nowadays, generally constituted in discursive terms, I have argued that our appreciation of the business of management has been framed within narrative accounts that tend to deny the grubby political realities of our organised existence.

Offering 'Climategate' as a case study I have suggested that the leak which precipitated this crisis carries echoes of debates which have been playing out in public since at least the 1950s. Indeed, I have argued that 'Climategate' represents, in fact, another play in the tobacco strategy, albeit with new and troubling twists. These twists, the descent into criminality and the associated development of narrative tactics, which assert that leading climate scientists have engaged in a fraudulent conspiracy, demonstrate:

- Our on-going failure to acknowledge the seamy side of social organization;
- The perils of leadership in this context;
- The need for changes that will enable reasoned public discourse on what amounts to an existential threat (Lynas, 2008).

Taking Climategate as a case study this chapter has been designed to reveal and to discuss the perils of scientific leadership in the green economy. My concern has been to reveal, not to resolve, these issues. Given my focus and given, too, limitations of space I cannot hope to offer detailed suggestions for change that might reverse or otherwise overcome the narrative strategy that has made scientific leadership in this context such a fraught endeavour. Yet to be silent on such matters is to be on the wrong side of history and there are some things that might be done now and in the light of my reflections.

Analysing the Climategate scandal and its immediate aftermath, Pearce (2010) argues that the scientists located within the Climatic Research Unit lost the media war because their employers failed to respond effectively to the storm. Given this it seems sensible to suggest that the field of climate science might develop dedicated media channels designed to challenge and to take down the preposterous claims that the 'contrarians' continue to peddle. These media channels, while focused upon the science need not, I suggest, shy away from a more direct and political engagement with their critics. Nor should they shy away from exposing the hypocrisy of those who demand transparency and accountability but refuse to act reciprocally. John Cox (see Schouten, 2016) has reflected upon this issue. He has suggested that we might develop a more active and questioning citizenry if our politicians were obliged – like NASCAR drivers and professional cyclists – to wear clothes displaying the names of their sponsors. I suggest that, through the media channels noted above, climate science might consider developing representations of their leading detractors, which demonstrate the presence of those vested which quietly fund and in so doing hide behind 'think tanks'. Furthermore I suggest that climate science should lead calls for more responsible forms of broadcasting. Indeed, I suggest that the climate scientists should demand that only those who can (a) establish their scientific credentials and who have (b) fully acknowledged the responsibility that they owe to their financial backers may be invited to comment or to participate in broadcast debate. Under circumstances where the broadcasters refuse to give this commitment I suggest that climate science should, live and on-air, loudly and publicly demand that this issue be made a key component of any ensuing discussion.

Finally, I suggest that climate science, while fighting back against the contrarians, should reach out to those such as the 'sceptics' who have, despite their questionable friendships, sought a genuine engagement with the science of climate change. Latour (1987) warns us that successful scientific projects build and depend upon the development and elaboration of heterogeneous networks, which extend the scientific domain beyond the closed world of the laboratory (see also Collins, 2016). If climate science is to take up its rightful leadership position in the green economy it will need to accept Latour's advice and, in doing so, will need to open itself up to a broader coalition of interest groups. This coalition-building activity, I suggest, should cultivate allies beyond the scientific academy who can call out the corporate shills that support climate change.

In short, the manifest perils of scientific leadership in the green economy demonstrate that our scientists require support and protection and must now be enabled to construct networks that can locate policy in science and science in policy.

Notes

1 Pearce (2010: 11) warns: 'This story is dark; there are few heroes. Neither mainstream climate scientists nor their critics come out of this very well'.
2 Since the Watergate scandal almost any major controversy soon acquires a '-gate' suffix. It has been suggested that it was James Delingpole who coined the term Climategate. Whatever would we do without this luminary of the fourth estate?
3 Taylor offers the following observation on the role which stories perform: 'Anthony Powell [author of *A Dance to the Music of Time*] once suggested

SPEAKING TRUTH TO POWER   35

that the crucial thing about the average human life is not what happens in it, but what the person experiencing it thinks happens in it – in other words, that the personal myths we construct around ourselves are just as, if not more, important than the verifiable facts of our existence'.

4 This is a golfing analogy. Golf courses are many things. They may be taken to be, for example, extensions of the Boardroom; sites of social exchange and indeed sites of social exclusion. That much is, of course, open to debate. What is clear, however, is that golf courses are, at root, linear queuing systems where the pace of play is, in effect, set by the slowest player(s) on the course. Recognising this limitation there is a social convention whereby slower players will invite those behind them on the course to 'play on through'. My suggestion is that corporate interests simply 'play on through' when their policies are challenged, for example, by academics and journalists.

5 The newspaper *Private Eye* suggests that, despite its PR, *Amazon* has done little to change its normal operating procedures and may, now, be taking steps to increase the surveillance of its workforce in order to enable further intensification of the labour process. *Private Eye* notes: 'to ensure its warehouses can keep processing orders at a frenzied pace during the Covid crisis [*Amazon*] is introducing social-distancing surveillance in its "fulfilment centres", positioning cameras and computing devices to ensure workers maintain a proper distance between each other while packing boxes. The workers will thus have all their movements captured on camera throughout their shift. With its track record of punishing efficiency targets, and a history of firing staff who don't make the grade it's not hard to imagine what else Amazon might use the cameras for'.

6 I am being too kind. Those on the receiving end of the hate-speak developed by certain climate contrarians have been informed that they deserve dismissal from their employment and death. Indeed, the spouses and children of leading scientists have also been threatened in similar ways.

7 I am of course engaging in a rhetorical projection here. For what it is worth I regard climate change 'sceptics' as just that. They are individuals who have a capacity to advance scientific understanding of anthropogenic climate change because they are prepared to probe the science. Climate change 'contrarians', in contrast, are for the most part non-specialists; they are 'unqualified voters', often in the pay of corporate masters, who advance their agenda, not by seeking to advance scientific understanding, but by attacking the scientists themselves.

8 This allusion to 'defence in depth' relates to a strategy developed by the German military in 1916. This strategy was highly reflexive, pragmatic and adaptable. It was consequently highly effective.

9 Oreskes and Conway (2010) observe that the tobacco industry undertook research to make tobacco smoke less visible when the hazards posed by passive smoking began to make themselves known!

10 It might be more appropriate to suggest that this and similar 'grass-roots' organisations are, in fact, 'astro-turfed' products of the tobacco industry.

11 A study undertaken by Peretti-Wattel et al. (2007) demonstrates that the scientific community has established a 'dose-response relationship' between smoking and disease. That is to say science has established that no level of smoking is safe. Indeed, the more one smokes the greater is the damage to health. Despite this many smokers continue to assert that there is a 'threshold effect' associated with tobacco smoke and only when this is breached that a hazard to health arises.

12 Pearce (2010) argues that this amounts to a false separation. Jones had been accused of subverting the peer review process to silence his dissenters and Pearce, quite correctly in my view, suggests that it would be impossible to deal with the issue of Jones's integrity in the absence of a consideration of his scientific practice.

13 I find it difficult to class these submissions as 'evidence'.

References

Boje D (1991) 'The storytelling organization: A study of performance in an office supply firm', *Administrative Science Quarterly*, 36: 106–126.

Boje D (1998) 'Amos Tuck's post-sweat Nike spin story', Paper presented to the International Academy of Business Disciplines Conference, San Francisco.

Boje D (2001) *Narrative Methods for Organizational and Communication Research*, Sage: London.

Bonazzo J (2018) 'Report: Amazon workers have to process 300 packages an hour and pee in bottles', *The Observer* 16/ 04/ 2018.

Clegg H A (1975) 'Pluralism in industrial relations', *British Journal of Industrial Relations*, 13 (3): 297–314.

Collins D (1998) *Organizational Change: Sociological Perspectives*, Routledge: London and New York.

Collins D (2000) *Management Fads and Buzzwords: Critical-practical perspectives*, Routledge: London and New York.

Collins D (2007) *Narrating the Management Guru: In Search of Tom Peters*, Routledge: London and New York.

Collins D (2016) 'Constituting best practice in management consulting', *Culture and Organization*, 22 (5): 409–429.

Collins D (2018) *Putting Stories to Work: The Power of Talk in Organizations*, Routledge: Abingdon, Oxon and New York.

Collins D (2021a) *Management Gurus: A Research Overview*, Routledge: Abingdon, Oxon and New York.

Collins D (2021b) *The Organizational Storytelling Workbook: How to Harness This Powerful Management and Communication Tool*, Routledge: Abingdon, Oxon and New York.

Collins D and Rainwater K (2005) 'Managing change at sears: A sideways look at a tale of corporate transformation', *Journal of Organizational Change Management*, 18 (1): 16–30.

Czarniawska B (1997) *Narrating the Organization: Dramas of Institutional Identity*, The University of Chicago Press: Chicago IL.

Czarniawska B (1999) *Writing Management: Organization Theory as a Literary Genre*, Oxford University Press: Oxford.

Deal T and Kennedy (1982) *Corporate Cultures: The Rites and Rituals of Corporate Life,* Addison-Wesley: Reading MA.

Deal T and Kennedy A (1999) *The New Corporate Cultures: Revitalizing the Workplace after Downsizing, Mergers and Reengineering*, Orion Business Books: London.

Delingpole J (2009) 'Climategate: The final nail in the coffin of anthropogenic global warming', *The Daily Telegraph* 20/ 11/ 2009.

Dickens C [1841] (1922) *A Christmas Carol*, Cecil Palmer: London.

Fairhurst G T and Sarr R A (1996) *The Art of Framing: Managing the Language of Leadership*, Jossey-Bass: San Francisco CA.

Fox A (1985) *Man Mismanagement*, Hutchinson: London.

Gabriel Y (1995) 'The unmanaged organization: Stories, fantasies and subjectivity', *Organization Studies*, 16 (3): 477–501.

Gabriel Y (1998) 'Same old story or changing stories? folkloric, modern and postmodern mutations' in Grant D, Keenoy T and Oswick C (eds) *Discourse and Organization*, Sage: London.

Gabriel Y (2000) *Storytelling in Organizations: Facts, Fictions and Fantasies*, Oxford University Press: Oxford.

Gabriel Y (2004) 'Narratives, stories and texts' in Grant D, Hardy C, Oswick C and Putnam L (eds) *The Sage Handbook of Organizational Discourse*, Sage: London.

Gioia D A and Chittipeddi K (1991) 'Sensemaking and sensegiving in strategic change initiation', *Strategic Management Journal*, 12: 433–448.

Grant D, Hardy C, Oswick C and Putnam L (2004) 'Introduction: Organizational discourse: Exploring the field' in Grant D, Hardy C,

Oswick C and Putnam L (eds) *The Sage Handbook of Organizational Discourse*, Sage: London.

House of Commons Science and Technology Committee (2010), The disclosure of climate date from the Climatic Research Unit at the University of East Anglia: Eighth Report of Session 2009-10, HC 387–1.

Huczynski A A (1993) *Management Gurus: What makes them and how to become one*, Routledge: London.

Kieser A (1997) 'Rhetoric and myth in management fashion', *Organization*, 4 (1): 49–74.

Latour B (1987) *Science in Action*, Harvard University Press: Cambridge MA.

Lynas M (2008) *Six Degrees: Our Future on a Hotter Planet*, National Geographic: Washington DC.

Oreskes N and Conway E (2010) *Merchants of Doubt: How a Handful of Scientist Obscured the Truth on Issues from Tobacco Smoke to Global Warning*, Bloomsbury: London and New York.

Pagel S and Westrefelhaus R (1999) 'Read the book or attend the seminar? Charting ironies in how managers prefer to read', *Journal of Business Communication*, 36: 136–193.

Pagel S and Westerfelhaus R (2005) 'Charting managerial reading preferences in relation to popular management theory books: A semiotic analysis', *Journal of Business Communication*, 42: 420–448.

Pascale R T and Athos A G [1981] (1986) *The Art of Japanese Management*, Sidgwick and Jackson: London.

Pearce F (2010) *The Climate Files: The Battle for the Truth About Global Warming*, Guardian Books: London.

Peretti-Wattel P, Constance J, Guilbert P, Gautier A, Beck F and Moatti J (2007) 'Smoking too few cigarettes to be at risk? Smokers' perceptions of risk and denial: A French study', *Tobacco Control* 16 (5): 351–356.

Peters T and Austin N (1985) *A Passion for Excellence: The Leadership Difference*, Fontana: London.

Peters T and Waterman R (1982) *In Search of Excellence: Lessons from America's Best Run Companies*, Harper and Row: New York.

Private Eye (2020) 'Money to burn', No. 1525, July 3-July 16, p.7.

Rüling C C (2005) 'Popular concepts and the business management press', *Scandinavian Journal of Management*, 21: 177–195.

Sainato M (2019a) 'Revealed: Amazon touts high wages while ignoring issues in its warehouses', *The Guardian* 07/ 08/ 2019.

Sainato M (2019b) 'Go back to work: Outcry over deaths on Amazon's warehouse floor', *The Guardian* 18/ 10/ 2019.

Schouten F (2016) 'Plan would require politicians to wear their donors' logos', *USA Today* 01/04/2016.

Scott J C (1990) *Domination and the Arts of Resistance*, Yale University Press: New Haven CT.

Sims D (2003) 'Between the Millstones: A narrative account of the vulnerability of middle managers storying', *Human Relations* 56 (10): 1195–1211.

Taylor D J (2019) *On nineteen eighty-four: A biography*, Abrams Books: New York, NY.

Watson T (2001) *In Search of Management: Culture, chaos and control in managerial work*, Thomson Learning: London.

Weick K (1995) *Sensemaking in Organizations*, Sage: London.

Wolfe T (1987) *The Bonfire of the vanities*, Farrar, Strauss and Giroux: New York.

3

VALUES AND LEADERSHIP IN THE ANTHROPOCENE

Chris Rose and Pat Dade

Humankind has now so changed the earth that it's less made by 'nature' than human beings, a situation popularised by the late earth-scientist Paul Crutzen[1] as a new geological-scale epoch: the 'Anthropocene'.

This new era is defined by the changes we have made to our environment, which now pose huge new challenges such as eliminating climate-heating and restoring nature, but it has not changed human nature.

Renowned biologist E. O. Wilson captured this dilemma when he wrote in *The Social Conquest of Earth:*[2]

> We have created a Star Wars civilization, with Stone Age emotions, medieval institutions, and godlike technology.

So if we are equipped with 'Stone Age emotions' and 'medieval institutions', is human leadership up to the task? There are many dimensions to leadership, but here we try to take a short excursion into one, taking a long view on leadership through the lens of human values.

DOI: 10.4324/9781003190820-4

Values

Sir Robert Worcester founded the polling research company MORI and was an investigator for the World Values Survey. He described values like this:

> Opinions are ripples on the surface of the public's consciousness, shallow ad easily changed. Attitudes are the currents below the surface, deeper and stronger. Values are the deep tides of the public mood, slow to change but powerful.

So by 'values' we mean the sets of deep-seated attitudes and beliefs which determine our world view of deep truths: how things 'really are'. Such values guide our most fundamental priorities, define what is 'common sense', and in turn influence our actions and frame our opinions in the shallower waters of day-to-day decisions, including all the important leadership issues.

Psychologists and social researchers have developed tools for detecting these powerful but subtle and largely unconscious motivational values, which operate at the level of every individual or group and, thus, nation.

Basic human nature may not have changed over time, but through painstaking measurement, survey and modelling we know that the proportions of these social motivating values (not to be confused with personality or philosophical values) have changed. In most countries, the values make-up of today's populations are radically different from those of even a few generations ago, and this gives rise to new 'social currents', and sometimes to splits or clashes within societies, which are often called 'culture wars'. Yet these are not ideas learnt or taught as cultural values so much as different priorities which then play out through human endeavours, such as politics, business or civil society. We bring different values to bear on problems and solutions at any scale, and solving the problems of the Anthropocene will be no exception.

One of us (Pat Dade) runs a research company called Cultural Dynamics (www.cultdyn.co.uk), which has been measuring these differences as 'Maslow Groups' and 'Values Modes' since the 1970s, and the other (Chris Rose) first came across Pat's work while trying to understand the evolving challenges facing Greenpeace in achieving change back in the 1990s. Later, Chris wrote a book about it: *What Makes People Tick: The Three Hidden Worlds of Settlers, Prospectors and Pioneers.*[3]

As it illustrates three profoundly different values-sets, the Cultural Dynamics model can easily be used to identify the different expectations of leaders and ideas of 'good leadership' alive in societies today. Pat Dade and his co-modeller Les Higgins have also produced a management-leadership version of their population model, used by organisations. But before having a look at that, let's wind back to the earliest forms of leadership, which of course are still with us today.

Fighting for land

It seems likely that the oldest style of leadership was first and foremost based on strength and force. There is an old joke about land-ownership in England in the form of a story, in which an aristocratic land-owner encounters a landless poacher. One version[4] has it:

> *Lord*: How dare you come on my land, sir?
>
> *Poacher*: Your land! How do you make that out?
>
> *Lord*: Because I inherited it from my father.
>
> *Poacher*: And pray, how did he come by it?
>
> *Lord*: It descended to him from his ancestors
>
> *Poacher*: But tell me how they came by it?
>
> *Lord*: Why they fought for it and won it, of course.
>
> *Poacher (taking off his coat)*: Then I'll fight you for it.

As E. O. Wilson pointed out, many of our institutions have their roots in medieval times, if not earlier. Land was the main gateway to resources, which we mostly derived straight from nature, and for millennia we fought for it, and other arrangements tended to flow from that. For example, land was gifted by tribal and then medieval and constitutional monarchs to keep them in power.

By studying historical evidence and contemporary societies in different stages of development, Professor Ron Inglehart, founder of the World Values Survey,[5] has traced stages in social development which have enabled change in expression of human values. He identifies pre-industrial or agrarian societies, secular industrialised societies and post-industrial societies.

The primacy of land was of course typical of settled agrarian societies which regarded land as territory and then legal property. We may think of the Magna Carta as about individual freedoms but it was really more of a land-rights pact between a monarch and his barons. Settled farmers displaced nomadic graziers and before them hunter gatherers who presumably had also fought for territory. In the modern era, fisheries policy is often still conducted along similar lines because, at sea, territory is more contested, though actual physical violence is now unusual.

Property rights are still an animating force in political ideology: for example, among right-wing US economists who would place it above the rights of citizens.[6]

But industrialisation has dramatically reduced the proportion of people directly engaged in land management and made it valuable for other purposes such as commerce, manufacturing, markets and playing golf. Attempts by one nation to acquire the land of another through violence are now unusual.

Numerous studies suggest that the number of wars and deaths arising from violent conflict have declined over time.[7] For instance, with its greater firepower and population, World War II (1939–1945) killed more people than the activities of Genghis Khan (1206–1927) but World War II killed only 2.6% of the global population, whereas Khan managed 11.1%.

For the average human, over time, the world has become a more peaceful place so far as conflict-related death goes. The toll exacted by disease and starvation has also declined, so life expectancy has increased.

Together with sanitation, education of girls and increased food security, per capita income and other factors measured by Swedish Professor of International Health, the late great Hans Rosling and his family,[8] over the long-run, these socio-economic improvements have made the world a safer place.

Inglehart has tracked the shift in human values resulting from these inter-generational changes in human experience on two main axes of survival v. self-expression, and traditional v. secular-rational.

In their epic 2005 book *Modernization, Cultural Change and Democracy: The Human Development Sequence*,[9] Ron Inglehart and Christian Welzel describe how predominantly security-driven 'traditional' societies with magical and religious beliefs gave way to 'materialist' organised industrial societies with secular-rational beliefs, and then to 'post-material' societies with rising 'self-expression' values, catalysed by the growing opportunities for autonomy and self-choice. This sequence, he argues, ultimately creates the conditions for democracy, which only becomes possible when self-expression values become so widespread that they lead security forces to no longer support autocratic leaders.

So Inglehart's work links change in individual human values to shifts in society, over generations and longer timescales. He first became well-known for the *Silent Revolution* published in 1977, explaining the values shift underlying the 'counter-culture' revolution in politics of the 1960s, archetypically remembered as starting in California.

Of course, it is not an entirely smooth process. In *Cultural Evolution* (2018)[10] Inglehart argues that interests and individuals feeling threatened by such values change can mount a 'counter-revolution'. (Manifest, for example, by the values most espoused in support of 'Brexit' and the election of Donald Trump – see below – a reaction against the 'new normal' arising from the earlier 'silent revolution'.)

Tackling the problems of the Anthropocene is going to be a long-term project, and the urgency of the climate and nature emergency means there is every reason to do everything possible to avoid triggering a 'counter-revolution' which causes fatal delay.

Inglehart's extraordinary body of work on inter-generational values shifts provides a historical perspective, but other tools for values analysis can also be useful tools in navigating, negotiating and managing change today. In particular, models which enable you to measure values at any scale from individual to a nation, and which also capture the distinct motivational group driven by the human needs for aspiration, success and esteem. One example is the 'Values Modes' or 'Cultural Dynamics' model.

The Cultural Dynamics model: 'Values Modes'

With his co-modeller Les Higgins, Pat has applied values analysis to management and communication issues in organisations ranging from the US Marines, to British design companies and football clubs, marketing ice cream and pubs,[11] the Australian military and numerous NGOs. Many examples applied to campaigning are at Chris's website,[12] including on the pivotal role of values in climate campaigns, and in the politics of

Brexit, and relating those to both the Cultural Dynamics model and work by Inglehart and others.

This values model is our primary lens. Other models are available but all are peering into the same well.

The 'Values Modes' model is calibrated against the well-known international academic Basic Human Values model,[13] developed by Shalom Schwartz of the Hebrew University, and the Pioneer–Settler axis in the 'Values Mode' model is essentially measuring much the same thing as the Security–Self-Expression axis in the World Values Survey (but the Prospectors are not visible as a distinct group in the Inglehart model).

The 'Values Modes' model divides the whole of any group or society into three large sectors called Maslow Groups (Settler, Prospector, Pioneer), and within those four smaller more coherent subgroups, the 'Values Modes' (you can take the survey yourself[14] to find out which you fall into).

Although the researchers behind this did not set out with Maslow's theories in mind, they discovered that, after identifying a vast number of 'deep driver' factors, the social groups this revealed looked more than anything else like Maslow's needs-based, three-part division. His idea was that we start life 'Security-Driven' (or Sustenance-Driven), and if we fully meet the needs for security, safety and identity, become 'Outer-Directed' (esteem-driven), and then if we fully meet the needs for first esteem of others and then self-esteem, become 'Inner-Directed', with a less easily defined set of needs, including innovation, a holistic view of society, experimentation and individual ethics.

Cultural Dynamics terms these big groups Settlers, Prospectors and Pioneers, summarised[15] like this:

The Settler (Sustenance-Driven) needs are:

- Core physiological needs;
- Safety and security;
- Belonging.

Some typical Settler characteristics are:

- Family and home, and caring for them, tend to be at the centre;
- For those living alone, friends take the place of family;
- Tradition and family structure are important;

- Prefer things to be 'normal';
- Naturally conservative (with a small 'c');
- Security conscious – wary of crime, violence and terrorism;
- Supportive of tough punishment for criminals;
- Wary of change, especially for its own sake;
- More comfortable with regular and routine situations;
- Concerned about what the future holds.

The Settler Values Modes are (in sequence) known as Roots, Smooth Sailing, Brave New World, Certainty First.

The Prospector (Outer-Directed) needs are:

- Esteem of others;
- Self-esteem.

Some typical Prospector characteristics are:

- Success-oriented;
- Always want to 'be the best' at what they are doing;
- Welcome opportunities to show their abilities;
- Take great pleasure in recognition and reward;
- Look to maximise opportunities;
- Will take opportunities for advancement and professional networking;
- Trend and fashion conscious;
- Like new ideas and new ways;
- Generally optimistic about the future.

The Prospector Values Modes are (in sequence): known as Golden Dreamers, Happy Followers, Now People and Tomorrow People.

The Pioneer (Inner-Directed) needs are:

- Aesthetic cognitive;
- Self-actualisation.

Some typical Pioneer characteristics are:

- Trying to put things together and understand the big picture;
- Concerned about the environment, society, world poverty, etc.;

VALUES AND LEADERSHIP IN THE ANTHROPOCENE   47

- Always looking for new questions and answers;
- Strong internal sense of what is right and what is wrong;
- Strong desire for fairness, justice and equality;
- Self-assured and sense of self-agency;
- Generally positive about change, if it seems worthwhile;
- Cautiously optimistic about the future.

The Pioneer Values Modes are (in sequence): Transitionals, Concerned Ethicals, Flexible Individualists and Transcenders.

Leadership

What is a leader? Someone who leads, followed by others. Why? Because directly or indirectly they provide for the needs of followers, or enable them to meet those needs. If all leaders and followers shared the same motivational values life would be simpler, but they often do not, and so have needs and priorities which can conflict. Understanding this can help resolve problems.

Given the drivers and orientations summarised above, it is obvious that the expectations of leadership vary between values groups.

Settlers want to follow a leader, who knows where they are going and commands authority and respect. The strength of the traditional 'strong' leader compensates for Settlers' comparatively low sense of self-agency: the feeling that the world can change them, but they cannot change the world. The group leader decides where to go and what to do. Followers are rewarded for loyalty by belonging. Settlers are society's bedrock and upkeep tradition, and this is true across all societies, although the form tradition takes of course varies from one society to another. Settlers are the most past-oriented group, in line with an unmet need for certainty and consequent distrust of change. This poses a challenge for any leader who needs to take society in a new direction.

Prospectors expect a leader to deliver success, be it national 'greatness' or personal success and advancement. Their world view sees life as a competition, personally, in business or between nations, and often a zero-sum game in which a gain for one is a loss for others. Competing is encouraged and winners are rewarded. The higher Prospector self-agency runs alongside optimism about the future as the place they will truly succeed.

Prospectors want leaders they can 'invest in' (and they tend to see politics in transactional terms rather than Settler loyalties) to enable their success as independent, no longer dependent, individuals. But, highly alert to the risk of failure, Prospectors want to see proof that change 'works' before embracing it: early adopters, not utter innovators.

Finally, Pioneers have the highest sense of self-agency, are not held back from change by a need to avoid failure or a desire to stay in the old certainties of the past, and are curious to innovate and explore complexity, even seemingly 'insoluble', wicked[16] problems such as climate change. Their idea of leadership is through ideas and they worry about whether these are the right ideas, ethically, and including everyone. Whereas Settlers tend to prefer not to engage with big-picture change (but can be engaged with specifics, practical, small actions on big ideas), and Prospectors want change to offer proven opportunities to succeed, Pioneers love the big picture and are sceptical about there being any definitive single 'right answer'. Pioneers embrace ambiguity and the open-ended. Their enthusiasm for change and complexity is not shared by the other groups and that can be the source of Pioneer leadership failures.

The unmet needs of each group work upon them like a psychological magnetic field only with three poles, subtle but exerting a constant draw in different directions, and each with its own emotional rationality. Any leader who needs to communicate to all three groups at once will have to show that any 'project' will bring safety and security, and that it will be successful and ethical (Figure 3.1).

Whereas Maslow conceived of a set of needs often shown as a pyramid-shaped hierarchy, plotting the statistical correlations and differences of all the data gathered from hundreds of surveys and studies of hundreds of thousands of individuals reveals a 'map' of values which most resembles a circle (simplified diagram above, map below) (Figure 3.2).

www.cultdyn.co.uk

The 'map' above shows the 100 most statistically significant 'Attributes' representing paired attitudinal statements (each explained on the Cultural Dynamics 'Alphabet').[17] This is like looking down on a motivational 'mind-map' of a society. Each Attribute is located on a 1000×1000 statistical grid at the point of its maximum espousal (statement agreement).

Plotted individually, most of these measures have some support across the whole map but those nearer the edge have the strongest values differences.

VALUES AND LEADERSHIP IN THE ANTHROPOCENE   49

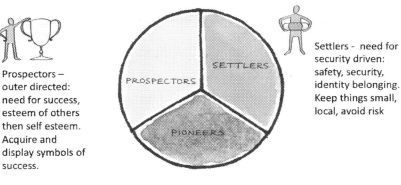

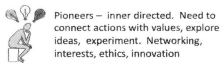

Figure 3.1 Unmet needs driving behaviours in the three 'Maslow Groups'.

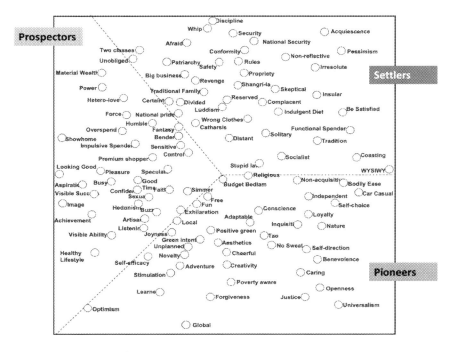

Figure 3.2 Values Map from the British Values Survey (BVS, 2017).

So, for instance, 'Budget Bedlam' (about failure to control one's expenditure) is close to population average and at the map centre: it's not going to cause a values split. In contrast, Discipline, Whip (about punishment) and National Security are strong Settler Attributes, whereas Global (an outlook measure), Universalism and Forgiveness (of oneself and others) are very Pioneer, and Showhome, Looking Good and Aspiration are strongly Prospector.

This highly detailed map covers the same space of human values as Shalom Schwartz's famous 'wheel' or 'Circumplex'), here orientated in the same 'Maslow Space' as the BVS map (Figure 3.3).

Broken out as Values Modes, the model looks like this: Figure 3.4.

There are several dynamics within the CDSM model. The two most important are the transition or 'conveyor' of individuals from Settler, to Prospector and Pioneer (anti-clockwise around the map), and the 'change

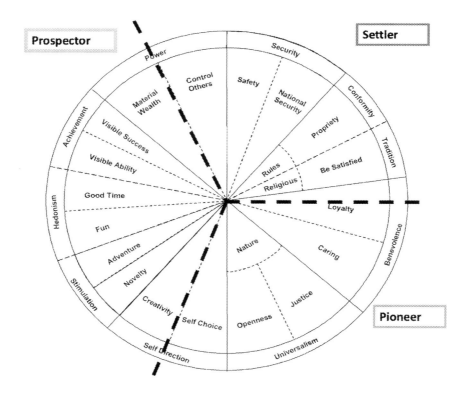

Figure 3.3 Schwartz in Maslow Space.

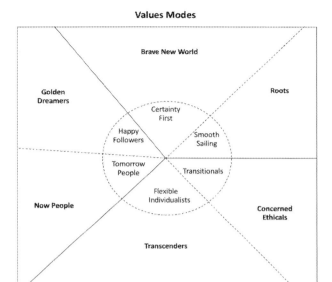

Figure 3.4 The outside Values Modes (VMs) are more different than the inside groups. These are the VMs that create disputes, politics and vigorous conversations in society and represent 50% of the model data.

dynamic' in the form of novel ideas or behaviours originating with Pioneers, and spreading, if they do, in the other direction, to Prospectors (by emulation) and then (by norming) to Settlers.

Both these dynamics are susceptible to intervention but to affect the mass movement of individuals (the conveyor) requires change at the level of a whole society. That is difficult to shift quickly, even for an all-powerful government and beyond the means of campaigners or advocates. In contrast, the change dynamic does not require individuals to change their Values Mode or Maslow Group in order for change to spread across the map, like a Mexican Wave spreading around a football stadium. Understanding how to make this happen will be vital if 'rapid transition' to succeed in coming to terms with the climate emergency and other aspects of the near-term Anthropocene (Figure 3.5 and Figure 3.6).

The critical step in achieving the spread of a new change across society's main values groups, rather than it staying stuck in the Pioneer area, is for

People can move – overall from Settlers> Prospectors > Pioneers

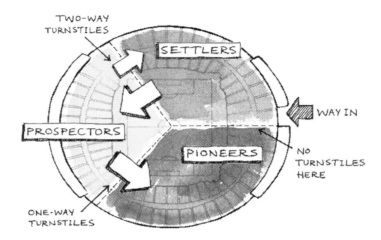

Figure 3.5 The potential movement of people as they transition from one group to another as a result of meeting needs through social experiences – using the population stadium metaphor (people get up and move seats). A slow process.

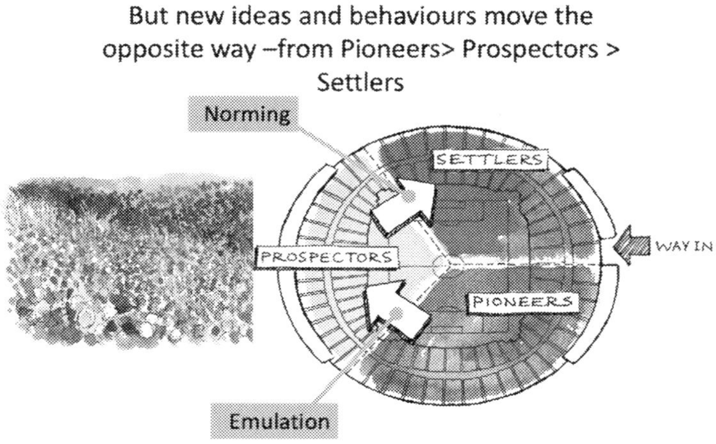

But new ideas and behaviours move the opposite way –from Pioneers> Prospectors > Settlers

Figure 3.6 The change dynamic runs in the opposite direction, always starts with Pioneers if it is a novel behaviour/idea, and does not require people to 'move seats' – the behaviour spreads like a Mexican Wave. (From *What Makes People Tick: The Three Hidden Worlds of Settlers, Prospectors and Pioneers*).

VALUES AND LEADERSHIP IN THE ANTHROPOCENE   53

it to appear 'successful' and thus attract emulation (often with adaptation) by the Prospectors. The two Values Modes essential to this bridge effect are the Transcender Pioneers and the Now People Prospectors. An example of the successful adoption of a new behaviour in the UK is the spread of solar PV technology (Figure 3.7).

The slower change in values groups in the UK from the 1970s to 2020s, caused by individual transitions, is shown below. The rise in the proportion of Settlers between 2005 and 2010 came after the financial crash of 2008 which temporarily slowed the 'values conveyor' transitioning Settlers to Prospectors (see slide 35)[18] (Figure 3.8).

Here's the 'management styles' (early version of Cultural Dynamics VOCS). Each of these VOCS Attributes is based on tested statements (Figure 3.9).

The range of statements tested to create the CDSM values model mean that it can often be used to identify connections between values and 'issues' we encounter in everyday life. For example, the idea that 'if I want

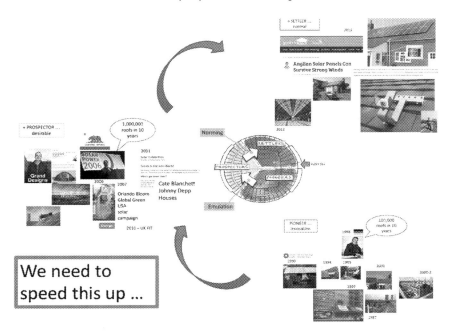

Figure 3.7 The adoption of solar PV from Pioneers to Prospector to Settler, 1990–2013, from the blog Brexit Values Story 2.2. http://threeworlds.campaignstrategy.org/?p=2305.

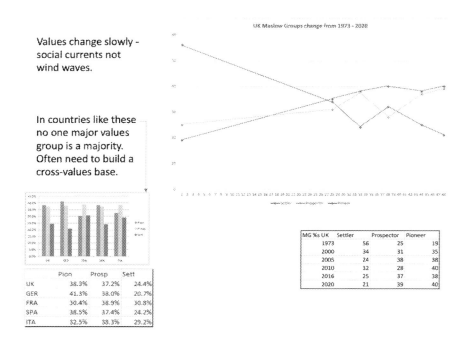

Figure 3.8 From Values Group Changes in the UK, 1973–2020.

something, it's OK to fight for it', discussed earlier, is close to agreement with the Attribute 'Force', which lies in the upper-left part of the map in the Prospector but Settler-like Values Mode 'Golden Dreamer' (Figure 3.10).

This is what agreement (measured on a six-point scale) looks like for the 'Force' Attribute on its own (Figure 3.11 and Figure 3.12).

Wider support for the idea does exist, but there isn't much of it: agreement is strongly centred in one part of the map. Just under 24% of the population agreed or strongly agreed with this idea (60% of whom were men, especially in the 18–34 age bracket).

These are the five Attributes most strongly correlated with 'Force' (Figure 3.13).

(i) Unobliged: I feel that people who meet with misfortune have brought it on themselves. I see no reason why rich people should feel obliged to help poor people.
(ii) Simmer: the thought of social disorder excites me. I would enjoy being involved in a street riot.

VALUES AND LEADERSHIP IN THE ANTHROPOCENE

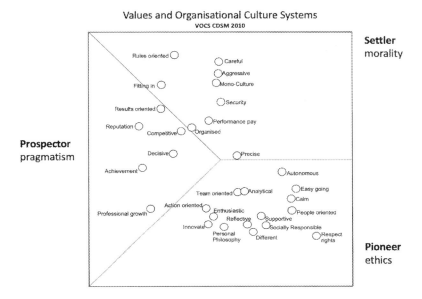

Figure 3.9 The VOCS model management version of the CDSM model (subsequently developed with 10,000 respondents in five European countries). Some management examples are described in *What Makes People Tick*. http://threeworlds.campaignstrategy.org/?p=2536.

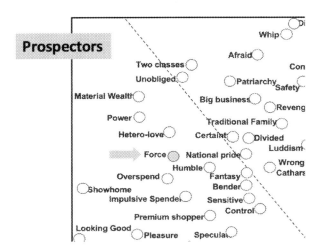

Figure 3.10 The 'Force' Attribute tests agreement with the statement: 'I believe it's acceptable to use physical force to get something I really want. I think the important thing is to get what I want'.

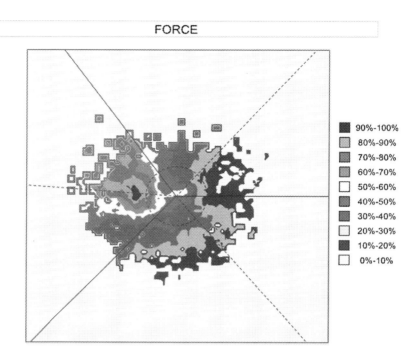

Figure 3.11 Values 'heat map' of Force Attribute.

	Maslow Group			
	Pion	Prosp	Sett	
1	127	262	87	476
	26.6%	55.1%	18.3%	23.6%
	70	148	75	
	774	752	493	2020
	38.3%	37.2%	24.4%	

Figure 3.12 Data for strong + weak agreement with the Force Attribute: it is disproportionate in the Prospectors (148 index against a population average of 100; 55% of Prospectors espouse this whereas they only made up 37% of the national sample).

CDSM's Attribute description[19] of Force notes:

This attitude can lead to great success in a range of business sectors. The threat of violence, from the most menial of levels to boardrooms, is enough for the majority of people to back off ideas that seem okay to

VALUES AND LEADERSHIP IN THE ANTHROPOCENE 57

Using *Force*

Demographic Skews:

1) Over-indexed: Male, under 45, mid-market

2) Under-indexed: Female, over 65

Force espousers also espouse other Attributes. The top five most highly correlated Attributes of *Force* espousers are, in order of the strength of relationship:

1) Catharsis
2) Simmer
3) Patriarchy
4) Bender
5) Unobliged

In total those who espouse *Force* also over-index significantly on 33 other Attributes.

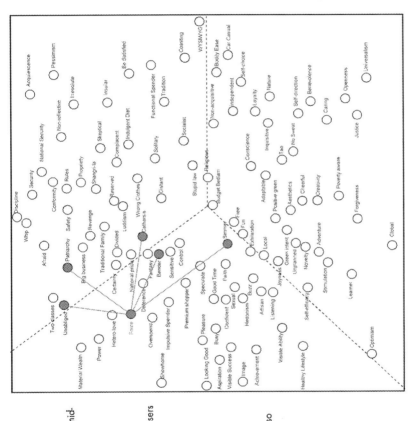

Figure 3.13 The 'Catharsis' Attribute means: I believe that violence is just a part of life. I think that, when you can't take it anymore and feel like you're about to explode, a little violent behaviour can relieve the tension.

them but are opposed vehemently by Force espousers. Bullying is a minor offshoot of this values-set.

The low empathy aspect of Force can lead to overt violence in localities where there are pre-existing situations of civil unrest. People who were previously law-abiding but are high on the Force Attribute, would be easily tempted by the disorder and chaos of the occasion to release some of the simmering tension brought on by the nature of their everyday life.

You can imagine that this may have played some part in the storming of the US Capitol following the speech by Donald Trump, and parts of the Gilets Jaune protests in France.

It should be noted that although Golden Dreamers are twice as likely as the population average to agree with the Force idea, most do not, and although more Prospectors than Settlers or Pioneers agree with it, an even smaller proportion do than among the Golden Dreamers.

There are several strategies which leaders or managers might use to avoid an attitude like 'Force' becoming a problem in the transitions needed in the Anthropocene (such as to a zero-carbon society).

One option is to simply outlaw behaviours and enforce the rules. This only works if there is wide and deep popular support for the laws concerned. Another option is to disincentivise use of force by giving greater esteem to those who avoid it. The big Golden Dreamer driver is to acquire the esteem of others, especially those in recognised positions of power and authority (which is why Donald Trump was a potent messenger). Golden Dreamers have just left the rule-abiding conformity and discipline of Settler World and are seeking the shortest routes to success. Above all, they do not want to be 'losers', so to channel their energy constructively, they need opportunities to win and gain self-esteem by doing 'the right thing'.

These options can work together, especially if the majority of other Golden Dreamers – 'people like us' in other respects (the heuristics of social proof and similarity) – are already avoiding this behaviour in favour of something else (see below).

The 'Force' attitude may never completely go away but well-designed change processes can avoid things reaching an entrenched and polarised position which can boil over into conflict. Brexit (in which Golden Dreamer voters were actually split more or less 50:50 and Settlers strongly

VALUES AND LEADERSHIP IN THE ANTHROPOCENE   59

skewed as pro-Leave and Pioneers leant pro-Remain) is an object lesson of what should be avoided if society is to succeed in achieving the wholesale restructuring necessary to become nature-friendly and zero-carbon.

The lesson of Brexit and political correctness

As CDSM surveys showed and Chris Rose detailed in a series of blogs[20] in 2017 and 2019, Brexit activated a latent political split along a values fault line, which ran more or less horizontally across the Values Map. This was an Inglehart 'counter-revolution' in action, and a long time in the making (explained in a 60- slide presentation).[21] Here is a grossly simplified explanation (Figure 3.14).

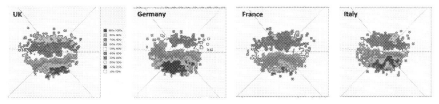

Figure 3.14 Top: the values split between Pioneer + Now Person and Golden Dreamer + Settler in the Brexit vote. Below – attitudes to the EU, prior to the vote. On this basis we anticipated (21 March 2016) that the Referendum of 23 June could give UKIP and the anti-Europeans in the UK, the opportunity sought by AfD in Germany. The values split seen in the UK also occurred in Germany, France and Italy (but not Spain) – it just wasn't activated there. http://threeworlds.campaignstrategy.org/?p=979 blog: the Brexit Values Battle.

Many indications suggest that after WW2 the UK, like many other 'developed' societies, saw a gradual increase in the number of Prospectors and then Pioneers, speeding up in the 1960s, as socio-economic conditions and opportunities (such as travel and education) increased. By 1973 they formed a significant but growing minority. 56% of the UK population was still traditionally minded Settlers.

Yet by 2016, as the EU Referendum approached, the Settlers were in a small minority of just 25% and the largest group (38%) were the change-attuned politically 'progressive' Pioneers. The values worlds had turned upside down. Settlers, who had tolerated but not generally welcomed change, were right when they said they no longer felt they recognised 'their country' (Figure 3.15).

The UK joined the EU (then the EEC, European Economic Community) in 1973. Britain was in decline and losing the last residues of its Empire. Environmentalism and feminism were novelties and Political Correctness almost unheard of. Then Reagan–Thatcher economics brought

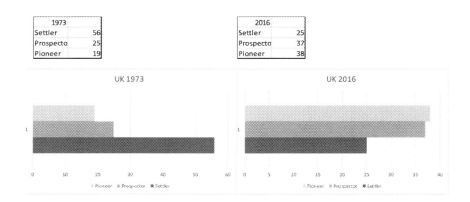

First CDSM type values UK survey in 1973 still found society was majority Settler but with many Pioneers and Prospectors

By 2016 Pioneers were the largest group and Settlers the smallest – a lot had changed and the 'pyramid' would be top-heavy

Figure 3.15 Inversion of the so-called 'Maslow Pyramid' in the UK, 1973–2019: Pioneers (Inner-Directeds) are now the largest group and Settlers (Security Driven) the smallest.

privatisation. Gradually, share- and asset-owners became relatively richer and wage earners poorer. A new consensus politics emerged around globalisation and smaller government. By the time of the 2016 Referendum, these and other 'isms' were mainstreamed, and rejection of them was found by Conservative pollster Lord Ashcroft to be a powerful predictor of voting Leave. In the US, the second strongest predictor of voting Trump was rejection of 'PC'. Eric Kaufmann of Kings College found that identity, not economics,[22] drove the Brexit vote and that in the UK support for the death penalty, linked to the CDSM Attribute 'Whip' (very Settler) was strongly associated with voting Leave, although the death penalty was not an issue in the campaign.

Slogans like 'Take Back Control' rather than 'Take Back The Money' were dog whistles to Settlers yearning to regain the past. Both left and right parties were split over Brexit. Much of the post-Brexit analysis focused on the idea that towns and cities which voted Brexit were economically left behind, which was true but the energising political force was values not economics.

Some lessons of Brexit for the future

If you were on the Leave side, the UK EU Referendum was an example of getting a values pitch right. If you were on the Remain side, it's an example of getting it wrong.

By default, most 'progressive' efforts are led or designed by Pioneers. Numerous surveys find that cause organisations are over-stuffed with Pioneers, especially Transcenders and sometimes Concerned Ethicals. The ways in which self-agency differences and (often unwitting) Pioneer framing combine to sieve out participation by other values groups are detailed in the 2018 blog *How Change Campaigns Get Populated By The Usual Suspects.*[23]

The 2019 blog *Brexit Warning*[24] drew three main conclusions from Brexit for future change efforts, and in particular those led by Pioneers.

1. The change model: for change to have sufficient legitimacy to last, it must respect values diversity. [This means] that it must be endorsed through adoption in all the main values groups of society (Pioneer, Prospector and Settler), on their own terms. Values bombing (e.g. PC-ness) does not do this.

2. Progressives should design and invest in campaigns to engage people unlike themselves and avoid the default mobilisation of their fund-raising base as the way to win campaigns.
3. Politicians, governments and campaigners must work actively to maintain the 'social elastic' of common experiences, inter-dependencies and behaviours with cross-values appeal to prevent society dividing into disconnected values silos, not just online but in real life.

By 'values bombing' we mean the projection of values-framed asks or demands projected ahead of the 'natural' wave of change caused by the change dynamic of innovation and experiment > success signal > emulation > norming (Figure 3.16).

In practical terms this means that 'advocacy' by Pioneers aimed at 'changing the minds' of Prospectors or Settlers by argument or coercion, is likely to backfire. Political Correctness has a long and complicated history, is almost a generic term for this approach (see the reckoning discussed in

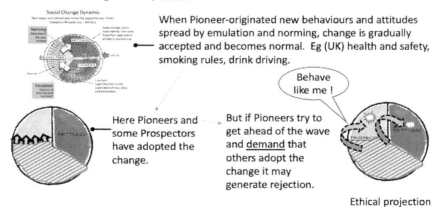

Figure 3.16 From Brexit Values Story 2.1. At http://threeworlds.campaignstrategy.org/?p=1462 and www.slideshare.net/tochrisrose/values-story-to-brexit-split-rev.

Political Correctness, Brexit, Trump and Campaigns).[25] Many early climate campaigns which were more about values-projection than matching solution-behaviours to values groups, not only failed but also probably slowed the uptake of solutions.

Engaging with people-unlike-us is now a common mantra among would-be change makers, spurred by many studies showing the exacerbating effects of social media and other aspects of contemporary lifestyles. A values lens reveals these differences at a deeper level than opinion, political affinity or demographics. Unfortunately for many NGOs, their reliance on a funding base which is maximally just like them, poses internal challenges to achieving this. Foundations or governments however which have a remit to think of the whole society, should find it easier to take a wider approach.

Perhaps the least addressed of these challenges is the need to rebuilt social connections and cohesion across values groups. For the UK the Brexit experience pulled back the curtain and revealed how stretched the social elastic had become. Many Pioneers living in Pioneer bubbles[26] were simply incredulous and shocked at the result. Here in conceptual terms, are some illustrations taken from the analysis for Brexit Story Part 1[27] (Figure 3.17, Figure 3.18 and Figure 3.19).

**Different in many ways so what holds them together ?
social elastic**

- Differences are significant but rarely absolute
- Many shared values eg 'being a parent'
- Attributes nearer the centre of the map are more in common
- With free-choice groups tend to self-select by values activities, social networks, venues etc and so avoid conflict
- Social bonds of family, friendship and culture & interests
- Utility eg at work: Settlers perfect essential functions, Prospectors are the turbo-boosters, Pioneers the experimenters
- Common experiences and interdependencies eg reliance on public services, common bonds formed in national or community wide efforts, common understanding eg from media
- Human contact and expecting to see one another again and needing to get along

Figure 3.17 Some ways in which social elastic is maintained.

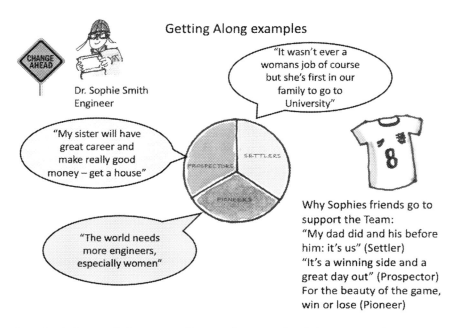

Figure 3.18 Some of the sorts of rationalisations for behaviours and accepting change that we come across in qualitative work with values groups.

A UK example of the importance of change rates is immigration. Academic studies[28] on immigration as a trigger to 'authoritarianism' (Karen Stenner, Eric Kaufmann, Jonathon Haidt) found that it was the experienced rate of change, rather than the absolute level of immigration, which provoked a reaction. Settlers are disproportionately likely to perceive such threats to their identity. This is exacerbated by policies and social effects which, by accident or design, concentrate such change in the very communities that are most Settler. An English example is the de facto practice of resettling refugees in poorer communities where accommodation is cheapest.

The increasingly separate lives lived online and in physical space played a role in Pioneers not even perceiving the existence of the divides that were opened over Brexit. After the EU Referendum two corporate executives asked one of us if the 'Bubble Print' of social media should be the 'new CSR [Corporate Social Responsibility] frontier for companies like Google and Facebook'.[29] Part of the answer must be 'yes'.

VALUES AND LEADERSHIP IN THE ANTHROPOCENE   65

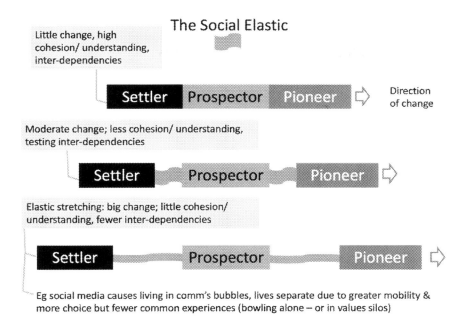

Figure 3.19 Perceived rate of change and the social elastic.

An interesting question is what impact the experience of the Covid pandemic will have. It generated more or less unavoidable common experiences, both good and bad. As in previous periods of acute existential threat, we all prioritised survival needs and experience suggests that Pioneers will revert to a Pioneer world view, and Prospectors to a Prospector world view, with their own priorities, if and when it's 'over'.

By definition the Anthropocene implies that Nature is no longer under self-management. To whatever extent this is true, it requires more systems thinking from human beings. At CDSM, Pat Dade and Les Higgins are updating their organisational management values tool to take account of 'infinite game' thinking, first developed by Professor James P. Carse in his 1986 treatise *Finite and Infinite Games: A Vision of Life as Play and Possibility*.[30] An obituary said of his ideas:

> The finite lens, is oriented around winning, achieving success and completion, and thus ultimately, the player is bound by past accomplishments. The other, with an infinite view of life, looks towards

possibility, renewal and ... enrichment. To play for the sake of keeping the game going, rather than playing to win.

Keeping nature and the planet going, rather than playing to win, is the challenge that now faces leaders of groups, organisations[31] and nations. Values are one of the tools we can use to understand ourselves and get the things done that we know we need to do.

Notes

1 The Man Who Invented the Anthropocene, India Bourke, *New Statesman*, 12–18 February 2021.
2 E. O. Wilson, *The Social Conquest of Earth* (2013), pub Liveright.
3 Chris Rose (2011) *What Makes People Tick: The Three Hidden Worlds of Settlers, Prospectors and Pioneers*; pub. Matador, available at http://three-worlds.campaignstrategy.org or as ebook on Apple or Kindle.
4 Guy Shrubsole, p. 79 in *Who Owns England?*, pub. William Collins (2019).
5 www.worldvaluessurvey.org/wvs.jsp.
6 Nancy MacClean, *Democracy in Chains*, pub. Scribe UK (2017); [the story of political economist James McGill Buchanan, whose ideas inspired the Koch Brothers].
7 See examples at https://ourworldindata.org/war-and-peace Max Roser. [https://archive.nytimes.com/www.nytimes.com/imagepages/2011/11/06/opinion/06atrocities_timeline.html - [Good graphic]]. (Data from atrociologist Matthew White, *The Great Big Book of Horrible Things* ISBN: 978-0-393-08192-3).
8 www.gapminder.org/fw/world-health-chart/ and *Factfulness*, Hans Rosling with Olga Rosling and Anna Rosling-Lund, pub. Spectre, 2018.
9 Ronald Inglehart and Christian Welzel, *Modernization, Cultural Change and Democracy: The Human Development Sequence*, pub. Cambridge University Press, 2005.
10 Ronald Inglehart, *Cultural Evolution: People's Motivations Are Changing, and Reshaping the World* (2018) pub. Cambridge University Press. His subsequent book with Pippa Norris is titled *Cultural Backlash*.
11 www.cultdyn.co.uk/ART067736u/PeopleBuyPubsNotBeer.pdf.
12 Links and Resources on Motivational Values http://threeworlds.campaignstrategy.org/?p=1420.
13 https://en.wikipedia.org/wiki/Theory_of_Basic_Human_Values.
14 www.cultdyn.co.uk/Process/indexAdagioGeneral.php.
15 www.cultdyn.co.uk/valuesmodes3.html.
16 https://en.wikipedia.org/wiki/Wicked_problem.
17 www.cultdyn.co.uk/alphabet/index.php.

18 www.slideshare.net/tochrisrose/values-story-to-brexit-split-rev.
19 www.cultdyn.co.uk/alphabet/ThrowItUp.php?What=force.
20 The Values Story of the Brexit Split (Part 1).
   http://threeworlds.campaignstrategy.org/?p=1462
   Brexit Values Story Part 2.1, http://threeworlds.campaignstrategy.org/?p=1601;
   Brexit Values Story 2.2: Brexit Warning, http://threeworlds.campaign-strategy.org/?p=2305.
21 at http://threeworlds.campaignstrategy.org/?p=1462 and www.slideshare.net/tochrisrose/values-story-to-brexit-split-rev.
22 https://blogs.lse.ac.uk/politicsandpolicy/personal-values-brexit-vote/.
23 http://threeworlds.campaignstrategy.org/?p=2104.
24 http://threeworlds.campaignstrategy.org/?p=2305.
25 http://threeworlds.campaignstrategy.org/?p=2191.
26 http://threeworlds.campaignstrategy.org/?p=1468.
27 at http://threeworlds.campaignstrategy.org/?p=1462 and www.slideshare.net/tochrisrose/values-story-to-brexit-split-rev.
28 http://threeworlds.campaignstrategy.org/?p=2305.
29 http://threeworlds.campaignstrategy.org/?p=1468.
30 www.amazon.co.uk/Finite-Infinite-Games-James-Carse/dp/1476731713.
31 See also Simon Sinek, who has developed this concept in terms of business in his 2019 book, *The Infinite Game*. https://simonsinek.com/the-infinite-game.

References

Carse, J., Finite-Infinite Games, 1986.

Crutzen, P., The Man Who Invented the Anthropocene, *New Statesman*, 12 – 18 February 2021.

Cultdyn (cultdyn.co.uk), http://www.cultdyn.co.uk/ART067736u/PeopleBuyPubsNotBeer.pdf, 2021A.

Cultdyn (cultdyn.co.uk), http://www.cultdyn.co.uk/Process/indexAdagioGeneral.php, 2021B.

Cultdyn (cultdyn.co.uk), http://www.cultdyn.co.uk/valuesmodes3.html, 2021C.

Cultdyn (cultdyn.co.uk), http://www.cultdyn.co.uk/alphabet/index.php, 2021D.

Cultdyn (cultdyn.co.uk), http://www.cultdyn.co.uk/alphabet/ThrowItUp.php?What=force, 2021E.

Inglehart, R., and Welzel, C., *Modernization, Cultural Change and Democracy: The Human Development Sequence*, Cambridge University Press, 2005.

Inglehart, R., *Cultural Evolution: People's Motivations Are Changing, and Reshaping the World*, Cambridge University Press, 2018.

LSE Blog, https://blogs.lse.ac.uk/politicsandpolicy/personal-values-brexit-vote/, 2021.

MacClean, N., Democracy in Chains, *Scribe UK*, 2017.

Our World Data (https://ourworldindata.org/war-and-peace Max Roser. [https://archive.nytimes.com/www.nytimes.com/imagepages/2011/11/06/opinion/06atrocities_timeline.html - [Good graphic]]. (Data from atrociologist Matthew White, *The Great Big Book of Horrible Things* ISBN: 978-0-393-08192-3).

Rose, C., *What Makes People Tick: The Three Hidden Worlds of Settlers*, Prospectors and Pioneers, Matador, 2011.

Rose, C., Links and Resources on Motivational Values Webiste.

Rosling, O., and Rosling, A., https://www.gapminder.org/fw/world-health-chart/ and Factfulness, Spectre, 2018

Shrubsole, G., *Who Owns England?*, William Collins, 2019

Sinek, S., *The Infinite Game*, 2019.

Slideshare, https://www.slideshare.net/tochrisrose/values-story-to-brexit-split-rev, 2021

Theory of basic Human Values, *Wiklipedia*, https://en.wikipedia.org/wiki/Theory_of_Basic_Human_Values, 2021.

Threeworlds, http://threeworlds.campaignstrategy.org, various pages, 2021.

Wicked Problem, *Wikipedia*, https://en.wikipedia.org/wiki/Wicked_problem, 2021.

Wilson, E. O., *The Social Conquest of Earth*, Liveright, 2013.

World Values Survey, https://www.worldvaluessurvey.org/wvs.jsp, 2021.

4

WHAT CAN YOUNG SOCIAL ENTREPRENEURS TELL US ABOUT ENVIRONMENTAL LEADERSHIP?

PERSPECTIVES FROM BRAZIL AND INDIA

Bharati Singh

Introduction

There is a divergence of opinion on available literature about social enterprise and the environment. Vickers (2010) stated that there is substantial literature connecting the two, whereas, more recently, in 2020, Fitzgerald and Darko, specifically talking about the United Kingdom (UK), stated that such literature was inadequate. However, a common theme that does emerge is confusion around the definition of 'social enterprise'. The other interpretational dilemma is about the term 'environmental leadership'. Whilst much has been written on environmental leadership (see Dechant et al., 1994; Portugal & Yukl, 1994; Case et al., 2015), in recent times, many youngsters or what is popularly known as Generation Z and the millennials

DOI: 10.4324/9781003190820-5

are also being hailed as environmental leaders for adopting a rhetoric against authority in the face of climate change.

Thus, this chapter aims to relook at the definition of a social enterprise and that of environmental leader/leadership. In the case of environmental leadership, the aim is to demarcate it from environmental activism in order to establish the role of the young environmental leader. The latter will be based upon two interviews with young social entrepreneurs. Both originating and now based out of separate emerging economies; thus, giving credence to south–south economic engagement or cooperation. Consideration will be accorded to their motivations, capabilities and available resources, challenges faced; and how they balance and integrate the 'triple bottom line' in pursuit of making a difference to the planet.

Social enterprise

Social enterprises are companies that want to bring about a change in the world. While the aim is profitability, utilisation of the profits thus generated is disparate from corporate enterprises that generate profits only towards enhancing shareholder or stockholder value. Social enterprises have a commitment towards creating social value both within and outside the organisational boundaries (Trivedi & Stokols, 2011). Corporate enterprises may also create social value but do so indirectly and not as a direct objective or mission of such enterprises.

Interpreting the social enterprise, Borzaga et al. (2012), state the following:

- Social enterprises provide goods and services that may not be easily accessible to less than affluent levels of society;
- Profit margin is not the only objective.;
- Public interventions are not adequate to service all levels of society, thus social enterprises have emerged; however, they are not substitutes for public, corporate or non-profit organisations;
- Social enterprises require analysis of both human behaviour and the role of the enterprise in itself; thus, confirming the multiple motivations of such enterprises which include intrinsic and social aspects.

Considering the above points, the authors suggest that a social enterprise 'can be regarded as an incentive structure that is consistent with the goal of producing goods or services to the advantage of the community or a group of citizens' (p. 8).

Social enterprises work in the open market, create employability, often produce products that are environment friendly, and help and support the communities wherein they are based (SE, UK, 2021). However, there is a tautological issue in clearly identifying the balance between social value and economic value outcomes perceived to come from social enterprises. To that extent, Stevens et. al. (2015) conducted a quantitative study to validate the relationship between the social and economic value and concluded that the two constructs were at divergent ends of a continuum. Thus, indicating that when integrating social good and economic value mindset and internal resources are key. Nonetheless, it is clear that social enterprises are motivated with social concerns. The social concerns can be both environmental and ethical; with environmental innovation to achieve sustainability at the heart of the social enterprise (Vickers, 2010); thus, making explicit that social enterprise and the environment have a positive correlation. Social enterprises can be a solution for the anthropogenic climate change-led 'market failures', providing both economic and social value but also requiring governmental support (Dean & McMullan, 2007). From a strategy perspective, given the unpredictability of the environmental factors, social enterprises can be considered as 'visionary', having innovative and creative ideas which lead to adapting and shaping through collaboration, which further leads to evolving as their paths proceed (Reeves et al., 2015).

With increasing climate concerns, it has become crucial that human and business activities are altered to reduce emissions linked with increasing temperatures, changing patterns of rainfall, melting glaciers and other environmental degradations (EEA, 2021). Hence, this then raises another question: if the managers at the helm of social enterprises clearly have a sustainability objective, can they be hailed as environmental leaders?

Environmental leader/leadership

Managers must be actively involved in any sustainability strategy of their organisations to counter ecological harms (Boiral et al., 2009). These managers should have the ability to lead and influence not only their co-workers but societies too. Leadership can be perceived as an influence mechanism between individuals and also processes that organise social reforms (Burns, 1978). Hence, when it comes to the environment, it is the realm of influence on activities that do not harm the environment – for people to think 'green'. To this extent, any individual who can persuade others to adopt green activities or even managers who can persuade senior management to have organisational policies to reduce harmful effect to the environment can be considered as 'environmental leaders' (Portugal & Yukl, 1994).

'Environmental Leadership is the ability to influence individuals and mobilise organisations to realise a vision of long-term ecological sustainability' (Egri & Herman, 2000, p. 2). One may ask why do we need to define environmental leadership and how is it different from leadership. Redekop (2010) claims that the physical environment, to a large extent, has been ignored in leadership studies. Given the serious issue of climate change being imminent, environmental concerns have become larger than life, and thus conventional leadership is often automatically assumed to translate into environmental leadership. From an environmental perspective, traditional notions of leadership in the singular sense are not favourable (Case et al., 2015), as it requires consideration of diverse social objectives. Nonetheless the practice of leadership today is more focused towards a global agenda emanating from environmental and social complexities, thus linking leadership to the natural environment (Akiyama et al. 2013). Thinking about the environment is not only limited to social enterprises but there is a growing shift amongst the mindset of profit-seeking businesses that environmentalism is not only about compliance but about overall company strategies to go 'green' which then renders product innovation and future technology (Dechant et al., 1994).

In face of the pandemic (Covid-19), when working from home became the new normal, there was also a loss of millions of jobs, negative growth rates for countries, the rise of extreme poverty and increases in malnourishment; however, the decrease in air travel and transport to work has largely reduced carbon emission levels around the world. Nonetheless, millions of job losses are perhaps not the most ethical way to reduce emissions (Jackson quoted in Myrick, 2020). Sustainability experts confirm that the focus on environmental issues will be of paramount importance as economies start re-opening and businesses reach their optimal output (Malmqvist, 2020). Companies need to build resilience to combat future shocks from Covid-19 by embedding environmental sustainability in their strategies now if not already considered in the past. Hence, the role of environmental leadership becomes even more pressing towards developing more lasting sustainability measures.

As stated above, anyone who can persuade others to be 'green' can be considered an environmental leader. Thus, many youngsters today are being hailed as environmental leaders, they are featured on various world forums, newspaper articles and magazines and are the centre of attention in climate change conversations. While history confirms that young people can be leaders (Ramey & Lawford, 2020), with reference to climate change, is it a case of just talking the talk and not walking the walk? While there is no doubt about the substantial social impact that has been created by students boycotting schools, the bigger question is if environmental goals can be achieved by such methods, thus leading to the question of whether the very young have the perceived intellect to understand the gravity of climate change. When the 'School Strike' took place in 2019, there was a rhetoric about the strikers using various gadgets that create pollution but not willing to give them up, travelling on diesel-powered school buses to head back to comfortable homes post the strike and questions about adequate knowledge or authority on climate issues (Feldman, 2020). The outbursts have been labelled more emotional than evidence-backed. Is participating in conferences and listening to climate experts' sufficient criteria to be hailed as an environmental leader? Notwithstanding the theory of Generativity, which is concerned for the future and mainly considers the middle aged (Ramey & Lawford, 2020), there is research that confirms the young can be generatively motivated; but there is little evidence of real impact and some of the actions are being labelled as disruptive and dangerous dissent (O'Brien et al., 2018). They can at best be considered as examples of environmental activism rather than environmental leadership.

'To do good, you actually have to do something' – Yvon Chouinard

Aspiring leaders must know what their 'walk' will emulate as that will link to the values origin of their 'talk', thus confirming success of social influence (Aitken 2007). Hence, environmental leaders are those who are walking the talk. They understand the challenges of sustainability and are leading the way towards sustainable goals that involve environmental performance in their product designs, supply chain and profitability; they are willing to take risks from the outset and try innovative ideas (Kashmanian et al., 2010). The modelling of the senior management concept known as 'tone at the top' (Byars & Stanberry, 2018), paves the path for any company – whether it be for ethical behaviours or towards sustainability. Environmental leaders are those who are making a change through real action where the companies or enterprises that they lead are clearly focused on environmental causes and have a sustainability agenda.

However, 26% of the world population today is under the age of 15 (Statista 2020), hence, it is essential to promote sustainability to the young. Linking it back to United Nations's 17 SDGs, the development and effectiveness of the goals depend on developing the youth through awareness, knowledge and education (Yahya, 2020). Billimoria (2016) has reported that involving the youth to achieve the SDGs require implementation of economic citizenship plans by policy makers towards feasible economic, social and environmental systems. Almost 30 years ago, in 1992, the UN had identified the youth to be key stakeholders in resolving environmental issues (Corriero, 2004). It is true that young people today have more exposure, due to advances in technology and communication, and thus have the power to make more instrumental changes than previous generations. Thus, the youth need to continue to be aware of sustainability issues and the earth's vulnerability to climate change and other environmental harms, which will be perilous for the future. They need to think about the actions that they can take today for a better tomorrow, which has been echoed by one of the interviewees and discussed later in this chapter.

Having established the role of the environmental leader, the next section discusses two companies being led by young people who are only in their twenties, their role as young environmental leaders and the sustainable action changes that they have undertaken.

The two companies and the two leaders
Company backgrounds

Carbon credit is not a new term in the 21st century. Many companies have and many others are in the process of undertaking activities that can offset their carbon footprint. The first company that we discuss here has introduced plastic credit and has created the world's first plastic credit platform. Every kilogram of plastic recycled equates to 1 plastic credit that then enables the company to finance waste management organisations. They also have a plastic footprint calculator akin to a carbon footprint calculator. Not only does this company tackle plastic waste that has already been generated but they are working with companies to reduce plastic in their packaging. While the company is registered in the US, the chief marketing officer (CMO) and co-founder (interviewed) is based out of Goa, India.

The second company has a mission and objective to convince other companies to switch to sustainable agriculture. They believe that nature and agriculture can work together. Farmers, with a focus on developing/emerging nations, should have the ability to be economically resilient, attain food security and be self-sufficient. This company feels that this can be attained through regenerative agriculture which means increasing the quality of the soil, water storage and also conserving forestry. This is then expected to lead to greater motivation amongst farmers to diversify, thus having both an economic output (increasing yield) and a social output (rural development and woman empowerment). This company is headquartered in the Netherlands and the chief commercial officer (CCO) and co-founder (interviewed) is based out of Brazil.

From the company profiles, it can be easily inferred that both these companies have a sustainability agenda. They are dedicated to reducing waste, reducing poverty, development of rural areas, empowering women, increasing food security, fostering self-sufficiency and economic resilience and, most importantly, restoring the environmental balance, or as stated on their websites, 'restoring nature's balance' and 'environmental enhancement'. Using the definition of the environmental leader provided in the earlier section, it can be accepted that these two young leaders are 'environmental leaders'. They are making a change through real action and their companies are clearly focused on environmental causes.

Area of operation

The main projects that both the companies run are in emerging economies, like Brazil, India, Chile, Haiti, Ghana, Kenya, Mexico, Malaysia, Uganda, Columbia, etc. UNESCO (2019) has categorically stated that economic growth in emerging economies has aided in poverty reduction. However, the economic growth has also led to mass urbanisation which in turn is counterposing environmental threats (Jayanti & Gowda, 2014). Rapid industrialisation is putting pressure on the environment. The governments in emerging economies, while adopting strategies towards an environmental objective, remain vulnerable to climate change and other bio-diversity damages. This, coupled with governance and institutional challenges, has led to a slow progress towards a sustainability agenda amongst the emerging economies (UNESCO, 2019). Nonetheless, some of the most attractive green stimulus packages by way of policy frameworks and eco innovation can be found in emerging economies (EcoAp, 2011). Undoubtedly, a sustainability agenda can help emerging economies achieve enhanced food security, reduce poverty and vulnerability to climate change and increase resource development.

An interesting point that emerges here is that the projects and main operations of both the companies are entirely in emerging or developing economies. This can be connected to the concept of south–south economic engagement or south–south cooperation. In the terms used by organisations like the United Nations (UN) or United Nations Conference on Trade and Development (UNCTAD), south–south cooperation is essentially trade and investment related. However, in this case it can be extended as innovative, technical and training cooperation and not only be limited to capacity building and trade and economic cooperation (Corrêa, 2017). South–south cooperation has been identified as an important aspect towards achieving the United Nations's 2030 sustainability agenda (UNCTAD, 2019).

Backgrounds of the two leaders and their motivations

The co-founder and chief marketing officer (CMO) for the plastic credit company grew up between China and Norway, and the co-founder and chief commercial officer (CCO) for the regenerative company grew up in Brazil. They both confirmed that they their exposure to the environmental cause was 'privileged'. The CMO went to the US for higher education and received a grant to work on a project in an emerging economy towards a sustainability objective. CCO's mother was environmentally conscious and instilled similar values in him from a young age. His father was associated with the finance industry for more than three decades and used his connections and expertise to procure seed funding for the venture.

YOUNG SOCIAL ENTREPRENEURS AND LEADERSHIP

While at university CMO participated in the Hult Prize Foundation North American regional competition. The Hult Prize Foundation, which is more than a decade old, is a competition that is held across more than 3,000 universities in 121 countries. The main aim is to transform young people's vision for the future and become impact leaders of change (Hult, 2021). That experience led CMO to work with an emerging economy on plastic waste management systems.

CCO, as a young adult, visited the Amazon forest and said the following about his experience:

> When I was 18, I went to Amazon to see with my own eyes how defor-estation is taking place for commodity use for industries like soybean cattle ranching and logging industries and this is really terrifying if we think about sustainability of landscapes in the future for coming generations.

For his final project, the CMO and his team at university decided to work on 'informal waste management' and the emerging economy that they selected was India. For them, the stark contrast between poverty and the glamour and glitz that coexisted was fascinating. In his words:

> It was an emotional awakening and a logical awakening ... the emo-tional awakening was when we visited one of the largest landfills in Mumbai ... and we were sort of standing in between these two very drastically contrasting things ... on the one side we had these massive mountains of plastic as far as the eyes can see, waste pickers and waste workers ... risk of collapse (mountains of waste) and burning happening ... and on the other side you have this shining metropolis that is India's financial capital ... with this endless concrete skyline ... that contrast was a shocking moment.

This experience led the CMO to contemplate starting the social enterprise and work on waste management systems.

For CCO, his mother, on a visit to India, was greatly influenced by the culture and was amazed that the majority of the population was vegetarian. She took to vegetarianism (this is different from veganism) and influenced him to also be a vegetarian. CCO, as a young adult was later able to associ-ate vegetarianism with the environmental cause since diets rich in animal products lead to environmental degradation and food insecurity, whereas plant-based diets reduce the strain on earth's resources (Fresán & Sabaté, 2019).

This association of depleting environment resources and increasing food insecurity led the CCO to start the regenerative agroforestry venture.

Resources and capabilities

For this section of the chapter, the Resource-Based View (RBV) will be considered to establish the specific capabilities that the young leaders possess and efficient use of resources available to them that make them successful environmental leaders.

RBV theory is based on the seminal work of Penrose (1959) (Barney, 1991). While her work is predominantly used to understand the nature of the firm, international business and strategy, the theory can be related to social enterprises too.

> Penrose stated that each firm was unique based on the services that its resources rendered. The resources when combined with other resources or used in different ways rather than what its initial use was or used in varying measurements provide distinctive services. These services are in the form of physical goods or intangible services which are sold to generate profits and expand or grow the firm.
>
> (Singh, 2017, p. 60)

As already established, social enterprises do have an objective to make profits but do so by providing both tangible and intangible services, the latter in the form of social values generated.

Capabilities and dynamic capabilities can also be attributed to the RBV (Nieves & Haller, 2014; Dunning & Lundan, 2008). Resources possessed can be adapted per the dynamic environment (both internal and external) (Helfat & Winter, 2011; Ambrosini & Bowman, 2009).

The dynamism of the young leaders (interviewed), environmental concerns leading to their social enterprises, their motivations, collaborations generating both social and economic values are indicative of dynamic capabilities combining both entrepreneurial activity and managerial capability. As Helfat et al. (2007) have confirmed, dynamic capabilities comprise of entrepreneurial action alongside organisational strategy. Teece (2014) substantiated that entrepreneurial management activity is the creation of new idea markets. In this case, both the enterprises are the first of their kind of operation, in that the company having the world's first plastic credit platform is registered in the US and the other company, having revitalised an ancient tradition of regenerative agro forestry that helps farmers across emerging economies, is registered in Netherlands.

'Teece further adds that entrepreneurial management activity also entails the creation of new knowledge and new opportunities to increase commercialised transactions' (Singh, 2017, p. 215). In the case of social enterprises, entrepreneurs can be considered as the firm's main resources and with their new ideas can create distinctive products and services (Penrose, 1959) which alluded by Teece (2014) confirms description of dynamic capabilities.

Strategic linkages is a crucial capability that helps the growth of social enterprises and builds legitimacy (Vickers & Lyon, 2012). Having a range of stakeholders with varying degrees of interests and demands on realising economic and social value (challenges are deliberated in the next section), networks are imperative for the survival of social enterprises. This is indicative in both the companies under discussion. CMO claimed that:

> Achieving scalable impact is important but there are too many silos ... we don't need silos ... there are too many silos even in the environmental space ... lot of criticism back and forth between organisations ... there is discourse with non-profit organisations, there is discourse with academia, there is discourse with brands, discourse with social entrepreneurs ... our business change model is built upon constructing communities and breaking down silos.

Whilst CCO said:

> We are trying to ... you know like build ... strong networks to make sure that we have the best business cases for the corporates and investors to see in regenerative agriculture, so that we don't fail and compromise the name of the regenerative agriculture.

These companies are operating in emerging markets which are highly unpredictable and are using new technologies, in such cases, companies do seek alliances which could be in the form of volunteers, business corporations, universities, policymakers and other stakeholders (Eisenhardt & Schoonhoven, 1996; Vickers & Lyon, 2012). The social impact of social enterprises requires engagement with different stakeholders including government support to generate income and this is highly dependent on their capabilities (Basque & Eddleston, 2018).

Social enterprise and its challenges

As defined earlier in this chapter, social enterprises are companies that want to bring about a change in the world. While the aim is profitability, the way the profit is used is far different from mere profit generating companies which only seek to enhance shareholder value. CMO described the nature of their social enterprise as follows:

> we are a profit based social enterprise, we don't hide behind that at all, we are a public benefit corporation ... legal charter is to achieve profits and to achieve impact ... there is not one above the other. Social entrepreneurship is not a panacea ... but is a really (really) amazing solution for market-based areas of social environmental impact ... scale comes with profit ....for us the theory of change is built upon constructing communities and breaking down silos (discourse of profit versus non-profit, academia, brands and social enterprises)..

He further explained that for the brands that they work with, generating profit is an important aspect; however, they are also trying to surpass the minimum CSR requirement and go beyond; and this can only be achieved through investments which in turn can be created only by generating profits. These brands want to exceed the 'conscious' customer's expectation of environmentally friendly products and also invest into employee well-being and retention (Figure 4.1).

For CCO, the non-profit motive preceded the for-profit company motive:

> The company is both the foundation and also a company, so it's both a non-profit and for profit; we started as a non-profit because our main, you know, purpose was impact ... we have mission that we have to empower farmers to regenerate nature. But of course, once we start seeing that there are a lot of like companies and you know commercial possible projects coming into our pipeline. We start thinking about

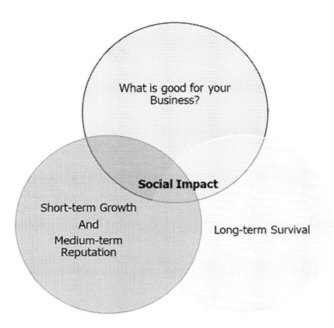

Figure 4.1 A sustainability agenda or what can be considered a green business strategy has social impact at the centre of its being, for the CMO it can be visually represented as follows.

> hey, maybe we should open also a business you know ... So today we have the foundation, which is, you know, receiving funds and grants for component. While we're doing also through the company and the business-like commercial projects with corporates.

In their conversation, both the young leaders emphasised the importance of 'social impact'. For hybrid companies such as social enterprises, the social impact is a focal point that can endorse the success of their missions and confirm if there is a positive change (Grieco et al., 2015) towards the well-being of the planet and the people while making profit; thus, satisfying the requirements of the Tripple Bottom Line (TBL). The concept of TBL (Elkington, 2018) was conceptualised in 1994 and was a framework that encompassed not only profit measures for companies but also social and environmental dimensions. It remains as relevant today given the UN Sustainable Goals for 2030 (SDG) to improve human lives and protect the earth (UN, 2015). 'To fulfil external accountability expectations social impact measurement has become an important practice for social enterprises' (Molecke & Pinkse, 2017, p. 550).

The main challenge that both stated was about managing stakeholder expectations. It was about managing divergent expectations raised by environmentally conscious groups which ranged from investors to customers. CMO said:

> It is about finding the nuggets of cooperation amongst the various stakeholders. They are far and few in between in the social entrepreneurship and social impact world but once found it is a go.

CCO had similar thoughts:

> The ones that we are the closest are the farmers and communities and these are the ones that we are giving priority. But for sure like the other ones in that ecosystem like buyers and then companies as well as the research institutes are stakeholders ... but in each particular project we try to identify which stakeholder belongs to the project context. And then we include them as a partner ... we see what is the alignment in the scope of the project. But in an overall like we always do this stakeholder analysis to understand for which project segmentation they fit in to.

There is evidence from research confirming that the success of business models based on sustainability strategies are dependent on cohesive stakeholder engagement (Abuzeinab & Arif, 2014). A study of 119 sustainability reports by Stocker et al. (2020) from 40 countries in the energy sector further confirms the importance of stakeholder engagement in the success of sustainability strategies by organisations. This is further reiterated in a systematic literature review of articles published between 1985 and 2015 in five separate databases that further substantiate that stakeholder engagement and management has become an integral part of organisational strategy (Pedrini & Feri, 2019). 'Formal and informal networks are important mechanisms for brokering cooperative relationships to meet shared ideals' (Vickers & Lyon, 2012, p. 14).

Main message from the two young environmental leaders

As already mentioned, both the young leaders are in their twenties belonging to Generation Z. A survey conducted by Amnesty International in 2019 of 10,000 Generation Z across 22 countries confirmed that the climate change issue was in the forefront of their minds (Barbiroglio, 2019).

CMO confirmed this, when they said that 'Gen Z is the first generation in the way we think about environmental activism. I see myself as that first generation to think differently'.

In both the companies the teams are young. There is no scarcity of young talent that want to make a difference. "Youngsters are looking for opportunities that are interesting and good for us [communities]" stated CMO. Whilst CCO said:

> We are receiving ... you know at least five CV's and motivation letters a week. There's a lot of young people wanting to work with us. We have already a long list of 800 volunteers [who have] applied in our website. And you know the interest is really big and the ones that we are currently working within the organization they are so passionate about [the cause]. Like working on something that has a meaningful purpose.

Both the young leaders emphasised the importance of embedding sustainability in education to build the foundation for the next generation of conscious consumers. As a UK-based survey on Generation Z summarised, global warming and air pollution was worrisome, and while they want to be eco-friendly where packaging is concerned, they worry that big businesses are still handing out plastics (Topić & Mitchell, 2019).

The regenerative farming company is collaborating with universities as the CCO confirmed:

> So, if we're going to start a project in Indonesia in Bogor, for example, we're going to partner with a University ... so we always try to engage with students from universities, local universities that are next to the project, and they always help with the measuring impact on the farms. Or you know, doing their own internship [and] getting their hands [dirty] on the farm or even doing economic analysis of the system. So, we always try to engage them in the process as well.

CMO reiterated:

> Exposure is privileged and I am very aware of that ... and the team have got that, and the international exposure, the thinking and the

> mentality, which a slum boy growing in Dharavi [made famous in the movie Slumdog Millionaire] Mumbai will not get and they will chuck plastic on the road and they will never get that consciousness as the system never taught them to do something differently.

A private school for the less privileged in Assam, India, which commenced in 2016, has been taking fees in the form of plastic, the students are expected to submit 200 pieces of plastic towards the cost of their education (Sindwani, 2019). The young couple who started the school again come from privileged backgrounds, having studied in New York and the best schools in India; however, through this venture, they are trying to increase the awareness of the harmful effects of plastic by educating the less privileged, they are embedding the sustainability cause into the curriculum.

As Yvon Chouinard, the very active environmentalist and founder of Patagonia has stated 'Everything we personally own that's made, sold, shipped, stored, cleaned, and ultimately thrown away does some environmental harm every step of the way, harm that we're either directly responsible for or is done on our behalf'.

The UK government introduced the Environment Bill in January 2020 which sets out a plan to protect and improve the natural environment in the country (Gov.UK, 2020). While sustainability and a green strategy has become part of organisational decision making, many companies are yet to embed the 'green cause' wholeheartedly and hence it has become crucial that governments introduce environmental policies as polluters do not bear the direct consequences of their actions and there is incorrect assumption that natural resources are infinite (Bueren, 2019).

As the CMO echoed: 'What is needed is Green Policy and a Green Mentality, they go side by side'. If companies have a sustainability strategy, they may not have a workforce with similar mentality; but if both a sustainability strategy and a workforce having a sustainability mindset are available, a broader governmental sustainability policy may be missing.

Further, governmental policy should not be restricted to only organisations but as stated in an earlier section, it should be embedded in the educational system too.

The CMO emphasised that youngsters needed to pick a cause as it is not possible for everyone to start a social enterprise:

> It's just not about posting in social media or going to protests ... or those sorts of activisms, right, like signatures ... young people particularly need to have a balance, a holistic view of what it takes to make our world a better place ... which will start by making changes in your own lives ... picking your cause.

The CCO went further to emphasise that educated people need to have the sustainability consciousness and educate others, starting from their own families and children:

> I do plan to have at least two [children] ... I think it's important. I think this argument of like let's not have children anymore ... Like it's not about that ... It's about us putting up on the positive impact on the planet because we live in abundant world. We are bringing scarcity because of our unconsciousness ... but I think we if we raise children with the you know, the mindset of like doing something positive for the planet and being a changemaker. It is the next generation ... we need more people who are aware of the environment.

As Mahatma Gandhi had said:
> 'We must become the change we want to see in the world'.

Conclusion

With access to advancements in communication and technology, the youth have a monumental role to play as influencers for policy changes towards protecting the earth. While there is youth activism present towards 'climate change' and its concerns, the sustainability cause is required to be embedded in schools and the higher education curriculum. The young generation are environmentally conscious, but it is somewhat restricted to the privileged. It is imperative that all echelons of society, especially in emerging economies, are made aware of the perils of environmental degradation.

This chapter has provided some clarification on the definition of social enterprises. While the main objective of such enterprises is sustainability, they also have a profit motive, thus fulfilling the requirements of the 'triple bottom line' concept. Such enterprises are not substitutes for non-profit organisations or public and private corporations. However, their presence cannot be denied as they create both social and economic value. The majority of such enterprises concern themselves with environmental causes and can be considered a solution for the human-led climate change challenges facing the earth and the future generations. Nonetheless, such enterprises cannot survive on their own merits and require both govern-mental support and extended networks. Social enterprises are innovative and creative in their ideas and have the ability to collaborate and evolve quickly.

The chapter then tackled the interpretation of environmental leader/leadership. Given that the term 'leadership' is constituted in discursive terms (see chapter by David Collins), it established that environmental leadership is different from environmental activism. Although a very lim-ited sample, the two young leaders interviewed have confirmed that the RBV is a useful tool to make sense of and support the development of environmental leadership. This was affirmed by their dynamism to co-found and lead enterprises with social and economic values and innova-tive ideas for sustained environmental protection while creating economic resilience for the less entitled. The entrepreneurial mindset of the two young leaders can be expressed as the main resources for the enterprises. Furthermore, stakeholder management was a key consideration for both the enterprises. While they were running social enterprises, stakehold-ers were key to success and challenges did arise as each stakeholder had a different requirement. They further emphasised that networks and col-laboration along with policy support was essential for meeting objectives of their enterprises.

Interestingly, both the social enterprises have their main operations in emerging economies, where the need to be sustainable is higher than the developed world due to lack of knowledge and education and rampant pov-erty. This is indicative of a south–south cooperation which is considered crucial to meet the UN's 2030 sustainability agenda. Although both the young leaders admitted that their upbringing was privileged, they were greatly motivated towards environmental causes based on their first-hand experience with the reality of waste management and environmental degradation.

References

Abuzeinab, A. & Arif, M. (2014). Stakeholder Engagement: A Green Business Model Indicator, *Procedia Economics and Finance*, 18.

Aitken, P. (2007). 'Walking the Talk': The Nature and Role of Leadership Culture within Organisation Culture/s, *Journal of General Management*, 32:4, pp. 17–37

Akiyama, T., An, K.J., Furumai, H. & Katayam, H. (2013). The Concept of Environmental Leader. In: Mino, T. & Hanaki, K. (eds) *Environmental Leadership Capacity Building in Higher Education*, pp. 19–40, Springer, Tokyo.

Ambrosini, V. & Bowman, C. (2009). What Are Dynamic Capabilities and are They a Useful Construct in Strategic Management? *International Journal of Management Reviews*, 11:1, pp. 29–49

Barbiroglio e. (2019). Generation Z fears Climate Change More than Anything Else, *Green Tech in Forbes*, Editor's Pick, December 09, 2019.

Barney, J.B. (1991). Firm Resources and Sustained Competitive Advantage, *Journal of Management*, 17:1, pp. 99–120.

Basque, S. & Eddleston, K.A. (2018). A Resource Based View of Social Entrepreneurship: How Stewardship Culture benefits Scale of Social Impact, *Journal of Business Ethics*, 152, pp. 589–611.

Billimoria, J. (2016). Why Young People Are Key to Achieving the SDGs, World Economic Forum, September 26, 2016.

Boiral, O., Cayer, M. & Baron, C.M. (2009). The Action Logics of Environmental Leadership – A Developmental Perspective, *Journal of Business Ethics*, 85, pp. 479–499.

Borzaga, C., Depefri, S. & Galera, Giulia, (2012). Interpreting social enterprises, *Revista de Administracao*, pp. 398–409

Bueren, E.v. (2019). Environmental Policy, *Encyclopedia Britannica*, 11 Feb. 2019, https://www.britannica.com/topic/environmental-policy

Burns, B.M. (1978). *Leadership*, New York, Harper and Row.

Byars, S.M. & Stanberry, K. (2018). *Business Ethics*, Open Stax, Rice University.

Case, P., Evans, L.S., Fabinyi, M., Cohen, P.J., Hicks, C.C. & Mills, D.J. (2015). Rethinking Environmental Leadership: The Social Construction of Leaders and Leadership in Discourses of Ecological Crisis, Development, and Conservation, *Leadership*, 11:4, pp. 396–423.

Corrêa, M. (2017). Quantification of South-South Cooperation and Its Implications to the Foreign Policy of Developing Countries, *Policy Brief, South Centre*, 41, July 2017.

Corriero, J. (2004). Role of Youth Survey. Retrieved January 30, 2004, from www.takingitglobal.com

Dean, T.J. & McMullen, J.S. (2007). Toward a Theory of Sustainable Entrepreneurship: Reducing Environmental Degradation Through Entrepreneurial Action, *Journal of Business Venturing*, 22:1, pp. 50–76,

Dechant, K., Altman, B., Dowining, R.M. & Keeny, T. (1994). Environmental Leadership: From Compliance to Competitive Advantage, *Academy of Management Executive*, 8:3, pp. 7.

Dunning, J.H. & Lundan, S.M. (2008). Institutions and the OLI Paradigm of the Multinational Enterprise, *Asia Pacific Journal of Management*, 25:4, pp. 573–593.

EcoAp (2011). 11th European Forum on Eco-Innovation Working with Emerging Economies for Green Growth, *Eco Innovation Action Plan*, 11th and 12th October 2011, Finland

EEA (2021). *Climate Change is One of the Biggest Challenges of Our Times*, European Environmental Agency, https://www.eea.europa.eu/themes/climate/climate-change-is-one-of

Egri, C. & Herman, S. (2000). Leadership in the North American Environmental Sector: Values, Leadership Styles and Contexts of Environmental Leaders and Their Organizations, *Academy of Management Journal*, 43:4, pp. 571–604.

Eisenhardt, K.M. & Schoonhoven, C.B. (1996). Resource-based View of Strategic Alliance Formation: Strategic and Social Effects in Entrepreneurial Firms, *Organization Science*, 7:2, pp. 136–150.

Elkington, J. (2018). 25 Years Ago I Coined the Phrase "Triple Bottom Line." Here's Why It's Time to Rethink It. *Harvard Business Review*, June 25, 2018.

Feldman, H.R. (2020). A Rhetorical Perspective on Youth Environmental Activism, *Journal of Science Communication*, 19:06, C07, https://doi.org/10.22323/2.19060307

Fresán, U. & Sabaté, J. (2019). Vegetarian Diets: Planetary Health and Its Alignment with Human Health. *Advances in nutrition (Bethesda, Md.)*, 10:4, pp. S380–S388, https://doi.org/10.1093/advances/nmz019

Grieco, C., Michelini, L. & Iasevoli, G. (2015). Measuring Value Creation in Social Enterprises: A Cluster Analysis of Social Impact Assessment Models, *Nonprofit and Voluntary Sector Quarterly*, 44:6, pp. 1173–1193.

Gov.UK (2020). *Environment Bill 2020 Policy Statement*, Department for Environment Food & Rural Affairs, 30 January 2020.

Helfat, C.E. & Winter, S.G. (2011). Untangling Dynamic and Operational Capabilities: Strategy for the (N) Ever-changing World, *Strategic Management Journal*, 32:11, pp. 1243–1250

Helfat, C.E., Finkelstein, S., Mitchell, W., Peteraf, M.A., Singh, H., Teece, D.J. & Winter, S., (2007). Dynamic Capabilities. Understanding Dynamic Change in Organizations, Blackwell Publishing

HULT (2021). Leading a Generation to Change the World, *HULT Website*, https://www.hultprize.org/

Jayanti, R.K. & Gowda. M.V.R. (2014). Sustainability Dilemmas in Emerging Economies, *IIMB Management Review*, 26:2, pp. 130–142, ISSN 0970-3896.

Kashmanian, R., Keenan, C. & Wells, R. (2010). Corporate Environmental Leadership: Drivers, Characteristics and Examples, *Environmental Quality Management*, 10:1002.

Malmqvist, T. (2020). Corporate Sustainability Leadership During a Pandemic, *GreenBiz*, November 2, 2020, https://www.greenbiz.com/article/corporate-sustainability-leadership-during-pandemic

Molecke, G. & Pinkse, J. (2017). Accountability for Social Impact: A Bricolage Perspective on Impact Measurement in Social Enterprises, *Journal of Business Venturing*, 32:5, pp. 550–568

Myrick, N. (2020). Environmental Leadership Will Be More in Demand Than Ever after COVID 19. Here's What You Need to Know to Be Prepared, *Tableau*, April 23, 2020, https://www.tableau.com/en-gb/about/blog/2020/4/environmental-leadership-after-covid-19

Nieves, J. & Haller, S. (2014). Building Dynamic Capabilities Through Knowledge Resources, *Tourism Management*, 40, pp. 224–232

O'Brien, K., Selboe, e. & Hayward, B.M. (2018). Exploring Youth Activism on Climate Change: Dutiful, Disruptive, and Dangerous Dissent, *Ecology and Society*, 23:3:42. https://doi.org/10.5751/ES-10287-230342

Pedrini, M. & Ferri, L.M. (2019). Stakeholder Management: A Systematic Literature Review, *Corporate Governance*, 19:1, pp. 44–59

Penrose, E. (1959). *The Theory of the Growth of the Firm*, Oxford, Basil Blackwell (1966).

Portugal, E. & Yukl, G. (1994). Perspectives on Environmental Leadership, *Leadership Quarterly*, 5:3/4, pp. 27–276

Ramey, H.R. & Lawford, H. (2020). Why Activism is Natural for Young People, *Greater Good Magazine*, 28 February 2020, https://greatergood.berkeley.edu/article/item/what_activism_is_natural_for_young_people

Redekop, B.W. (2010). *Leadership for Environmental Sustainability*, Routledge, New York and Oxon.

Reeves, M., Haanaes, K., & Sinha, J. (2015). *Your Strategy Needs a Strategy: How to Choose and Execute the Right Approach*, Harvard Business Press, Boston.

SE, UK (2021). *What Is It All About?*, Social Enterprise, UK, https://www.socialenterprise.org.uk/what-is-it-all-about/

Sindwani, P. (2019). Plastic Waste as School Fees: A School in Assam Adopts a Novel Idea, *The Business Insider*, 26 July 2019, https://www.businessinsider.in/assam-school-offers-education-in-exchange-for-plastic-waste/articleshow/70397399.cms

Singh, B. (2017). The Internationalisation of Emerging Market Firms: A Study of the Indian Service Sector, UoY PhD Thesis, October 2017.

Statista (2020). World Population by Age and Region 2020, Statista Research Department, December 02, 2020, https://www.statista.com/statistics/265759/world-population-by-age-and-region/

Stevens, R., Moray, N. & Bruneel, J. (2015). The Social and Economic Mission of social Enterprises: Dimensions, Measurement, Validation, and Relation, *Entrepreneurship Theory and Practice*, 39:5, pp. 1051–1082.

Stocker, F., de Arruda, M.P., de Mascena, K.M.C. & Boaventura, J.M.G. (2020) Stakeholder Engagement in Sustainability Reporting: A Classification Model. *Corporate Social Responsibility Environment Managemental*, 27, pp. 2071–2080.

Teece, D. J. (2014). A Dynamic Capabilities-based Entrepreneurial Theory of the Multinational Enterprise, *Journal of International Business Studies*, 45:1, pp. 8–37.

Topić, M. & Mitchell, B. (2019). *Generation Z & Consumer Trends in Environmental Packaging, Project Report*, The Retail Institute, Leeds.

Trivedi, C. & Stokols, D. (2011). Social Enterprise and Corporate Enterprises: Fundamental Difference and Definign Features, *The Journal of Entrepreneurship*, 20:1, pp. 1–32

UN (2015). The 17 Goals, United Nations, https://sdgs.un.org/goals

UNCTAD (2019). South-South Cooperation for Trade, Investment and Structural Transformation, TD/B/66/6, June 2019.

UNESCO (2019). Towards Green Growth in Emerging Economies: Evidence from Environmental Performance Reviews, *OECD Green Growth Papers*, 2019–01.

Vickers, I. (2010). *Social Enterprise and the Environment: A Review of Literature*, Third Sector Research Centre, 22.

Vickers, I. & Lyon, F. (2012). Beyond Green Niches? Growth Strategies of Environmentally-motivated Social Enterprises, *International Samll Business Journal*, 32:4, pp. 449–470

Yahya, W.K., (2020). Engaging Youth Participation in Making Sustainability Work. In: Leal Filho, W., Wall, T., Azul, A., Brandli, L., & Özuyar, P. (eds) *Good Health and Well-Being. Encyclopedia of the UN Sustainable Development Goals*, Springer, Cham, https://doi.org/10.1007/978-3-319-69627-0_130-1

5

FRONTIERS OF FREEDOM

US ENVIRONMENTAL LEADERSHIP

Heather Crawford and Adam Bronstone

Introduction to the complexities

Wild spaces have, for as long as humankind has existed, held fears. Fear of the unknown, fear of the dark, fear of 'things' that could harm us. In modern times (time that stretches back several hundred years) the need to conquer the wild, to tame it, has been the definition of the pioneering spirit, of the move to the 'West' that sits in the American psyche. But what is the concept of pioneering in the modern world? As Louv (2010 p. 146) says 'the difference is one of degree, one way excites the senses, the other drowns the senses in noise and fumes and leaves tracks that last a thousand years'.

The dominance of 'flat' tradition – the largely horizontal world view of 'resolutely flat perspectives' which is as much a political failure as a perceptual one (Graham, 2016 pp. 4–7) is part of the problem. As a world society we do see things in the horizontal, questioning is tough, it forces us to look at the uncomfortable truths that lie beneath and entwined with our supposedly comfortable existence. For the most part this is not something 'we' want to do. The Anthropocene age in which we are living demonstrates

DOI: 10.4324/9781003190820-6

environmental change at a frightening rate 'in which crisis exists not as an ever deferred future apocalypse but rather as an ongoing occurrence experienced most severely by the most vulnerable' (Macfarlane, 2019 p. 14). But how much will people, governments, organisations do or take active responsibility for if the consequences are not those they have to face on a personal level?

How do we stop the denuding of wild spaces for coal or roads unless we ensure young people's unfettered connection to nature. Globalisation may bring its own problems but the close connections it forms through ease of communication brings benefits – witness the power of Greta Thunberg's school strike for climate change. 'As care of nature increasingly becomes an intellectual concept severed from the joyful experience of the outdoors where will the next environmentalists come from?' (Louv, 2010 p. 142).

America has long been torn between encouragement for personal connections to wilderness, seen in the idea of summer camp, for example, and the desire to exploit that same wilderness for profit. Leadership of the question of wilderness has see-sawed between a powerful business lobby and a burgeoning interest in environmental issues from environmental groups and cultural icons. Nowhere do these tensions emerge more clearly than in bad-tempered and contested constructions of the idea of the West.

Pioneering, ownership and environmental racism

For the US, the 'West' is held as being the anchoring sense of place, the origin of the pioneering spirit, captured by Edward Abbey as 'the West of my deep imaginings ... where the tangible and mythical become the same' (Abbey 1975).

Abraham Lincoln stated that 'every man should have the means and opportunity of benefitting his condition' (www.history.com/topics/american-civil-war/homestead-act). What he did with the Homestead Act 1862, perhaps unwittingly, was unleash environmental racism on a grand scale. The Dawes General Allotment Act (1887) formalised the injustices already taking place. The issues of water rights have history with the diverting of Milk River, Montana in 1900 affecting the Fort Belknap Reservation. The diversion and damming of the Truckee and Carson Rivers for agricultural irrigation and subsequent localised near extinction of Lohantan Trout from Pyramid Lake in the early 1900s was a direct attack on the Pyramid Lake

Paiute tribe which was dependant on the lake for food and water, and the Fallon whose access to water was severely disrupted without promised reparation (NRC, 1992).

Understanding of the need to protect communities harks back to the New Deal of the 1930s with projects such as the Missouri Flood Protection Scheme (Bureau of Reclamation) designed to protect large tracts of Louisiana and in particular the big cities. All well and good it would seem, except that it actually resulted in the flooding of agricultural land, villages and burial grounds in Native American tribal reservations (Lewis, 1995) – the protection of one sector of society at the expense of another.

The term 'environmental racism' (Bullard, 1993) was coined in the early 1980s in reference to what appeared to be the disproportionately high level of industrial complex siting near low-income and non-white areas with the 'racial correlation being stronger than the economic one' (Lartey and Laughland, 2019), with examples including 'Cancer Alley' and the contaminated waste burial site at Point Hope, Alaska. These issues yet again raise the question of the definition of 'environment' and where humans of all races sit. Too often it is a case of 'out of sight, out of mind', and inequality prevails where justice and basic human rights should take precedence.

The Dakota Access Pipeline protests at Standing Rock (Worland, 2016) highlights, yet again, the dilemma facing America: the 'American Dream' of economic wealth and self-sufficiency versus the environmental urgency and lack of care about people, basic rights (in this case access to unpolluted drinking water) and respect for heritage. The desecration of historic lands and culturally important sites returns us to the 'conqueror' view. The fact that almost no national airtime was afforded to such an important event which was 'reshaping the national conversation for any environmental project that would cross Native American land' (Lui, 2016) until a video showing the protest action was shared on YouTube (https://www.youtube.com/watch?v=15YAD0Us4N4) says much about political control of the media and how far down the agenda environmental issues, particularly regarding Native American and non-white American issues, truly are.

The management of land and water for profit has caused huge issues over the years with the state and federal movement of tribes off traditional lands highlighting the lack of learning from traditional practice (Lewis, 1995). That is not to say there has not been any transfer and that traditional practice cannot be profitable. The White Mountain and San Carlos

Apache have demonstrated successful, long-term ranching on reservations and National Forest locations. Whilst the Jicarilla Apache have developed a wildlife management system model of New Mexico resulting in significant income. (Lewis, 1995 p. 428) In fishery management however, the US vs. State of Washington (1974) saw what seemed to be an effective solution to access to fish and protection of traditional spawning grounds only for this to have replicated the initial issues but with different players (Knutson, 1987), demonstrating the complexity of environmental sustainability in its widest form.

And yet, sustainability, which is the true heart of forward-thinking conservation and environmentalism, cannot ignore human factors. From the genocide of Native American tribes during the land grab of the 1800s made possible by the Homestead Act 1862, to the Dust Bowl and the huge inequalities highlighted by Hurricane Katrina, habitat conservation has to take humans into account. Policies that favour massive political funders (and thus lobbyists) such as the NRA and the Hunting Lobby, unsustainable agricultural practices which result in massive food recalls on a weekly basis (Ducharme, 2019), plus water and logging violations undermine almost every effort to ensure sustainability.

In The Winning of the West (1889), Roosevelt tracks the westward movement of the incomers and in its very title hints at the future GOP approach to land as a possession. Yet his beliefs were those that would still today be thought of as essential to conversation and nurturing of the land for future generations. Such legislation as the American Antiquities Act 1906 were paramount in preserving heritage that millions think of as the essence of America. Roosevelt was unusual in his thinking (though perhaps not by modern standards) holding membership of the Stockman's Association and being a founding member of the Boone and Crockett Club. The latter being influential in the creation of the National Forest service, National Wildlife Service, National Parks, wildlife refuges and reserves – hugely influential work with lasting impact. Perhaps more hard hitting was its responsibility for the elimination of commercial hunting in the US, which, given the power held by hunters up until that time and the catastrophic effect on ecology, was truly groundbreaking.

The two major influences in all this, however, were Thoreau and Emerson, who can truly be called the fathers of environmentalism in the US. In Nature a series of essays and lectures, Emerson depicted nature as the source of spiritual and ethical wisdom (Emerson, 1836). His view was that humans could not see themselves as separate to nature, rather it was essential to understand how we work with and in nature rather than seeking to master it. There are echoes of this in Thoreau's *Walden* (1854) in which he advocates simple living, spirituality and conservation. His experiments at Walden Pond, the observations of his seasonal records (largely ignored in America for half a century after his death) serve as a source for scientific measurement of climate change and formed the basis for environmental decision-making that still holds influence today.

The establishment of Earth Day in 1970 (see www.earthday.org/history/) as a direct response to the Union Oil Platform, a blowout off California in 1969, was proclaimed by the United Nations as a way to honour the planet and the concept of peace. The decade marked a continuance of the grassroots movements around environmental issues and in the US heralded a series of bills that ushered in 'clean' legislation in a number of areas. It could be asserted that Nixon's legislative record was a result of forces acting upon him, including the spirit of the times, pressure from Democratic legislators and polling indicating the importance of such issues to the electorate. Nixon's statement that

> what is involved is something much bigger ... [and concerns] the use of our resources ... in a more effective way, and with more concern for preserving the beauty and natural resources that are so important to any kind of society that we want for the future ... We are going to do a better job that we have in the past
>
> (Barkdull, 1998)

has echoes of Kennedy's words; however, he seemed unable to convince the powerful environmental lobby with the Sierra Club stating, 'I don't believe in what you believe in' (Rinde, 2017).

Abbey was a fierce critic of what he saw as the industrial tourism of national parks with society's over-reliance on vehicles and technology which turned the parks into little more than parking lots; feeling strongly that modernisation was making society as a whole forget what was truly important (Abbey, 1968 p. 52). What he'd make of adventure tourism and the theme park approach to wilderness now evident in some areas is anyone's guess. Though perhaps Theodore Roosevelt, together with John

FRONTIERS OF FREEDOM 97

Waynes in myriad Westerns, can truly be credited with the popularisation of the 'West' in the American psyche.

The 'West' in popular culture

This idea of the West influences on many levels, which perhaps explains the enduring popularity of country and western and folk music, particularly through the midwest and southern USA. John Denver's *Take Me Home Country Roads* and *Rocky Mountain High* speak to the sense of longing and need to belong that appears to permeate so much of American culture. The crossover of folk music into mainstream is particularly poignant with Joni Mitchell's *Big Yellow Taxi* referencing the concretisation of the world to satisfy human cravings and is perhaps for many their first awareness of environmental activism through popular music.

The 1995 release of Michael Jackson's *Earth Song* was a questioning of the promises made by successive governments. With Jackson's humanitarian and children's charity work, these lyrics are a call for understanding of the need to learn the lessons and create a world fit for future generations. Jackson's global fan base meant that the track brought wide awareness of the global nature of environmental problems. The younger 'Disney' generation was specifically targeted by the release from Disney in 2009 of *Send it On* which, although purporting to be an environmental song, doesn't hold any references to it. What Disney did was to hook into their demographic to raise money for various environmental causes; whether it was successful or had a long-term effect on that generation is arguable. It is questionable, too, whether a global organisation could hold any legitimacy in an environmental debate. However, it can be argued that any method of raising environmental leadership awareness in each generation is positive.

Perhaps the godfather of environmental music is Pete Seeger whose numerous musical offerings include the anthemic 'Where have all the flowers gone?', which although an anti-war song, has environmental overtones reinforcing the message of lessons not learned which in the current climate 60 years on from the track's release seems particularly relevant. However, his most influential work, the *God Bless the Grass* album, was the first to be composed entirely of songs dedicated to the environmental movement including, in the best tradition of folk music, songs from across the world that celebrate nature.

The idea of positioning people within ecological webs rather than masters of them through their relationship to the land is what has established Aldo Leopold at the forefront of eco-centric ethics. His approach led him to use 'wilderness' as a way to describe his idea of preservation; an ethical sensitivity which encouraged a deep examination of our interpersonal relationships, links to society as a whole and thus to our relationships with the land which lead to a reduction in actions based on self-interest. His life was deeply influenced by his outdoor-focused childhood, leading him to become the foremost expert on wildlife management, favouring a scientific management of habitats to produce healthy biotic communities. He developed the first comprehensive management plan for the Grand Canyon together with the first Forest service Game and Fish Handbook and the formation of the Wilderness Society, which used an intelligent humility towards man's place in nature have had a lasting effect in which his approach is still felt across the USA in various research institutes and through his writings in 'A Sand County Almanac'; 'Land then is not merely soil; it is a fountain of energy flowing through a circuit of soils, plants and animals' (Leopold, 1949 p. 216), prescient words for those who sought to learn from the disasters that had brought the Dust Bowl. Leopold had shown through his purchase of a denuded farm that planting of trees, formation of lakes to capture water provided a hold for the land to recover and thus prosperity to return to a devastated landscape. The influence of Leopold's work is felt today in such institutions as the Center for Sustainable Agriculture at Iowa State University and the Wilderness Research Institute at the University of Montana, which is the only federal research group dedicated to the dissemination of knowledge needed to improve management of wilderness, parks and other protected areas.

The importance of his acknowledgement of the issues of overgrazing and work to address the problems caused were to have devastating relevance in the Dust Bowl crisis of the 1930s; ironically, work that was to influence many of the policies of FDR's New Deal in 1933 and which continues to influence the focus of the NRCS. The rupture of connections described in Steinbeck's *Grapes of Wrath* so perfectly capture the tensions that lie at the heart of America that it has become almost a biography of the American story.

The idea of connectedness as espoused by Leopold, Emerson and others is perhaps best summed up in popular culture by Woody Guthrie, who experienced first-hand the Dust Bowl. In 1940 he wrote his best known song 'This Land is Your Land'. True, it was a rebellion against 'God Bless America', which was hugely popular on radio at the time, but the most telling line:

> By the relief office I saw my people
> As they stood there hungry, I stood wondering if
> This land was made for you and me

suggests that his experiences of the Dust Bowl, the divides he saw across the nation, were questions that the country as a whole needed to be asking itself. The echoes of that seem apposite to modern issues. The question is, where are the voices of the people – the Dylans and Guthries of today? More importantly, where are the politicians who are paying attention to the cries of the nation? The investigation of agricultural destruction which lead to the Dust Bowl, and the damage still played out today by such things as widespread use of chemicals, industrial-scale agriculture and the huge number of food safety issues all massively impacting environmental sustainability (Mendelsohn et al., 1991; Schlenker et al. 2004, US Geological Survey) is too widespread for this discussion but is, nevertheless, important in the consideration of a political approach to environmental sustainability.

Non-governmental leadership

The true battles for the American wilderness have been played out not so much in the political sphere, but in the myriad organisations formed and reformed since the mid-1800s. Influencing political agenda but not wanting to be part of it, or more truthfully, not wanting to be seen to be part of it.

The Dust Bowl of the 1930s is an enduring case of poor political leadership in the face of rapidly changing technology versus known good practice and ecological stewardship (McLeman et al., 2014).

So who are the non-governmental leaders? Despite the long history of environmental leadership, the USA, unlike many other countries does not have a credible national figurehead for environmentalism who is also perceived to be independent of the political whims that pervade American issues. France for instance has Jacques Cousteau, Canada has David Suzuki and David Attenborough of the United Kingdom is held as a national treasure and held in high esteem at all levels of society. In the US it seems this position is held by organisations. The conversation surrounding environmentalism, be it political, corporate or organisational, can be contextualised by 'shades of green'. There are those of 'deep' green who believe in the intrinsic value of the planet of the sake of the planet, whereas those of 'light' green are concerned about the environment for human needs.

In 1892 the Sierra Club – perhaps the most politically savvy of the various environmental organisations, was founded on the principles of environmental preservation by John Muir, amongst others, who through his persuasion of Teddy Roosevelt, was responsible for the formation of the first national parks in the US (Sierra Club, 2020). The club leans towards the progressive and liberal in terms of political endorsement and have been active since 2004 in advertising candidate positions on the environment. Their stance is for land management to be equitable, encouraging environmentally friendly use of public lands; hence their opposition to dams in particular within national parks. They have been vocal in opposition to coal with their Beyond Coal programme attracting significant funding from such people as Michael Bloomberg and the CEO of Chesapeake Energy (Sierra Club). Despite this leadership, they have courted controversy by their association with the Wilderness Society to allow logging in the South Dakota Black Hills, a position that met with significant ire from members. The opposition to fossil fuels notwithstanding, they do though have history in successful blue collar joint-working; for example, with the United Steelworkers International Union in opposition to the Keystone pipeline. This led to the formation of the BlueGreen Alliance in 2006 as an effort to find sustainable environmental solutions to some of the most pressing problems by harnessing environmental and industrial knowledge and expertise. If history and observation of successful organisms and organisations teach us anything it is only by cooperation and pooling of talent and resources that sustainable change is made.

Frustration with lack of action by the traditional organisations, suspicion of the links to political mainstream and a growing understanding of the power of media lead to the eco-terrorist approach of organisations such as Sea Shepherd (Hoek, 2010) elements of Earth First! and Earth Liberation Front which have drawn attention to significant areas of ecocide but, by their nature, alienate the US public who's 'circling of the wagons' reaction against threats (perceived or real) has arguably allowed politicians of both sides to get away with not implementing policies due to 'lack of public appetite'. However, these organisations bear further understanding to show the spread of environmental concern and the depth of leadership in a non-political context.

Earth First! took some of their beliefs and tactics directly from Abbey's 'The Monkey Wrench Gang' and its ideas of sabotage as a means of protest (Abbey had once stated, 'if wilderness is outlawed, then only outlaws can save wilderness' KAET-TV interview, Dec, 1982), the term 'monkey-wrenching' is still used on their website. They focus on the preservation of large tracts of forests, in particular the old growth areas, and were inspired by the Roadless Area Review and Evaluation (RARE II) (1979) of the US Forest Service: the aspiration was the formation of a multi-million acre ecological preserve across the USA. Their pledge of 'No compromise in defense of Mother Earth' lead to the direct action for which they are known, particularly that of tree-sitting as a means of preventing felling. This approach attracted membership from those with an anarchist or countercultural background, including Judi Bari who was a key figure in advocating and organising direct action across many of the California logging sites. Her leadership role was not always to the taste of members and the more hardcore actions, including uncertainty around possible bombing action, was too much for some, leading to questions over the direction of the organisation (Coleman, 2005). However, the direct action approach is not so far removed from Washington DC, or lacking in appreciation of efforts, as evidenced by a letter sent by President Clinton to a long-term activist thanking him for his efforts, indicating that perhaps political will is more hampered by outside forces than is given credit (Durbin, 1998, pp. 269–271). The influence of such organisations goes beyond national borders, with direct action of the kind employed by Earth First! and ELF directly influencing protests in the UK over the past several decades.

From the late 1990s Earth First! have increasingly identified with deep ecology and the work of Arne Naess (himself noted for direct action) which seeks to provide an alternative to the one-size-fits-all industrial culture. However, some of the proclamations and justifications made by Earth First! are at odds with Naess's actual beliefs.

Climate change and myriad environmental disasters of all sizes have led many to question the environmental approach which sees humans as separate to the natural world. The work of Naess was simply highlighting aboriginal traditions and grassroots approaches by stating that

> we don't say that every living being has the same value as a human, but that it has an intrinsic value which is not quantifiable. It is not equal or unequal. It has a right to live and blossom. I may kill a mosquito if it is on the face of my baby but I will never say I have a higher right to life than a mosquito.
>
> (Schwartz, 2009)

By its very nature direct action does court publicity and as a result political action. The Sea Shepherd – whose founder, Paul Watson, was (ironically) ousted from the board of Greenpeace for his direct activism – saw their role as being to 'document and report violations of conservation' (Sea Shepherd, 2020), including ramming of Japanese whalers. This resulted in their branding as eco-terrorists by the US courts, however it did also contribute to the International Court for Justice 2014 ruling requiring Japan to cease her activities, which raises the question about how much influence such activity has, or can have, on political will. Despite this, Sea Shepherd increasingly works with the government to ensure law enforcement and the organisation's influence and operation has spread worldwide.

These organisations, along with the Audubon Society (founded in 1905), are some of the heavyweights in a field of many voices, all who demonstrate varying shades of green. How do we separate those who wish to preserve Yellowstone for its own sake from those who wish to conserve it to allow tourism? Or those hardcore environmentalists who believe the only good whaling ship is one that is sunk against those who believe whaling should be stopped but protest by picketing an embassy? And where do we place groups such as Young Evangelists for Climate Action, who we know are extremely unlikely to chain themselves to the side of a nuclear power plant or burn down a ski resort in the name of the planet, but equally may not be the people who speak of the environment on Monday and go hunting on Saturday. How do we make sense of all the 'voices' to find compelling leadership?

What is evident is that all these groups struggle to raise funds, find a compelling story and develop and sustain leadership. Some are marked by various divisions of mission which highlight the struggles with the environmental movement to stay true to its mission. The issues faced by the Sierra Club and Earth First! are clear examples of the tugs-of-war where

FRONTIERS OF FREEDOM 103

some members want to stay aloof to the political scene in Washington to be able to criticise it, and others who believe that the organisation can be more effective at the table rather than throwing rocks from the outside. The greatest organisational conflict within the environmental movement comes from those who purport to be one thing but who's own work appears to undermine such efforts. For example, those that eulogise about a focus on conservation efforts most beneficial to wildlife, but who actively support and indulge in hunting of those species. Perhaps what is needed is not a wider spectrum to make sense of a complex world, but a coming together under one banner to acknowledge that the end goal is more important than the arguments about how to achieve it. Perhaps in this there will be found leadership and direction.

Political leadership

Voting in the US can be highlighted by many things but it is fairly consistently true that those who live on the coasts will vote for environmental issues whilst those in the middle will vote for jobs over environment (Starr, 2021). What is abundantly clear to all observers is that money plays a huge part in all policy-making and attempting to stand out from this takes courage.

With the world in the midst of ever-hastening environmental crises and 200 years after Native American leaders, Thoreau and Emerson first highlighted the need to live in harmony with the earth, questions are increasingly asked about the lack of effective American environmental leadership and how the US can limit the already-considerable damage inflicted. As traditionally styled 'leaders of the free world', the USA has long had the opportunity to be at the forefront of such development, but slavish dedication to industrial development, materialism, profit and political infighting have ignored decades of grassroots pressure and left a yearning gap in solid and effective, high-level pioneering action. Donald Trump's desire to erase from government any trace of information concerning climate change (BBC, 2018) and the equally strong desire to seek out and 'put on the shelf' career civil servants who had spent the Obama administration working on these issues (Eilperin & Cameron, 2018) are only two indicates of the see-saw, back-and-forth, politics-related twists that have befallen environmental issues. To move forward and make positive, long-lasting and sustainable changes across the world, it is essential to understand the history and wider context.

Trump's attitude is completely at odds with (arguably) one of the GOP giants who 120 years ago did so much to put into public protection such wonders of the American dream as Yosemite and the Grand Canyon. Teddy Roosevelt can perhaps be called the best environmentalist the GOP have ever had, not something that fits with the usual image of the Republican approach. Together with Aldo Leopard, who put into practice many of the ideas developed at that time; i.e., the plan for the Grand Canyon, the first Game and Fish Handbook, to the first true definitions of wilderness and the relationship of land to society as a whole; and with significant influence from John Muir, significant protections were put in place in a relatively short space of time (U.S. Department of Labor, 2020).

Leadership is often best demonstrated by how one lives as a whole – true integrity. President Jimmy Carter's long-term support and action for Habitat for Humanity and his quiet understanding that respect for community, citizenship are at the heart of efforts to preserve and conserve the environment. In his 23 May 1977 speech he stated, 'intelligent stewardship of the environment is a prime responsibility of government'. In dealing with issues as wide-ranging as pollution and health, wetlands, the environment and the workplace and energy he firmly stated his deep commitment to ensuring generations of Americans inherited a healthier and more resilient environment. (The American Presidency Project, 1977). Whatever his political legacy, his personal one is something that serves as practical inspiration where so often rhetoric is what is offered.

Prior to him, Lyndon Johnson, not a man to be confused with a Northern-based liberal, commented that 'this generation has altered the composition of the atmosphere on a global scale through … a steady increase in carbon dioxide from burning fossil fuels' (Rosier, 2017). Johnson's Great Society plan effectively put into place many of the conservation plans initiated by Kennedy, who had asserted, 'Our task … is to make science the servant of conservation, and to devise new programs of land stewardship that will enable us to preserve this green environment' (Miller C, 2013). Kennedy, though an advocate for a green future, leaned heavily on technology as the way forward with projects that raised significant concerns amongst conservationists even before Rachel Carson warned that humans are 'custodians not owners of the earth'.

Rachel Carson's 'Silent Spring' (1962) was heralded as a wakeup call as to what could happen, whereas it was actually a documentary of the (irreparable) damage already taking place and an urge to action by US and world leaders. That it is still being quoted tells us much about the relative silence in the ensuing decades. According to H. Patricia Hynes, 'Silent Spring altered the balance of power in the world. No one since would be able to sell pollution as the necessary underside of progress so easily or uncritically' (Pennsylvania Conservation Heritage Project, 2020). Among the legacies of Carson's work were the formation of the Environmental Defense fund, which enabled lawsuits against the government to 'enable a citizen's right to a clean environment' and the establishment of the EPA by the Nixon administration.

Given the track record of Trump with respect to environmental issues it is sometimes difficult to remember that not all GOP administrations of modern times have been so ego-centric. One of Reagan's enduring legacies is the addition of 10.6 million acres of forests, mountains, deserts and wetlands to the National Wilderness Preservation System (NY Times, 1982, p. 14) Though this is significantly tempered by, as the Wilderness Society put it, 'an extraordinarily aggressive policy of issuing oil, gas and coal development on tens of millions of acres of national lands' (Bradshaw & Erhlich, 2015 p. 41). All this is evidenced by the reductions in overall budget of the EPA by 25% and similar attempts to reduce the enforcement component of the EPA. As a result there was a 79% decline in the number of enforcement cases filed from regional offices and a 69% decline in the cases filed from EPA to the Department of Justice. Hardly surprising when the effectiveness of the Clean Air Act and Clean Water Act had been effectively gutted by the markedly anti-environment heads of the Department of the Interior and EPA.

With eight years of pillaging, the environmental lobby could be forgiven for expecting more of the same was in store from George H. Bush. However, it seemed that the future Vice President Quayle was somewhat of a dark horse and in a debate with Bentsen asserted that 'the greenhouse effect is an important environmental issue. It is important for us to get the data in, to see what alternatives we might have to fossil fuels and make sure we know what we're doing' (Commission on Presidential Debates, 1988). To add weight to the environmental credentials of the administration President Bush, with all his links to Texas and oil, created the US Global Change Research Program. An initiative which spurred Congress to develop a research programme designed to 'understand, assess, predict and respond to human-induced and natural processes of global change' as it relates to global warming and possibly 'alter world climate patterns and increase global sea levels' (Rosier, 2017).

The Clinton years are remembered for many things that unfortunately overshadow the administration's achievements, mainly in what didn't happen. With the GOP holding Congress after the first mid-term elections it is of some note that the GOP failed to open up drilling in the National Arctic Wildlife Refuge, place a radioactive waste dump in the Mojave desert, sell protected forests to private developments and eliminate tax-incentives for renewable energy use (Peak, 2015). However, becoming a signatory to the UN Law of the Sea, increasing the number of environmental cases to 250, raising gas mileage standards and preserving the number of wetlands across the US are to be celebrated, despite transgressions including allowing more logging in national forests, calling greenhouse standards in other countries 'too restrictive' and a lack of strong environmental provisions in the NAFTA. Such failures led one critic to state 'when Democrats were out of office, at least liberals could console themselves that someone was speaking out on their behalf. Now, no-one is'(Hove, 1997).

Al Gore brought a political focus, central to the election campaign, that at once galvanised support and also forced organisations to re-evaluate their stances and allegiances. Whether Gore could actually be called a political and environmental heavyweight can be argued in other fora; what cannot be denied is that with his appointment as Clinton's running mate the environment issue in America was catapulted into the spotlight, forcing examination of the nation's attitude to its heritage and questioning its leadership. Gore's mentor at Harvard, Dr Roger Revelle, was a direct influence on him, calling the first Congressional hearing on global warming in 1976 (Scripps Institution of Oceanography, 2007). This mentorship, together with themes from 'The problems of advanced industrial society' seminar delivered by Prof Martin Peretz and his reading of Rachel Carson, formed the basis of Gore's belief.

The seeds of hope?

The environmental record of the Clinton administration was in no small measure due to the presence and passion brought by Al Gore and the publication of his book *The Inconvenient Truth*. This laid the groundwork for an even more radical approach by the Democrats to environmentalism, the Green New Deal, launched in February 2019.

The context of the proposal being the United States and the planet

> face a 'perfect storm' of economic and environmental crises that threaten not only the global economy, but life on Earth as we know it ... require bold and visionary solutions if we are to leave a liveable world for the next generation and beyond.
>
> (Green Party, 2019)

Representing a new era in bold legislative efforts by the Democrats, the general goal is to 'convert the decaying fossil fuel economy into a new, green economy that is environmentally sustainable, economically secure and socially just ... transitioning to 100% green renewable energy by 2030 ... halt any investment in fossil fuels'. Like Roosevelt's New Deal during the Great Depression, the deal also encompasses non-environmental issues to 'guarantee full employment and generate up to 20 million new, living wage jobs'. Unsurprisingly, the Republican response was immediate and obvious, with claims that the components of the deal are 'tantamount to genocide for rural residents' (Adragno, 2019). A more measured statement from Mitch McConnell asserted that 'the proposal is frankly delusional [and] ... so unserious that it ought to be beneath our two major political parties to line up behind it'.

With the GOP traditionally being supported by big industry – oil, gas, coal, steel – the attempted move away from fossil fuels was always going to be contentious and with the decision in 2019 to withdraw from the Paris Agreement due to 'unfair economic burden', highlighted the lack of under-standing by Trump, if not those in his administration, about the leadership required for America to be world-leading (Farand, 2019). The influence of money in US politics and the significant power that lobby wields over Washington has devastating climatic effects.

Years of wildfires in the American West – some admittedly through negligence; chronic water shortages in California, caused in part by rap-idly increasing mono-culture – primarily Avocado and Almond planta-tions (Gerretson, 2019) to fuel an unsustainable, 'healthy' lifestyle; the Washington State wildfires in 2020, caused by prolonged periods of high temperatures and the devastation caused by an increasing number of

L5 hurricanes making landfall, i.e., Katrina and Irma, to name just two (National Science Foundation) are directly attributable to climate change and crisis. These are catastrophes that no amount of carbon off-setting can alter. The damage done to environmentally critical areas such as the Florida mangroves in pursuit of coastal development and repeated damage by hurricanes along with the threat by rising sea levels due to climate change are already showing significant levels in terms of habitat and species loss and increased pollution levels (The Nature Conservatory). All of which actually threaten communities by raising the risk of severe flooding, reducing to unsustainable levels the fishing which sustains some local communities and threatens the extinction of a number of flora and fauna species.

Which makes the Great American Outdoors Act (enacted 4 August 2020) perhaps the most surprising legacy of the Trump administration. An incredible signing for a President who actively campaigns on issues for 'energy dominance' such as coal mines, increased oil drilling in environmentally sensitive areas and does not care if the water of thousands of his fellow countrymen is polluted. Stated by Senator Alexander as being 'the most significant conservation legislation in half a century' (www.chatanoogan.com, 14 July 2020), the safeguarding, protections and hope this Act provides is utterly contrary to Trump's very public desecration of the protections formerly enshrined. It could be see as forward-thinking, socially conscious and a significant act of leadership … until one understands that party support for this was nothing more than a cynical political ploy to secure the Senate in the forthcoming election and support the political hopes of GOP candidates in Montana and Colorado (Tamborini & Adragna, 2020). Nevertheless, permanent protections have been put in place and go some way to reversing the monumental damage done to funding and thus futures of millions of acres of habitat. This achievement by the Trump administration, one that at the time was hailed as highly progressive by Republicans and Democrats alike, and given what has been mentioned above, which a public desire to allow almost unfettered drilling on public lands, including in ANWAR, starkly represents the long-standing flipping and flopping on environmentalism that has taken place in American politics for many decades (Jaffe, 2007).

At the moment the GOP is the only major political party in the world that is not convinced climate change exists. Catholic Climate Covenant remarked that, once Republicans 'accept the reality and science of climate change we will have reached a tipping point in the political will for solutions'. A 2019 poll across 23 countries found the US had the highest percentage (13%) of people who agreed with the statement that the climate is changing 'but human activity is not responsible at all'. A further 5% said that the climate is not changing (Milman & Harvey, 2019). Simultaneously, however, an increasing number of Americans are coming to believe that climate change is caused by human activity. In a Pew poll (2020), two-thirds of adults say 'protecting the environment should be a top priority for the president and Congress', and 52% believe the same about climate change. A majority also exists in respect to the role that should be played by the federal government and that stricter regulations are worth the economic cost, if (and this is the kicker) such regulations prove to be effective with respect to slowing the progress of climate change (Funk & Kennedy, 2020). Unsurprisingly, the same polling indicates a substantial divide between Democrats and Republicans who have a high level of science knowledge. In this, almost 90% of Democrats believe in climate change and its negative impact on the planet against 17% of Republicans. It is evident that ideological sway is more important than one's grasp of and belief in science and scientists when it comes to environmental perspective.

The surprising face of future political influence

It seems that the future of climate leadership may lie not in the hands of politicians but in the heartland of American religious belief. The one caveat to polling is among the younger Republicans (be they religiously based or not) who are more in favour of making alternative energy sources a priority because of climate change by a margin of 25%. The growing influence of groups such as Young Evangelists for Climate Action (YECA) highlight this divergence. Their mission is to 'take action to overcome the climate crisis as part of our Christian discipleship and witness' (YECA, 2020). Representatives of YECA are quite clear that this environmental position does not conflict with their religious beliefs. Rather it is *because* of the latter that they believe in the former. Ben Lowe has publicly stated that he is 'called to love my neighbour as I love myself, and I can't do that … if I can't address how climate change is impacting communities around the US and all over the world' (Thomas, 2014). Evidencing the group's mission, its leadership met with senior White House officials on climate change policy during the Obama administration.

Groups such as this are a new phenomenon on the Christian Right – young adults (under 30 years of age), fully committed to their faith, conservative in social values and political action and also believing in the existence of climate change and the need to take decisive action. In 2006 more than 60 evangelical leaders supported the Evangelical Climate Initiative – a direct challenge to the existing and continuing evangelical position. Within a year, a further 100 leaders added support (Redden, 2011), followed by 45 members of the Southern Baptist Convention voicing support and leading conservative commentator E. J. Dionne to state, 'creation came as part of a larger reformation disentangling a great religious movement from a partisan political machine'. In 2008, however, the reaction to the climate change initiative was far more of the 'business as usual' in the older-age group GOP, with hugely influential voices such as Marco Rubio being openly sceptical, leading Grover Norquist to opine that 'formerly environmentally minded GOP candidates … better have an explanation, an excuse or *mea culpa* [for their pro-environmental position]' (Benen, 2011) Yet despite such a high-level opposition, groups such as YECA remain with a strengthening commitment. Many of the leadership see the word 'dominion' in Genesis not as an excuse to use the earth but rather to be stewards of the planet. This understanding is more the historical reading of the word and drives younger evangelicals – conservative, liberal and independent – to recognise that climate change is a moral calling, not a political issue. A direct move against the traditional conservative view, which for many is a divide too far.

It was Hurricane Sandy and its aftermath that helped make it easier for this younger generation to become more climate change oriented and more open to the message Al Gore was promoting. The reason was quite simple – Gore spoke about the real possibility of such an event – it happened, thus making his claims real and irrefutable. Of interesting and significant note is YECA support for the bi-partisan Green New Deal, stating 'we welcome the principles … as a helpful framework that centres communities of colour, displaced workers, frontline communities and indigenous right, and we are committed to working toward translating these principles into viable, bi-partisan bills'. The rationale for this is based on recognition that 'biblical principles … are embedded … including justice (Micah 6:8; Amos 5:24,

Isaiah 1:17), neighbour-love (Matthew 22:34-40); and meaningful protection of the earth (Genesis 2:15). These are principles that YECA Christians and all people of good will can and must affirm' (YECA, 2019). An interesting reference, intended or not, to the principles of Emerson, Roosevelt and Native Indian teachings. Their call is for climate change to be given the highest level of political action with policies that are equitable, just, bold, reasonable and transformative. Although this appears to be at odds with long-held Republican thinking, YECA cite the environmental record of the Nixon administration as evidence of how to be conservative and pro-environment; a view not generally expounded by the older generation.

So why is YECA important in this discussion of the past, present and future of environment and political action? They represent a confluence of three trends within conservative right-of-centre community – young, active and decidedly conservative on almost every issue – and *also* pro-climate change. The challenge to date has been not only the rejection of science within the GOP and evangelicals, but also a rejection of anything that has, is and will be supported by the Democrats. Hence why, despite Al Gore making a compelling, articulate case regarding climate change, there are many on the right of the political spectrum who will not give him time simply *because* he is Al Gore and (at the time) was the very definition of the Democratic Party. Anything to do with the Democrats is the 'kiss of death', as witnessed by the ex-Florida Governor Crist changing allegiance simply because his thanks for help given by Obama in the wake of Hurricane Sandy was a step too far for many within the GOP.

Therefore, YECA who 'look like one of us' are able to connect with the wider Republican electorate since it speaks the same language of faith with authenticity, making it acceptable to be openly pro-climate change. By doing this the gaps between political parties and in the country as a whole on this issue will shrink and *may* (I say may with great caution) create a realignment in environmental political behaviour that could in time move the party itself to an environmental position more closely allied to that of the majority of Americans and the wider world. Finally, YECA is heading a growing landscape of religious environmental groups including CRC Office of Social Justice, Climate Caretakers, Eden Vigil, Blessed Earth and the National Religious Partnership for the Environment (of which YECA is a member) as well as the Evangelical Environmental Network. Given the demographic and the rise of pro-climate evangelical young adults, the tide is changing with potential repercussions for the entire environmental movement and most particularly for the political landscape that may in the near future be significantly disruptive.

Parting shots

It seems that the younger GOP generation are fighting, ideologically, a tough rear guard action from their elders. Almost as a parting gift to Trump, possibly the most devastating decision to undermine the environmental message and campaigning came from the EPA (supposedly set up to protect all Americans from harm in the environment in which they work and live) to strip the 38 tribes in Oklahoma of their sovereignty over environmental issues – a right that enshrined by a Supreme Court ruling. What this effectively means is that no human or place is sacred in environmental terms. Not even the Supreme Court has jurisdiction due to a bizarre situation where federal legislation can nullify the Court's rulings. This ruling effectively makes a mockery of any legislation that claims to protect tribal lands as 'destroying all environmental protection has been ramped up to give fossil fuel industry life support as it takes its last dying breath' (Camp-Horineck, 2020). The truth demonstrated by this is that no matter the hype, or pretence, money talks in the USA; no matter the consequences. It also demonstrates that the EPA is subject to political whims and has no real independence or clout. This decision is effectively the death knell for the organisation (Volcovivi, 2020).

Conclusions

From the deep understanding of human relationships with land brought by Native traditions, to the exploitation of resources, through to the cultural sense of freedom that underpins the idea of the American dream, the West continues to define, actually and metaphorically, America's turbulent relationship with its environment. The tension between the call to conserve and the desire to exploit continues, as seen in the powerful well of ideas and organisations that have emerged from America to protect the environment and the endless controversy over the lobbying power of business on US politics.

It may be that the emergence of groups like YECA, the election of Biden and the impact of the pandemic serve to counter America's current and unsustainable view of itself and its people as conquerors. Certainly with its tradition of 'camp', Spring Break and wilderness trips there is a historic willingness to ensure knowledge of and engagement with nature, but, today, is this just a form of 'Disneyfication' (Louv, 2010 p. 149) or what Loynes (1998) termed 'adventure in a bun'? The question facing Americans is not whether they care about their environment. The voice and global impact of NGOs, musicians and artists indicate that they clearly do. It is whether Americans are ready to adopt a joined-up strategy to treading more lightly with their lifestyle, or will continue to simply react to events.

Hurricane Katrina and the recent fires in California may be causing people to think about the consequences of an American lifestyle that reach beyond previous concerns; flowing more directly than from specific incidents and actions, such as the Three Mile Island nuclear accident or ongoing debate about the environmental consequences of fracking. Yet it remains to be seen whether the accidental signing of significant legislation (in the Great Outdoors Act), or if Joe Biden's rejoining of the Paris Agreement on 'Day 1' of his Presidency will result in action that demonstrates US ambition (Daventry, 2020).

It is tempting to view flat tradition as comforting – after all, we as humans are here for a short term in epoch terms – what does destruction of an ecosystem or societal tradition matter as long as we survive now? But, as Macfarlane (2019 p. 15) states, we should resist such internal thinking, 'deep time' as a radical perspective should provoke us to 'action not apathy'. We are part of a greater web, the view that Native Americans lived by, and perhaps it is time for a deep reconnection at societal and political levels with wilderness while there is still time to protect what we have. Now is the time for debate and division to end and co-ordinated action to take precedence. As the Doomsday Clock notes, we are at '100 seconds to midnight' (Bulletin of the Atomic Scientist, 2021) and lessons of the past which may hold sustainable direction and learning for the future are running out of time.

References

Abbey E. (1968) *Desert Solitaire* New York: McGraw Hill
Abbey E. (1975) *The Monkey Wrench Gang*, Philadelphia, PA: Lippincott Williams &Wilkins.

Abbey E. (1982) Personal interview December 1982, by Eric Temple KAET-TV of Arizona.

Adragna A. (2019) GOP lawmaker: Green new deal 'tantamount to genocide' Politico 03/14/2019.

Alexander L. Sen. (2020) 'Alexander says most important conservation legislation in half a century' www.chatanoogan.com Wednesday, July 22, 2020.

The American Presidency Project (1977) 'The environment message to congress by Jimmy Carter' May 23, 1977 (The Environment Message to the Congress. | The American Presidency Project (ucsb.edu)).

Anders A. & Hassman N. (2009) *Send it on Hollywood: Disney*.

Barkdull J. (1998) "Nixon and the marine environment" *Presidential Studies Quarterly*, vol. 28, no. 3, pp. 587–605. JSTOR, www.jstor.org/stable /27551903. Accessed January 27, 2021.

BBC (2018) I would reference as: BBC. 'Trump on climate change report: 'I don't believe it' 26th November.

Benen S. (2011) 'The new litmus test' *Washington Monthly*, January 3, 2011.

Blimes L. (2020) 'The biggest land conservation legislation in a generation' *The Harvard Gazette*, July 27, 2020.

Bradshaw Corey J.A. & Erlich P.A. (2015) *Killing the Koala and Poisoning the Prairie: Australia, America and the Environment*. Chicago: Chicago University Press, p. 41.

Bullard R. (ed.) (1993) *Confronting Environmental Racism: Voices from the Grassroots*. Boston, MA: South End Press, p. 31.

Bulletin of the Atomic Scientists (2021) 'This is your Covid wake-up call: It is 100 seconds to midnight' January 27, 2021.

Bureau of Reclamation 'The inception of the Pick Sloan Missouri basin program' www.usbr.org.

Camp-Horinek C. (October 5, 2020) https://tyt.com/stories/4vZLCHuQrYE 4uKagyooyMA/65Oa5aonYl4rljnOqxhUto

Carson R. (1962) *Silent Spring*. Boston, MA: Houghton Mifflin.

Coleman K. (2005) *The Secret Wars of Judi Bari: A Car Bomb, the Fight for the Redwoods and the End of Earth First!* Encounter Books.

Commission on Presidential Debates (1988) 'The bentsen-quayle vice presidential debate' October 5, 1988 (CPD: October 5, 1988 Debate Transcripts (debates.org)).

Danhoff B. Nivert T. & Denver J. (1971) *Take Me Home Country Roads USA: RCA*.

Daventry M. (2020) 'Joe Biden vows to rejoin Paris Accord on climate change on his first day in office' in www.euronews.com 05/11/2020.

Denver J. & Taylor M. (1972) *Rocky Mountain High USA: RCA.*

Diamond J. (2005) *Collapse*, New York: Viking Press.

Ducharme J. (2019) 'You're not imagining it: Food recalls are getting more common. Here's why' www.time.com January 17, 2019.

Durbin K. (1998) *TreeHuggers: Victory, Defeat & Renewal in the Northwest Ancient Forest Campaign*, Kathie Durbin. The Mountaineers Press Seattle, pp. 269–271.

Elperin J. & Cameron D. (2018) 'How trump is rolling back Obama's legacy' *Washington Post*, January 20, 2018.

Emerson R.W. (1836) *Nature*, Boston, MA: James Munroe & Company.

EPA (United States Environmental Protection Agency (nd) 'The Origins of EPA', https://www.epa.gov/history/origins-epa

Farand C. (2019) 'Trump begins formal US withdrawal from Paris agreement' *Climate Change News* 04/11/2020.

Funk C. & Kennedy B. (2020) 'How Americans see climate change and environmentalism in seven charts' in www.pewsearch.com April 21 2020.

Gerretson I. (2019) '5 everyday foods that are making droughts worse' *CNN* April 8, 2019.

Gore A. (2006) *An Inconvenient Truth*, Hollywood: Lawrence Bender Productions.

Graham S. (2016) *Vertical: The City From Satellites to Bunkers*, London: Verson, p. 47.

Green Party (2019) https://www.gp.org.gnd_full.

Hoek A. (2010) 'Sea Shepherd Conservation Society v. Japanese Whalers, the Showdown: Who is the real villain?' *Stanford Journal of Animal Law and Policy*, vol. 3, p. 159.

Hove A. (1997) 'Clinton environmental record justifies criticism' *The Tech online edition* http://tech.mit.edu/V117/N28/hove.28o.html, vol. 117, no. 28, Wednesday, June 25, 1997.

Jackson M. (1995) *Earth Song*, New York: Epic Records.

Jaffe C. (2007) 'Melting the polarization around climate change politics' *The Georgetown Environmental Law Review*, vol. 30, p. 455. https://www.law.georgetown.edu/environmental-law-review/wp-content/uploads/sites/18/2018/07/melting-_GT-GELR180017.pdf

Knutson P. (1987) 'The unintended consequences of the boldt decision' *Cultural Survival Quarterly*, June 1987 11–2 Fishing Communities.

Lartey J. & Laughland O. (2019) 'Almost every household has someone that has died from cancer' *The Guardian* May 6, 2019.

Leopold A. (1949) *A Sand County Almanac*. New York: Oxford University Press, p. 216.

Lewis D.R. (Summer 1995) 'Native Americans and the environment: A survey of twentieth century issues' *American Indian Quarterly*, vol. 19, no. 3, pp. 423–450.

Louv R. (2010) *Last Child in the Woods: Saving Our Children from Nature Deficit Disorder*, London: Atlantic Books, pp. 142–148, 312–313.

Loynes C. (1998) 'Adventure in a bun' *Journal of Experiential Education*, vol. 21, no. 1, pp. 35–39. downloaded from http://insight.cumbria.ac.uk//id/eprint/795

Lui L. (2016) 'Thousands of protesters are gathering in North Dakota – and it could lead to 'nationwide reform'' www.businessinsider.com September 13, 2016.

Macfarlane R. (2019) *Underland: A Deep Time Journey*, London: Hamish Hamilton, p. 14.

McLeman R.A., Dupre J., Berrang Ford L., Ford J., Gajewski K. & Marchildon G. (2014) 'What we learned from the Dust Bowl: lessons in science, policy, and adaptation' *Popul Environment*, vol. 35, no. 4, pp. 417–440. doi:10.1007/s11111-013-0190-z

Mendelsohn R., Nordham W. & Shaw D. (1991) 'The impact of climate variation on US agriculture' in Mendelsohn R. & Neumann J.E. (eds) *The Impact of Climate Change on the United States Economy*.

Miller C. (2013) 'Green urbanism: Remembering JFK's major environmental achievements' www.kcet.org November 19. 2013.

Milman O. & Harvey F. (2019) 'US is a hotbed of climate change denial, major global survey finds' *The Guardian* May 8, 2019.

Mitchell J. (1970) *Big Yellow Taxi USA: Reprise Records*.

National Archives The Homestead Act 1862.

National Research Council (1992) *Water Transfer in the west: Efficiency, Equity and the Environment*, Washington, DC: The National Academies Trust.

National Science Foundation 'Number of category 4 and 5 hurricanes has doubled over the past 35 years' *News Release* 05–162.

The Nature Conservatory 'Valuing the flood risk reduction benefits of Florida's mangroves'.

New York Times (1982) 'Reagan asks additions to wilderness system' September 15 1982 Section A, p. 14.

Peak (2015) 'Which presidents are the greenest in U.S history?' in www
.Nationswell.com September 16, 2015.

Pennsylvania Conservation Heritage Project (2020) 'Rachel louise carson'
https://paconservationheritage.org/stories/rachel-louise-carson-3

Redden M. (2011) 'Whatever happened to the evangelical-environmental
alliance?' *The New Republic*, November 2, 2011.

Rinde M. (2017) 'Richard nixon and the rise of american environmentalism'
www.sciencehistory.org June 2, 2017.

Roosevelt T. (1889) *The Winning of the West*, New York: G.Putnam & Sons.

Rosier P. (2017) 'Politics and the environment: A historical perspective'
Hindsights December 16, 2017.

Schlenker W., Hanemann W.M. & Fischer A.C. 'The impact of global warming on
US agriculture: An econometric analysis of optimal growing conditions'
https://escholarship.org/us/item/0801/7sQ published 2004-10-01.

Schwartz W. (2009) 'Arne Naess – obituary' The Guardian January 15 2009

Scripps Institution of Oceanography (2007) 'Around the pier: Gore: Roger
revelle was my inspiration', June 1, 2007.

Sea Shepherd, 'Our story', *Our Story – Sea Shepherd Conservation Society*.

Seeger P. & Hickleson J. (1955) *Where Have All The Flowers Gone?* New York:
Colombia.

Seeger P. (1966) *God Bless The Grass*. New York: Colombia.

Skelton R. & Miller V. (2016) 'The environmental justice movement' www
.NRDC.org March 12, 2016.

Sierra Club, 'America, let's move beyond coal' (America, Let's Move Beyond
Coal | Beyond Coal (sierraclub.org).

Starr S. (2021) 'How Democrats scientific approach lost them US's industrial
heartland' *Irish Times* Wed February 3, 2021 www.irishtimes.com

Tamborino K. & Adragno A. (2020) 'Trumps 'Unforced error' puts Western
Senate Republicans in an election jam' *Politico* 07/17/2020.

Thoreau H.D. (1854) *Walden; or Life in the Woods*, Boston, MA: Ticknor & Fields.

Thomas M. (2014) 'Pro-life equals pro-planet for this green evangelical leader'
Grist, December 26, 2014.

Turner F. (2003) 'Still ahead of his time' *Smithsonian Magazine*, May 2003.

U.S. Dept of Agriculture Forest Service (1979) *RARE II Final Environmental
Statement Roadless Area Review & Evaluation*, January 1979.

U.S. Department of Labor (2020) 'The conservation legacy of theodore
roosevelt', February 14, 2020 (www.doi.gov/blog/conservation-legacy
-theodore-roosevelt).

Volcovici V. (2020) 'Tribes slam EPA move to give Oklahoma control of environmental rules' www.Reuters.com October 7 2020.

Weldman W. & Diters C. (2007) *The Legacy of Project Chariot*, Bureau of Indian Affairs Alaska Region, regional archaeology report under the National Historic Preservation Act c. 2007.

Worland J. (2016) 'What to know about the Dakota Access Pipeline protests' *Time*, October 28 2016.

YECA (2019) 'Young evangelicals support principles of green new deal and call for bipartisan legislation to enact them' www.yecaction.org

YECA (Young Evangelicals for Climate Change) (2020) 'Organizational website' https://yecaction.org/

Additional Information

https://www.youtube.com/watch?v=15YADoUs4N4

http://www.conservationgateway.org/pages/Florida-Mangroves.aspx

https://www.doi.gov/blog/conservation-legacy-theodore-roosevelt

http://sierraclub.org

https://coal.sierraclub.org

https://seashepherd.org/our-story/

https://www.presidency.ucsb.edu/documents/the-environment-message-the -congress

https://medium.com/hindsights/politics-and-the-environment-a-historical -perspective-60d7c43c2e65

https://paconservationheritage.org/stories/rachel-louise-carson-3/

https://www.earthday.org/history/

http://debates.org/voter-education/debate-transcripts/october-5-1988-debate -transcripts/

https://medium.com/hindsights/politics-and-the-environment-a-historical -perspective-60d7c43c2e65

https://tech.mit.edu/V117/N28/hove.28o.html

https://scripps.ucsd.edu/news/around-pier-gore-roger-revelle-was-my -inspiration

https://www.gp.org.gnd_full

https://yecaction.org/

https://grist.org/living/pro-life-equals-pro-planet-for-this-green-evangelical -leader/

https://newrepublic.com/article/97007/evangelical-climate-initiative-creation
-care

https://yecaction.org/blog/overview.html/article/2019/07/09/young
-evangelicals-support-pronciples-of-green-new-deal-call-for-bipartisan
-legislation-to-enact-them

https://doi.org/10.17226/180

https://www.aldoleopold.org/about/

https://emersoncentral.com/texts/nature-addresses-lectures/nature2/
chapter1-nature/

https://www.counterpunch.org/2002/08/01/dark-deeds-in-the-black-hills/

https://thebulletin.org/doomsday-clock/

https://leopold.wilderness.net

https://pubs.usgs.gov/fs/2007/3001/pdf/5

6

THE WEAPONISATION OF CLIMATE CHANGE

ENVIRONMENTAL LEADERSHIP IN THE AGE OF TRUMP

Elesa Zehndorfer

The weaponisation of climate change

On 8 October 2020, leading science journal *Nature* took the unprecedented step of publishing a consciously politically focused editorial, in which they stated that 'Science and politics are inseparable' (2020, p. 169). The journal, widely respected as one of the best scientific journals in the world, committed at the same time to include political content in future editions, a reflection of how interlinked politics and science had, in their view, become. As noted by the editors of the journal, 'The conventions that have guided the relationship between science and politics are under threat, and *Nature* cannot stand by in silence' (p. 170).

The same day, the *New England Journal of Medicine* ran an editorial focusing on the existential threat faced by science, a threat enabled in large part by what they perceived to be systemic political failings at the uppermost echelons of government. Titled 'Dying in a Leadership Vacuum', it addressed the magnitude of the Trump administration's failure to manage the Covid-19 pandemic, a failure so significant as to place US testing capabilities significantly

DOI: 10.4324/9781003190820-7

behind those of developing nations such as Kazakhstan, Zimbabwe and Ethiopia. 'the magnitude of this failure', noted the journal, 'is astonishing' (2020, p. 1479).

Trump's failures in the context of the recent Covid-19 pandemic echo those of other right-wing populist administrations, including Boris Johnson's Conservative Party in the UK and Jair Bolsonaro's Alliance for Brazil (e.g. CNN, July 2020),[1] and are in fact somewhat predictable given the strategically and traditionally anti-science stance adopted by most right-wing (RW) populist administrations. A cornerstone of RW populism remains the fervent demonisation of science, and the often highly profitable opportunities for clientelism that emerge from it. It is a strategic approach that forms a central focus of this chapter.

The chapter subsequently begins by outlining Trump's treatment of the EPA, the FDA and other governmental organisations as part of wider strategy to demonise and dismantle scientific authority, clarifying the way in which clientelism (i.e. patronage – the funding of a politician in exchange for access) plays a key role. We then move to the positioning of a highly divisive faith vs. science discourse in a RW charismatic populist's advancement of their own charismatic authority, alongside a greater polarisation of the electorate. Finally, the central role of propaganda, including the concepts of 'deep state' and alt-realities, in the obfuscation of environmental as well as wider scientific goals are presented, alongside an explanation as to why an anti-science agenda remains a key imperative in the intended dismantling of democratic checks-and-balances. It is an imperative that seeks to achieve what former White House Chief Strategist Steve Bannon referred to as the 'deconstruction of the administrative state'.[2]

Throughout the chapter, the potentially ruinous implications of such a powerful anti-science agenda are made clear – not only in terms of its impact on the urgent threat of anthropogenic climate change, but also in terms of the damage that such a strategy stands to wreak on democracy.

A historic reversal

The Trump administration's reversal of environmental protections is, itself, unprecedented. The administration pulled the US from the Paris Climate Agreement in 2017, for example, rolled back the Obama-era Clean Power Plan, loosened regulations on toxic air pollution, rescinded methane-flaring rules, revoked flooding standards, narrowed definitions of what constituted a federally protected river or wetland, allowed seismic airgun blasts for oil and gas drilling (a procedure that risks marine life), relaxed regulations designed to protect endangered species, and reinterpreted the Migratory Bird Treaty Act to allow energy companies to install large wind turbines, power lines and/or to leave oil exposed that might otherwise have been ruled as unlawful due to the threat that they pose to its bird life (National Geographic, 2017).[3]

The Trump administration dramatically sought to downsize national monuments (e.g. Bears Ears and Grand Staircase-Escalante in Utah, which have now been opened up for mining and drilling companies) and enabled a 30% increase in logging on public lands, dropped climate change from the list of US national security threats (delisting is significant because it excludes climate change projects from prioritised Department of Defence funding).

Perhaps the most ruinous decision thus far has been the sustained campaign to auction off a 19-million-acre Arctic national wildlife refuge located in north-eastern Alaska to oil and gas drilling companies in 2020, an area that had previously fallen under the protection of the federal government since 1980. In a recent article for The Guardian,[4] Kristen Monsell, an attorney with the Center for Biological Diversity's oceans program, warned that 'An oil spill in this special sanctuary could devastate polar bears and caribou and cause irreparable harm to a pristine Arctic ecosystem'. Monsell went on: 'We've reached a dangerous new low in the Trump administration's obsession with expanding the extraction of dirty fossil fuels'. According to Reuters (2019), every single environmental roll-back made by the Trump administration seems to be linked to improving conditions for the oil, gas and coal industries.[5]

If Trump had won a second term in November 2020, the EPA would have received a 26% cut in funding at a time that it was already struggling; John O'Grady, head of a union representing EPA employees commented in an interview with CNN that 'The U.S. EPA is already on a starvation diet, with a bare-bones budget and staffing level. The administration's proposed budget will be akin to taking away the agency's bread and water'. The Agency also faced a concomitant elimination of 50 EPA programs, and a proposed 97% budget cut for the Land and Water Conservation Fund if the Trump administration had entered a second term. Similarly, The Bureau of Land Management would have stood to lose around US$144 million in funding in the same proposals, with the Fish and Wildlife Service losing around US$265 million in funding. Similarly, the National Park Service would have lost around US$581 million in funds.

Environmental damage caused by cutbacks would be impacted further by a ramping up of energy sector investment; the administration had planned to combine those deep-seated environmental cuts whilst concomitantly pledging US$195.5 million for oil and gas activity via the Bureau of Land Management and US$18.9 million for the development coal management programs.[6]

Internally, the administration had actively sought to dismantle the power of the EPA by promoting individuals to run the EPA who were not only prominent anthropogenic climate change deniers (Scott Pruitt, Andrew Wheeler), but who also possessed a clear track record of powerful engagement in the oil and gas industries (Wheeler is a former coal lobbyist, whilst Pruitt is now engaged as a coal consultant) (Gibbens, 2019).

Weaponising science

Climate change denial forms a central part of a wider anti-science agenda that has been weaponised by the administration – a concept that we see play out intensively at the current time in the context of the Covid-19 pandemic. Citing the politicisation of mask wearing, the clear denigration of scientific experts by the Trump administration, the exclusion of key organisations such as the National Institutes of Health and the utilisation of 'opinion leaders' and charlatans' (p. 1480) over the expertise and data-led opinions of scientists, the editors of the *New England Journal of Medicine*, cited earlier, echo attorney Monsell's concerns, cited earlier, in their statement that Trump has presided over 'the promulgation of outright lies' (ibid.).

The administration ultimately built consistently on an anti-science discourse of which denial of anthropogenic climate change formed a key part, actively seeking to dismantle work done by the previous Obama administration. The attacks were both external (e.g. denouncing climate change scientists) and internal (appointing Pruitt and Wheeler, both allies of the oil, gas and coal industries, to head up the EPA, or withholding funds – at the time of writing, US$43 billion of funding approved by an Obama-era Congress for low-interest clean-energy loans had still not been disbursed).[7]

Trump and the EPA

Trump's speed at attempting to dismantle climate change activity was rapid; within a week of his inauguration in 2016, he introduced a bill to cut funding to the IPCC, the Green Climate Fund and the UNFCCC (the United Nations Framework – Convention on Climate Change).

One of Trump's first notable appointments following his election was the selection of Scott Pruitt (mentioned earlier) as Head of the EPA (Environmental Protection Agency). Pruitt was, at that time, an attorney general from Oklahoma known for his outspoken views as a climate change denier. He was also a leading figure in enacting legislation to fight President Obama's climate change policies. He is known to be a close ally of the fossil fuel industry (the co-chairman of Pruitt's re-election campaign in 2013 was Harold Hamm, CEO of Continental Energy, an oil and gas corporation). The oxymoronic nature of Pruitt's advancement within government to head up the EPA is clear; when Pruitt was appointed to lead the EPA, his resume literally included his role in leading major lawsuits *against* the EPA. His appointment accompanied that of Rex Tillerson, former CEO of energy giant ExxonMobil to Secretary of State.

Placing the Environmental Protection Agency (EPA) in the hands of a man who declared President Obama's Clean Power Plan as a 'war on coal' clearly threatened the existence and reach of the EPA from the inside. Ken Cook, former Head of the Environmental Working Group, referred to Pruitt as 'the most hostile EPA administrator toward clean air and safe drinking water in history' (Davenport & Lipton, 7 December 2016).

Multiple investigations uncovered malfeasant actions by Pruitt in the context of pushing the interests of energy companies whilst at the EPA. In fact, by July 2018, the date that Pruitt resigned, Pruitt was under at least 14 separate federal investigations led by the Government Accountability Office, the EPA inspector general, two House committees, the US Office of Special Counsel and the White House Office of Management and Budget. Amongst many accusations, Pruitt reportedly allowed energy lobbyists to draft letters on his behalf using official state stationary, which he would then sign. These letters were sent to multiple governmental institutions, including the Office of Management and Budget, directly to President Obama, to the EPA and to the Interior Department.

Pruitt's appointment reflects the denigration of the EPA as part of a wider anti-science agenda so common to RW charismatic populists (see later in the chapter for more detail). In a bid to control the narrative, RW populists seek to discredit all respected expert opinion, thereby removing the power of the scientific community to hold their actions to account. By offhandedly characterising climate change research as 'bullshit' (see opening Trump tweet), Trump signalled to his base and to the GOP his permission that, by inference, scientists and the scientific process could also be viewed as 'bullshit'.

The pushback from the scientific community in terms of a wilful politicisation of science has been resounding: Philip Duffy, President of the Woods Hole Research Center, for example, states that 'What we have here is a pretty blatant attempt to politicize the science – to push the science in a direction that's consistent with their politics. It reminds me of the Soviet Union' (Davenport & Landler, 2019). What Duffy references in his Soviet Union comment is a RW populist practice that clearly betrays an underlying authoritarian ideological agenda – to control the narrative, to remove the independent scientific voice that holds a democratic government to account – and to denigrate the expertise and data-led opinion of anyone who contradicts the words and beliefs of the leader.

In a RW populist administration, an anti-science agenda enables a natural shift towards authoritarianism when

> facts no longer provide a compelling epistemic base for presenting and resolving disputes. Instead, a partisan base provides the discursive and institutional support for a parallel universe of alt-news, alt-facts, and alt-reality.
>
> (Lynch, 2017)

We have seen a more explicit acknowledgement of Trump's authoritarian ambitions in recent weeks; Republican senator Mike Lee recently stated, pre-election, that 'Democracy isn't the objective' (8 October 2020).

The role of anti-science rhetoric in right-wing populism

Climate change denial has been found to correlate positively with right-wing ideological political beliefs, according to a recent multi-nation study by Jylhä & Hellmer (2020), with political narratives that focus on climate change observed to be a polarising subject (e.g. Whitmarsh & Cornel, 2017). In embracing this denial, Trump was able to appeal directly to a conservative base.

Populist right-wing parties, usually led by a charismatic individual, also tend to dismiss climate change (e.g. Lockwood, 2018, Forchtner, Kroneder &Wetzel, 2018) as part of a wider strategy that embraces socially conservative ideologies (Mudde, 2007). RW charismatic populism tends to embrace the communication of traditional values whilst romanticising nationalistic notions, usually to the detriment of minority groups. Given that RW populism tends to focus on denigrating attacks on the 'other' – that is, minority groups (such as Jews in 1930s Germany, and Muslims and Mexicans under the Trump administration) (e.g. Lobban et al., 2020), the conscious effort to reject liberal, egalitarian values might represent not only an ideological approach but an associated, conscious strategic effort to appeal to a conservative base.

Charisma, populism and climate change denial

Right-wing populism, interestingly, is generally characterised by a scepticism towards climate policy and a far lower readiness to support action on climate change (e.g. Lockwood, 2018, McCright et al., 2016) with a recent 12-country study of 13 right-wing populist parties demonstrating a clear anti-environmental bias (Gemenis et al., 2012). Further, Hamilton and Saito (2015) and Shao (2017) found intra-party differences in the US Republican Party where Tea Party members (a far-right faction of the Republican Party) held far more pronounced views that related to climate scepticism than their more moderate conservative counterparts.

It is interesting that 'aversion to wealth distribution partly mediates the correlation between Trump support and climate change denial' (Jylhä & Hellmer (2020, p. 3) and that climate change denial also correlates with racist and anti-immigrant views, Social Dominance Orientation and Right-Wing Authoritarianism (ibid., p. 12). They are also most likely to hold anti-immigration views, which Trump's aggressive anti-immigration stance courts and amplifies powerfully.[8]

It also appears to be linked with a pro-conspiracy mindset (Lewandowsky, Oberauer & Gignac, 2013) and is predicted by anti-establishment attitudes, traditional values and anti-egalitarian practices, which in turn were found to be positive predictors of pseudoscientific beliefs (Jylhä & Hellmer 2020, p. 8). Together, the conflagration of these observed beliefs forms a strong likelihood of climate change and anti-science denial (Rutjens, Sutton & van der Lee, 2017) alongside a willingness to instead invest in, and welcome, conspiracies and pseudo-science. Trump's rhetoric clearly plays to and amplifies these preferences and descriptors whilst seemingly also betraying a personal tendency to conform to these cognitive descriptors (e.g. 'Any and all weather events are used by the GLOBAL WARMING HOAXSTERS to justify higher taxes to save our planet! They don't believe it! $$$$' (@realdonaldtrump, 26 January 2014). The administration utilises propagandist techniques to amplify Trump's environmental narrative; a recent Brown University doctoral study found that roughly 25% of all climate change denial tweets are in fact produced by mechanised bot activity (Marlow et al., 2020).

Research also identifies that the Big Five trait of 'openness' (McCrae & Costa, 2008) correlates negatively with climate change denial, likely because it reflects a greater acceptance of the status quo and predicts acceptance of group-based hierarchies (Jylhä, 2016), whilst dampening a readiness to reject novel, complex ideas (such as those that emerge throughout the scientific process). Since the early 1990s, there is evidence that conservative think tanks explicitly formed to counter environmental decision-making (De Pryck & Gemenne, 2017), engaging with a wider network of actors in manufacturing uncertainty (e.g. Dunlap, 2013) such as energy giants Koch Industries and the George C. Marshall Institute think tank. Thus, the Trump administration is capitalising on the anti-environmental work of a powerful, existing sub-culture (the Republican Party and associated actors). The party has (as it currently appears) largely ceded control to Trump, and it is Trump who is now capitalising on that work, and on the embedded anti-environmental beliefs of its followers.

Science vs. rhetoric

Comparing scientific consensus relating to anthropogenic climate change with Republican commentary offers a compelling insight into the forces that drive both beliefs: Republican senator for Kentucky, Rand Paul, for example, recently shared his disdain for scientific evidence of climate change (e.g. Brulle, 2018; Dunlap & McCright, 2008; Kool, 2010) by saying that:

> I think this debate has become so dumbed down beyond belief ... We have real data [for] about 100 years. So somebody tell me what 100 years' data is in an Earth that is 4.6 billion years old? My guess is that the conclusions you make from that are not conclusive.

Politicians might make guesses about science, but scientists, of course, do not. Anthropogenic climate change simply describes 'a statistically significant variation in either the mean state of the climate or in its variability, persisting for an extended period' (VijayaVenkataRaman, Iniyan & Goic, 2012, p. 879). It is apolitical but has been rendered political, at least in the perceptions of right-wing voters, who now view climate change as a 'liberal' concept. The evidence for, and broad scientific consensus around, the concept of climate change is immense (e.g. NASA, n.d.),[9] yet it runs counter to RW populist ambitions to acknowledge it.

Creationism vs. climate change

Creationist education policy has grown notably during Trump's presidency (National Law Review, 2019),[10] representing a favouring of Christian protestant evangelism and a courting of faith-based agencies by the administration at the same time as the scientific and academic organisations have been attacked and vilified. The strategic favouring of religion is a common feature of authoritarian and totalitarian states, as is the denigration of science (Linz, 2004).

The movement to support creationism and faith-based academic approaches in favour of scientific content has received high-level support within the Republican Party; former Vice President Mike Pence and Secretary of Education Betsy DeVos both vigorously supported the teaching of creationist theory, falsely communicating the supposition that creationism simply offers a competing theory to evolution. Both have furthered this narrative despite a US Supreme Court ruling that forcing a requirement to teach creationism in schools would represent a clear violation of the First Amendment's Establishment Clause (a clause which exists to prevent 'sponsorship, financial support, and active involvement of the sovereign in religious activity').[11]

The weaponisation of truth: religion vs. science

Trump's relationship with religion, most notably the Evangelical Christian movement, remained a powerful boon to his continued position as POTUS, even in the face of a recent impeachment (a reported 81% of US Christian Evangelicals voted for Trump in 2016).[12] This enthusiastic support, confusing to many observers, might hold its roots in American Evangelical history. Science denial first gained traction in the context of Darwinism in the late 1800s in the USA, and less than a century ago, teaching evolutionary science was still illegal in Texas.

The GOP has historically formed a close bond with the Protestant Evangelical movement – a bond that the current administration is exploiting effectively. White American Evangelical Protestants are most likely amongst all religious groups to be sceptical of climate change, with only 27% believing that climate change is real (Jones, Cox & Navarro-Rivera, 2014). It is this sector of the GOP votership that is often described as the 'base' of the Republican Party (Brint & Abrutyn, 2010).

If the campaign slogan 'Make America Great Again' is to be considered, rightly, a form of revivalist nationalism, then it would be sensible to include creationism and the removal of evolution theory as one key part of that patchwork American revivalist nostalgia that the MAGA campaign has tapped so powerfully into.

Science, God and a cult of charisma

The powerfully symbiotic relationship that the Republican Party has historically enjoyed with the conservative Christian right has undoubtedly strengthened further under the Trump administration: 3 January 2020, for example, saw the launch of Evangelicals for Trump in Florida, a key battleground state, with President Trump promoting a powerful and popular Pentacostal mega-church evangelist named Paula White-Cain to lead the White House Faith and Opportunity Initiative. White is a major presence in the Evangelicals for Trump organisation, often hosting religious prayer events where various Evangelical pastors pray openly for Trump, sometimes even engaging in a 'laying on hands' activity when Trump himself is present.

As Trump's Presidential tenure progressed and accusations of moral turpitude increased, support from mainstream religion waned. The influential religious publication *Christianity Today*, for example, denounced Trump as 'grossly immoral' (Galli, 2019). A rejection by some in mainstream religion may explain in part Trump's higher engagement with mega-church pastors such as Paula White-Cain over more orthodox figures in the mainstream Christian movement; it removes the bureaucratic checks-and-balances of an established religious organisation, further removing limits on his behaviour, yet still conveys an image of a high-profile, close relationship with religion. As the relationship has been cultivated, so references to Trump's Messianic status have also increased; Trump, for example, referred to his recent Covid-19 diagnosis as a 'blessing from God' in a video posted to Twitter (@realdonaldtrump, 7 October 2020). According to Eatwell (2004), the leader is driven by a special mission (p. 106); he positions himself as a superman, a Messiah figure, endowed with special powers (Weber, 1968). Trump's self-positioning as a man endowed by supernatural qualities can thus be considered a common charismatic leadership strategy. The 'laying on hands' imagery and the direct equation of Trump with God himself invokes powerfully the Weberian 'Messiah' image so sought after by the charismatic populist leader (Weber, 1968).

Controlling the narrative

The goal of RW charismatic populists is to control the political narrative and to transfer expert power from experts (e.g. scientists) to that of his own voice and coterie (e.g. Homolar & Scholz, 2019). Science has long been viewed as a pillar of democracy, exerting key checks-and-balances that act to constrain (and facilitate) executive power (Collins & Evans, 2019) – thus it makes sense that it would become a natural target to a leader of this kind.

In order to understand Trump's vociferous climate change denial, we must also understand its symbiotic and crucial role in both facilitating, and being facilitated by, charismatic populist appeal, and why 'The Trump folks have poured an acid on public institutions that is much more powerful than anything we've seen before' (David Victor, political scientist at the University of California, in Tollefson, p. 194). Former EPA chief for the George W. Bush administration, Christine Todd Whitman, noted that, in the case of the Trump administration, 'I've never seen such an orchestrated war on the environment or science' (Tollefson, 2020), p. 191). The use of combative rhetoric in this 'war against science' has been extensive, with the Trump administration relying heavily on the conceptualisation of a 'deep state' and on the normalisation of 'alternative facts' to denigrate and attack scientific bodies such as the EPA; it is to both that we now turn in order to understand the phenomenon further.

Deep state

Mike Lofgren, a former Republican civil servant and congressional staffer, created the term 'deep state' after leaving the Republican Party (Myre & Treisman, 2019). His decision to leave in 2011 was based on his growing disillusionment with the rise of the Tea Party within the ranks of the Republican Party which represented what he felt to be a hard shift to the right.

'Deep state' was a term that Lofgren first noticed in a John Le Carré work of fiction titled *A Delicate Truth*. Lofgren adopted it in his own writing — a move that he now regrets. Lofgren believes that his utilisation of the phrase in a political context has been manipulated and abused to such an extent that 'It's like I released this species into the wild ... maybe it's a Frankenstein ... what it does is not within my control'. Trump uses the term to refer to any political opponent (e.g. Democratic politicians) or even members of his own party when he feels held back by bureaucratic processes, or if the individual in question contradicts him in some way.

In the context of science, Trump recently used the term to refer negatively to the Food and Drink administration (FDA). In the tweet, Trump inferred that the FDA was part of a pro-Democrat 'deep state' that was working nefariously against him to prevent him from enabling a vaccine before the Presidential elections had taken place:

> The deep state, or whoever, over at the FDA is making it very difficult for drug companies to get people in order to test the vaccines and therapeutics. Obviously, they are hoping to delay the answer until after November 3rd. Must focus on speed, and saving lives! (@realdonald trump, 22 August 2020)

Trump's former trade advisor, Peter Navarro, had reportedly accused the FDA of the same five days earlier at a meeting with the FDA. Ex-White House Chief of Staff Mark Meadows followed up Trump's remarks soon after by voicing his frustration with the 'bureaucrats' who would not endorse Covid-19 vaccines endorsed by Trump.

John McLaughlin, the former deputy director of the CIA, noted that the notion of a deep state is laughable. McLaughlin stated recently that what Trump referred to as a deep state was simply a conflagration of normal democratic, bureaucratic processes and organisations; 'the American civil service, social security, the people who fix the roads, health and human services, Medicare'.[13] Department of Health and Human Services spokesman Michael Caputo recently defended his attempts to alter CDC (Center for Disease Control and Prevention) reporting data as a means of combatting '"ulterior deep state motives in the bowels" of the CDC'. In Caputo's case, he reportedly tried to halt the release of a report discussing the dangers of using hydroxychloroquine as a treatment for Covid-19, because it contradicted Donald Trump's endorsement of the drug (Weiland, 2020). CDC employees have since spoken of a five-month campaign of intimidation and bullying meted out at the hands of Caputo and of a general silencing of the CDC.

Alternative facts

Following Trump's inauguration ceremony, then Press Secretary Sean Spicer referred to the event as having the largest crowd of any Presidential inauguration in history. It was a clearly provable falsehood, yet spokeswoman Kellyanne Conway defended the statement, commenting that 'we feel compelled to go out and clear the air and put alternative facts out there' (Marshall, K. L., 2020, p. 172). In just that utterance Conway opened a pathway to the normalisation and legitimisation of the rejection of robust empirical data in favour of a version that the administration preferred. It is a pattern that has continued throughout the 2016–2020 Presidential term.

The establishment of an 'alternative fact' discourse was thus set out in the very first days of the administration. Collins and Evans (2019) note that the 'locus of legitimate interpretation' (p. 210) is in this scenario thus moves from experts (e.g. scientists) to the political leader. It represents an effective means of controlling the political (or scientific) narrative and, in Trump's case, has been strategically strengthened by the appointment of Trump loyalists – what Weber termed 'disciples' in the charismatic literature (Weber, 1968, p. 242).

It is commonly acknowledged that charisma is an enduring trait found amongst right-wing populist authoritarian leaders (e.g. Zaslove, 2008, p. 324; Zehndorfer, 2019; Zehndorfer, 2015; McDonnell, 2015, p. 1) with Max

THE WEAPONISATION OF CLIMATE CHANGE   133

Weber's 'disciples' (1968, p. 242) required to demonstrate 'absolute trust in the leader' as 'a duty' (Weber, 1968, pp. 243–244). 'Disciples' of this nature often display remarkable loyalty. A level of inexperience usually inconsistent with a governmental role of such stature (e.g. Ivanka Trump, Jared Kushner, Hope Hicks, Kellyanne Conway, Sarah Huckabee-Sanders, Kayleigh McEnany), combined with an associated sensation of gratitude directed towards the leader for his patronage reflects a consistency with follower behaviour in the destructive leadership literature (e.g. Thoroughgood et al., 2012). Pushing or defending an 'alternative facts' discourse has constituted a key responsibility for these followers, which has often required a refutation or denigration of scientific data (according to The Washington Post's Fact Checker Column, Trump has lied or made misleading statements around 20,000 times since entering office). These refutations regularly spiralled into attacks on governmental health organisations run by scientists, such as the CDC (Center for Disease Control and Prevention). Former Department of Health and Human Services spokesman Michael Caputo, for example, stated that CDC scientists are part of a 'deep state' engaging in 'sedition' (Franiere, 2020), whilst a recent investigation by Politico (Diamond, 2020) uncovered attempts by politically appointed aides working for the Department of Health and Human Services to intimidate CDC scientists into adapting weekly scientific reports that did not corral with Trump's positive Covid-19 messaging.

These attacks have not been limited to organisation; individuals have been targeted, too. National Institute of Allergy and Infectious Disease Director Dr Anthony Fauci has been consistently targeted by Trump after his Covid-19 messaging quickly diverted from that of the Trump administration. On Sunday, 12 April 2020, Trump retweeted a message posted by DeAnna Lorraine, a former Republican congressional candidate reading 'Time to #FireFauci'.

A recent major *Science* study (Piller, 2020) found that public levels of trust in the CDC have dropped from 70% in 2015 to only 19% in September 2020, likely reflecting a dual perception that the CDC has failed to control the virus (partly a reflection of the administration's hostility to scientific work, and attempts to undermine it) and as a result of ongoing public attacks by the Trump administration that have sought to discredit it. As long as scientists fail to endorse alternative facts in favour or scientifically rigorous data, they will, sadly, remain a target.

A failure to respect scientific data over alternative facts has come at a price; in 2020, the US recorded more than seven million Covid-19 cases, experiencing a death toll greater than that of any other nation. The USA currently accounts for roughly one-fifth of Covid-19 deaths globally, yet is home to only 4% of the global population (Tollefson, 2020).

Charisma and the quasi-individual nature of populism

As noted by Josh Chafetz, Professor of Law at Cornell University, 'We might be in trouble' (Chafetz, 2019, p. 17).

Chafetz's words reference the interpolation of charismatic authority and constitutional maturity during the Trump era. The interpolation of the power of charismatic authority with the constitutional maturity of the state might in some scenarios allow the strengthening of the democratic process alongside the realisation of socially orientated goals (e.g. the socialised charisma of President Barack Obama in the creation of the Affordable Healthcare Act ('Obamacare')) (McClelland, 1976). However, in some cases, charisma is personalised – that is, charisma is utilised in in pursuit of personally beneficial goals. Right-wing populism engages more closely to this model of charisma via the utilisation of a symbiotic clientelistic relationship (as we have seen, for example, in the Trump administration's favouring of oil, gas and coal contracts over environmental protection). Trump himself rejects the notion of the importance of constitutional maturity (this can be observed a number of ways – multiple indictments and arrests amongst his inner circle, for example, Trump's tweets relating to his perceived sense of absolute authority, suggestions that he would not stand down if the US Democratic Party won the November 3rd US Presidential election). Trump displays a disdain for any organisation that exerts democratic checks-and-balances central to a constitutionally mature government (e.g. the EPA, FDA), choosing instead to actively seek to dismantle any voices (including those possessing scientific authority), alongside the display of a damaging level of personal aggrandisement. As Weber notes, the combination is toxic:

> [T]here is no more destructive distortion of political energy than when the parvenu swaggers around, boasting of his power, conceitedly reveling in its reflected glory.
>
> (Max Weber, Politics as a Vocation (1919), cited in Chafetz, 2019, p. 35)

THE WEAPONISATION OF CLIMATE CHANGE   135

Science remains, as noted by Collins and Evans (2019), a 'loyal opposition, a second chamber, a free press and an independent judiciary' in the face of politics (p. 210), which is exactly why right-wing populists seek to attack and discredit it. It is also because Trump relies so heavily on this aggrandised form of charismatic authority that he cannot accept to be contradicted. As an individual with no scientific background, scientists offer a valuable source of knowledge and expertise to whom he could regularly turn; he has decided, instead, to attack any scientific voice who does not display a deference to his alternate-fact based rhetoric.

Right-wing populism as a rational investment strategy

Gurov and Zankina (2013) argue that populism is not a consequence, primarily, of voter disengagement and disenfranchisement, but as an investment strategy, where a charismatic candidate adopts right-wing populism as the fastest and most effective means of entering the political fray, thus opening up opportunities for the acquisition of resources that would otherwise not have been available to him. It is a strategy that requires clientelism (e.g. campaigning funding by high-net-worth individuals or companies) whose investment will assist the inexperienced candidate in reaching office, whilst at the same time 'buying' access and future access to resources for those benefactors (in Trump's case, these include energy billionaires Harold Hamm, Kelcy Warren, John and Margo Catsimatidis, Jeffery and Melinda Hildebrand, Jim Justice, Dan, Farris and Jo Ann Wilks). Whilst donating to a campaign is legal, it nevertheless raises significant ethical questions, particularly when historic environmental rollbacks are executed which stand to benefit high-value benefactors. As stated by the authors,

> Instead of treating populism mainly as a dysfunction of democratic politics caused by a sheeplike electorate or a rise in extremist attitudes, we argue that populism may also be viewed as a rational strategy for investing in politics.
>
> (2013, p. 4)

Gurov and Zankina (2013) argue that crises (e.g. an economic recession) might increase the success of a populist charismatic leader because privately acquired resources might become far more scarce during that period;

> In conditions of severe economic crisis and without virtual alternatives to investment except for state-controlled funds, the incentive for promoting special interests through the faster and cheaper means of personalistic politics becomes ever more accentuated.
>
> (p. 14, 2013)

Such a strategy represents a pure form of 'opportunity-based, procedural democratic politics' (Gurov & Zankina, 2013, p. 4) that can quickly disintegrate into populist authoritarianism as the leader continues to dismantle the institutional checks-and-balances that are limiting his ability to engage in clientelism and resource acquisition. Environmental leadership under the Trump administration embodies such an approach; the dismantling of environmental protection to facilitate lucrative oil, gas and coal resource acquisition during Trump's 2016–2020 Presidential term has left the US in a far more precarious position in terms of its ability to counter the devastating effects of global warming. It has also led to FBI investigations; Scott Pruitt was arrested in 2018 on felony charges, and to charges of preferential treatment for big money donors; Energy Transfer CEO Kelcy Warren, a major Trump donor, faced the closure of his Dakota Access Pipeline but a federal appeals court blocked the order; Warren was been given an appeal date of 4 November 2020, the day after the 2020 US Presidential election took place.

In summary: truth is neither liberal nor conservative

As noted by the *New England Journal of Medicine*, 'Truth is neither liberal nor conservative' (2020, p. 1480). The reader will note, however, that its denigration and exploitation in the context of environmental and wider science represents a pure politicisation of the scientific voice where alt-right voices have sought to re-position science as a Democratic liberal hoax or enemy, in an effort to demonise and discredit it. It also reflects a wider, traditional right-wing populist aim of establishing an 'alternative truth', where the voices of politicians or religious leaders are prioritised in the environmental and wider scientific sphere over those of qualified scientists and high-quality scientific data. Such an approach is formulaic in the context of those – including Donald Trump – who have adopted right-wing

THE WEAPONISATION OF CLIMATE CHANGE   137

charismatic populism as a political and investment strategy. It comes, sadly, at a price, one in which outcomes for our planetary ecosystem remain critically endangered, ignored and cast aside in favour of short-term financial gain for a small sub-section of human society.

Notes

1   https://edition.cnn.com/2020/07/12/health/britain-masks-intl-gbr/index.html
2   https://www.washingtonpost.com/politics/top-wh-strategist-vows-a-daily-fight-for-deconstruction-of-the-administrative-state/2017/02/23/03f6b8da-f9ea-11e6-bf01-d47f8cf9b643_story.html
3   https://www.nationalgeographic.com/news/2017/03/how-trump-is-changing-science-environment/
4   https://www.theguardian.com/us-news/2020/aug/17/trump-alaska-arctic-wildlife-refuge-drilling
5   https://www.reuters.com/article/us-usa-climate-regulations-factbox-idUSKCN1VJ2BP
6   https://thehill.com/policy/energy-environment/482352-trump-budget-slashes-funding-for-epa-environmental-programs
7   https://www.rechargenews.com/transition/about-43bn-set-aside-for-clean-energy-loans-being-withheld-by-trump-administration/2-1-802198
8   https://bulletin.hds.harvard.edu/understanding-white-evangelical-views-on-immigration/#Notes
9   https://climate.nasa.gov/scientific-consensus/
10   https://www.natlawreview.com/article/alternative-facts-classroom-creationist-educational-policy-and-trump-administration
11   https://www.natlawreview.com/article/alternative-facts-classroom-creationist-educational-policy-and-trump-administration
12   https://www.nytimes.com/2019/10/07/books/review/who-is-an-evangelical-thomas-s-kidd.html
13   https://www.npr.org/2019/11/06/776852841/the-man-who-popularized-the-deep-state-doesnt-like-the-way-its-used?t=1602160292811

References

Brint, S., & Abrutyn, S. (2010). Who's Right About the Right? Comparing Competing Explanations of the Link Between White Evangelicals and Conservative Politics in the United States. *Journal for the Scientific Study of Religion*, 49, 2, pp. 328–350.

Chafetz, J. (2019). Constitutional Maturity, or Reading Weber in the Age of Trump. *Constitutional Commentary*, 34, pp. 17–41. Cornell Legal Studies Research Paper No. 19-19.

Collins, H., & Evans, R. (2019). Populism and Science. *Epistemology & Philosophy of Science*, 56, 4, pp. 200–218.

Davenport, C., & Landler, M. (2019). Trump Administration Hardens its Attack on Climate Science. *Brandon Thibodeaux for The New York Times* (May 27, 2019).

De Pryck, K., & Gemenne, F. (2017). The Denier-in-Chief: Climate Change, Science and the Election of Donald J. Trump. *Law Critique*. Springer Science + Business Media Dordrecht.

Diamond, D. (11th September, 2020). Trump Officials Interfered with CDC Reports on Covid-19. *Politico*. Available online at: https://www.politico .com/news/2020/09/11/exclusive-trump-officials-interfered-with-cdc -reports-on-covid-19-412809

Dunlap, R.R. (2013). Climate Change Skepticism and Denial: An Introduction. *American Behavioural Scientist*, 57, 6, 691–698.

Eatwell, R. (2004) Charisma and the Revival of the European Extreme Right. In J. Rydgren (ed.)., *Movements of Exclusion: Radical RightoWing Populism in the Western World*. New York: Nova Science. Pp. 101–120.

Forchtner, B., Kroneder, A., & Wetzel, D. (2018). Being Skeptical? Exploring Far-Right Climate Change Denial in Germany. *Environmental Communication*, 12, 589–604.

Gally, M. (19th December, 2019). Trump Should Be Removed from Office. Editorial. *Christianity Today*.

Gemenis, K., Katsanidou, A., & Vasilopoulou, S. (2012). The Politics of Anti-Environmentalism: Positional Issue Framing by the European Radical Right [online]. *Paper prepared for the MPSA Annual Conference*, 12–15 April 2012, Chicago.

Gurov, D., & Zankina, E. (2013). Populism and the Construction of Political Charisma. Post-Transition Politics in Bulgaria. *Problems of Post-Communism*, 60, 1, 3–17.

Hamilton, L.C., & Saito, K. (2015). A Four-Party View of US Environmental Concern. *Environmental Politics*, 24, 2, 212–227.

Homolar, A., & Scholz, R. (2019) The Power of Trump-Speak: Populist Crisis Narratives and Ontological Security. *Cambridge Review of International Affairs*, 32, 3, 344–364.

Jones, R.P., Cox, D., & Navarro-Rivera, J. (2014). *Believers, Sympathizers, and Skeptics: Why Americans Are Conflicted about Climate Change, Environmental Policy, and Science* (Public Religion Research Institute, 2014). Available online at http://publicreligion.org/site/wp-content/uploads/2014/11/2014-Climate-Change-FINAL1.pdf.

Jylhä, K.M. (2016). Ideological Roots of Climate-Change Denial: Resistance to Change, Acceptance of Inequality, or Both? (Doctoral thesis). Uppsala, Sweden: Uppsala University.

Jylhä, K.M., & Hellmer, K. (2020). Right Wing Populism and Climate Change Denial: The Roles of Exclusionary and Anti-Egalitarian Preferences, Conservative Ideology, and Anti-Establishment Attitudes. *Analyses of Social Issues and Public Policy*, 20, 1, 315–335.

LaFraniere, S. (14th September, 2020). Trump Aide Pushes Bizarre Conspiracies and Warns of Armed Revolt. *The New York Times*. Available online at: https://www.nytimes.com/2020/09/14/us/politics/caputo-virus.html

Lewandowsky, S., Oberauer, K., & Gignac, G.E. (2013). NASA Faked the Moon Landing – Therefore (Climate) Science is a Hoax: An Anatomy of the Motivated Rejection of Science. *Psychological Science*, 24, 622–633.

Linz, J.J. (2004). The Religious Use of Politics and/or the Political Use of Religion: Ersatz Ideology versus Ersatz Religion. In Maier, Hans, ed., Bruhn, Jodi, trans., *Totalitarianism and Political Religions Volume 1: Concepts for the Comparison of Dictatorships*. Abingdon, UK: Routledge.

Lobban, R., Luyt, R., Martin, S., Brooks, A., McDermott, D., & Zawisza-Riley, M. (2020). Right-Wing Populism and Safe Identities, NORMA. *International Journal for Masculinity Studies*, 15, 1, 76–93.

Lockwood, M. (2018). Right-Wing Populism and the Climate Change Agenda: Exploring the Linkages. *Environmental Politics*, 27, 4, 712–732.

Marlow, T., Miller, S., & Roberts, J.T. (2020). *Twitter Discourses on Climate Change: Exploring Topics, Presence of Bots*. Doctoral thesis: Draft. Brown University.

Marshall, K.L. (2020). *Faith and Oil: How the Alaska Pipeline Shaped America's Religious Right*. Eugene, OR: Wipf & Stock Publishers.

McCrae, R.R., & Costa, P.T. Jr. (2008). The Five-Factor Theory of Personality. In O.P. John, R.W. Robins, and L. A. Pervin. (Eds)., *Handbook of Personality: Theory and Research*. (3rd ed., pp. 159–180). New York: Guilford.

McCright, A.M., Dunlap, R.E., & Marquart-Pyatt, S.T. (2016). Political Ideology and Views About Climate Change in the European Union. *Environmental Politics*, 25, 2, 338–358.

McDonnell, D. (2015). Populist Leaders and Coterie Charisma. *Political Studies*. The Political Studies Association. 64, 3, 1–15.

Mudde, C., & Kaltwasser, R. (2013). Exclusionary vs. Inclusionary Populism: Comparing Contemporary Europe and Latin America. *Governments and Opposition*, 48, 147–174.

Mudde, C. (2007). *Populist Radical Right Parties in Europe*. Cambridge: Cambridge University Press.

Myre, G., & Treisman, R. (9th November, 2019). *The Man Who Popularized the 'Deep State' Doesn't Like the Way It's Used*. NPR.

Piller, C. (14th October, 2020). The Inside Story of How Trump's COVID-19 Coordinator Undermined the World's Top Health Agency. *Science Magazine*. AAAS. Available online at: https://www.sciencemag.org/news/2020/10/inside-story-how-trumps-covid-19-coordinator-undermined-cdc

Public Religion Research Institute (PRRI) (2014). *National Survey on Religion, Values, and Climate Change*. PRRI.

Rutjens, B.T., Sutton, R., & van der Lee, R. (2017). Not All Skepticism is Equal: Exploring the Ideological Antecedents of Science Acceptance and Rejection. *Personality and Social Psychology Bulletin*, 44, 384–405.

Schjoedt, U., Stødkilde-Jørgensen, H., Geertz, A.W., Lund, T.E., & Roepstorff, A. (2011). The Power of Charisma--Perceived Charisma Inhibits the Frontal Executive Network of Believers in Intercessory Prayer. *Soc Cogn Affect Neuroscience*, 6, 1, 119–127.

Shao, W. (2017) Weather, Climate, Politics, or God? Determinants of American Public Opinions Toward Global Warming. *Environmental Politics*, 26, 1, 71–96.

Smith, P. (2000). Culture and Charisma: Outline of a Theory. *Acta Sociologica*, 43, 2, 101–111.

Thoroughgood, C.N., Padilla, A., Hunter, S.T., & Tate, B.W. (2012). The Susceptible Circle: A Taxonomy of Followers Associated with Destructive Leadership. *The Leadership Quarterly*, 23, 5, 897–917.

Tollefson, J. (2020). How Trump Damaged Science. *Nature*, 586, 190–194. 8th October 2020.

Van der Brug, W., & Mughan, A. (2007). Charisma, Leader Effects and Support for Right-Wing Populist Parties. *Party Politics*, 13, 1, 29–51.

VijayaVenkataRaman, S., Iniyan, S., & Goic, R. (2012). A Review of Climate Change, Mitigation and Adaptation. *Renewable and Sustainable Energy Reviews*, 16, 1, 878–897.

Weber, M. (1968). Max Weber on Charisma and Institution Building: Selected Papers/Edited and with an Introduction by S.N. Eisenstadt. Chicago: University of Chicago Press.

Weber, M. (1978). *Economy and Society*. Berkeley, CA: University of California Press.

Weiland, N. (18th September, 2020). Emails Detail Effort to Silence C.D.C. and Question Its Science. *The New York Times*. Available online at: https://www.nytimes.com/2020/09/18/us/politics/trump-cdc-coronavirus.html

Zaslove, A. (2008). Here to Stay? Populism as a New Party Type. *European Review*. 16, 3, 319–336.

Zehndorfer, E. (2015). *Charismatic Leadership: The Role of Charisma in the Global Financial Crisis*. London: Routledge.

Zehndorfer, E. (2019). *Evolution, Politics & Charisma: Why do Populists Win?* New York: Routledge.

Part II

SYSTEMS AND COMPLEXITY

7

COMPLEX SYSTEMS LITERACY

SOCIAL DILEMMAS – THE SETUP FOR MANAGERIAL DECISION-MAKING IN A COMPLEX WORLD

Ligia Cremene

Introduction: living in complex systems

This chapter offers a multi-disciplinary perspective on managerial decision-making in the current global context. It identifies social dilemmas as the frequent setup for managerial decision-making and synthesises the main approaches for solving them. The chapter presents the main Systemic Leadership traits – a skill set that is connecting us to the future and is required for the new, green business leaders of the planet, if we are to create a world in which we all want to be a part of.

We live in complex systems. Not in cities, countries, organisations, but in complex systems. Networked in interdependent roles, tasks and processes, our actions are rippling further into the future, and present, than ever before. We can no longer ignore, or escape, the consequences of our actions. Multidimensional, highly interconnected layers of biological, social, technical structures influencing each other, as they evolve and transform.

As leaders and managers of our lives, our companies and our communities, we find ourselves facing complicated decisions, dilemmas (conflicting

DOI: 10.4324/9781003190820-9

goals) and conundrums, that generations before us had to face perhaps only once or twice in a lifetime. Business models and industries that ran for decades are now facing ruin and the natural environment is giving us all the signs of exhaustion. Well established educational paradigms are turned upside down in every corner of the world. Indeed, the whole landscape of value creation is changing as the 4th Industrial Revolution breaks down traditional ideas governing globalisation.

In the post-information-revolution era, leaders and managers are pressed to make faster decisions considering huge amounts of data and ever-changing contexts. Sustainability is essential, and companies are starting to understand that if they do not change, they will die. The intuitions that served us well when managing deterministic systems are no longer valid, no longer helping us, and can lead to fatal errors in complex systems, which are being characterised by emergent phenomena and self-organisation.

There is growing awareness that the systems we live in are in fact fundamentally complex and such systemic phenomena require a whole new, networked and evolutionary approach, and a new strategic toolbox, if we are to start shifting things around and shaping a more sustainable way of living on planet Earth.

The Covid-19 pandemic has given us the final warning and pushed us into a great reset. The crisis has highlighted the interconnectedness of business, society and environment, more than ever before, acting as a magnifying glass for all the existing vulnerabilities and compulsive social behaviours. We either start strategising for sustainability and a fairer society, or we continue the downward spiral into a very gloomy future for the human race.

Are managers and leaders ready to embrace a new kind of thinking and integrate it into their day-to-day business decisions? Will they be brave enough to implement new, externalities-aware business models?

Social dilemmas – the frequent setup for managerial decision-making

In the highly interconnected world we live in, social dilemmas are ubiquitous and have become a frequent setup for decision-making (Weber & Messick, 2004). Whether in organisations, communities, individual households or small businesses, we can no longer escape the consequences of our actions.

COMPLEX SYSTEMS LITERACY   147

Social dilemmas capture the core dynamic within groups requiring collective action where there is a conflict between an individual's short-term personal or selfish interest and the actions that maximise the longer-term interests of the group they are part of (Olson, 1965; Ostrom et al., 1999; Weber & Messick, 2004).

Social dilemmas are characterised by two properties (Dawes, 1980):

(a) the social payoff to each individual for defecting behaviour is higher than the payoff for cooperative behaviour, regardless of what the other society members do, yet

(b) all individuals in the society receive a lower payoff if all defect than if all cooperate.

Kollock identifies social dilemmas as situations '*in which individual rationality leads to collective irrationality*' (Kollock, 1998, p. 183). '*Why do we collectively create results nobody wants?*' is the question Otto Scharmer and Katrin Kaufer ask in their 2013 eye-opening book, *Leading from the Emerging Future: From Ego-system to Eco-system Economies* (Scharmer & Kaufer, 2013).

Externalities: what's not counted – the seeds for crises

Externalities are at the core of any social dilemma. Externalities cannot be effectively managed by the immediate cost–benefit analysis of the individual agents, and thus the social dilemma arises.

> When we measure the wrong things, the result is perverse. Today, what matters most to a thriving life is not counted at all in our dominant economic performance indicators. A natural environment that will continue to provide us with fresh air, clean water, rich soil – not counted. Communities that educate and nurture their members – not counted. Forms of governance with a stable degree of accountability – not counted. In the end: our ability to continue life on Earth (what is meant by the word sustainability) – not counted.
>
> (Phillipsen, 2020)

Environmental problems are largely problems of externalities, consequences of human activity that are shifted from the producer to others, often the rest of society.

> The separation of production from capital removes the immediacy of responsibility for inevitable externalities which flow from production.
>
> (Taylor & Bronstone, 2019)

The problem is that most times positive externalities are flowing to the top, whereas negative externalities are flowing to the bottom (Scharmer & Kaufer, 2013; Mazzucato, 2018).

> For too long, governments have socialized risks but privatized rewards: the public has paid the price for cleaning up messes, but the benefits of those clean-ups have accrued largely to companies and their investors. [...] We socialize bailouts, we should socialize successes, too.
>
> (Mazzucato, 2020)

Many large businesses have neglected long-term investments in favour of short-term gains and short-term shareholder interests.

> Obsessed with quarterly returns and stock prices, CEOs and corporate boards have rewarded shareholders by buying back stocks [...] These buybacks come at the expense of investment in wages, worker training, and research and development.
>
> (Mazzucato, 2020)

Externalities-unaware financial systems have led the global economy into crisis after crisis (Scharmer & Kaufer, 2013).

Making decisions 'the old way' – blind spots

It took more than 40 years since its 'discovery', at the maternity clinic at the General Hospital in Vienna, for hand-washing with a chlorinated solution to become a common, mandatory, practice in hospitals and one of the main tools in public health. Regardless of the benefits, even today, convincing healthcare providers, and the general public, to take hand-washing seriously can sometimes be a challenge (see general behaviour at the beginning of the Covid-19 crisis, when we all re-learned to wash our hands correctly).

The same seems to be true for climate change. As early as the 19th century, scientists first argued that human emissions of greenhouse gases could alter the climate. Many theories of climate change were advanced, and a consensus was formed by the end of the 1980s: greenhouse gases were deeply involved in most climate changes and human-caused emissions were bringing discernible global warming (Hansen et al., 1981). More than 40 years have passed since the first public alerts and calls for action were voiced, for climate change to be considered one of the greatest threats to human health and survival (Nicholls, 2007).

A paradox of the information age is that when 'information is plentiful, we often use it not to make better decisions based on the intrinsic characteristics of a situation, but rather to imitate others – and their mistakes' (Bonabeau, 2004). Moreover, efforts of training or stimulating people to improve decision-making competencies have not been very successful so far.

The 2015 World Bank Group *World Development Report*: 'Mind, Society, and Behavior' (World Bank, 2015) offers numerous world-wide examples of public policy success stories that are based on bypassing people's cognitive biases (Tversky & Kahneman, 1974; Gigerenzer & Selten, 2002) that would not let them act in their favour and for the common benefit of their respective societies. Similar efforts were previously highlighted in *Nudge* (Thaler & Sunstein, 2008) which discusses ways in which public or private organisations can help people make better decisions. Although *Nudge* has brought about a major shift in public policy design – the behavioural approach – and 'many psychologists discovered that the name of their trade had changed even if its content had not' (Kahneman, 2013), to a very large extent people are still making decisions 'the old way'.

Because we can – the right to consume more

The most common argument legitimising socially defecting choices (e.g. tax evasion, polluting, etc.) is that those in leading positions in society violate the social norms. (Mazar et al., 2008; Hammar et al., 2009, as cited by Gächter & Renner, 2018). Reports of socially defecting behaviour are part of our daily lives, with a large range of exposure in the media.

The financial crisis of 2008 illustrates the effects of socially defecting behaviour. Toxic and risky financial products have been used only because they offered huge profits for banks and investment funds. The lack of regulation and control made this possible. When the tailors of such speculative schemes were questioned about their deeds, the answer was most often: because we can, because the control is loose, because state authorities lack the resources to catch people like me – see the declarations of Bernard Madoff, operator of the largest financial fraud in US history (Soltes, 2016).

When asked to explain their choices, the participants in a 'commons dilemma' experiment – where they could buy out others' access to a resource (White, 1994, as cited by Weber & Messick, 2004), viewed their buyout costs 'not [...] *as a cost of consumption but as the purchase of the right to consume more'*. The parties who bought out others consumed more and exhausted the resource more quickly, not occurring to them that the cost of the buyout makes the need for conservation more salient.

Exxon knew about climate change almost 40 years ago. As investigations have shown, the oil company understood the science before it became a public issue and spent millions to promote misinformation (Scientific American, 2015).

According to Mazar et al. (2008), the standard external cost–benefit perspective – rooted in the philosophies of Thomas Hobbes, Adam Smith, and the standard economic model of rational and selfish human behaviour (i.e., *homo economicus*) – generates three hypotheses as to the forces that are expected to increase the frequency and magnitude of socially defecting behaviour: (i) higher magnitude of external rewards (payoffs), (ii) lower probability of being caught (punishment probability) and (iii) lower magnitude of punishment.

As Dirk Philipsen expresses it:

> perhaps it is, then, unrealistic to expect individuals to make smarter choices, when dominant economic reasoning rewards them for moving in the wrong direction.
>
> (Philipsen, 2020)

What Game Theory teaches us about promoting green principles

Promoting green principles requires the cooperation of many actors: citizens, institutions, organisations. Adopting green principles and solving major environmental problems cannot rely solely on isolated, individual efforts. Global issues require global effort, and global effort requires large-scale cooperation.

COMPLEX SYSTEMS LITERACY   151

Both *competition and cooperation* have been the driving biological and social mechanisms of evolution on planet Earth and can be witnessed in every species. In human societies, cooperation is a massive resource for advancing individual and group capabilities and over the course of thousands of years people evolved complex networks for collaboration and cooperation. Curry argues that morality could be seen as 'the *product of a suite of "adaptations for cooperation" that evolved to solve the problems of cooperation and conflict recurrent in the lives of our ancestors*' – and sees '*morality as cooperation*' (Curry, 2016).

The emergence of social cooperation has been extensively studied in the framework of public goods games, tragedy of the commons, prisoner's dilemma, collective action logic, etc. (Olson, 1965; Hardin, 1968; Dawes, 1980; Binmore, 1990; Ostrom, 1990, 1999, 2015; Axelrod, 2006; Rand et al., 2009; Roca & Helbing, 2011).

For a situation to be modelled as *a game*, a correct identification of the following elements is needed: (i) *players* – decision-making agents, (ii) *strategies* – sets of actions that are available to each player (choices, decisions) and (iii) *payoffs* – one player's gain depends entirely on her choice and on the number of players who choose a certain strategy. 'A game is simply a system of payoffs depending on the combination of choices made by the players' (Dawes, 1980, p. 178).

In dilemma games, each player makes one of two choices: *defecting* or *cooperating*. Pro-social or pro-self behaviour translates into cooperation/defection in *social dilemma games* (Weber & Messick, 2004; Cremene & Cremene, 2021).

There are several ways of promoting and enabling cooperation:

(a)   *Natural forms of cooperation intertwined in human evolution*

People cooperate more with those whom they are closely connected to, members of their group, more than with those who are of a different group, cultural society and with whom they do not perceive they have a connection. In small groups, cooperation is typically maintained by a reciprocity system (individuals having personal connections with other group members, helping each other and exchanging favours). In larger groups, patterns of interaction may differ significantly; people often feel less responsible for the common good as they are more removed from it and less connected with the other people with whom they share a certain resource.

All members experience the benefits of the large group, including 'free-riders' – those who stop contributing but continue to enjoy the benefits. Yet, most members of large groups cooperate.

Game Theory highlights the role of punishment in maintaining cooperation, which reduces the benefits to free-riding (Binmore, 2006; Boyd et al., 2010). Finding an efficient balance between punishment severity and punishment probability is key. Empirical evidence and reported experiments reveal that punishment probability is more important than punishment severity (Gladwell, 2000; Cremene et al., 2014). Moreover, social experience indicates that a low punishment probability is inefficient even when punishment severity is very high (Binmore, 2006). A classic example is the US Prohibition at the beginning of the 20th century.

(b)   *Regulation and rule adherence*

Regulation involves limiting undesirable behaviour. This is usually done by an external, third party imposing sanctions or giving rewards to groups and individuals. Regulation aims to connect the individual's externalities with the costs and benefits they pay, by imposing extra costs on them for certain negative externalities, while providing them with subsidies and payments for certain activities that generates positive externalities. It is common for people to choose or appoint a leader to look after a common resource, to the benefit of all the individuals involved (e.g. grazing land, forests, fisheries) (Ostrom, 1999).

Regulation can be very effective in situations of independence between actors. On the other hand, the external, third party approach has overhead costs and is also prone to corruption. Legitimacy and fair procedures are extremely important for citizens' willingness to accept the authority.

(c)   *Norms and social influence*

Individuals are decision-makers embedded in social networks, where they constantly extract information from, and against which they constantly calibrate their behaviour. These social networks create the social capital that individuals use in their decision-making processes (Fukuyama, 2000; Binmore, 2006; Pentland, 2014). Social influence is the way in which individual behaviour is influenced by the presence (real or imaginary) of other individuals, groups or institutions.

Social norms often serve to regulate the use of a common resource (Ostrom, 1999). Identity keeps social norms from breaking down and social norms arise by repeated interactions (Fukuyama, 2000; Akerlof & Kranton, 2010). Social conformity, the need for safety, greed and the fear of missing out induce powerful incentives for imitation (Bonabeau, 2004).

> *Strong social ties create the conditions in which peer pressure is the most effective mechanism for promoting cooperation.*
>
> (Pentland, 2014)

An individual's incentive to engage in socially defecting behaviour depends largely on social norms. Yet, in our modern-day society we have quasi-anonymous users and fluid groups. In most cases, there are no guarantees that they are likely to interact with one another on a regular basis. The social capital is eroded when norms deteriorate (Fukuyama, 2000).

(d)   *Positive interdependence and repeated interaction*

Cooperation increases when people are given a chance to talk to each other. Communication, transparency and feedback mechanisms that build positive interdependence are a way to foster cooperation (Sally, 1995; Axelrod, 2006; Pentland, 2014).

Solving social dilemmas

When the individual pays the full cost for their actions, there is no social dilemma. The community or organisation should be sustainable. The tragedy with social dilemmas is that they are not a feature of the actors involved but of the structure of the game. It is the setup, the nature of the systems of interaction, that causes the dilemma, not the individual personalities or motives of the players. The outcome is predictable, yet no one, individually, can do anything to prevent it. That seems to be the case with the self-devouring growth our economic systems have generated.

(a)   Norms and interdependence

As soon as externalities go above a certain level we need to think and act collectively. Norms and interdependence are two mechanisms for dealing with social dilemmas.

One way is for organisations to create some *top-down structures* that regulate the systems through norms, incentives, rewards and penalties, to ensure that those who create negative externalities pay for them and those who create positive externalities in turn get reimbursed for them (e.g. carbon credits, benefits). This integrates the externalities into the cost–benefit analysis of the agents, making them visible and harder to ignore.

Another way is to increase *connectivity and interdependence* among actors: what happens to an actor happens to another (breathing the same air, using the same roads, airports, etc.). When there is low connectivity, there will likely be low interdependence.

When actors are independent, they can do things that affect others without that effect returning to themselves. For example, if I live in Italy and pollute the atmosphere, water and land in Romania by dumping waste through clandestine transportation and burning, then what happens there does not affect me too much; this negative correlation can go on existing. Turning up the connectivity and interdependence will, however, change the dynamic. For instance, if I have business partners in Romania and I happen to take my family on holiday there, there is a much greater possibility for a positive correlation between my experience and what happens in Romania. This means that I increasingly have to factor my negative externalities into my cost–benefit analysis.

Connectivity and interdependence can be used to create self-regulating, sustainable cooperative organisations and platforms. Furthermore, enabling ongoing interaction with identifiable others, with some knowledge of previous behaviour and reputation, is key to fostering constructive interdependence and thus to helping solve, or even avoid social dilemmas from the start.

Complex systems literacy: Systemic Leadership traits

Making decisions in complex systems requires more of leaders. Only a few years ago, five- to ten-year strategic plans were considered the norm, until crisis after crisis forced us to embrace uncertainty, agility, reinvention and reconfigurability. We do not live in cities, we do not work in companies, we live and work in social networks. Social networks are complex adaptive systems (Woolley et al., 2010; Pentland, 2014; Barabási, 2002, 2018) where cause and effect are not always obvious, visible or trackable.

COMPLEX SYSTEMS LITERACY   155

We find ourselves in an information age, a new reality in which we are scaling networks and digital platforms and customising experiences and services. Today the major value creators are networks like Google and Alibaba, and platforms like Haier and Amazon. The information era sees products transformed into services.

(Haanaes, 2020)

Today's problems are yesterday's solutions

Adaptation builds complexity (Holland, 1995; Atkins, 2003). The very mechanisms that helped a system develop and thrive, for a while, are the ones that can choke it and bring it at the edge of reset or irreversible decline. We call this *the vicious circle of adaptation*; it is identifiable in various systems, from biological to technical ones (Cremene, 2011).

Behind the organisational chart, or of any structure that interacts with the environment for that matter, the vicious circle of adaptation takes shape. To cope with change, we implement adaptive, short-term effective solutions; over time, they become redundant or conflicting and, by accumulation, increase complexity. Increased complexity leads to decreased efficiency (higher resource consumption, redundancy, inability to decide, confusion, delays, missed opportunities). Temporary adaptation capacity also decreases, which again leads to implementing new adaptation strategies and mechanisms. This is, in short, the vicious circle of adaptation.

If changes are not implemented in a timely manner – or they are not brave enough but merely incremental, complexity builds and becomes difficult to manage, seizes the entire system, and exhausts those involved, no matter how successful they have been until that point.

Adaptive solutions can be effective in the short run (in the context that led to their creation) but the structures created for the purpose of adaptation may be unnecessary or redundant on the long-term evolution. In biological organisms, structures resulting from adaptation without anticipation (e.g. the appendix, respiratory ways intersecting with the digestive airways) are a potential hazard – infection, inflammation, asphyxia (Atkins, 2003).

Similarly, the invention of plastics may have been a great solution at the time, with a wide range of advantages, yet a few decades later, plastic waste is suffocating our planet's oceans, rivers, marine life and was recently found in human placenta (Ragusa et al., 2021). Like many modern technological advances this is a 'social trap' (Platt, 1973, as cited by Dawes,

1980); it occurs when a behaviour that results in immediate reward leads to long-term punishment. Today's problems are yesterday's solutions.

> Design of sustainable adaptive solutions requires extended time effort and involves dealing with greater complexity. A unitary, yet flexible approach is needed, so that local problems can be solved locally and global problems globally, considering the effects of local actions at global level, and vice-versa.
>
> (Cremene, 2011)

Deterministic vs. complex systems: what characterises a complex system?

A system is a collection of parts that interact with each other to function as a whole. A system has a purpose that defines it and keeps it together. A vehicle, for instance, has the purpose of taking people and objects from A to B. This purpose is a property of the vehicle as a whole and cannot be detected in the component parts (engine, wheels, etc.). A deterministic system can be fully described, either by mathematical equations, diagrams, algorithms and so on. The link between cause and effect can be clearly established. Take for instance a computer, or a TV set, a gas, water or electrical installation. Any malfunctioning can be detected, repaired and even predicted and avoided by careful design, operation and maintenance. There is a finite set of patterns and behaviours that can occur, and they can all be previously described and learned. Expertise can therefore be developed.

On the other hand, a complex system may take us by surprise. We usually name 'complex' systems whose behaviour has proved difficult to predict and control, such as the human brain, the world economy or the global climate. There are various attempts to characterise a complex system. However, there is no concise definition of a complex system, let alone a definition that all disciplines agree on (Ladyman et al., 2013).

A core set of features that are widely associated with complexity, necessary but not sufficient, are: *numerosity, non-linearity, feedback, emergence, local organisation, robustness, hierarchical organisation*. Narrowing even more, the two main properties that help us identify a complex system are *emergence* and *self-organisation* (Holland, 1995; Merali & Allen, 2011).

Local actions produce global outcomes: charging your smartphone every night or buying a new sweater doesn't seem like much; one can say it is a simple,

COMPLEX SYSTEMS LITERACY   157

insignificant gesture, but when billions of people are charging their phones every night and buying cloths frequently, their local actions contribute to global CO_2 emissions and climate change (Edenhofer, Pichs-Madruga et al., 2014).

Small local changes may lead to large global changes: local deforestation leads to barren lands, changes in the local climate and climate refugees. Local re-greening interventions (e.g. hydrologic corridors), on the other hand, have the potential of generating large-scale changes in regional climate, ecosystems and people well-being (MEA, 2005).

Simple rules generate complex behaviour: a hive of bees, or a murmuration of starlings, exhibit complex behaviour which is not controlled by the queen or by some other member of the group, but is generated by the members themselves, who follow relatively simple rules of behaviour: attraction, avoidance and alignment (e.g. fly to the nectar, avoid obstacles, stay close to other bees, do not bump into each other, follow the foragers, etc.) (Dawkins, 1986).

The dynamic nature of chaotic systems is a consequence of the sensitivity of complex systems to initial conditions and perturbations (change), which can result in disproportionate subsequent effects on the entire system: phase shifts (the transition of a system from one state of operation to an entirely different state), tipping-points (Gladwell, 2000), black swans (Taleb, 2007).

Systems thinking is a tool for managing complexity (Merali & Allen, 2011), an adjustable lens – zooming in and out on events and daily issues – that we people can use to look at the interconnected functioning of things in the attempt to *manage complexity*. The only difference is that before we were used to looking mostly at deterministic systems (where you can identity cause and effect) whereas now we need to look at *complex adaptive systems*, because that is our surrounding reality, and we can no longer ignore the consequences of living in interconnectedness. And that requires challenging our intuitions and adapting our tools and methods.

Green business leaders: managing complexity

Almost 50% of the Fortune 500 from 1999 had disappeared from the list just 10 years later (Goodburn, 2015). Today's rate of change is at a faster pace than ever. We live in the VUCA world, where VUCA stands for volatility, uncertainty, complexity and ambiguity.

A lack of systems thinking and of Systemic Leadership skills

The most frequently mentioned internal causes of a corporate crisis were: the management held on to strategies that were no longer working, the management did not want to adapt to external changes, the management had no vision, the internal communication was insufficient, changes in the market were underestimated (Lymbersky, 2014).

In almost a third of all situations, the fact that the management of the company was not very well educated in business matters played a big part in fostering the crisis. Yet, underlying all of these reasons, there is a lack of systems thinking and of Systemic Leadership skills.

An organisation's services are delivered to customers and markets by systems, not by individuals. It is ultimately an integrated system that gets things done. Organisations succeed or fail as systems. The job of the organisational leadership is to optimize that system (Tate, 2013).

Change is the new constant

Change is the new constant. The typical organization today has undertaken five major firmwide changes in the past three years. [...] Yet half of change initiatives fail, and only 34% are a clear success (Gartner, 2020).

Increased rate of change initiatives is one of the indicators that many organisations have reached a complexity level they can no longer manage.

Managing the current level of complexity requires new skill sets, new thinking, new approaches, new language (Senge, 2006; Scharmer, 2007; Merali & Allen, 2011; Espinosa & Walker, 2011). All these have come to be known under the umbrella of Systems Leadership (von Bertalanffy, 1974; Forrester, 1968; Meadows, 2008; Dreier et al., 2019) or Systemic Leadership (Tate, 2013; Pinnow, 2011; Stam & Hoogenboom, 2018). Both terms have surfaced during the past decade, attracting increasing interest from diverse stakeholders seeking new approaches to address complex, systemic challenges. Google search result count in January 2021 reached 99,300,000 for 'Systemic Leadership' and 607,000,000 for 'systems leadership'. The two are intertwined and draw from the same roots. 'Systems leadership' is used more in the context of solving global environmental challenges, whereas 'Systemic Leadership' is used in management and organisational development contexts. Sometimes the terms are used interchangeably.

COMPLEX SYSTEMS LITERACY   159

The systemic approach to leadership considers managers, first and foremost, as a part of a complex system, which is constantly at change. It does not consider the art of leadership as one who manages these systems themselves, but rather one who manages the relations and networks within these systems.

(Pinnow, 2011)

Both individual leadership and Systemic Leadership are important and are intertwined. They are not binary polarities. Leadership is at the service of the organisation's needs.

(Tate, 2013)

Organisations talk to us through symptoms: turnover, burnout, delays, low performance, not delivering, lack of leadership, not achieving goals, lack of direction, conflicts. Symptoms are just the events, the tip of the iceberg. We further need to look at the patterns and the underlying systemic structures (Senge, 2006; Pinnow, 2011).

Epic fails

Increased complexity leaves many gaps uncovered and blind spots that lead to epic fails.

A story of an epic failure is that of The Electric Company in the early 1900s in New York. In 1900, there were more electric automobiles on New York City streets than cars powered by gasoline (Yergin, 2012) and around a third of all cars in the US were electric (Schiffer et al., 1994). By 1920 the electric car had all but vanished and gas-powered cars dominated the market. There was even a NY Taxi company having an all-electric fleet and charging stations (Schiffer et al., 1994). The electric car was especially advertised for women. Photos of the time pictured elegant women, in nymph-like dresses, charging their electric cars at their home charging stations. Pictures of magnates perched atop their electric cars were also popular in the age.

Fast forward to the 21st century, electric cars are 'the latest innovation' and a consumer trend. What happened in the meanwhile, for almost a hundred years? The Electric Company has failed. The case was a living illustration of the, by now famous, adage by Peter Senge:

Technology is not the final frontier, human systems are.

A brief analysis of the company's story reveals expansion from 13 cars to 1,600 in only 2 years. Yet this occurred without proportional investment in batteries and charging systems (Schiffer et al., 1994). External factors were also at play: oil had been discovered in Texas and gasoline price went down. Competitors, like Ford, started producing more affordable cars and there were also electric car patent litigations.

Among all these factors, sociocultural norms and biases had also their say, and eventually sealed the fate of the company and of the electric vehicle altogether (Schiffer et al., 1994). The electric car was considered 'too feminine' (in a time when women were still fighting for their right to vote): no noise, no smoke, no dirt, no oil; it was too clean, too easy, too elegant, too soft, not rough enough. Moreover, women themselves wanted to prove their fathers wrong: they wanted to show them that they were capable of driving a stick shift (manual transmission gasoline cars). And the rest is history.

More recently, successful companies that fell prey to confirmation bias and missed the connection with the emergent future were Kodak and Nokia. Kodak continued to believe that film photography was superior to digital photography, even if they built the first self-contained digital camera in 1975. Nokia continued to believe that 'hardware is more important than software', even if they produced their first touchscreen smartphone in the 1990s.

While these failures seem to be about those bets that can change the course of a company, they are actually examples of lack of systems thinking which lead to the inability to manage complexity and make the right decisions in the wider context.

Systemic leaders – born or trained?

Systemic Leadership manages complexity, builds organisational fitness and solves multi-levelled issues. It is about how we make decisions regarding the whole and the systems we are part of: family, company, team, department, community, society, etc. The systemic perspective adds to all the other ways of looking at an organisation: legal, financial, business, psychological, operational, managerial, strategic and developmental.

(b)   Systemic perception

People tend to have an inner knowing about systems. They feel when they truly belong to a group or not, when they have a place, when they are accepted or merely tolerated. People feel when they are connected with others, exchanging information, non-verbal signals, ideas, material goods, emotions, thoughts, flows of communication or when they are disconnected. *Systemic perception* is present at birth, yet for some reason, it is later ignored or not fully tapped into by many people when making decisions.

There are people in this world who see things in their interconnectedness by default. They are natural born system thinkers who cannot understand an action or a concept if they do not see how it is connected to the whole, why, and what does it do. There are others who are terrified at the prospect that everything is interconnected with everything and one's actions have consequences that they might not be aware of. As one of my students once expressed it:

> And what now? What am I supposed to do? If I take this 'systems thinking mumbo-jumbo' into consideration, then I'll end up doing nothing: I can't even drive my car without thinking it causes draught in some other part of the world?!

The discomfort of being aware of the ripples of our actions can be significant, and, for some, unmanageable. Interdependence awareness can be painful. Running away from this discomfort is what makes many people ignore the evidence and remain in denial.

> For those who stake their identity on the role of omniscient conqueror, the uncertainty exposed by systems thinking is hard to take. If you can't understand, predict, and control, what is there to do? (Donella Meadows, Dancing with Systems)

(c)   A different sort of doing

> Systems thinking leads to another conclusion – obvious as soon as we stop being blinded by the illusion of control. [...] there is plenty to do, of a different sort of 'doing.' Systems can't be controlled, but they can be designed and redesigned. [...] We can't control systems or figure them out. But we can dance with them (Donella Meadows, Dancing with Systems)

(d)   Learning to manage complexity

Managing complexity first requires thinking outside of the paradigm of deterministic systems – linear cause and effect, 'command and control', 'if-then-else' type of reasoning – and switching to the complex systems paradigm, where fundamental properties of emergence and self-organisation need to be understood and considered. The most important tool we have for managing complexity is systems thinking (Merali & Allen, 2011). Yet, learning the specific set of skills under the umbrella of systems thinking is not an easy task. Tom Grimes of Hanover Insurance Company observes: 'We have such a capacity to think linearly in our lives, that it's going to take a major learning experience to turn it around'.

Professor Barry Richmond, who has dedicated many years of his life to teaching system dynamics and the systems thinking method, once explained (thesystemsthinker.com):

> Despite significant advances in personal computers and systems thinking software over the last decade, learning to apply systems thinking effectively remains a tough nut to crack. Many intelligent people continue to struggle far too long with the systems thinking paradigm, thinking process, and methodology.
>
> While the concept of Systems Leadership makes intuitive sense to many stakeholders, it is not yet widely embraced and practiced. Mainstreaming its application will require a broader and more coordinated effort to develop research, share knowledge and build capacity.
>
> (Dreier et al., 2019)

Managers around the world are increasingly aware of the need to build up expertise in systems thinking.

'Without that internal expertise, it's unlikely any new thinking mentality will infiltrate the organization very well', explains Dan Simpson, Director of Planning at The Clorox Company. He adds that a more intensive course may be necessary to train the facilitators who will continue the systems thinking learning process inside their companies. 'These people will continually make the translation from what is an academic field of study into operational action inside an organization' (thesystemsthinker .com).

Systemic Leadership skill set – connecting to the future

Creating self-regulating, sustainable cooperative organisations and platforms to deal with social dilemmas requires a different approach than those of traditional management and leadership. Prominent systems thinker Donella Meadows once wrote:

> Living successfully in a world of systems requires more of us than our ability to calculate. It requires our full humanity—our rationality, our ability to sort out truth from falsehood, our intuition, our compassion, our vision, and our morality.

If after all, morality is cooperation (Curry, 2016), then what are some qualities and skills of systemic leaders? The following is a list, not by far exhaustive, of intertwined Systemic Leadership skills to which many nuances and concepts may be added.

(e) Self-awareness

The quality of our awareness determines the quality of our decisions and therefore our outer reality (Senge et al., 2005; Senge, 2006; Scharmer, 2007; Taylor & Bronstone, 2019). From ancient philosophers to modern-day system thinkers, this was expressed in various ways and contexts.

> The quality of the results in any kind of system is a function of the awareness that people in the system are operating from. Even though our world is interconnected in ways unimaginable even a decade ago, in many cases our awareness whether as individuals, organizations or nations is still limited and local.
>
> (Scharmer, 2007)

Knowing yourself well enough to understand your motives, your values, your inner drives, beliefs and goals, and not getting drawn into the deep traps of complex environments, is an important capacity of systemic leaders.

Our actions are driven from the subconscious. This is no longer an 'esoteric observation' but rather the main line of experimentation in Moral and Social Psychology (Haidt, 2013) and Behavioural Economics (Camerer, 2003; Thaler & Sunstein, 2008; Ariely, 2008; Akerlof & Shiller, 2009;

Kahneman, 2011). Being capable of truly seeing one's actions can be transformative. Also, at a collective level, helping people become aware of how they interact, brings about amazing transformations (Pentland, 2014).

(f)   Emotional and mental flexibility

Managing complexity requires inner work (Senge, 2006; Scharmer & Kaufer, 2013). Inner work towards achieving clarity of thought and 'an emotional flexibility that allows for constant reinvention' (Harari, 2018).

> we need to get to know ourselves better and we need to develop this mental flexibility. Not as a kind of hobby on the side. This is really the most important quality or skill to just survive the upheavals in the coming decades.
>
> (Harari, 2018)

This flexibility of the mind enables systemic leaders to simultaneously be creative, systematic and practical.

(g)   Listening and holding space

Many failures in management, leadership, politics and society in general, can be attributed to a lack of listening, and therefore a lack of understanding. Considered a fundamental 'soft-skill', listening helps leaders understand what is going on with their people and organisations. Although rather hard to achieve, non-defensive and non-judgemental listening creates safety and a sense of trust – the space for new solutions to arise.

The Four Levels of Listening (Scharmer & Kaufer, 2013) is a valuable model for developing effective leadership skills, self-awareness and driving change. Scharmer and his team identify four levels of listening: (1) *downloading* – listening to confirm what you already know, (2) *factual listening* – listening with an open mind without prior judgements, (3) *empathic* – seeing the world through the other's eyes and connecting on an emotional level and (4) *generative listening* – connecting with an emerging future, the highest level of listening at which leaders can gain a broader strategic perspective and far greater awareness of situations.

(h)   Role modelling

COMPLEX SYSTEMS LITERACY 165

Whether they like it or not, systemic leaders become role models, and this is something they have to internally manage all the time. Their influence is larger than their humbleness would care to admit.

> Leaders strongly shape their followers' initial beliefs and contributions. In later rounds, followers put more weight on other followers' past behaviour than on the leader's current action. This creates a path dependency the leader can hardly correct.
>
> (Gächter & Renner, 2018)

(i) Integrative complexity

Integrative complexity is the capacity of holding multiple perspectives, and the ability to develop and hold opposing traits, values and ideas and then integrate them into larger ones (Suedfeld, 2010, as cited by Békés & Suedfeld, 2019).

> *In general, low integrative complexity is characterized by rigid, black-and-white thinking, intolerance for ambiguity and uncertainty, a desire for rapid closure, and not recognizing the validity of other viewpoints. Conversely, high integrative complexity is marked by flexible, broad thinking that recognizes multiple aspects and possible interpretations of an issue and sees connections and dynamic tensions between perspectives.*
>
> (Suedfeld, 1985, as cited by Békés & Suedfeld, 2019)

Eminent psychologist Mihaly Csikszentmihalyi describes what creative geniuses, from Nobel laureates to business tycoons to renowned artists, have in common:

> If I had to express in one word what makes their personalities different from others, it would be complexity. By this I mean that they show tendencies of thought and action that in most people are segregated. They contain contradictory extremes — instead of being an 'individual,' each of them is a 'multitude'.
>
> (Csikszentmihalyi, 1996)

(j) Dilemma wizarding

The capacity to work towards apparently contradicting goals – for instance, combining purpose and profit. Systemic leaders are passionate about the dual goals being served and are on the constant look out for new innovative solutions that can help achieve both goals simultaneously, (e.g. improving financial performance through energy conservation, scaling-up and remaining locally significant for the community).

Csikszentmihalyi observes that:

> these qualities are present in all of us, but usually we are trained to develop only one pole of the dialectic. We might grow up cultivating the aggressive, competitive side. Having a complex personality means being able to express the full range of traits that are potentially present in the human repertoire but usually atrophy because we think that one or the other pole is 'good,' whereas the other extreme is 'bad'.
>
> (Csikszentmihalyi, 1996)

(k)   Systems thinking. Discernment

Straight-line answers do not work for complex problems. Interdependence builds non-linearity and non-linearity requires a different kind of thinking. Systemic leaders understand their context and tailor their actions accordingly.

The new perspective on leadership and decision-making based on complexity science is illustrated by the Cynefin framework (Snowden & Boone, 2007) which helps executives sort issues into five contexts: *simple, complicated, complex, chaotic* and *disorder*.

> Simple contexts are characterized by stability and cause-and-effect relationships that are clear to everyone. Often, the right answer is self-evident. [...] Complicated contexts may contain multiple right answers, and though there is a clear relationship between cause and effect, not everyone can see it. [...] In a complex context, right answers can't be ferreted out at all; rather, instructive patterns emerge if the leader conducts experiments that can safely fail. [...] In a chaotic context, searching for right answers is pointless. The relationships between cause and effect are impossible to determine because they shift constantly and no manageable patterns exist. The fifth context, disorder, applies when it is unclear which of the other four contexts is predominant. The way out is to break the situation into its constituent

parts and assign each to one of the other four realms. Leaders can then make decisions and intervene in contextually appropriate ways.

(Snowden & Boone, 2007)

(l) Zooming in, zooming out

Systemic leaders are able to look at the whole, across space and time, as well as other multiple dimensions of human activity. They are able to look at past, present and future, with discernment and compassion. They are able to see both big pictures and granular details, synthesise and convey the perspectives they gain at different levels.

Looking behind the events, they identify patterns and discover the underlying structures that have generated the events. Most often, the answer is at a different level than the one where the problem arose. To influence events and outcomes, they act at the level of systemic structures (framework, infrastructure, processes). Connecting with the emergent future, systemic leaders can anticipate and embrace rapid change and futureproof opportunities presented by the new normal.

> a systemic leader does not focus on the superficial symptoms of the system, but rather looks at what is happening underneath its surface. He or she analyses the factual, social and timely patterns and processes out of which the system consists. This enables a systemic leader to lead his staff in an indirect way, rather than being directive and patronizing.
>
> (Pinnow, 2011)

(m) Humbleness. Navigating uncertainty. Facilitation

Unlike traditional leaders, systemic leaders are humble, acting as skilled facilitators who can successfully engage diverse stakeholders, with divergent priorities and perspectives. Their role is a catalysing one, enabling widespread action, without occupying the spotlight themselves (Dreier et al., 2019).

In recognition to uncertainty, and to the fact that the future is unknown and unpredictable, leaders of a green world need to be comfortable with not knowing. They allow themselves and their teams time for *exploration*

− exploration of certain questions or well-defined problems, pre-testing business decisions in a systemic exploration setup. The insights they gain help them distil the right solutions for their business or projects, at any given moment. Any professional or organisational dilemma they might face can be explored in a systemic setup that will bring unforeseen value and clarity to their decision-making process. Once they discover this way of working, navigating uncertainty becomes their super-skill.

(n)   Design thinking and multi-disciplinarity

Solving systemic problems calls for a multi-disciplinary approach to human-centred design. 'No problem can be solved from the same level of consciousness that created it' is a quote attributed to Albert Einstein. Design thinking is actually designing for system transformation − new business models, new processes, new products and services − based on empathic observation to understand the needs embedded in a specific problem, developing and testing innovative solutions through experience prototyping. Systemic leaders encourage creativity, experimentation and flexibility to make business products and services more human-centred and innovative.

(o)   Tapping into collective intelligence

Systemic leaders have the ability to orchestrate and harness collective intelligence. Collective intelligence is a concept that defines a group's general ability to perform a wide range of tasks and reflects how well groups problem-solve together (Woolley et al., 2010).

Sociometric data shows that the pattern of the flow of ideas is more important for team performance than all other factors − and in fact is just as important as all other factors taken together: individual intelligence, personality, abilities and skills (Pentland, 2014).

The most important predictor of group intelligence is *the equality of conversational turn taking* − a balanced number of interventions in a conversation. Groups in which only a few members dominated the conversation proved to be less collectively intelligent than those with a more balanced distribution of conversation interventions (Pentland, 2014). The second predictor of group intelligence is members' *social intelligence*, measured as the ability

COMPLEX SYSTEMS LITERACY   169

to read social signals. Women tend to do better at reading social signals, therefore groups with more women performed better (Pentland, 2014; Curşeu et al., 2015).

(p)   Orchestrating communication flows

Beyond company structure, beyond rules and processes, the only aspect that if you improve, it will increase performance, productivity and organisational health, is the flow of ideas (Pentland, 2014). Organisational health is the system's ability to respond to change by developing new constructive patterns in adaptation to the outside world. It is said that the best indicator of an organisation's health is 'feedback delay' – how much time passes since an event occurred and feedback is received, whether positive or negative. Interactions and flows of ideas are the blood of the system and how well they circulate is a sign of vitality and organisational fitness.

In his book *Social Physics*, Alex Pentland talks about the chemistry of high-performing teams. In the numerous research experiments he and his group at MIT have conducted, they observed the phenomenon of *synchronicity*, of *resonance*, which accompanies performance: 'the higher the performance of a group, the more people shared a common rhythm, including body movement, speech, and tone of voice. The best performing groups were in synch, literally moving in synchrony with each other' (Pentland, 2014).

Operating in the complex systems paradigm does not necessarily involve more complex reasoning or action. On the contrary, the identification of those simple rules or mechanisms that applied locally, at the micro level, lead to the desired effects globally, at macro level (community, organisational, global). Choosing the right goals around which groups can self-organise, creating contexts in which people interact, being aware of how they interact and evaluating larger-scale outcomes rather than individual outcomes, are some of the successful mechanisms in managing the complexity of our social structures.

Conclusion

Many countries around the globe are linking post-pandemic recovery to climate goals. When the world changes, what keeps us going needs to change as well.

Reassessing the targets by which we gauge success is key to the shift. Designing new business models that count in a healthy natural environment, communities that educate and nurture their members, accountable forms of governance and sustainability will see us moving forward into a green, new world. This change begins with the recognition that value is created collectively and that new skills are needed to manage and navigate the emerging complexity of human activities on Earth.

Complex systems literacy becomes a necessity if we are to shorten the learning curve and see good decisions being made in the new, highly interconnected paradigm. Systemic Leadership is a skill set required for the new, green business leaders of the planet, if we are to create a world in which we all want to be a part of.

References

Akerlof, G.A., Shiller, R., *Animal Spirits: How Human Psychology Drives the Economy, and Why It Matters for Global Capitalism*, Princeton University Press, 2009.

Akerlof, G.A., Kranton, R.E., *Identity Economics: How Our Identities Shape Our Work, Wages, and Well-Being*, Princeton University Press, 2010.

Ariely, D., *Predictably Irrational: The Hidden Forces That Shape Our Decisions*, HarperCollins, 2008.

Ariely, D., *The Honest Truth About Dishonesty: How We Lie to Everyone—Especially Ourselves*, HarperCollins, 2012.

Atkins, P., *Galileo's Finger. The Ten Great Ideas of Science*, Oxford University Press, 2003.

Axelrod, R., *The Evolution of Cooperation*, New York: Basic Books, 2006.

Barabási, A.L., *Linked: The New Science of Networks*, Perseus Books Group, May 2002.

Barabási, A.L., *The Formula: The Universal Laws of Success*, Little, Brown and Company, November 2018.

Békés, V., Suedfeld, P., 'Integrative Complexity', In Zeigler-Hill, V., Shackelford, T. (Eds.), *Encyclopedia of Personality and Individual Differences*, Cham: Springer, 2019.

Binmore, K., *Game Theory and the Social Contract*. MIT Press Series on Economic Learning and Social Evolution. MIT Press, 1990.

COMPLEX SYSTEMS LITERACY   171

Binmore, K., 'The Origins of Fair Play', *Papers on Economics and Evolution*, 2006–14, Max Planck Institute of Economics, Evolutionary Economics Group, 2006.

Bonabeau, E., 'The Perils of the Imitation Age', *Harv Bus Review*, 82: 45–54, 2004.

Boyd, R., Gintis, H., Bowles, S., 'Coordinated Punishment of Defectors Sustains Cooperation and Can Proliferate When Rare', *Science*, 328(5978): 617, 2010.

Camerer, C., *Behavioral Game Theory: Experiments in Strategic Interaction*, Princeton University Press, March 2003.

Cook, F.H., *Hua-Yen Buddhism: The Jewel Net of Indra*, Penn State Press, 1977.

Cremene, L., 'Managing Complexity in Communications Systems', In Dumitrescu, D., Lung, R.I., Cremene, L. (Eds.), *Coping with Complexity*, Cluj-Napoca, Romania: Casa Cărții de Știință, 2011.

Cremene, M., Dumitrescu, D., Cremene, L., 'A Strategic Interaction Model of Punishment Favoring Contagion of Honest Behavior', *PLoS ONE*, 9(1): e87471, 2014.

Cremene, L., Cremene, M., 'The Social Honesty Game – A Computational Analysis of the Impact of Conformity and Identity on Honest Behavior Contagion in Complex Social Systems', to be published in: *Chaos, Solitons and Fractals: The Interdisciplinary Journal of Nonlinear Science, and Nonequilibrium and Complex Phenomena*, Elsevier, 2021.

Csikszentmihalyi, M., *Creativity: Flow and the Psychology of Discovery and Invention*, Harpercollins, 1996, 2013.

Curşeu, P.L., Meşlec, N., Pluut, H., Lucas, G.J.M., 'Cognitive Synergy in Groups and Group-to-Individual Transfer of Decision-Making Competencies', *Frontiers in Psychology*, 6(1375), 2015.

Curşeu, P.L., Pluut, H., Boroş, S., Meşlec, N., 'The Magic of Collective Emotional Intelligence in Learning Groups: No Guys Needed for the Spell!', *British Journal of Psychology*, 106(2): 217–234, 2015.

Curry, O.S., 'Morality as Cooperation: A Problem-Centred Approach', In Shackelford, T., Hansen, R. (Eds.), *The Evolution of Morality. Evolutionary Psychology*. Cham: Springer, 2016.

Dawkins, R., *The Blind Watchmaker: Why the Evidence of Evolution Reveals a Universe without Design*, Oxford Publishing, 1986.

Dawes, R.M., 'Social dilemmas'. *Annual Review of Psychology* 31: 169–193, 1980.

Dreier, L., Nabarro, D., Nelson, J., *Systems Leadership for Sustainable Development: Strategies for Achieving Systemic Change*, Corporate Responsibility Initiative Harvard Kennedy School, 2019.

Edenhofer, O., Pichs-Madruga, R., et al., 'Summary for Policymakers', In IPCC (Ed.). *Climate Change 2014: Mitigation of Climate Change. Contribution of Working Group III to the Fifth Assessment Report of the Intergovernmental Panel on Climate Change*, Cambridge, UK and New York, NY, USA: Cambridge University Press, 2014.

Sir Eliot, Ch., *Hinduism and Buddhism: An Historical Sketch*, I-III, London: Edward Arnold & Co., 1921.

Espinosa, A., Walker, J., *A Complexity Approach to Sustainability: Theory and Application*, Imperial College Press (World Scientific Press), Jensen, H. (Ed.), Series on Complexity Science: 1, 2011.

Forrester, J.W., *Principle of Systems*, Productivity Press, 1968.

Fukuyama, F., *The Great Disruption: Human Nature and the Reconstitution of Social Order*, Free Press, 2000.

Gartner Insights, www.gartner.com/en/human-resources/insights/organizational-change-management, retrieved 2020.

Gächter, S., Renner, E., 'Leaders as Role Models and 'Belief Managers' in Social Dilemmas', *Journal of Economic Behavior & Organization*, 154: 321–334, August 2018.

Gigerenzer, G., Selten, R., *Bounded Rationality: The Adaptive Toolbox*, MIT Press, 2002.

Gladwell, M., *The Tipping Point: How Little Things can Make a Big Difference*, Boston, MA: Little Brown, 2000.

Goodburn, M., KPMG International, 'What is the Life Expectancy of Your Company?', www.weforum.org/agenda/2015/01/what-is-the-life-expectancy-of-your-company, 2015.

Haanaes, K., 'Reshaping Industries: Embracing the New Normal', *A New Mini Case Study Series, IMD*, August 2020, www.imd.org/research-knowledge/videos/reshaping-industries-embracing-new-normal, retrieved 2021.

Haidt, J., *The Righteous Mind: Why Good People are Divided by Politics and Religion*, Penguin Books Ltd., 2013.

Hammar, H., Jagers, S.C., Nordblom, K., 'Perceived Tax Evasion and the Importance of Trust', *The Journal of Socio-Economics*, 38(2): 238–245, 2009.

Hansen, J., Johnson, D., Lacis, A., Lebedeff, S., Lee, P., Rind, D., Russell, G., 'Climate Impact of Increasing Atmospheric Carbon Dioxide', *Science*, 231(4511): 957–966, 1981.

Harari, Y.N., *21 Lessons for the 21st Century*, Spiegel & Grau (US), Jonathan Cape (UK), 2018.

Hardin, G., 'The Tragedy of the Commons', *Science*, 162: 1243–1248, 1968.

Hofstadter, D.R., *Gödel, Escher, Bach*, Basic Books, p. 266, 1999.

Holland, J., *Hidden Order: How Adaptation Builds Complexity*, Cambridge, MA, Perseus, 1995.

Kahneman, D., Foreword. In E. Shafir (Ed.), *The Behavioural Foundations of Public Policy, VII–IX*, Princeton University Press, 2013.

Kollock, P., 'Social Dilemmas: The Anatomy of Cooperation', *Annual Review of Sociology*, 24, 183–214, 1998.

Ladyman, J., Lambert, J., Wiesner, K., 'What is a Complex System?', *European Journal for Philosophy of Science*, 3(1), 2013.

Lymbersky, Ch., 'Why Do Companies Fail', Survey, The Turnaround Management Society, 2014, https://www.prweb.com/releases/2014/02/prweb11550376.htm

Malhotra, R., *Indra's Net: Defending Hinduism's Philosophical Unity*, Noida: HarperCollins Publishers India, 2014.

Mazar, N., Amir, O., Ariely, D., 'The Dishonesty of Honest People: A Theory of Self-Concept Maintenance', *Journal of Marketing Research*, XLV, 633–644, 2008.

Mazzucato, M., *The Value of Everything: Making and Taking in the Global Economy*, Public Affairs, 2018.

Mazzucato, M., 'Capitalism after the COVID-19 Pandemic', *Foreign Affairs*, July 1, 2020, www.foreignaffairs.com/articles/united-states/2020-10-02/capitalism-after-covid-19-pandemic

Meadows, D., *Thinking in Systems*, Chelsea Green Publishing, 2008.

Meadows, D., 'Dancing with Systems', donellameadows.org/archives/dancing-with-systems/, retrieved 2020.

Merali, Y., Allen, P.M., 'Complexity and Systems Thinking', In Allen, P., Maguire, S., McKelvey, B., (Eds.), *The Sage Handbook of Complexity and Management*, SAGE Publications Ltd., 2011.

Millennium Ecosystem Assessment (MEA), *Ecosystems and Human Well-being: Desertification Synthesis*, Washington, DC: World Resources Institute, 2005, retrieved 2020. www.millenniumassessment.org/documents/document.355.aspx.pdf

Nicholls, N., 'Climate: Sawyer Predicted Rate of Warming in 1972', *Nature*, 448, 992, 2007.

Olson, M., *The Logic of Collective Action: Public Goods and the Theory of Groups*, Harvard University Press, 1965.

Ostrom, E., *Governing the Commons: The Evolution of Institutions for Collective Action*. Cambridge Univ. Press, 1990.

Ostrom, E., Burger, J., Field, Ch. B., Norgaard, R.B., Policansky, D., 'Revisiting the Commons: Local Lessons, Global Challenges', *Science*, 284(5412), 278–282, 1999.

Ostrom, E., 'Frontmatter', In *Governing the Commons: The Evolution of Institutions for Collective Action* (Canto Classics, pp. I-Iv). Cambridge: Cambridge University Press, 2015.

Pentland, A., *Social Physics: How Good Ideas Spread – The New Lessons from a New Science*, New York: Penguin Press, 2014.

Pinnow, D.F., *Leadership – What Really Matters. A Handbook on Systemic Leadership*, Berlin: Springer, 2011.

Philipsen, D., 'The Challenge of Reclaiming the Commons from Capitalism', https://aeon.co/essays/the-challenge-of-reclaiming-the-commons-from -capitalism, 2020.

Platt, J., 'Social traps', *American Psychologist* 28(8): 641–651, 1973.

Ragusa, A., Svelato, A., Santacroce, C., Catalano, P., Notarstefano, V., Carnevali, O., Papa, F., Ciro, M., Rongioletti, A., Baiocco, F., Draghi, S., D'Amore, E., Rinaldo, D., Matta, M., Giorgini, E., 'Plasticenta: First Evidence of Microplastics in Human Placenta', *Environment International*, 146, 106274, January 2021.

Rand, D.G., Dreber, A., Ellingsen, T., Fudenberg, D., Nowak, M.A., 'Positive Interactions Promote Public Cooperation', *Science* 325: 1272–1275, 2009.

Richmond, B., 'The "Thinking"', In *Systems Thinking: How Can We Make It Easier To Master?* thesystemsthinker.com/the-thinking-in-systems-thin king-how-can-we-make-it-easier-to-master/, retrieved 2020.

Roca, C.P., Helbing, D., 'Emergence of Social Cohesion in a Model Society of Greedy, Mobile Individuals', *Proceedings of the National Academy of Sciences*, 108: 11370—11374, 2011.

Sally, D., 'Conversation and Cooperation in Social Dilemmas. A Meta-Analysis of Experiments from 1958 to 1992', *Rationality and Society*, 7(1), 58–92, 1995.

Scharmer, O.C., *Theory U: Leading from the Future as it Emerges*, SoL, the Society for Organizational Learning, 2007.

Scharmer, O.C., Kaufer, K., *Leading from the Emerging Future: From Ego-System to Eco-System Economies*, Berrett-Koehler Publishers, 2013.

Schiffer, M., Butts, T.C., Grimm, K.K., *Taking Charge: The Electric Automobile in America*, Smithsonian, 1994.

COMPLEX SYSTEMS LITERACY

Senge, P.M., Scharmer, O.C., Jaworski, J., Flowers, B.S., *Presence: An Exploration of Profound Change in People, Organizations, and Society*, Currency, 2005.

Senge, P.M., *The Fifth Discipline: The Art & Practice of The Learning Organization*, Currency, 2006.

Snowden, D.J., Boone, M.E., 'A Leader's Framework for Decision Making', *Harvard Business Review*, 85(11): 68, November 2007.

Soltes, E., *Why They Do It: Inside the Mind of the White-Collar Criminal*, PublicAffairs, 2016.

Stam, J.J., Hoogenboom, B., *Systemic Leadership*, Systemic Books, 2018.

Suedfeld, P., 'APA Presidential Addresses: 'The Relation of Integrative Complexity to Historical, Professional, and Personal Factors'', *Journal of Personality and Social Psychology*, 49(6), 1643, 1985.

Taleb, N., *The Black Swan: The Impact of the Highly Improbable*, Random House (U.S.) Allen Lane (U.K.), 2007.

Tate, W., *Managing Leadership from a Systemic Perspective*, London Metropolitan University: Centre for Progressive Leadership, White Paper, 2013.

Taylor, A., Bronstone, A., *People, Place and Global Order: Foundations of a Networked Political Economy*, First Edition, New York: Routledge, 2019.

Thaler, R., Sunstein, C., *Nudge: Improving Decisions about Health, Wealth, and Happiness*, New Haven: Yale University Press, 2008.

Tversky, A., Kahneman, D., 'Judgment under Uncertainty: Heuristics and Biases', *Science*, 185, 1124–1131, 1974.

von Bertalanffy, L., *Perspectives on General Systems Theory*, Edgar Taschdijan (Ed.), New York: George Braziller, 1974.

Weber, J.M., Messick, D.M., Conflicting Interests in Social Life: Understanding Social Dilemma Dynamics, Chapter 18, In Gelfand, M.J. & Brett, J.M. (Eds.), *The Handbook of Negotiation and Culture*, Stanford University Press, 2004.

White, S.B., 'Testing an economic approach to resource dilemmas'. *Organizational Behavior & Human Decision Processes*, 58: 428–456, 1994.

Woolley, A.W., Chabris, Ch. F., Pentland, A., Hashmi, N., Malone, Th. W., 'Evidence for a Collective Intelligence Factor in the Performance of Human Groups', *Science*, 330(6004), 686–688, 2010.

World Bank. *World Development Report 2015: 'Mind, Society, and Behavior'*, Washington, DC: World Bank. License: Creative Commons Attribution CC BY 3.0 IGO, 2015.

Yergin, D., *The Quest: Energy, Security, and the Remaking of the Modern World*, Penguin Books, 2012.

8

GREEN SHOOTS

EMERGENT SYSTEMIC LEADERSHIP AND CRITICAL SYSTEMS PRACTICE

Amanda J. Gregory and Jonathan P. Atkins

Introduction

Climate change is recognised by many to be the defining adaptive challenge of our time. Despite such recognition, the failure of many world leaders to comprehend the scale, scope (bringing a complex mix of environmental, economic and social dimensions) and urgency of this challenge has created a space which has been taken up by a number of young people. As such, these young people are not just protesting about climate change or signalling their potential to lead in the future, they are leading the climate change agenda in the present. Whilst they may be known for seeking to bring about change on a global scale and/or for their activities within their own local communities, the emergence of these young leaders is not easily explained with reference to traditional theories of leadership. In part, this is because traditional theories do not adequately differentiate between leadership and authority and regard the terms as almost, if not fully, synonymous. The creation of definitional distinction between leadership and authority provides the basis for a more systemic understanding of

DOI: 10.4324/9781003190820-10

the complementary nature of leadership and authority which is better able to explain the emergence of young leaders focused on the more issue-based agendas associated with the wicked problems or adaptive challenges of complex systems. The proposal of a systems-based understanding of leadership provides the opportunity for the suggestion of how some approaches associated with this discipline can be put in the service of young leaders with the will to make a difference on a global and local scale.

Climate change, wicked problems and adaptive challenges

Climate change is one of the defining challenges of our time. On the basis of a substantial evidence base, it can be said that anthropogenic activities are changing the Earth's climate, leading to more extreme types of weather and causing events such as heatwaves, hurricanes and storm surges. While the impacts of such extreme events on people and nature are often experienced most profoundly at the local level, affecting the quality of life and of habitats, the cumulative effects are global. No longer can extreme weather be regarded as exceptional and isolated events; indeed, the regularity and speed with which such events occur, often invoking the declaration of a state of emergency, brings a sense of urgency that something needs to be done at the global level. But the complexity of climate change, involving the engagement of a mix of stakeholders with associated environmental, economic and social concerns, introduces many different perspectives and opposing views to the decision-making process about what needs to be done. Indeed, there is often a lack of clarity to the decision-making process, involving international negotiation, compromise and agreement, which leads some stakeholders to dispute that anything needs to be done at all. Given the competing pulls of environmental, economic and social concerns, it is difficult for established leaders to agree what to prioritise and a reluctance on the part of some to take the type of radical decision, fundamentally affecting peoples' lives and businesses operations, that some declare to be necessary to prevent a deepening of the climate crisis. Indeed, Heifetz, in conversation with Senge and Torbert (Senge et al., 2000), suggests that 'People would prefer to avoid wrestling with ecological values because they involve trade-offs in terms of prosperity and ways of life' (p. 61). Such decisions are also difficult because adaptive change, particularly ecological change, implies that losses and gains may not be equitably distributed, for example, across the globe or between generations. Heifetz (2011, p. 308) outlines three kinds of losses:

- Jobs, money and status;
- Loyalty to families and heritage by changing ways of life to adapt to new realities;
- Competency in how to do things and what to do in an environment characterised by new norms of behaviour and values.

In short, the losses associated with decisions about how to tackle climate change make it a very wicked problem.

The notion of a 'wicked problem' can be traced back to the work of Churchman (1967), who refers to the earlier use of the term by Rittel (later discussed in Rittel and Webber, 1973). Churchman recalls that Rittel used the term 'wicked problem' to refer

> to that class of social system problems which are ill-formulated, where the information is confusing, where there are many clients and decision makers with conflicting values, and where the ramifications in the whole system are thoroughly confusing. The adjective "wicked" is supposed to describe the mischievous and even evil quality of these problems, where proposed "solutions" often turn out to be worse than the symptoms.
>
> (p. B-141)

In contrast, with a tame problem the mission is clear, as is whether or not the problem has been solved (Rittel and Webber, 1973). Churchman (1967) went on to discuss the Operations Research profession's role in tackling such problems and how 'whoever attempts to tame a part of a wicked problem, but not the whole, is morally wrong' (p. B-142). Strong words, indeed, but highly relevant to the wicked problem of climate change and leadership.

Heifetz (1994) makes a similar distinction to the tame and wicked problem, in distinguishing between technical and adaptive challenges. Like tame problems, technical challenges are relatively straightforward problems that we already know how to solve. In contrast, adaptive challenges cannot be resolved through the use of current knowledge and potential options for their resolution may be contentious in bringing about changes in dominant values and established behaviours; hence adaptive challenges are akin to wicked problems.

The leadership/authority distinction

In contrast to the wicked problem of adaptive challenge is the relatively tame problem of definitional clarity but, according to Senge, 'There are few better examples of the debilitating or dysfunctional consequences of ambiguity than in the area of leadership.' (Senge et al., 2000, p. 57). On the basis of this insight, Heifetz takes up the challenge of bringing definitional clarity by making the distinction between leadership and the related concept of authority. Leadership is about deciding what changes need to be made in response to a problem or issue in recognition that this will cause wins for some and losses for others (Senge et al., 2000, p. 63). In contrast, authority involves holding a formal position since 'Authority relationships are essentially a contract for services in which somebody entrusts power to somebody else in exchange for service' (Heifetz, 2011, p. 306). Very often that service is focused on change management – the effective and efficient implementation of decisions. Defined in this way, leadership and authority can be regarded as complementary terms and practices but are they both necessary for change? According to Heifetz (2011) it depends:

> This system of looking to authority works so long as the ecosystem remains stable or changes very slowly. In a stable ecosystem you don't really need leadership at all. All you need are people in authority providing authoritative expertise to deal with straightforward problems: where's the food; how do we protect ourselves; how do we maintain order? We need leadership when the ecosystem changes. Unless we learn a new strategy quickly enough to thrive in our changed environment, we could be looking at extinction.
>
> (Heifetz, 2011, p. 306)

However, depicting change in such a slow–fast way, informed by the organic metaphor, rather underplays consideration of the nature of change in complex systems and important related concepts such as weak signals (advanced signs of future trends often unstructured and fragmented bits of information), inflexion points (when trends shift sharply) and megatrends (large-scale changes that are slow to form but have wide-scale influence over future decades). In order to make explicit what these concepts might imply for leadership and authority, it is perhaps relevant to refer to the work of Baik (2003), who suggests that 'an issue leader is required to exhibit three distinctive behaviors: issue-creating, audience-involving, and issue-implementing.' (p. 37). Taking each of these behaviours in turn:

- Issue-creating may be taken to refer to making sense of weak signals, conceptualising and presenting signals as advanced warnings of emergent issues and future trends, and understanding how power relations may affect whose voice is heard and whose is not;
- Audience-involving implies raising awareness of an emergent issue and to seizing the moment to convince others to protest.

In contrast, issue-implementing perhaps more relates to authority given that it involves mobilizing others, often in the face of opposition, to reconfigure systems and established patterns of organisation. We will return to these behaviours later in this chapter.

Climate change and young leaders

Greta Thunberg, the Swedish environmental activist, came to prominence in 2018 when, at the age of 15, she began her '*Skolstrejk för klimatet*' (School strike for climate) protest outside the Swedish parliament calling for stronger action on climate change. Other students emulated her actions in their own communities and, together, they organised a school climate strike movement under the name '*Fridays for Future*'. After Thunberg addressed the 2018 United Nations Climate Change Conference, student strikes took place every week somewhere in the world and by 2019 there were multiple co-ordinated multi-city protests involving millions of students. Thunberg's approach has attracted both ridicule (for example, alleged Twitter bullying by ex US President Donald Trump) and praise. As O'Keeffe (2020) reflects, 'In perhaps her most impressive fearless appearance to date, she confronted world leaders at a UN climate summit in New York September 2019, thundering "*How dare you?*" in accusation of their failure to take action'. Thunberg's numerous awards are testimony to her influence; for example, being the youngest *Time* 'Person of the Year 2019', inclusion in the *Forbes* list of 'The World's 100 Most Powerful Women (2019)', and two consecutive nominations for the Nobel Peace Prize (2019 and 2020).

Recognition of Thunberg's efforts has not only taken the form of awards, though, as she has inspired other young people to take up a leadership role when it comes to environmental issues. Licypriya Kangujam, born in 2011, has campaigned for years for climate action, urging the Indian government to pass new laws to curb the country's high pollution levels and to make climate change literacy mandatory in schools. Helena Gualinga, born in 2002, has become a spokesperson for Ecuador's indigenous Kichwa Sarayaku community. She exposes how indigenous communities in the Amazon have experienced climate change, promoting an empowering message among the youth in local Ecuadorian schools and reaching out to the international community. To take one further example, in this case from an earlier period, Severn Cullis-Suzuki, born in 1979, founded the Environmental Children's Organization (ECO) at the age of nine, a group of children dedicated to learning and teaching other young people about environmental issues. Cullis-Suzuki raised money with other ECO members to attend the 1992 Earth Summit in Rio de Janeiro, presenting a youth perspective on environmental issues including an address to the Summit. Cullis-Suzuki continues to be a culture and environmental activist and writer, and an Earth Charter International Council Member.

It is not only as individuals that young leaders are tackling climate change issues; they are realising their impact can be far greater when they act together and make use of new technologies and ways of thinking to leverage the resources they have at their disposal to maximum impact. 'We decided we had to do something because we are in a climate emergency... We are not the leaders of the future. We are the leaders of today'. These are the words of Dom Jaramillo, in an interview with the BBC (2020). Jaramillo was a co-organiser of the youth-led Mock COP, organised when the international climate talks that were due to be held in Glasgow were delayed a year because of the coronavirus pandemic. In organising the event both leadership and authority were demonstrated providing an illustration of young people doing far more than merely protesting about critical issues. They walked the talk in delivering a Mock COP that:

- Was not based anywhere physical, with workshops and talks hosted virtually across multiple time zones, reducing carbon emissions by

1,500 times that of previous COP events which involved delegates flying in from around the world;

- Addressed complaints about a lack of diversity in the climate movement and fears that countries most affected by climate change were not being heard. They gave countries from the Global South more young delegates and speaking time than given to richer countries.

More than 350 young environmental activists from 150 countries participated in discussions and heard from a range of climate experts. The event culminated in the production of a final statement of demands. Working with environmental law charity ClientEarth, it has been suggested that the final statement of demands could be developed into a legal treaty for countries to consider adopting into law.

Pushing the boundaries of engagement out in the Mock COP in an effort to explicitly address the issue of diversity was an important move to support understanding of how different decisions involve changes that will cause wins for some and losses for others. Such moves are necessary but not sufficient as they need to be supported by research of a critical orientation. As Heifetz (Senge et al., 2000) states, 'we need to do research to find a more sophisticated framework for the normative inquiry that tackles radical questions about whether our diagnosis is capturing reality or is denying critical parts of reality.' (p. 62). He elaborates that this involves inquiry at the level of 'higher abstractions' of assumptions, values and action logic, as well as grappling with the realities of people's everyday lives and the value trade-offs implied by adaptive change. Enter Critical Systems Practice as a framework and theory to support such inquiry.

Putting Critical Systems Practice in the service of young leaders

A ten-year Carnegie Foundation study examined 120 youth-based organisations located across the United States. The research found a profound disconnect between youth leadership educational provision and the experiences and needs of young leaders (Klau, 2003). In reflecting on these findings, Klau refers to Roach et al.'s (1999) suggestion that many programmes 'often depend, at best, on implicit unexamined ideas about how young people develop leadership traits and what being a leader entails.' (Klau, 2003, p. 60).

The traditional approach often treats leadership as if it were a property of the individual and this is in stark contrast with what has become known as emergent leadership. The latter type of leadership is informed by systems theory and, whilst some theorists choose to situate it within the organisational context (see, for example, Tate, 2009), we attempt to focus on systemic cross-cutting issues that go beyond organisational boundaries. A systemic perspective of leadership encourages understanding of the contextual relationships that give rise to a leader as an emergent force and catalyst for action. In recent years, there has been a significant rise in the number of prominent young leaders who have not undergone traditional leadership training and yet their words and actions are effectively shaping the response to environmental crisis at international, national and local levels. Being free from years of training in the reductionist method, they appear to intuitively grasp systemic issues. Mindful of Klau's comments on the disconnect between educational provision and the experiences and needs of young leaders, we tentatively suggest that perhaps an understanding of systems methodologies and how they can be used in a flexible way might enhance their practice of leadership behaviours, including 'issue-creating, audience-involving, and issue-implementing.' (Baik, 2003), necessary to address change in complex systems.

Critical Systems Practice (CSP) (Jackson, 2000, 2003, 2019) is a development of Critical Systems Thinking (CST) which serves to bring to light the underlying theoretical assumptions, with associated strengths and weaknesses, of the different systems methodologies. The critical orientation of CST is important in uncovering 'what aspects of complexity they are able to address and which they hide.' (Jackson, 2019, p. 142). This theoretical orientation is complemented with CSP which 'addresses what to do with the outputs of critical systems theory in order to bring about "improvement" broadly defined. It concludes that it is best to use the variety of systems approaches in combination...' (p. 142). Here, for the purposes of illustrating the relevance of CSP to the theme of our discussion, we will tentatively suggest how and for what purpose young leaders might use different systems approaches (unfortunately, it is beyond the scope of this chapter to go into the detail of the different approaches discussed):

Issue-creating: making sense of weak signals and power relations

One of Churchman's (1968, 1971) greatest contributions to systems thinking was establishing the idea that the drawing of system boundaries is crucial for determining how improvement is to be defined and what action should be taken. He also saw it as the system designer's responsibility to redraw boundaries to 'sweep in' stakeholder views to ensure that the system comes to serve the interests of more than just the powerful. Midgley (2000) reflects on this in suggesting that you have to deal with power up-front, because if you do not then its use may be hidden by the powerful in manipulating the definition of system boundaries to ensure that their interests are best served. Ulrich (1983), however, did not believe that this important task should just be left to the system designer but rather the question of determining where to draw the system's boundaries should be established through a dialogue between those involved and those affected by a system's design (referred to as the process of boundary critique). Another notion that Ulrich draws from Churchman is the need for systems design to take on the whole system because localised action based on partial understanding can lead to unexpected consequences for the wider system. Of course, to attempt to understand the whole system is an impossible task. What is important, therefore, is to accept an inevitable lack of comprehensiveness in our designs and planning but to make this transparent so that we can reflect critically on their limitations and the likely implications of boundary decisions.

Audience-involving: awareness raising and seizing the moment

'Soft systems methodology (SSM) is an approach for tackling problematical, messy situations of all kinds.' (Checkland and Poulter, 2006, p. 191). It supports users in learning about a problematic situation in a participatory and creative way and in taking action to improve it (Checkland, 1981). Learning emerges through the exploration of the situation structured around the use of a set of tools to inform and structure discussion about a situation and how it might be improved. The tools, such as rich picturing, are creative, engaging and rigorous and support participants in articulating their views of the situation, sharing their views, debating systemically desirable

GREEN SHOOTS   185

and culturally feasible changes and, finally, taking action to improve the situation.

According to Eden (1992), who has done groundbreaking work in this field, how views are elicited and shared is significant because:

> if we take seriously Karl Weick's aphorism that we do not know what we think until we hear what we say, then the process of articulation is a significant influence on present and future cognition. If articulation and thinking interact, then an elicitation of cognition that depends upon articulation is always out of step with cognition before, during, and after the elicitation process. Indeed it is this process of reflective mapping that often gives mapping its utility (Eden et al., 1979). The elicitation process is designed to be a cathartic experience which provides 'added value' because it changes thinking...
>
> (Eden, 1992, p. 261)

Convincing and engaging others: facing opposition and planning for action

Heifetz and Linsky (2002) provide a survival guide for leaders in recognition of the inevitable attempts to place hazards in the way of anyone adopting a leadership role and to thwart their efforts to bring about change. We suggest the bolstering of this survival guide with methodological support in the form of Strategic Assumption Surfacing and Testing (SAST) (Mason and Mitroff, 1981). This methodology serves to systematically reveal the assumptions on which any plans for change are based on and to present them with the opposing argument, the deadliest enemy. SAST is based on four principles:

- Adversarial – the best way to test an assumption is to oppose it;
- Participative – the knowledge and resources necessary to create and implement a solution to a complex problem is distributed among a group of individuals;
- Integrative – emerging out of the adversarial and participative processes is a unified plan at a higher level of understanding;
- Managerial mind supporting – exposure to underlying assumptions deepens the manager's insight into an issue or situation.

Given the focus of this chapter, it is relevant to suggest that SAST has wider applicability than the organisational domain, hence we suggest that it might usefully be considered to be leadership mind supporting.

Good and bad leaders and the commitments of Critical Systems Practice

Having placed CSP and associated systems methodologies at the service of young leaders, it is worth finally reflecting on the normative aspects of good and bad leadership. In doing so, we highlight the ethical commitments that those who use the power of CSP are expected to adhere to.

Whether a leader is regarded as good or bad is essentially a value call. The potential for leadership to have a 'dark side' was discussed by Bass and Steidlmeier (1999). Four components of leadership can be used to exploit or deceive followers:

- Idealised influence: the leader is egotistical and uses their articulation of a vision to manipulate followers;
- Inspirational motivation: the leader encourages dependence and so fails to support the empowerment of followers;
- Intellectual stimulation: the leader discourages independent thought and creativity;
- Individualised consideration: the leader is not concerned with the well-being of followers, regarding them to be a means to an end.

The need for good leaders to be ethical is recognised by Burns (1978), who defines the process of transformational leadership as raising both leaders and followers to 'higher levels of motivation and morality.' (p. 20). In the previous section, we have seen how CSP can be put in the service of such endeavour but merely having an understanding of the systems methodologies is necessary but not sufficient for good systems practice which depends on a deep appreciation of the underpinning philosophy. Jackson (2000) suggests three important commitments:

- *Critical awareness* relates to the critique of the different systems methodologies and contextual sensitivity;

- Improvement refers to the achievement of 'something beneficial' reflecting a circumspect aspiration in the light of the postmodernist challenge to the notion of universal liberation;
- Pluralism recognises the requirement to work with multiple paradigms, to use methods disconnected from the paradigm of their origin but with an understanding of the paradigm that they are being put in the service of, and that there are many ways of being pluralistic.

To become systems thinkers requires young leaders to not only understand the above commitments but also to be able to practise them when addressing wicked issues within their own contexts. Good leaders should find these commitments reassuring, bad leaders may walk away as CSP is not for them.

Concluding reflections

The creation of definitional distinction between leadership and authority provides the basis for a more systemic understanding of the complementary nature of leadership and authority. On the basis of this understanding, we are better able to explain the emergence of young leaders focused on the more issue-based agendas associated with the wicked problems or adaptive challenges, such as climate change, of complex systems. Tentatively, we suggest how CSP might be used in support of young leaders with the will to do good and make a difference on a global and local scale.

References

Baik, K. (2003). Issue leadership theory and its implications in global settings, *Advances in Global Leadership*, 3: 37–62.

Bass, B.M., and Steidlmeier, P. (1999). Ethics, character, and authentic transformational leadership behaviour, *The Leadership Quarterly*, 10(2): 181–217.

Burns, J.M. (1978). *Leadership*. Harper & Row, New York.

BBC (2020). COP26: Frustrated by delay, young activists stage virtual Mock COP, 19th November, available at: https://www.bbc.co.uk/news/science-environment-54990281.

Checkland, P.B. (1981). *Systems Thinking, Systems Practice*. Wiley, Chichester, UK.

Checkland, P., and Poulter, J. (2006). *Learning for Action: A Short Definitive Account of Soft Systems Methodology and its Use, for Practitioners, Teachers and Students*. John Wiley and Sons, Chichester, UK.

Churchman, C.W. (1967). Wicked problems, *Management Science*, 14(4): B141–B142.

Churchman, C.W. (1968). *The Systems Approach* (Reprinted 1979). Delta Books, New York.

Churchman, C.W. (1971). *The Design of Inquiring Systems*. Basic Books, New York.

Eden, C., Jones, S. and Sims, D. (1979). *Thinking in Organizations*. London: Macmillan

Eden, C. (1992). On the nature of cognitive maps, *Journal of Management Studies*, 29(3): 261–265.

Heifetz, R.A. (1994). *Leadership Without Easy Answers*, Harvard University Press, Cambridge, Mass.

Heifetz, R., and Linsky, M. (2002). A survival guide for leaders, *Harvard Business Review*, June.

Heifetz, R. (2011). Debate: Leadership and authority, *Public Money & Management*, 31(5): 305–308.

Jackson, M.C. (2000). *Systems Approaches to Management*. Kluwer/Plenum, London, UK.

Jackson, M.C. (2003). *Systems Thinking: Creative Holism for Managers*. Wiley, Chichester, UK.

Jackson, M.C. (2019). *Critical Systems Thinking and the Management of Complexity: Responsible Leadership for a Complex World*. Wiley, Chichester, UK.

Klau, M. (2003). Exploring youth leadership in theory and practice, in: W.H. Mobley and P.W. Dorfman (eds.), *Advances in Global Leadership*, Volume 3, 37–62. Emerald Group Publishing Limited, Bingley, UK.

Mason, R.O., and Mitroff, I.I. (1981). *Challenging Strategic Planning Assumptions*. John Wiley and Sons, Chichester, UK.

Midgley, G. (2000). *Systemic Intervention: Philosophy, Methodology, and Practice*. Kluwer Academic/Plenum Publishers, London, UK.

O'Keeffe, N. (2020). *Iconic Future Shaper – Greta Thunberg*, Prosper Leadership Academy, available at: https://prosperleadershipacademy.com/2020/02/28/iconic-future-shaper-greta-thunberg/.

Rittel, H.W.J., and Webber, M. M. (1973). Dilemmas in a general theory of planning, *Policy Sciences*, 4: 155–169.

Roach, A.A., Wyman, L.T., Brookes, H., Chavez, C., Heath, S.B., Valdes, G. (1999). Leadership giftedness: Models revisited. *Gifted Child Quarterly*, 43(1): 13–24.

Senge, P.M., Heifetz, R.A., and Torbert, B. (2000). A conversation on leadership, *Reflections*, 2(1): 57–68.

Tate, W. (2009). From systemic failure to systemic leadership, available at: https://www.triarchypress.net/uploads/1/4/0/0/14002490/from -systemic-failure-to-systemic-leadership.pdf.

Ulrich, W. (1983). *Critical Heuristics of Social Planning*. John Wiley and Sons, Chichester, UK.

9

COMPLEXITY AND NETWORKS

Yasmin Merali

Introduction

Climate change, the Covid-19 pandemic and the financial crash of 2018 all highlight the importance of recognising the interconnected, networked nature of the landscape that we operate in. The *systemic* impact of these phenomena accentuates the urgency of attending to the social, economic, geopolitical and physical dimensions of sustainable development at all scales across national and geographic boundaries.

The notion of ecosystems is a popular one in contemporary management discourse, used with varying degrees of rigour, but generally acknowledging the existence of a web of a diverse collection of interdependent entities, occupying distinctive niches on the competitive landscape. It is heavily used as a metaphor across the board, but most accounts do not engage fully with the systemic elegance of the multidimensional, multi-layered organisational complexity embodied in the ecosystems of the natural world.

In taking the ecosystem perspective it is not uncommon for managers to limit themselves to thinking about their immediate competitive landscape,

DOI: 10.4324/9781003190820-11

COMPLEXITY AND NETWORKS   191

trusting in the market mechanism to maintain the equilibrium between supply and demand. When considerations of corporate social responsibility (CSR) are directed towards broadening the frame to admit social and environmental considerations, mental models are highly modularised, compartmentalising the social, economic and environmental 'systems' as distinct, bounded domains for impact or intervention.

The Covid-19 pandemic has demonstrated the inadequacy of this framing for apprehending the complex web of interdependences between the economic, social, political, technological and biological dimensions of the world we live in. Media coverage of the evolving crisis demonstrated the failure of nation states to effectively address the evolving dynamics of the interactions between the mutating virus, social practices and behaviours of the populations it spread through, the political dimensions of state-imposed governance measures to contain the spread, and the economic impact of implementing the measures. This underlines the importance of attending to the intersectionality of the social, economic and environmental 'systems' and adopting a multidimensional, holistic perspective.

We *are* part of the bio-physical ecosystem: the natural world is not a separate ecosystem 'out there'. Central to the viability of natural (bio-physical) ecosystems is the diversity of species, the emergence of niches, and the dynamics of the *system-wide* network interactions and feedback loops *over time* to maintain systemic stability efficiently and effectively. As one of the species in that web, we cannot control the evolution of the entire system, but we can, and have, used our superior intelligence and technological capabilities to create perturbations that destabilise the system, and set in motion a complex web of interactions that (literally) change the face of the planet Earth irreversibly.

Anthropogenic factors affecting the ecosystem and climate change (e.g. via species extinction, habitat loss, pollution, carbon emissions) have been clearly identified, and their collective systemic impact is manifested through the cascading networks of decline resulting in what is becoming recognised as the Sixth Catastrophic Extinction. The planet's CO_2 record shows that over the million years up to the 1950s, from the ice age through the interglacial period, the atmospheric CO_2 levels never varied by more 130 ppm, and always stayed below 300 ppm. By comparison, in the short period between 1958 and 2016 the levels shot up to 400.97 ppm and the global temperature rose by 0.8°C, largely due to accelerated growth of human activity and patterns of consumption (Lüthi et al 2008). This vastly accelerated rate of change is accompanied by an unprecedented rate of species loss. Over 400 vertebrate species became extinct in the last century, something that would have taken up to 10,000 years in the normal course of evolution, and 515 are on the brink of extinction according to a 2019 study of 29,400 species of vertebrates. It is likely that the species on the brink will become extinct soon, and because of the complex networked nature of the ecosystem, their disappearance will move other species towards annihilation – 'extinction breeds extinctions' (Ceballosa, Ehrlich and Raven, 2020).

The imperative for taking collective action today to address the progress of climate change is clear when we look at the evidence, but the will to act lacks the requisite energy and urgency. A major impediment to the mobilisation of individuals, organisations, institutions and political will is the failure of the actors to recognise the speed with which non-linear, cascading network effects (of anthropogenic factors and natural cyclical planetary temperature fluctuations) are leading to the mass extinction of species and the degradation of conditions for human life on Earth. An antidote to this lackadaisical stance would be to get people to understand their role in climate change directly and indirectly through the networked ecosystem that they are part of. This (a) requires the ability to conceptualise how network interactions work in the complex ecosystem, and (b) a recalibration of our *Weltanschauung* to fully appreciate our role and impact on the networked world that we are part of, and exercise our agency to realise a better future.

The next sections of the paper introduce some fundamental network concepts, before moving on to discuss the challenge of inculcating cognitive frames and organising principles for enabling the transition to a viable future for humankind on Earth.

Network effects

The conceptualisation of the ecosystem as a complex network of interactions between species is not new. As Bascompte (2009) points out, we see it in Darwin's contemplation of the tangled bank:

> It is interesting to contemplate a tangled bank, clothed with many plants of many kinds, with birds singing on the bushes, with various insects flitting about, and with worms crawling through the damp

earth, and to reflect that these elaborately constructed forms, so different from each other, and dependent upon each other in so complex a manner, have all been produced by laws acting around us.

Charles Darwin, On the Origin of Species by Means of Natural Selection

The network approach today is a transdisciplinary one, bringing together thinkers and researchers from the pure and applied sciences with formal modelling and simulation approaches drawing on advances in the mathematical and physical sciences, and the observations of network organisation in ecological, biological and social systems. This collaborative endeavour reveals a number of generalisable insights about the organisation of networks and the associated systemic behaviours, which have been used to analyse the observed dynamics and evolution of ecosystems (Bascompti, 2009).

Structure and stability: lessons from ecology

In ecosystems large networks are built from combinations of smaller networks embodying a small number of motifs (recurring patterns of interrelations). How motifs combine into larger networks can influence the stability of the larger network (May, 1972).

Biodiversity is an essential feature of healthy ecosystems, with different species able to flourish in particular niches. An ecological niche describes the position of a species within an ecosystem, defining both the range of conditions necessary for persistence of the species and its ecological role in the ecosystem (Polechova and Storch, 2019). Changes in the biotic and abiotic environment affect the species (e.g. observed as adaptations when the species coevolves with its environment) and concurrently the species has an effect on its environment. These impacts may be directly observable locally or may manifest indirectly through network interactions, generating observable effects at a distant time or place.

Interactions with other species may be collaborative or competitive in nature. The stability of the ecosystem rests on a complex web of feedback loops and interactions of different types. Perhaps the most familiar textbook example is the food web, where we consistently see the recurring motif of the tri-trophic food chains (in which a predator eats a consumer who in turn eats a resource), as well as a pattern of ominivory (in which the predator eats both the consumer and the resource) (Bascompti, 2009). The strength of predator–prey interactions and the microdiversity within populations are important in the fine tuning of the feedback loops for maintaining stability of the system and viability of the populations.

Also observable are mutually beneficial relationships (e.g. between plants and pollinators, or seed dispersers) which play a major role in generating biodiversity, and give rise to communities organised around a network of mutual dependencies (Thompson 2005) with groups of species coevolving in time and space.

Network analysis of the ecosystem shows the importance of the differentiated network structure (i.e. not every species is connected with the same number of other species, and the number and nature of connections they have is not uniform). Theoretical models (May 1972) and observations in the field (Margalef, 1968) suggest that, within a web, species which interact with many others do so weakly, and, conversely, those which interact strongly do so with but a few species. May (1972) also showed that multispecies communities will do better if the interactions tend to be arranged in 'blocks', a feature observed in natural ecosystems.

The overall picture, then, is that in the organisation of ecosystems we essentially have an arrangement that can be described as a network of networks of different sizes, composition and connectivity. The heterogeneity and differentiated structure embodied in the whole network underpin the maintenance of stability, co-evolution and generative potential over time.

Humans in the mix

The *accelerating pace* of our technological advances, population expansion and invasion of habitats has outstripped the capacity of the ecosystem network to accommodate the anthropogenic impact gracefully.

Perhaps the greatest challenge of our time is our collective failure to see ourselves as just another species in the ecosystem, a part of the web of life. Pathogens and natural disasters do not respect man-made boundaries – the changing weather patterns will affect us all. On the other hand, our economic and political instruments have moved *Homo sapiens* onto a fitness landscape where the criteria for Darwinian selection rest on economic and financial viability, not on biological fitness. Consequently, we

COMPLEXITY AND NETWORKS   195

find that if we cannot slow down (or even reverse) the impact of anthropogenic stressors and climate change, the hardest hit will be the poorest countries, with large parts of the population perishing from things like treatable diseases, starvation and lack of access to water unless they are able to migrate to more habitable lands (which in turn will incur the environmental cost of supporting an increased population). This will bring to the table of the richer countries issues of ideology and ethics, which are arguably things that we should be addressing *now* if we are serious about halting the cascading descent into a Hobbesian state of nature, *bellum omnium contra omnes* (Hobbes, 1651) which is discernible in the Covid vaccine wars (*The Economist*, 2021a, 2021b).

Resetting cognitive constructs

It has been said that the slow-burning nature of climate change makes it difficult to mobilise individuals and governments to respond with the urgency that is needed if we are to avoid catastrophic extinction. To overcome this inertia, a primary leadership challenge is that of changing perceptions and dispositions to act in concert, and to create conditions where ecologically responsible behaviour permeates business and society. The *Cognitive Congruence Framework* (Merali, 2000, 2001) (Figure 9.1) is a construct for articulating the knowledge structures (including assumptions and beliefs) and relationships that underpin the interactions of people in social organisations (see Merali, 2000, 2001, for a full description). Apprehending the integral role that we play as active agents constituting a significant force in our evolving ecosystem entails developing a coherent action-perception cycle through every part of the *Cognitive Congruence Framework*.

An individual's schema is unique and is developed through the individual's experience and interactions with his social environment. Similarly, the collective schema underpins the collective consciousness and is established through the collective being and sensemaking process, which are socially situated. The *Cognitive Congruence Framework* is founded on the importance of the social dimension of knowledge creation and leveraging, and on the notion of the collective consciousness (Durkheim, 1933). Thus, an individual is an effective part of the collective only to the extent to which there is a congruence between the individual and collective schemata. Relationship scripts and enactment (described below) provide the mechanisms for developing

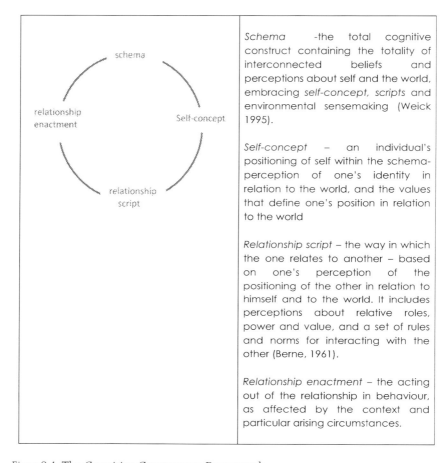

Figure 9.1 The Cognitive Congruence Framework.

and maintaining a degree of congruence between the individual and collective schemata.

The next sections outline some of the changes that are necessary for the adaptation of our society to exist in harmony with the rest of our ecosystem, entailing: the extension of our schemas to articulate the social, economic and environmental 'systems' into a multidimensional whole; transforming our self-concept from *homo economicus* to *homo reciprocans*; and the requisite changes in our relationship scripts and enactment in a global context where our destinies are intertwined with the viability of our planet.

COMPLEXITY AND NETWORKS   197

Rethinking capitalism

The weaponisation of information has occupied a great deal of media attention over recent years. Expositions of 'fake news', conspiracy theories and misinformation campaigns on social media deploying malicious bots are commonplace, demonstrating the power of networks for enhancing the speed and extent of communication. Climate change denial has emerged as a persistent theme on this landscape, often woven into a web of conspiracy theories and rationalisations about the necessity of fossil-based fuels for the survival of local or national economies.

Movements like Extinction Rebellion and GreenPeace have gone some way towards countering this effect with positive messaging about the need to take climate change seriously. In the richer countries of the West, there is significant pressure on governments to invest in green infrastructure development and legislation for emissions control. When it comes down to individual behaviours, there have been exhortations for lifestyle changes, such as switching to fair trade goods, vegan diets and electric cars. All these are important advances, but to have an impact on the global ecosystem, these movements need to be grounded in more fundamental *systemic* changes. In the rich countries, national strategies for meeting commitments to the COP21 Paris Agreement (13 December 2015) need to be coupled with policies for foreign aid and trade investments to advance clean energy production and biodiversity in the countries that fall into the United Nations categories of Least Developed Countries (LDCs) and Heavily Indebted Poor Countries (HIPSs) (United Nations, 2020).

Whilst government commitment, leadership and action are essential, timely, impactful change can only come through harnessing the energy of citizens, and rethinking our engagement with the institutions of capitalism, and, as Mark Carney puts it, looking at the relationship between how markets value things versus the broader values of society:

> Markets have come to the narrow view that only things that can be given a price have value. We can price Amazon, the company – its current market value is almost \$1.7 trillion – but value is only ascribed to the Amazon, the region, when the ecosystem is destroyed for the purposes of agriculture or harvesting timber. Meanwhile, the market view of value applies not only to material goods, but increasingly to the whole of life, from the allocation of healthcare to education

> and environmental protection. The seeds of the crises we have experienced lie here ... My point is that, if we're conscious about it, we can build an architecture where you have a kind of artisanal globalisation that spreads activity in a way that not only creates jobs, but promotes good jobs and reduces inequalities, both between regions and between individuals.
>
> Mark Carney, cited New Scientist Newsletters interview (Webb, 2021)

There are a number of other observations that highlight the unsatisfactory relationship between the current dominant models of 'business ecosystems' propelled by the mindset that Carney is so critical of.

Large corporations and power dynamics: the domination of the economy by large corporations has received a great deal of attention from environmentalists, economists and in critiques of neoliberalism (e.g. Galbraith, 2004; Klein, 2015). The trickle-down model for wealth distribution has been shown not to work (Stiglitz, 2016), and there is a substantial literature on the negative environmental and social impact that individual multinational corporations have at home, and, more acutely, on developing countries. Developing countries often feel that the scope for their independent policy-making is constrained as a result of conditionalities imposed by the World Bank and the IMF. Moreover, aid-dependent countries are vulnerable to political pressure because of the potential threat of reduced monetary assistance necessary for survival. Multinational Corporations (MNCs) often leverage their own economic power with the power of their governments. The asymmetry of wealth, information and power between developed and developing countries leads to the drafting of country-level trade agreements that can be instrumental in jeopardising the long-term welfare of developing countries. These agreements can allow MNCs to deploy lower environmental and welfare standards in their foreign operations compared to those required in their home country, and allow special protections that can undermine economic efficiency and be contrary to basic principles of social justice (Stiglitz, 2007). The dynamic is one of a downward spiral:

> Developing countries are in competition for investment from the advanced industrial countries. Even if it could be shown that signing

COMPLEXITY AND NETWORKS   199

such an agreement led to more investment in a cross-section empirical study, it does not mean that developing countries as a whole benefit. As in other areas of competition, there can be a race to the bottom. The Nash equilibrium entails each developing country 'sacrificing its own interests' (for example, with lower environmental or worker protections) in hope that it will gain enough additional investment to more than offset the losses. But, of course, when they all do so, none gain.

(Stiglitz, 2007, p. 490)

Global supply chains: technological advances coupled with globalisation have spawned complex global outsourcing and supply networks. In manufacturing, their efficiency supports lean and economically advantageous models of production. However, the way in which greenhouse gas emissions associated with these networks are allocated to the different countries from production to final consumption is controversial (Kagawa et al., 2015), and may allow developed countries to assign the emissions associated with their consumption to the developing countries where the environmental cost of production is incurred. In the case of agricultural and horticultural imports, the challenge is one of justifying the air miles and carbon footprint associated with their transport, and there are also concerns about the impact that the industry has on the farming practices, land use and social welfare in developing countries (Gonzalez, 2006). In the UK, the Brexit impasse over the Irish border and the Covid vaccine crisis has highlighted the fragility of long supply chains and the potential for political grandstanding and brinkmanship to disrupt them.

Consumer capitalism: the synergistic impact of planned obsolescence and throw-away culture, the power of brands, and the invasiveness of advertising, have long been criticised for escalating consumerism and waste. The introduction of social media into this mix has generated a cyber-social space in which

We're more globally connected than ever before, and also less connected to who makes our clothes, who grows our food, and I think part of that is down to information overload. And in terms of what social media is doing to our ability to stay focused, to not see the world in terms of these matrices of our own marketability and consumability,

> whether it's views or likes or retweets ... It's not that people don't care, it's that they care for five seconds. That acceleration of emotion, and attention – it's a pretty big shift.
>
> (Naomi Klein, cited in The *Guardian*, 2019)

The consumer–brand relationship and the projection of the self-concept in terms of consumption and taste preferences disconnects individuals from the fundamentals of the impact of individual consumption on the wider ecosystem.

These observations call for alternative models of growth and development. Carney's observations resonate with Schumacher's (Schumacher, 1973) principle of 'small is beautiful'. Whilst there is clearly a role for large corporations in the ecosystem, their current dominance suppresses the extent to which we can leverage the diversity embodied in the population of small- and medium-sized enterprises, and of community-based co-operative ventures. From the ecological perspective this constitutes a major welfare cost, and the next sections outline an alternative approach that overcomes this limitation, aligned with what we know about the resilience and generative potential of ecosystems in the natural world.

Organising in the networked world

In addressing the role of our species in the ecosystem, the Covid-19 pandemic highlights the importance of attending to the patterns of network connectivity and the multi-layered temporal dimension when devising strategies that accommodate the complex, evolving dynamics of the networked world. To do this, it is essential to understand and leverage the affordances of the network form of organisation to align the social, economic, technological and political dimensions of our way of life with the well-being of our ecosystem.

Network forms of organisation

For what follows in this chapter, the term 'socio-economic' embraces the economic, social, political and technological facets of human existence on Earth. Like the ecosystems within which they are nested, socio-economic systems are Complex Adaptive Systems, embodying a network form of organisation:

> The network form (of Complex Adaptive Systems) is integral to self-organisation: network connectivity is instrumental for both, sustaining stability and for propagating transformational state changes. It is the capacity for self-organisation and adaptation that confers robustness upon organisational forms in dynamic environments. This resonates with Ashby's law of requisite variety ... the system has the generative capacity to respond to contingencies in the environment by realising its adaptive potential for transformation and coevolution.
>
> (Merali, 2006, p. 222)

It is the network form of organisation that confers on Complex Adaptive Systems the capacity to either maintain a steady state through adaptation, or transform themselves in the face of environmental perturbations. The networks are characterised by

- Heterogeneity of nodes and connectivity;
- Dynamically configuring network topology.

As illustrated by the discussion on ecosystems architecture, such networks are 'lumpy' – we can visualise them as networks of networks of different sizes and compositions. The resilience of networked systems derives from the combinatorial potential they embody: recombination of different components in different constellations as and when appropriate, enables access to a large option space for the adaptation and transformational change in the face of unforeseen environmental perturbations (Merali, 2021). The key capabilities afforded by the network form of organising are:

Speed of communication (and co-ordination capacity): the multiplier network effect enables non-linear escalation in the speed with which information and resources can be transmitted across the network, and in the number of nodes that can be reached.

Fine tuning for control and co-ordination: the potential for selective activation of pathways and constellations (i.e. groups of connected nodes, or groups of connected network clusters) at different times and for different durations enables fine control of the behaviour of the network in real time.

The overall system essentially comprises a network of networks (we can think of them as hubs) of different sizes and connectivity: there can be very large hubs with lots of connections, some small ones with very few connections, and others in-between. This lumpy structure has been shown to be a universal feature of viable systems across biological, social, economic and technological domains (Barabasi, 2002), furnishing the structural foundations for resilience and robustness.

Hyper-network configuration and differentiation: the behaviour of the Complex Adaptive Systems at the whole systems level emerges from multiple interacting networks. The spatio-temporal variation in hub connectivity is also associated with a hierarchical relationship of hubs and modularisation for regulation and co-ordination of global/local network activity. This allows for efficient co-ordination of processes at multi-level spatial and temporal scales, so, for example, in a differentiated multicellular organism, local repair adjustments to local perturbations may be fast paced and instantaneous, and happen against the backdrop of a continuous cell renewal cycle.

These capabilities become particularly significant when we turn to the challenge of how to organise our institutions and communities to address the contingencies of climate change and other unconscionable anthropogenic consequences.

Harnessing the networkness of networks for sustainable development

Delivering to the COP21 Paris Agreement undertaking to strive to limit global temperature rise to 1.5°C would enable us to slow down (or even reverse) the Earth's trajectory towards a full-blown catastrophic extinction. On the positive side of the equation, we have the technologies for renewable energy, the possibilities of conservation associated with the circular economy, and the hope that the Extinction Rebellion generation will translate rhetoric into constructive action, displacing consumerism with more eco-friendly, sustainable life choices. Less promising is the mobilisation of political will to invest in the requisite renewable energy infrastructures, or in legislation curbing the harmful externalities (such as deforestation and habitat loss, environmental pollution, etc.).

COMPLEXITY AND NETWORKS

The urgency for action demands the mobilisation of integrated individual, country, regional and global strategies for rapid, sustainable reductions in carbon emissions. 'One-size-fits-all' solutions are not possible because of significant differences in:

- The levels and types of social, material and cultural resources available in different locations;
- Competing ideologies and perspectives on globalisation;
- The degree to which the knowledge, disposition and agency to act is shared between public, private and third sector organisations and civil society.

Under these conditions, it makes sense to turn to the network model of ecosystems: from a Complex Adaptive Systems perspective, the natural way to move forward would be to design and orchestrate programmes in diverse settings as an integrated *network of networks* (Figure 9.2).

The overall architecture would be one combining

- Multiple place-based clusters embodying the requisite heterogeneity afforded by public, private and third-sector institutions collaborating and competing to make the best use of local resources, within

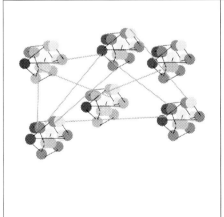

The "Networks of Networks" Approach

- local programmes or projects are themselves treated as heterogeneous networks rooted in local communities or spaces, and
- the overall approach delivers a network in which distributed, place-based programmes are linked to each other through relationships of interdependence for mutual benefit, e.g. resource sharing, infrastructure development, knowledge exchange etc.

Figure 9.2 Network of networks.

- An overarching national network providing the requisite connectivity between clusters in the form of infrastructure provision, policy, legislation and resource allocation.

The Complex Adaptive Systems approach for sustainable development (Merali, 2021) entails integrated development, attending to economic, social and environmental aspects *simultaneously* to achieve a synergistic, place-based enhancement of well-being. There are three features important for enhancing the viability of the community, and the sustainability of programmes:

Local agency and positive freedom (with reference to Berlin's conceptualisation);[1]

1. Generative capacity and evolutionary mechanisms;
2. Retention of microdiversity.

The role of centralised resource allocation is to create the context within which

- Networks of the requisite diversity and capability are seeded, and
- Support is in place for local *agency* in articulating goals and strategies for achieving them by
- Harnessing the collective generative capacity for innovation by using indigenous knowledge and resources co-specialised with requisite external inputs to develop distinctive, locally rooted development trajectories.

Network effects and synergies can be realised over time within the local clusters and through the wider network to accelerate the adoption of advantageous traits, whilst retaining the flexibility to adjust the scope, scale and nature of exchanges at a pace that is aligned with the capacity of the ecosystem to support diversity and co-evolution.

This design avoids the pitfalls of 'one-size-fits-all' strategies and allows the best use of local resources to satisfy place-based development needs and priorities whilst achieving improved quality of life and livelihoods at the scale of the integrated network. It also allows for multiple, 'experiments' and innovative practices to emerge in *parallel*, and the capacity for rapid knowledge transfer across clusters for the diffusion of good practice.

Conclusion

Merali's (2000) *Cognitive Congruence Framework* and the distributed network form of organising introduced in this paper furnish a conceptual frame that accommodates many of the key issues raised in the wider sustainability literature on socio-ecological systems (SES).

Ostrom (2009) points out that government-led 'one-size-fits-all' solutions have been shown to fail (i) because of a lack of congruence between the centrally set rules and local conditions (Dietz et al., 2003), and (ii) when conditions do not support the establishment of locally developed rules and norms for managing and using place-based resources in diverse contexts when there is a diversity of resource harvesters. In her framework for analysing the sustainability of socio-ecological systems, she identifies ten variables associated with self-organisation that may affect the likelihood of particular policies for enhancing sustainability. Five of these (collective agency and autonomy, norms and social capital, local leadership and knowledge of socio-ecological systems) resonate with the realisation of the *Cognitive Congruence Framework*: they are about the ability of place-based community mechanisms to develop congruence between the members' collective understanding of the wider ecosystem and the impact of their actions, their identification with the need to invest themselves in ensuring the sustainability of that resource, the relationships that diverse resource users have with each other, and the way in which they communicate and co-ordinate their activities over time.

Ostrom and others emphasise the importance of social capital and trust in lowering the transaction cost for achieving co-ordinated action to ensure the sustainability of a resource, and value that is collectively placed on that resource. The willingness of collectives to invest in such action even when that may lead to a loss of short-term speaks to Mark Carney's distinction between economic value and the value to broader society. Ostrom's treatment also suggests that the value that a community places on a particular resource will be positively related to the effort that its members are willing to invest in ensuring its sustainability, and locally devised governance provisions rooted in that understanding are more likely to succeed when implemented. A failure to appreciate this dynamic can be costly, and Ostrom cites the example of colonial powers in Africa, Asia and Latin America: they did not recognise local resource institutions that had been developed over centuries and imposed their own rules, which frequently led to overuse if not destruction (Berkes and Folke, 1988; Mwangi, 2007; National Research Council, 2002).

The distributed network form of organising overcomes the deficiency of centrally determined 'one-size-fits-all' policies. The local place-based networks provide the context within which local knowledge can be retained, and collective agency can be exercised, valuing social capital and trust in a manner consistent with Ostrom's analysis. The overall architecture allows the retention of place-based diversity whilst allowing flexibility in the degree to which local clusters collaborate – for example, in order to achieve economies of scale for particular outcomes, or to access complementary resources, or realise synergies between distinctive resource/capability endowments. The retention of diversity is key for ecological resilience and sustainability, and an important property for the generation of innovation and adaptive responses in dynamic contexts.

In the case of climate change, we need to respond with urgency, but we need to embark on a journey that we can sustain for generations to come. The network form of organising is perhaps the most promising model for allowing our species to stay systemically connected with the rest of our ecosystem whilst adapting and investing for a future that we cannot control.

Note

1 Isaiah Berlin's (Berlin, 1969) concept of positive liberty, with intrinsic factors affecting the degree to which individuals or groups act autonomously.

References

Barabási, A.L. (2002) *Linked: The New Science of Networks*, Perseus Books Group, 200.

Bascompte, J. (2009) Disentangling the Web of Life, *Science* **Vol 35**, 416–419.

Berkes, F., Folke, C. (1988) *Linking Social and Ecological Systems*, Cambridge: Cambridge Univ. Press.

Berlin, I., (1969) Two Concepts of Liberty, in I. Berlin (Ed.), *Four Essays on Liberty*, London: Oxford University Press.

Ceballosa, G., Ehrlich, P.R. and Raven, P.H. (2020) Vertebrates on the brink as indicators of biological annihilation and the sixth mass extinction, *PNAS* **Vol. 117** no. 24, 13596–13602 https://doi.org/10.1073/pnas.1922686117

Darwin, C. (1859) *On the Origin of Species by Means of Natural Selection*, London: John Murray.

Dietz, T., Ostrom, E. and Stern, P. (2003) The Struggle to Govern the Commons, *Science* **Vol 302**, 1907–1911.

Durkheim, E. (1933) *The Division of Labor in Society*. George Simpson (trans.). New York: Free Press.

Economist (2021a) https://www.economist.com/graphic-detail/2021/01/28/vaccine-nationalism-means-that-poor-countries-will-be-left-behind Economist, Daily Chart 1st Jan 2021.

Economist (2021b) The Next Calamity: The Coronavirus Could Devastate Poor Countries, *The Economist*, 28th March 2021 Issue.

Galbraith, J. K. (2004) *The Economics of Innocent Fraud*. New York: Houghton Mifflin Company.

Gonzalez, C. (2006) Markets, Monocultures, and Malnutrition: Agricultural Trade Policy Through an Environmental Justice Lens, *Mich. St. J. Int'l L.* **Vol 14**, 345. https://digitalcommons.law.seattleu.edu/faculty/569

Guardian (2019) No Logo at 20: Have We Lost the Battle Against the Total Branding of Our Lives? at https://www.theguardian.com/books/2019/aug/11/no-logo-naomi-klein-20-years-on-interview

Hobbes, T. (1651) *Leviathan: Or the Matter, Forme, and Power of a Commonwealth Ecclesiasticall and Civill*, ed. by Ian Shapiro, Yale University Press, 2010.

Kagawa, S., Suh, S., Hubacek, K., Wiedmann, T., Nansai, K. and Minx, J (2015) CO_2 Emission Clusters Within Global Supply Chain Networks: Implications for Climate Change Mitigation, *Global Environmental Change* **Vol 35**, 486–496.

Klein, N. (2015) *This changes everything: Capitalism vs. the climate*. Simon and Schuster.

Lüthi, D., Le Floch, M., Bereiter, B., Blunier, T., Barnola, J.-M., Siegenthaler, U., Raynaud, D., Jouzel, J., Fischer, H., Kawamura, K. and Stocker, T.F. (2008) High-Resolution Carbon Dioxide Concentration Record 650,000–800,000 Years Before Present, *Nature* **Vol 453**, 379–382, 15 May 2008.

Margalef, R. (1968) *Perspectives in Ecological Theory*, University of Chicago.

May, R.M. (1972) Will a Large Complex System be Stable? *Nature* **Vol 238**, 413–414.

Merali, Y. (2000) Individual and Collective Congruence in the Knowledge Management Process, *Journal of Strategic Information Systems* **Vol 9**, 213–234.

Merali, Y. (2001) 'Individual and collective congruence in the knowledge management process' *Journal of Strategic Information Systems* **Vol 9**, Issue 2–3, 213–234.

Merali, Y. (2006) Complexity and Information Systems: The Emergent Domain, *Journal of Information Technology* **Vol 21**, 216–228.

Merali, Y. (2021) *Network Thinking for Sustainable Development*, forthcoming.

Mwangi, E. (2007) *Socioeconomic Change and Land Use in Africa*, New York: Palgrave MacMillan.

National Research Council (2002) *The Drama of the Commons*, Washington, DC: National Academies Press.

New Scientist (2021) Mark Carney Interview: Rethink Capitalism to Solve the Climate Crisis, *New Scientist Newsletter* 18/03/2021, https://www.newscientist.com/article/mg24933260-900-mark-carney-interview-rethink-capitalism-to-solve-the-climate-crisis/#ixzz6pT8xxVbh

Ostrom, E. (2009) A General Framework for Analyzing Sustainability of Social-Ecological Systems, *Science* **Vol 325**, 419–422.

Paris Agreement (Dec. 13, 2015) *UNFCCC*, COP Report No. 21, *Addenum*, at 21, U.N. Doc. FCCC/CP/2015/10/Add, 1 (Jan. 29, 2016).

Polechová, J. and Storch (2019) D Ecological Niche, in Fath, B. (Ed), Encyclopedia *of* Ecology (Second Edition), Elsevier.

Schumacher, E.F. (1973) *Small Is Beautiful: Economics As If People Mattered*.

Stiglitz, J.E. (2016) *Inequality and Economic Growth. Rethinking Capitalism.* Wiley-Blackwell.

Stiglitz, J.E. (2007) Regulating Multinational Corporations: Towards Principles of Cross-Border Legal Frameworks in a Globalized World Balancing Rights with Responsibilities, *American University International Law Review* **Vol 23** Issue 3, 451–558.

Thompson, J.N. (2005) *The Geographic Mosaic of Coevolution*, Chicago: Univ. of Chicago Press.

United Nations (2020) World Economic Situation Prospect Report. https://www.un.org/development/desa/dpad/wp-content/uploads/sites/45/WESP2020_FullReport.pdf

Webb, R. (2021) Mark Carney interview: Rethink Capitalism to Solve the Climate Crisis in New Scientist Newsletters, Technology 17 Mar 2021 at https://www.newscientist.com/article/mg24933260-900-mark-carney-interview-rethink-capitalism-to-solve-the-climate-crisis/

Part III

LOOKING FORWARD

10

STEWARDSHIP AND STRATEGY IN TURBULENT TIMES

Andrew Taylor

Introduction

Discussions in business school classrooms, corporate headquarters and their journals tend to implicitly assume that the search for profit is an end in itself and that the earth's resources are no more than tokens in a giant game called global trade. Tullis (2019), for example, describes the consumer goods giant Unilever's decision to switch from trans fats to palm oil as a response to shifting consumer and regulatory patterns. The switch may have solved a marketing problem for Unilever, but it has produced 'devastating environmental consequences' (Tullis 2019):

> Forests destroyed for oil palm plantations are among the most carbon-rich in the world. When they are burned, that carbon is released.
> (Tullis, 2019)

The trouble is that, in a globalised world, not only is it hard for consumers to actually know what is happening at the other end of global supply

DOI: 10.4324/9781003190820-13

chains, but the rise of e-commerce's global search for the lowest cost is destroying the planet. Few consumers have much idea of where the components of things that are bought online come from and, as Tullis (2019) puts it, 'When it's out of sight, it's difficult to get enough of them to care'.

Unilever's switch to palm oil was devastating, not just because palm oil quickly became a key component of global supply chains, but also because, in a digitally networked world, that switch, Tullis reports, took place in under three months. It was a switch that has been followed by competitors and led to the deforestation of countries from Malaysia to Papua New Guinea, which has mirrored the widening demand for palm oil from global food and cosmetics giants. It continues apace.

This chapter will explore first how true sustainability flows from a sense of stewardship that recasts humans as a connected part of nature, rather than its conqueror. Second, how the convergence of technology and globalisation have altered strategies for value creation with significant consequences for environmental impact. Third, it will reveal how globalisation is leaving many people behind. People who are quietly but actively resisting the process whilst offering a historical reminder of how the Merchant Princes (Kennedy 2000) developed the idea of business as a source of both social change and competitive advantage. Fourth, we will explore contemporary examples of enterprises that celebrate and nurture ideas of local sustainability and who are consciously constructing networked, perhaps even polycentric (Ostrom 2015), systems.

Stewardship

The corollary of property rights – duties flowing from ownership – have historically been grouped together under the headings of stewardship or custodianship. Mostly defined by philosophers as obligations towards contemporary non-owners or future generations (Ryan 1984, Scruton 2012, Bollier 2014), they may be socially and/or legally codified, but are a response to problems of externalities (see Jacobs 1991 and described by Cremene in this book). Stewardship defines (often implicitly) a code of virtue that, in its rejection of pure, short-term utilitarianism, provides a foundation for cultural relations and practices that holds a group of people together in common cause to nurture and cherish the environment that enables them to flourish. As such they have been a means to inject ideas of sustainability into the human search for economic development and have acted as a brake upon economic greed throughout history.

Intellectually, stewardship can be traced back to 'primitive' peoples (McLuhan 1989), but was most influentially, in the modern age, captured by Locke (1991) who, in the words of Ryan (1984), described resource owners as '*pro tem*' custodians and managers of 'God's property'. In biblical terms, Shaiiko claims that:

> The steward was God's deputy or representative in a symbolic sense, who recognized God's omnipotence, but applied intelligence, reason and moral responsibility in his care of his surroundings. The execution of stewardship was therefore the ultimate act of God's will on earth through his designated manager, man.
>
> (Shaiiko 1987, p. 258)

This is a statement which captures the ethical dimensions of stewardship, which reaches beyond transactional obligations only to people, to convey the idea that success is about using advances in knowledge to develop sustainability and not just achieve growth of output efficiency for its own sake. Thus, stewardship can be a means to temper human excess. This raises a key question as to the purpose of why we might put aside our economic ambition to care for the environment and also asks when we will know the limits of exploitation.

At core, questions of purpose are about linking actions to ethics so that we may be able to make sense of patterns of behaviours and construct norms that allow us to navigate day-to-day experience. Whilst academics and philosophers might argue about the details, there are broadly three principal schools of ethics. Deontology was developed by Kant around the idea of duty as a rational choice. Thus, for Kant, duties and rights are inseparable 'because your duty to treat the other person as you would wish to be treated is his or her right to be treated thus, and vice versa' (Curry 2011). Kant's focus upon duty is, from an ecological point of view, interesting in an age and 'in a culture increasingly dominated by rights alone' (Curry 2011). However, it rests upon an underlying belief that ethics can only be rooted in individual rationality and thus only applies to rational beings. Thereby positioning all of nature behind human beings and, inevitably, also allowing the rational to be defined by prevailing elites. Whilst attempts have been made to extend deontology even to non-sentient organisms (Taylor 1986), such as plants, there remains no scope for either the common good, beyond individual rationality, or how to overcome the tendency to separate rights from duties (Curry 2011) and as such its value to our discussion is limited.

Consequentialism, which finds its most common expression as Utilitarianism, and virtue ethics are the major alternative schools of ethics. They are often simplistically contrasted about whether we do things because they are useful in some instrumental way or because they are right or wrong morally. Utilitarianism is a broad stream of thought, but dominated by Bentham, who argued that ethics should be about the greatest happiness of the greatest number. Bentham claimed that ethics is essentially mathematics, made famous with his *felicific calculus* – pleasure minus pain, and as such, requires sentient capacity. If an action gives more pleasure than pain it is a good thing. If it should give less pleasure than pain then it is a bad thing (Sabine & Thorson 1973, Berki 1977). The trouble with this view of ethics is threefold. First, as the Marquis de Sade (Parekh 1973, Berki 1977) famously described, some people get pleasure from pain, whilst others derive pleasure from causing others pain. Second, in assuming free will, it takes no account of power (Berki 1977). For example, a person may not get pleasure from their work, but if it is the only alternative to poverty, do they really have the luxury of ethical choice? Third, the association between utility, or usefulness, based upon sentient capacity (Wenz 2001) clearly prioritises human needs. Although 'glaringly at odds with Bentham's use of pleasure and pain' (Sabine & Thorson 1973, p. 625) and despite the interest of important contemporary thinkers such as Peter Singer (1975), over time utility has been increasingly defined and measured in economic terms. We see this with GDP as the primary measure of national progress and development, for example, and how many times have you witnessed the need for jobs and economic growth used to justify environmental loss?

Virtue ethics is the oldest of the three schools, rooted primarily in the work of the Greek philosopher Aristotle. For him, life was a journey to develop a virtuous character, based upon temperance, justice, courage and practical wisdom, which good actions flow naturally from and result in happiness, or, as Curry (2011) prefers to define it, as well-being. With the rise of economics associated with modernism, utilitarianism has tended to eclipse ideas of virtue. Nonetheless virtue ethics remains a compelling story, retold by Christians around faith, hope and charity (Curry 2011). Central to sporting ideals, it is visible in questions about money and drugs in sport and stubbornly insists on a place in business with community-owned enterprises, mutual enterprises, cooperatives and torrid debates over the value and importance of corporate social responsibility. Whilst virtue ethics do not offer the simplicity of Bentham's utilitarianism, or the rationality of Kant, they do not require humankind to be the centre of the universe and position economics and business as a means to something virtuous and not ends in themselves.

Based upon utilitarian principles and Kantian rationality, much recent contemporary thinking about the environment is essentially anthropocentric (human-centred); based upon the idea that 'human beings ought to care for the environment because it is in our interest to do so' (Dobson 1990, p. 19). Whilst this is self-evidently true over the long-term, in the real world, people have a track record of discounting the future (Jacobs 1991). For example, few would today argue that gains in agricultural productivity have not been, to some degree, at the expense of ecological richness, quality and diversity. Indeed it was Rachel Carson (1965) who famously described the use of agricultural chemicals to achieve greater productivity as producing a 'Silent Spring'. Thirty years later, Lowe et al. (1997) found that farmers were jettisoning their duties to care in favour of a utilitarian drive to improve yields. There are few reasons to believe that the underlying ethic has changed today.

Anthropocentric (so-called light green) thinking, based upon a requirement for rational sentient being, implicitly draws the limits of exploitation at the point where it clearly impacts upon human well-being (Eckersley 1992). In contrast, and rejecting Cartesian modernism, so-called deep greens 'wish to de-centre the human being, to question mechanistic science and its technological consequences, to refuse to believe that the world was made for human beings' (Dobson 1990, p. 9). Thus for both deep greens and many 'primitive' peoples a society which does not place duties to care before rights to take is inherently unsustainable. In this sense stewardship is a means to express our responsibility to be the first among equals (with other species) in contributing to a more sustainable environment. As Shaiiko (1987) put it, virtue flows from caring for the earth as Managers for God. Throughout history this belief has been transmitted through narratives.

In almost every society popular music such as Woody Guthrie's *This Land Is Our Land*, stories such as Steinbeck's *The Grapes of Wrath*, well-known hymns such as *All Things Bright & Beautiful, Morning has Broken*, the writing of prophets such as Kahlil Gibran (1991), fables such as Miorita (in Romania) all utilise narratives to convey ideas of stewardship. Intellectually it is clearly and directly expressed in Leopold's (1966) land ethic, where the author describes belonging to the land and work as a means to cherish the past, nurture the future and recognise the interdependence of life. Such narratives exist to convey values of stewardship grounded in culturally specific ideas of place (Newby 1985, Scruton 2012, Collins 2020), whose virtuous character invites and encourages us to accept that rights flow from fulfilment of duties.

Stewardship comes to life through the ability of narratives to connect people to places and each other that crosses historical time but remains rooted in place. To date, technology has not proven a suitable substitute, and despite corporate claims to the contrary, technology is neither representative of, nor an actual experience of, the good life itself. During the pandemic, communication platforms, such as Teams, Zoom and so forth provided functional utility, but few shoppers, students or business executives are likely to describe the experience as nurturing or virtuous, certainly compared to the face-to-face alternative. They simply lack what we might crudely call soul. Without grounding in an ethic of stewardship, technology's claims to offer freedom confuses utility with virtue.

In contrast, stewardship relations have historically been built upon physical proximity as the means to hold people to account to a shared set of ethics. Stewardship is not simply a commitment to a set of abstract ideas but has historically been contextualised around a specific place to create an identity that transcends both (Scruton 2012). It is this that leads Scruton to describe (the English) people as 'inseparable at every point from the attachment to the land and the desire to endow the land with the character of home' (Scruton 2017, p. 16). Fables and metaphors have been used throughout history to capture the relationship between people and place that is at the centre of how stewardship is constructed as an act of virtue. A simple shorthand example that conveys so much more than the words themselves is Scruton's statement that 'who we are is where we are' (Scruton 2017, p. 23). Proximity between action and consequence has an immediacy that touches people in a way that intellectual responsibility for externalities does not always. If your identity is wrapped up with a way of life that reproduces proximate sustainable outcomes, that is likely to be a nurturing experience and matter far more than decisions made that affect people and places remote to you. As Taylor and Krouwel (2013, p. 93) rather bluntly put it, 'No one wants to defecate on their own doorstep'.

The rise of industrial production-expanded supply chains has distanced individuals from the consequences of their collective actions (Schumacher 1993, Taylor & Krouwel 2013). Furthermore, scale drives economic efficiencies by denying employed labour the capacity to exercise moral reasoning when that has an impact upon margins and profits (Engels 1935). A process which has been extended greatly in a digital global village (Bloodworth 2018). As Kohr (1957) famously put it, 'the world's one and only problem is not wickedness but bigness' (Kohr 1957, p. 95). The trouble is that, as scale grows, the opportunities for efficiency gains present multiplier effects that are very tempting for those in search of profit margins. Even *Harvard Business Review* recently expressed concern that the emphasis upon efficiency may have gone too far (Martin 2019). The problem, as we see with the pandemic, is that the more things are stripped back and streamlined to deliver greater robustness of what is predictable, the less resilient our models of organisation become and the more vulnerable to unpredictable change we become. As Snowden and Boone (2007) demonstrated with their Cynefin Framework, efficiency is fine in settled and predictable spaces, but disastrous during periods of radical change. Complex change requires us to put aside traditional utilitarian management thinking, learn from nature, embrace emergence and conduct safe-to-fail experiments (Snowden & Boone 2007). Thus underlining the relationship between practical day-to-day management practice and underlying ethics. The Covid-19 pandemic crisis, for example, is, according to Shiva (2020) based upon an 'anthropocentric worldview of humans as separate from and superior to other beings we can own, manipulate and control [and] … instead of being connected through biodiversity we become connected through disease' (Shiva 2020, p. 11).

Convergence

Globalisation and technology are coming together to enable and create global patterns of consumption but, in doing so, are destroying local production relationships. The ability to move production to lowest-cost locations and often even replace it completely with close to zero marginal costs of delivery (think iTunes, eBay, etc.) is not only revolutionising markets (Mason, 2015). The shift to an economy where value lies in knowledge and not products (Argyris 1991, Evans & Wurster 1997) and based upon dynamic networks and not internal corporate structures is empowering some and disempowering many.

Back in the days before the internet, strategy was about securing value creation within business processes, products and brands (Porter 1979). However, Prahalad and Hamel (1990) recognised that technological change requires a focus upon core competence to be able to adapt a business to markets evolution. As the internet started to take hold, Hammer (1990) realised that global connectivity would wipe whole layers of processes and people from organisations. To prove his point, he cited how Ford salespeople now entered purchase data such that they could reduce accounts payable staff by 75%! This led to a noisy fad for so-called business process re-engineering (BPR). A process which, with its ruthless focus upon efficiency and productivity, simultaneously enabled globalisation whilst implicitly defining work, and the resources used for work, in productive, instrumental and utilitarian terms. Technology enabled supply chains to become longer and more complex as production shifted to lower-cost locations around the world. The ethical consequences of utilitarian global supply chains were seen in fires in Bangladeshi sweatshops (Hickman 2010), but they reached their most recent zenith in the discovery that Chinese factories were using political prisoners as forced labour to supply Western markets (Kuo 2019), both cases where virtue took a back seat to productive utility. Equally in Eastern Europe the arrival of multinationals has in the case of some industries brought investment in cleaner and safer technologies, but in many industries investment was attracted by lower costs flowing from reduced labour costs and more lax regulatory environments. The results can be seen in the river Tisza cyanide spill, which took place in Romania during 2000. Described by the BBC as 'the worst environmental disaster since the Chernobyl nuclear leak in 1986' (Batha 2000) caused by gold miners using a method of separating gold that would simply not be permitted in more developed economies. The chairman of Hungary's environment committee accused Esmeralda Exploration of 'engaging in 'eco-colonisation' ... Nature is being destroyed here in central Europe', he said. 'The health of hundreds of thousands is being endangered with technologies which may not be permitted in ... Australia or ... in western Europe' (Thorpe 2000).

The devastating environmental consequences of the growth in digital devices can be seen in the destructive search for rare earths, metals and chemicals needed to produce them. Kaiman (2014) reports Ma Jun, director of the Beijing-based Institute of Public and Environmental Affairs, as saying that 'we basically export the resources at a rather cheap price, and much of the environmental cost is externalised to local communities'. As a miner put it to Kaiman 'We don't understand these things', he said. 'We're just here to make a living' (Kaiman 2014). In actual fact:

> Globally, rare earths are not, in fact, that rare, but they are expensive to extract if done in ways that cause less harm to the environment. The mining industry in southern Jiangxi Province [China] was largely unregulated until recently, with illegal mining operations proliferating.
>
> (Standaert 2019)

The global search for cheap tech's true cost is being borne by the planet's poorest workers, who are poisoning the planet itself on our behalf. Significant quantities of rare earths have recently been discovered in Africa, which, for the tech producers, is an appealing alternative to dependence upon China, but is likely to lead to the kind of conflict, exploitation and despoliation that has followed discovery of every other mineral resource on the continent.

Arthur (1996) has shown how the convergence of technology and globalisation is not just extending the reach of capitalism. It is actually undermining the law of diminishing returns so that those that are ahead move further ahead and those that are behind are left behind. The fear that we once had of larger grocers' market dominance (Blythman 2004) is dwarfed by the monopolistic power that businesses like Amazon marketplace have assumed.

Iansiti and Lakhani claim that:

> the global economy is coalescing around a few digital superpowers. Thereby embedding and legitimising a global search for lowest cost. We see unmistakable evidence that a winner-take-all world is emerging in which a small number of 'hub firms' – including Alibaba, Alphabet/Google, Amazon, Apple, Baidu, Facebook, Microsoft, and Tencent occupy central positions.
>
> (Iansiti & Lakhani, 2017, p. 86)

The combination of growing computer processing power, near-zero marginal cost of digital distribution and 'Metcalf's law [which] states that a network's value increases with the number of nodes' (ibid., p. 87), the digital network economy will continue to grow rapidly. Furthermore, the rise of monopolistic hub companies is creating information bottlenecks that are clearly open to abuse and concentrating value in the hands of a small number of firms (Iansiti & Lakhani, 2017). Digital hubs, such as Amazon Market, Alibaba, eBay, etc., are actually starting to replace whole markets. Companies are being forced to work with digital hubs or risk irrelevance. The consequences for the laws of economics are unclear, but profound:

> The centralizing forces of digitization are not going to slow down anytime soon. The emergence of powerful hub firms is well under way, and the threats to global economic well-being are unmistakable. All actors in the economy—but particularly the hub firms themselves—should work to sustain the entire ecosystem and observe new principles, for both strategic and ethical reasons. Otherwise, we are all in serious trouble.
>
> (Iansiti & Lakhani 2017, p. 10)

As the capture of value concentrates into a small number of tech hubs, the share of that value left for producers is squeezed even harder. Whilst companies like Amazon and Alibaba have provided consumers with global reach, the algorithms that they are based upon are purely utilitarian, with no moral compass, resulting in a global shopping frenzy and the rise of so-called fast fashion (Schlossberg 2019, Davis 2020). A term which has become shorthand for a society based upon treating clothes, and those who make them, as if they were disposable (Hunter 2015). Pearhouse describing the centre of the Bangladeshi tannery business claims 'It's hard to overstate how polluted Hazaribagh is' (PBS 2017). Whilst, in the same report, Sreenivasan states that 'The Bangladeshi government has acknowledged that 21,000 cubic meters of untreated tannery wastewater is dumped every day into the Buriganga River that runs through Dhaka, one of the world's most densely populated cities' (PBS 2017). Impersonal electronic platforms, through their anonymous transactional search for low cost, don't just enable externalities, they implicitly encourage the search for them. Both the human and environmental cost of cheap and fast fashion is toxic and mostly invisible to consumers who don't have to live with its consequences

(Tynan 2012). As Band Aid famously sang, 'Thank God it's them instead of you'. Sadly, this frenzy has not been limited to clothes.

From clothing and footwear sweatshops to the destructive search for rare earths required for tech devices, the burning of fossil fuels and the pollution and despoliation of land, sea and air, the consequences of industrialism are now being globally turbo charged in an orgy of utilitarian consumption. Meanwhile the global trade in wildlife, the over-fishing of oceans to feed global demand and the rising rate of disease from the industrialisation of agriculture all underline an ethical assumption that flora and fauna are primarily units of production to serve the needs of humans as conquerors of nature. As McBurney (1990) wryly observed, however, ecology cannot be stuffed into the concept of economics. Yet it is the reduction of all life to its economic value that the digital hubs enable, encourage and legitimise by their transactional nature. We are using technology, in the words of Lovelock (2007, 2009), to destroy the richness of Gaia. The digital revolution may offer hope for technological solutions to our resource overshoot, but, in the meantime, it is simply fast-forwarding the rate of destruction.

Sadly, it is not only the non-human world that is being reduced to a data node waiting to be mined in the new economy. Many people are being left behind too. Whilst there has been much debate about how technology is driving not only the marginal cost of distribution close to zero (how much does it cost iTunes to send you a song?), it is also enabling the cost of production to move close to zero (Mason 2015). China has been accused of using forced labour to supply products at the lowest cost imaginable (Kuo 2019), whilst the treatment, by firms like Amazon, of workers as units of production (Bloodworth 2018) has been described as little better than the concomitant rise of modern slavery (Young 2019). Even *Harvard Business Review* is concerned that 'in a painfully ironic turn, after creating unprecedented opportunity across the global economy, digitization and the trends it has given rise to – could exacerbate already dangerous levels of income inequality, undermine the economy, and even lead to social instability' (Iansiti & Lakhani, 2017, p. 86).

Left behind – the human dimension

A casual glance at the Brexit vote, the election of Trump or the surge of support for LePen reveal a widespread rejection of a utilitarian global village, one without roots or responsibilities. 'The old distinction of class and economic interest have not disappeared but are increasingly over-laid by a larger and looser one – between the people who see the world from Anywhere and the people who see it from Somewhere' (Goodhart 2017, p. 3). Both Goodhart (2017) and Rose (2011) describe how class structures have been replaced by motivational values, attitudes towards change and attachment to place. Based upon relationships between values and behaviour, Rose has identified three types:

> For Settlers, the deep forces draw people to seek out safety, security, identity and belonging. For Prospectors, it is the yearning for success, the search for esteem of others and self-esteem, while for Pioneers, the constant drive is for new ideas, the quest for connections waiting to be made, and living a life based on ethics.
>
> (Rose, 2011, p. 16)

Rose and Dade develop this model and how it has influenced relationships between people and environment further in their own chapter of this book. In short, whilst the global village has empowered Prospectors and Pioneers the dynamic ambiguity of the network economy has created an instability of both work and place that is profoundly disturbing to Settlers' sense of well-being (Taylor & Bronstone 2019). The excitement of digital opportunities rests upon a sense of agency that Settlers simply do not possess. Rather than expanded rights, Settlers crave belonging and attachment to tradition (Rose 2011, Scruton 2017). As Goodhart says, 'Anywheres regard society as a shop, while Somewheres regard it as home' (Goodhart 2017, p. xix). Furthermore, Settlers' rejection of the global village, witnessed in the votes for Trump, Brexit and LePen, is a clear sign that they perceive political economies to have lost their anchors.

The growing irrelevance of place in the global village, with its emphasis upon the global, is undermining any sense of place that the word village implies. Towns and villages across the developed world are being hollowed out by e-commerce. Belonging and identity that are defined beyond productive or consumptive status and connected to past and future generations are being subsumed under the networked ability to search out the lowest price. A search which is often no more than a global means of identifying the most exploitative means of production and distribution. With electronic distribution costs close to zero, the pressure to lower the cost of any value creation is immense in a global marketplace (Mason 2015). Of course, wherever possible, people will be replaced: with driver-less cars, drones, robots or outsourced to cheaper locations. Even supposedly higher-value functions, such as HR and finance, are now being outsourced, in so-called shared service centres in low-cost locations around the world.

The Covid-19 pandemic has, as I write, shattered the idea of a global village. First, because the immediate response of countries, even within the EU's supposed bloc of cooperation and single market, was to close national borders. Second, the fact that the virus is piggybacking upon global connections to spread cannot be ignored and has caused many to shift their gaze and look to create more personal, familial, local and national resilience (Gallagher 2020). The UK government has, for example, made it clear that it must not be dependent upon global trade for the supply of essential products and services again (Woodcock 2020, Serhan & Gilsinan 2020, Burden 2020).

Where, until recently, suburban and provincial living were looked down upon by ambitious executives, the pandemic has caused many to re-think. As I write, property agents are reporting a surge in demand for such properties (Bloom 2020, Macaskill 2020, Mowat 2020). In many ways 'The health emergency is forcing us to deglobalise' (Shiva, p. 11). In the shadow of the pandemic, the exit from cities in search of an imagined rural idyll (Pahl 1965, Marsden et.al 1993, Taylor & Krouwel 2013) reveals a renewed search for a place to cherish; what the philosopher Scruton (2012) called Oikophilia. Pushing back against what James (2007) called affluenza, people, Prospectors especially (Rose 2011), are, implicitly at least, questioning their global ambitions and thinking beyond consumption to the sort of environment that they may thrive in and even what it means to thrive. The pandemic was preceded by similar outbreaks of disease amongst animals. Mad cow disease, swine flu and bird flu were all direct products of claiming ethical superiority that in 1975 Singer (1975) described as speciesism. In the name of economic progress, we are now treating many more animals than in 1975 as units of production to be exploited with maximum efficiency and productivity with little thought to the systemic consequences flowing from treating creation as no more than ingredients in profit processes.

Despite corporate PR to the contrary, the simple fact is that analysis of species diversity, water quality, air quality, climate change, soil quality reveals that the triumph of industrialism is decimating the earth's ecology (Lovelock 2007, 2009, Porritt 2020, Webster 2020). Arguing whether the US, China, Russia or the EU should set the parameters in this orgy of consumption is rather like fighting for control of the first-class deck of the Titanic. All the cocktails in the world will not alter the fact that the ship is sinking under the hubris of human invincibility. The current dash out of cities is no more than recognition that the ship of globalisation is experiencing very turbulent water and may be holed below the water line.

Virtue as competitive advantage

Perhaps now is the time to remember that, as 'The Merchant Princes' (Kennedy 2000) showed, work can be a chance to express a commitment to cherish, nurture and sustain such that economy and society become inseparable parts of a whole, that we might describe as virtuous. During the nineteenth century, the idea of stewardship was rediscovered amidst the transformation that was the industrial revolution. It was reinvented by the non-conformist industrialists, like the Cadbury brothers, Rowntree, the Lever brothers and Reckitt. Driven by religious vision (most were non-conformists, often Quakers), they believed that the commitment of their employees was more valuable than their mere compliance. That commitment was obtained through defining work as a religious act in which people were equal in their common humanity (Hunt 2006). Business was, for these 'Princes' (Kennedy 2000), a means to finance a better world, a model of an alternative future. They built worker's villages, provided education, healthcare, sports facilities and saw their employees as a kind of extended family (Kennedy 2000). The idea that the commitment of employees could be a powerful source of competitive advantage became known as the human relations school or soft HR model (Mayo 1933). In recent times Pink (2009) has popularised the scientific evidence that a focus upon quantitative targets and efficiency has a negative impact upon both performance and motivation. The soft HR model (Pink 2009) delivers excellence through the power of intrinsic motivation, rather than the transactional nature of carrots and sticks (Taylor & Krouwel, 2013). In a digital age, it is not just network connectivity that matters, but also the intensity of connections

STEWARDSHIP AND STRATEGY 225

that matters. This is especially true for Rose's (2011) Pioneers who 'work because they love what they do' (Taylor & Krouwel, 2013, p. 97).

Out of fashion since the ideological and management focus upon efficiency during the 1980s, these ideas are making a comeback for people for whom work is either an expression of identity rooted in place (Scruton 2017) or is a contribution to something transformational (MacGregor Burns 2004, Rose 2011, Goodhart 2017). There has been a surge in employee-owned (Creasey 2018) cooperative enterprises; and, according to a partnership between NatWest Bank and the social enterprise news site pioneerpost .com, there has been a 355% growth in social enterprise in the year to May 2020. Even the likes of former Conservative Prime Minister David Cameron, through his 'big society' idea, became interested in ideas like employee ownership and community engagement as more than peripheral to the search for profit (Taylor & Bronstone 2019). What we are seeing is digital networks being used to disrupt established markets and empower communities to develop sustainable patterns of behaviour (Taylor & Bronstone 2019).

Stewardship in a digital world

The fulfilment of Handy's (2002) vision of fleas competing with elephants, the rise of a technology driven long tail economy (Anderson 2006), is tailor-made for differentiating value creation (Mason 2015) around scale, ownership and identity of place (Taylor & Bronstone 2019).

Digital networks can enable community and commons enterprise to leverage a pride connecting relations between people and place to produce a sense of virtue, that is central to Scrutons (2012) Oikophilia, and blurs the line between production and consumption. In so doing the opportunity exists for Rose's (2011) Settlers to participate in global markets through celebrating the very values that make them feel secure and engaged. Competitive advantage, for the local or commons to thrive in digital markets is often a commitment that goes beyond the processes of corporate business (Taylor & Krouwel 2013). Increasingly it goes beyond tighter collaboration with customers (Wenger & Snyder 2000) to include cooperation with other companies sharing similar scale and values, in conscious bids to develop alternative ecosystems of enterprise (Taylor & Bronstone 2019). Small businesses have often cooperated with one another both on the basis of shared values and project need (Taylor & Krouwel 2013). However, digital markets are driving a surge of interest in commons and community enterprise that goes beyond enlightened self-interest. Not only is enterprise being defined as a transformational activity, its configuration, as creating value from the fulfilment of duties to people and place, goes beyond the remit of the Merchant Princes (Kennedy 2000). Often explicitly including environmental sustainability, goods or benefits[1], such enterprise is not only virtuous, but, depending upon your point of view, expanding the reach of ethics or restoring humans position within wider ethical obligations to the world around us.

There is recognition, amongst thinkers, that there is a blurring of boundaries between words like cooperative, commons and community and that local systems may well also include private enterprises that share key values (Taylor & Bronstone 2019, Ostrom 2012). Examples include village shops, pubs and renewable energy projects. Community enterprise typically sustains assets which hold cultural and symbolic value in reproducing constructions of locality. As such they are highly relevant to Rose's (2011) Settlers. Moreover, both commons and community enterprise tend to be structures for extending a shared transformative vision (Bollier 2002) that is 'a cultural practice and outlook that seeks to understand the world in different terms' (Bollier 2014, p. 122). Community enterprise projects are different because they 'are being done by the community not being done to the community' (Cowtan 2017).

Nobel Prize winner Elinor Ostrom (2015) describes overlapping commons regimes as polycentric, 'where [commons] systems exist at multiple levels with some autonomy at each level' (Ostrom 2012, p. 82), which provides for systemic resilience. Vincent Ostrom provides a more detailed and nuanced definition of overlapping commons:

> Polycentric' connotes many centers of decision making that are formally independent of each other. Whether they actually function independently, or instead constitute an interdependent system of relations, is an empirical question in particular cases. To the extent that they take each other into account in competitive relationships, enter into various contractual and cooperative undertakings or have recourse to central mechanisms to resolve conflicts, the various political jurisdictions in a metropolitan area may function in a coherent

manner with consistent and predictable patterns of interacting behavior. To the extent that this is so, they may be said to function as a 'system'.

(from Ostrom, Vincent, Tiebout & Warren 1961, quoted in Ostrom 2009, p. 3)

Interestingly, such 'nested' (Ostrom 2015) enterprise can and does occur organically, from the bottom up and reaches beyond commons enterprise. Taylor and Bronstone (2019) found that commons, community and employee-owned enterprises deliberately sought to lever one another into commercial relationships to develop and widen their reach. The explosion of interest in commons and community enterprise, which is often cutting out bankers, consultants and intermediaries as it digitally joins together commons and local enterprise with individuals and communities sharing common values globally, has often occurred organically, but is increasingly structured, explicitly, as an interlocking system (Taylor & Bronstone 2019). Whether we are witnessing the emergent development of digital polycentric enterprise requires further research to be sure. However, these emergent systems do exist to cherish and nurture the local, yet leverage global networks for resources, markets and ideas required to flourish.

Community and commons enterprise

The Phone Coop (UK) pioneered the use of the internet to develop a successful enterprise community of shared values. Not only have they provided a living example of how digital cooperatives can thrive, but the networked nature of their initial mobile telecoms business has enabled them to bridge their network (Zhu & Iansiti 2019, Taylor & Bronstone 2019) into new markets for themselves[2] and other commons type businesses. Thereby acting explicitly as a catalyst for both deepening and widening commons and community trade systems (Taylor & Bronstone 2019). Whether such networks can be described as polycentric, or not, can be debated, but they are certainly gaining traction and demonstrating that business as virtue is possible in a digital age.

What seems to hold such networks together is the idea that the organisation of work is a moral challenge, often limited by scale and defined by people and place, as much as it is an economic one. Thus the products and services provided, be they fair trade, renewable or recycled, are the ethical output of a relationship between people and place that is socially constructed to nurture the idea of stewardship and work as an act of service. Myriad small enterprises are being explicitly constructed to offer 'man a chance to utilize his faculties; to overcome his egocentredness by joining together with other people in a common task; and to bring forth the goods and services needed for a becoming existence' (Schumacher 1993). Like the Merchant Princes before them, they are trying to show that work can be an act of virtue as much as it is a utilitarian necessity and still be competitive.

There are now numerous examples of community energy enterprises seeking to utilise locally available wind, hydro and solar power. Such enterprises typically provide free, or low-cost, electricity and sell any surplus, through guaranteed uptake prices, to create additional value for the community to invest elsewhere. The challenge with such enterprise is that the initial capital costs – of purchasing the wind turbine, solar panels, etc. – are high. Thus, they have sourced finance from both the local community itself and used digital platforms to crowd source investment capital (Cowtan 2017).

Triodos Bank is but one example of how community enterprises have created opportunity by reconceptualising risk. Their relationship managers (they have no branches) work with communities to construct a community enterprise. Then the bank loans a minority of the money and it structures a bond or equity offering which is marketed on their website and through digital networks that transcend frontiers. This enables small investors from anywhere in the world to invest, with a guaranteed return based upon things like fixed energy prices for typically five years. Thus, cutting out intermediaries, enabling a more diverse energy grid and enriching and empowering communities. The key to the Triodos model is that they have been able to construct trust around the idea that, rather than using a crowdfunding platform, investors are sharing risk with a bank, an organisation that, in the minds of most people, ought to be better at evaluating risk than they are able to do. That trust is matched up to the desire to obtain a financial return from investing in sustainable transformations. As Triodos themselves say:

> We create direct investment opportunities with businesses, charities and social enterprises spanning a range of sectors and industries.

STEWARDSHIP AND STRATEGY   229

> We work with these organisations to get them ready for investment and provide you with all of the information you need to make your decision.
>
> (Triodos 2020)

Whilst community enterprises have tended to issue bonds with Triodos (2020), an increasing number of small (non-community) enterprises are issuing equity-based offerings with Triodos. In all cases value is established around the bank as a gatekeeper between global networks of small ethical investors and enterprise clients. At the time of writing, they claimed to have raised £161,330,000 (Triodos 2020) to invest in small enterprises, through global digital networks.

As enterprises and enterprise hubs, such as the Phone Coop and Triodos, cooperate to create wider socio-economic relationships, myriad overlapping interlocking systems are beginning to emerge (Taylor & Bronstone 2019). Organisations such as Triodos, the Phone Coop, Ecotricity and others have gone from fringe businesses to respected and credible market disruptors in themselves. Just as the likes of Amazon continue to seek out opportunities to bridge their monopolistic networks into new markets, the rise of what is, or may become, polycentric commercial space is establishing itself as a legitimate alternative means of constructing digital markets.

Conclusion

The digital economy is changing the world; creating both economic opportunity and ecological havoc and, whilst it has empowered many, it has also left many more behind. The hollowing out of communities, outsourcing of jobs, digitalisation of interactions and the perceived complicity of elites in this process (Goodhart 2017) is alienating Rose's (2012) Settlers to the point where, across the developed world, they are using the ballot box to reject the global village (Taylor & Bronstone 2019). From both socio-economic and ecological perspectives, leadership that enables stewardship to flourish is needed. Using digital networks as bridges to finance and markets can enable communities to thrive. The digital economy, structured appropriately, is giving rise to a form of networked stewardship. It is not true that all the enterprises described above are entirely ecocentric. However, in defining enterprise as something more than an end in itself, most do take an ethical account of relationships between people, place and environment, that was previously not the case. This is most effective when adopting a systemic approach, using digital networks to connect values-based enterprise across people and place. Up until recently most enterprises in this space have relied upon individual Pioneers (Rose 2011) to step up and, just as with Cadbury, provide a template. What is clear now, though, is that channelling commitment to people, place and community can create systemic value and enable sustainability by aligning ethical resources with local needs such that it disrupts existing corporate organisations and efficiencies. Could it be that, whilst the ruthless utilitarian Goliaths of the digital economy have not met their Davids, Scruton's (2012) little platoons are quietly plotting a different way forward?

Notes

1 See the web pages of almost all community energy and retail businesses.
2 They now offer home broadband and energy.

References

Anderson, C. (2006), *The Long Tail: Why the Future of Business Is Selling Less of More*, New York: Hyperion.

Argyris C. (1991), 'Teaching Smart People to Learn', *Harvard Business Review*, May–June.

Arthur W. B. (1996), 'Increasing Returns and The New World of Business', *Harvard Business Review*, July–August.

Batha E. (2000), 'Death of a River', *BBC News*, February 15th.

Berki R. (1977), *The History of Political Thought: A Short Introduction*, London: Dent.

Bloodworth J. (2018), *Hired: Six Months Undercover in Low-Wage Britain*. London: Atlantic Books.

Bloom J. (2020), 'Coronavirus May Have Huge Impact on Property Markets', *BBC Website*, June 11th.

Blythman J. (2004), *Shopped: The Shocking Power of British Supermarkets*, London: HarperCollins.

Bollier, D. (2014), *Think Like A Commoner: A Short Introduction To The Commons*, Gabriola Island, Canada, New Society Publishers.

Burden (2020), 'Global Trade Restrictions Surge in Pandemic', *The Telegraph*, November 17th.

Carson R. (1965), *Silent Spring*, London: Penguin.

Collins D. (2020), *The Organizational Storytelling Workbook How to Harness this Powerful Communication and Management Tool*, London: Routledge.

Cowtan G. (2017), *Community Energy: A Guide to Community-Based Renewable Energy Projects*, Cambridge, UK: Green Books.

Curry P. (2011), *Ecological Ethics: An Introduction* (2nd Ed.), Cambridge, UK: Polity Press.

Davis N. (2020), 'Fast Fashion Speeding Toward Environmental Disaster, Report Warns', *The Guardian*, April 7th.

Dobson, A. (1990), *Green Political Thought*, London, HarperCollins.

Eckersley R. (1992), *Environmentalism and Political Theory: Toward an Ecocentric Approach*, New York: State University of New York Press.

Engels F. (1935), 'Anti-Duhring', In *The Handbook of Marxism*, New York: Random House.

Evans P., & Wurster S. (September–October 1997), 'New Economics of Information', *Harvard Business Review*.

Gallagher S. (2020), 'Escape to the Country: Will People Leave Cities Behind Post-Pandemic?' *The Independent*, August 12th.

Gibran K. (1991), *A Treasury of Kahlil Gibran*, London: Mandarin.

Goodhart D. (2017), *The Road to Somewhere*, London: Hurst and Company.

Hammer G. (1990), 'Reengineering Work: Don't Automate, Obliterate', *Harvard Business Review*, May–June.

Handy C. (2002), *The Elephant and the Flea: New Thinking for a New World*, New York: Random House.

Hickman M. (2010), '21 Workers Die in Fire at H&M Factory', *The Independent*, March 2nd.

Hunt T. (2006), 'The Protestant Revolution', *A TV Documentary Series for the BBC*.

Hunter I. (2015), 'Crammed Into Squalid Factories to Produce Clothes for the West on Just 20p a Day, the Children Forced to Work in Horrific Unregulated Workshops of Bangladesh', *Mail Online*, November 30th.

Iansiti M., & Lakhani K. (2017), 'Managing Our Hub Economy: Strategy, Ethics and Network Competition in an Age of Digital Superpowers', *Harvard Business Review*, September.

Jacobs M. (1991), *The Green Economy*, London: Pluto Press.

Kaiman J. (2014), 'Rare Earth Mining in China: The Bleak Social and Environmental Costs', *The Guardian*, March 20th.

Kennedy C. (2000), *The Merchant Prices, Family, Fortune and Philanthropy: Cadbury, Sainsbury and John Lewis*, London: Hutchinson.

Kohr. L. (1957), *The Breakdown of Nations*. Croydon, UK, Green Books, 2001. Originally published by Routledge & Kegan Paul.

Kuo L. (2019), 'Inside the Chinese Jail Behind the Christmas Card Scandal', *The Guardian*, December 28th.

Leopold A. (1966), *A Sand County Almanac*, New York: Oxford University Press.

Locke J. (1991), *Two Treaties of Government*, London: Dent.

Lovelock J. (2007), *The Revenge of Gaia*, London: Penguin.

Lovelock J. (2009), *A Final Warning: The Vanishing Face of Gaia*, London: Penguin.

Lowe P., Clark J., Seymour S., & Ward N. (1997), *Moralizing The Environment: Countryside Change, Farming and Pollution*, London: UCL Press.

Macaskill M. (2020), 'Pandemic Pushes Interest in Rural Scottish properties', *The Times*, March 29th.

Macgregor Burns J. (2004), Transforming leadership. New York: Grove Press.

Marsden T., Murdoch J., Lowe P., Munton R., & Flynn A. (1993), *Constructing The Countryside*, London: UCL Press.

Martin R. L. (2019), 'The High Price of Efficiency', *Harvard Business Review*, January–February.

Mason P. (2015), *Postcapitalism: A Guide to Our Future*, London: Allen Lane.

Mayo E. (1933), *The Human Problems of an Industrial Civilization*, Cambridge, MA: Harvard University Press.

McBurney S. (1990), *Ecology Into Economics Won't Go: Or Life is Not a Concept*, Hartland, Devon: Green Books.

McLuhan T. (1989), *Touch the Earth: A Self Portrait of Indian Existence*, London: Abacus.

Mowat L. (2020), 'UK Property: Demand for the Countryside Soars as Londoners Look to Flee the Capital', *The Express*, May 28th.

Newby H. (1985), *Green and Pleasant Land?: Social Change in Rural England*, Farnham, Surrey, UK: Ashagte.

Ostrom E. (2012), *The Future of The Commons: Beyond Market Failure and Government Regulation*, London: IEA.

Ostrom E. (2015), *Governing the Commons: The Evolution of Institutions for Collective Action*, Cambridge: University Press.

Pahl R. (1965), *Urbs in Rure: The Metropolitan Fringe in Hertfordshire*, London: Weidenfeld & Nicolson.

Parekh B. (ed) (1973), *Bentham's Political Thought*, New York: Barnes & Noble.

PBS NewsHour (2017), 'Bangladesh's Leather Industry Exposes Workers & Children to Toxic Hazards', March 29th.

Pink D. (2009), *Drive: The Surprising Truth about What Motivates Us*, London: Penguin.

Pioneers Post (2020), 'Top 100 social enterprises in UK revealed: NatWest SE100 2020', https://www.pioneerspost.com/news-views/20200514/top-100-social-enterprises-uk-revealed-natwest-se100-2020#NatWest%20SE100%20Top%20100, viewed on December 24th 2020.

Porritt J. (2020), *Hope in Hell: A Decade to Confront the Climate Emergency*, London: Simon & Schuster.

Porter M. (1979), 'How Competitive Forces Shape Strategy', *Harvard Business Review*, March.

Prahalad, C. K., & Hamel, G. (1990), 'The Core Competence of the Corporation', *Harvard Business Review*, May–June.

Reasey S. (2018), 'The Rise of the Employee-owned Business', *HR Magazine*, 29th January.

Rose, C. (2011), *What Makes People Tick: The Hidden World of Settlers, Prospectors and Pioneers*. Leicester, UK: Matador.

Ryan A. (1984), *Property & Political Theory*, Oxford: Blackwell.

Sabine G., & Thorson T. (1973), *A History of Political Theory* (4th Ed.), Orlando, FL: Holt, Rinehart & Winston.

Schlossberg T. (2019), 'How Fast Fashion is Destroying the Planet', *The New York Times*, September 3rd.

Schumacher E. (1993), *Small is Beautiful: A Study of Economics as if People Mattered*, London: Vintage.

Scruton R. (2012), *Green Philosophy: How to Think Seriously About the Planet*, London: Atlantic Books.

Scruton R. (2017), *Where We Are: The State of Britain Now*, London: Bloomsbury.

Serhan Y., & Gilsinan K. (2020), 'Can the West Actually Ditch China?' *The Atlantic*, April 24th.

Shaiiko R. (1987), 'Religion, Politics, and Environmental Concern: A Powerful Mix of Passions', *Social Science Quarterly*, 68, 244. June 1987.

Shiva V. (2020), 'One Planet: One Health', *Resurgence & Ecologist*, Issue 321, May/June.

Singer P. (1975), *Animal Liberation*, New York: HarperCollins.

Snowden D., & Boone M. E. (2007), 'A Leader's Framework for Decision Making', *Harvard Business Review*, November.

Standaert (2019), 'China Wrestles with the Toxic Aftermath of Rare Earth Mining'. Yale Environment 360, July 2nd.

Taylor, A. & Krouwel W. (2013), *Taking Care of Business: Innovation, Ethics & Sustainability*. Cluj-Napoca (Romania): Risoprint.

Taylor A & Bronstone A. (2019), *People Place and Global order: Foundations of a Networked Political Economy*. London: Routledge.

Taylor P. (1986), *Respect for Nature*, Princeton, NJ: Princeton University Press.

Thorpe N. (2000), 'River of Cyanide Runs Through Europe', *The Guardian*, February 11th 2000.

Triodos Bank (nd), 'Investment opportunities', https://www.triodoscrowd funding.co.uk/investments, viewed July 4th 2020.

Tullis P. (2019), 'How the World Got Hooked on Palm Oil', *The Guardian*, February 19th.

Tynan E. (2012), 'The Fire in Bangladesh is a Fashion Scandal', *The Guardian*, December 5th.

Webster B. (2020), 'Ten Times' More Plastic in Atlantic Than Feared', *The Times*, August 19th.

Wenger E., & Snyder W. (2000), 'Communities of Practice: The Organizational Frontier', *Harvard Business Review*, January–February.

Wenz P. (2001), *Environmental Ethics Today*, Oxford: Oxford University Press.

Woodcock A. (2020), 'Coronavirus: UK Cannot Go Back to 'Business as Usual' with China after Pandemic, Raab Warns', *The Independent*, April 16th.

Young M. (2019), 'Amazon Warehouse Staff 'Treated Like Slaves with 10-hour Shifts and Short Breaks', *The Mirror*, October 20th.

Zhu F., & Iansiti M. (2019), 'Why Some Platforms Thrive and Others Don't', *Harvard Business Review*, January–February.

11

THE 'UNDERGROWTH MOVEMENT' AND THE VIRTUES OF LEADERSHIP

Sr Margaret Atkins

Only by cultivating sound virtues will people be able to make a selfless ecological commitment (Pope Francis)

Introduction

We are facing not only an ecological crisis, but multiple planetary crises, economic, political, social and personal. They arise from the way of life we have lived since the Industrial Revolution, which has intensified greatly over the last half-century. Responding to them will demand of us an enormous change in our global political and economic goals and in the focus of big business and manufacturing. Politicians, engineers and corporations are beginning to make the urgent changes we need, if not, perhaps, as quickly as would be wise. It is arguable, however, that we need more than changes to the way we work within the existing system. Indeed, a prophet might argue that the existing system is on the verge of a dramatic transformation, of an upheaval on the scale of the Reformation or the Enlightenment. The epoch of large-scale industrialisation was characterised by technocratic

DOI: 10.4324/9781003190820-14

command and centralised control; the age of the factory, of efficiency, of Rational Economic Man. The new epoch will need to make room for other ways of living, animated by a different spirit, one that is organic, flexible, spontaneous, evolutionary, creative, democratic, resilient, networked, rooted in the local but embracing the global. Arguably, only communities shaped and animated by such a spirit will be able to change whole societies in the way that is necessary.

This chapter will explore the limitations and dangers of the mindset, shaped by technology, that has done much to shape our recent industrial past, and argue that if we are aiming at large-scale social changes we need to attend to virtues of character, in our leaders and in wider society. Political leaders in a renewed society will need to see themselves more as enablers than controllers, with a primary responsibility to encourage and facilitate both leadership and success in others. New groups, animated by the sort of spirit just described, can not only themselves constitute an important element in a renewed society, but also provide a training-ground for such virtues.

Every writer is influenced by tradition (even those who self-consciously reject it). My own influences are primarily Classical and Christian, philosophical and theological, with a strong interest, rooted in the Catholic respect for human reason, in integrating the best from all sources of wisdom and understanding.[1] It is intriguing and encouraging that much of what I argue might well have been argued in a similar way, citing different authorities, by writers in quite different religious or non-religious traditions. One of the real signs of hope over the last few decades has been a convergence of ideas among people whose intellectual roots are very different; such a convergence is most easily explained if what they are converging upon are deep truths about the world and the human condition.

Reforming business as usual

Mark Carney's final Reith Lecture of 2020 provides a very thoughtful example of how to rethink business and politics to meet the challenge of climate change, while keeping a fairly conventional focus on large-scale financial economics and productivity (Carney 2020). He argues that the regulation of finance and business needs to align more closely with the widely held desire for a net-zero economy, while the general public need to invest in

THE VIRTUES OF THE 'UNDERGROWTH MOVEMENT'   237

ways that support this goal, which is also their own. In this way, he is confident that private finance will be able to drive the continued growth, through green innovation, that he sees as an effective solution to the climate crisis. Surely, he is right that we need to shift our political focus from abstract money to the real goals we wish to achieve, and enable, as he puts it, 'values to drive value'. However, his lecture, which anticipated COP26, prompts further questions about the ways in which large institutions interrelate not only with individuals, but also with what we might broadly call 'civil society'. I identify four of these:

- What are the limits and dangers of top-down planning intended to produce predetermined outcomes in the behaviour of whole populations?
- How do we nurture the kind of morality in which markets, innovation and investment (as Carney argues) need to be embedded?
- How does political regulation relate with the mass of grassroots initiatives[2] that are already responding to climate change and other social challenges from the bottom up?
- What is the appropriate size and scale for each different kind of economic activity, in its own geographical and social context?

I will explore these four questions in order to suggest an outline of the kind of politics and political leadership that might facilitate the flourishing small- and medium-sized community projects that could complement, and sometimes replace, big business and big politics. Such community projects, I will argue, will provide a hopeful source of the kind of leaders we need to guide and coordinate our transition to a better future.

The 'Technocratic Paradigm'

The industrial age was marked by an interlinked mesh of centralised sources of energy (fossil fuels), increasingly centralised and influential communication (newspapers, televisions), increasingly powerful technology and increasingly large commercial institutions of production (from factories to multinationals). The latter had to be balanced by an increasingly centralised and powerful state. These various factors combined to produce exponentially increasing speed and ever expanding distances between individuals, their families, and their original homes.

These changes have shaped the way we viewed the world. The point made clearly by Joseph Ratzinger, later Pope Benedict XVI:

> Technological civilisation is not in fact religiously neutral, even if it believes it is. It changes people's standards and their attitudes and behavior. It changes the way people interpret the world, from the very bottom up.
>
> (2002, pp. 76–77)

His successor, Pope Francis, put it this way:

> Humanity has taken up technology and its development according to an undifferentiated and one-dimensional paradigm. This paradigm exalts the concept of a subject who, using logical and rational procedures, progressively gains control over an external object. This subject makes every effort to establish the scientific and experimental method, which in itself is already a technique of possession, mastery and transformation. It is as if the subject were to find itself in the presence of something formless, completely open to manipulation.
>
> (Francis 2015, 106)[3]

This 'technocratic' way of thinking trains us to choose a single predetermined goal and to work out a method (usually highly dependent on numbers) for achieving that goal. Both human beings and natural objects are viewed through the lens of control (the language of 'quality control', for example, has moved from the factory even into the universities, once bastions of creative, independent thinking). The technocratic method is an exercise of power, and our technological powers are now immense. However, to quote the book which inspired both of these popes:

> recent years have been marked by a monstrous growth in man's power over being, over things and over men, but the grave responsibility, the clear consciousness, the strong character needed for exercising this power well have not kept pace with its growth at all.
>
> (Guardini 1998, p. 82)[4]

At any rate, after two or three centuries of steadily increasing the size and power of institutions, their impersonal nature, and the speed and distance at which they function, we are facing a daunting set of crises: the collapse

THE VIRTUES OF THE 'UNDERGROWTH MOVEMENT'   239

of biodiversity and climate change; economic instability, increasing inequalities in wealth and intensified economic migration; bitter political divisions and the collapse of trust in political figures; the poorly examined influence of virtual communication and Big Data over nearly every aspect of our lives; the alarming increase (at least in the West) of loneliness, isolation, substance addictions and other mental health problems; and finally, of course, the present reality and future threat of global pandemics.[5] For many of our major collective problems, however, there is little evidence that they can be solved by top-down systems of authority applying technological power. However many switches we flick or triggers we pull, commerce in illegal drugs, for example, remains one of the biggest industries in the world. Centralised technological fixes such as 'dimming the sun' (Klein 2015, ch. 8), far from providing safe solutions to climate change, are exceptionally risky.

Perhaps, then, we need to look more deeply into the mindset that both shapes and is shaped by the technological lens through which we tend to view the world. It begins by failing to attend to the moral responsibilities of our power, as if it is simply our own possession, there to achieve whatever goals we wish. It then tends to shape those very goals, so that success is reckoned in ways that can be measured with technology and with numbers, and consequently size ('growth') and speed seem desirable for their own sake. It specifies problems individually, in order to focus its methods of solving them. It expects a pre-defined outcome, and anything else counts as failure.

All of us in the West are shaped by this mindset. To illustrate this, here is a simple example. I sometimes show a slide which has on one the left side a photo of an advertisement for a mobile-operated system for turning on your home heating, and on the right pictures of someone chopping wood and of a log fire. I ask the audience, 'Which is less work?' Behind the first picture, of course, lies hidden the control of the coordinated labour of hundreds, even thousands, of people (leaving aside the mass of materials and their environmental impact of their production) that has been required to turn that tiny gesture into a warm living room. Chopping wood, by contrast, when the labour is largely one's own and the log is recognisably part of a tree, forces you to confront the reality of the objects and the truth of the effort involved. Most people in the audience, of course, give the apparently obvious answer. The technocratic mindset which blinkers them concentrates on its own goals and sees only the effect it aims to achieve.

Why does this matter politically? I suggest that the technocratic paradigm is largely responsible for certain weaknesses of vision that have contributed to our current crises. First, we have been focusing on monetary outcomes (in part because they are easily measurable, in part because they fit with the illusion that bigger is better), corporate profit and GDP, which distort our purposes and distract us from asking what are our real goods. One result of this is that we have often been very slow to notice, even when alerted by prophetic voices, many of the unwelcome side-effects of our projects, from the wiping out of our invertebrates through pesticides, to the interwoven destruction of local communities and their environments by the oil industry, to the dumping of our plastic waste in the oceans.

Second, when we have focused our attention on real goods, such as health or education or food, we have tended to treat them as separate problems, each to be tackled by a system with its associated industry. Consequently, it is only recently that we have begun to attend to the interconnectedness of our problems, and therefore of their solutions: to the ways, for example, in which town planning might affect both the local ecology and the mental and physical health of its inhabitants, or agricultural methods might either foster or destroy flourishing communities. Such separation leads, third, to striking inconsistencies in political decisions, such as continuing to allow the destruction of ancient forests for the building of HS2, while planning to plant 'a million trees'. Relatedly, the personal inconsistency which all of us experience in relation to ecologically sensitive living is greatly magnified for decision-makers at the political level: no minister who overrides a local fracking ban, or allows the application of neonicotinoids to crops, wants his or her grandchildren to live in a world devoid of clean air, fertile land, safe drinking water or butterflies.

The measuring of success by size and power, combined with the resultant accumulations of such power in fewer hands, has, in the words of Pope Benedict, 'brought about that division of the world into north and south, into rich and poor, which represents the real emergency of our time' (2002, p. 58). Relatedly, it is one important cause of the political conflict, often rooted in economic problems, that has become so obvious: Brexiteers versus Europhiles, Democrats versus Republicans, fossil fuel companies versus Extinction Rebellion, *gilets jaunes* versus the establishment, Islamicist terrorists versus the rest of the world. Rabbi Jonathan Sacks characterises such conflict as 'The Death of Civility' (2020, ch. 16), for it seems as if there is no longer space to settle public differences through patient, reasoned, attentive and charitable discussion. Such polarisation, combined with the centrally facilitated power of digital technology, has also led to high levels of distrust towards politicians and other powerful people, often with good reason, when public words, on the one hand, have become so cheap, while the hidden words of lobbyists, on the other, can be so influential (e.g. Klein 2015, p. 149; Sayer 2016, pp. 245–253).

Finally, if we focus only on top-down approaches, free countries will rightly tend to shy away from the question of serious changes in personal lifestyles: we will be happy to legislate for LED-lighting, or even perhaps for low-carbon investment portfolios, but not for low-meat diets or low-fuel holidays. Yet a realistic response to ecological problems demands of us far more radical changes than we have yet embraced.[6] It also demands these of all of us: to quote the polar explorer Robert Swan, 'The greatest threat to our planet is the belief that someone else will save it'.[7] Such truths pose a challenge to the technocratic mind, used to thinking of problems as ones for which solutions can be 'delivered' by appropriate methods: human beings in their ordinary lives, in a healthy society, are free. A sane politics can only enable and facilitate, not command and predict, the kind of behaviour for which the enlightened might hope, just as, in fact, a sane agriculture can only enable and facilitate, not fully control, the fruits of the earth.

Hardly any of us (and explicitly not the two popes I have quoted) will fail to be grateful for the benefits of much modern technology. However, as long as we possess this, with its apparently effortless power over other people and things, we will never be free of the temptation to slip into the technocratic mindset, with all its dangers.[8] We can only guard ourselves against it, by vigilance against the seductive power of machines, by awareness of our weaknesses, by the prudent and intentional selection of which technologies to use, by a disciplined willingness to resist and abstain from risky usages, and by a culture which supports us in this. None of these defences can be created by political fiat. The Amish, who have preserved the religious and moral structures to nurture such a culture, provide one living example of such discerning usage, from which we might learn, even while, for mainstream society, innovative methods of communication and of energy-production remain essential tools to meet our ecological challenges. For unless we use such tools with great wisdom and discernment, even they will be double-edged. In other words, Mark Carney's powerful appeal to root finance in values needs to be extended to all areas of our life, with a keen awareness of the way in which our values shape not only our choices of specific projects but our very capacity to read the evidence on which such choices are based.

Virtues and communities

In other words, we need to think about virtues. In fact, all of us who use words such as 'kind', 'sensible', 'honest', 'brave', 'gentle', 'reliable' or 'friendly', as novelists or sports writers, barristers or teachers, or simply (and most commonly) as friends and neighbours enjoying a gossip, are already noticing virtues. We value such dispositions in each other because, as St Thomas Aquinas (2005), pp. 7–8, explained, they enable us to act consistently, readily and with pleasure. A kind person, for example, responds spontaneously to her friend in need; it is normal for her to do so; she does so happily, without being forced. 'We know where we are', as we say, with someone whose good character is stable.

How do we acquire such dispositions? They are grounded in both mind and heart, in an interplay among our thoughts and beliefs, our feelings and emotions. For this reason, virtuous individuals are nurtured in virtuous communities. Learning the virtues, through the training of our minds and hearts, which happens primarily through example and imitation, is hard to achieve if it does not begin in childhood. Although our families are normally our first teachers, every parent knows the insidious pressures that come from peer groups and from the wider culture ('But it's not fair – everyone else in my class has got one!'). Like it or not, we cannot but learn from our society. Indeed, the very language that we use, to identify and teach the virtues, to blame and to praise, is of its essence something social. An important moral task, in a culture that honours a distorted view of human success, is simply to keep a rich language of virtue alive.

Moreover, the determination of what counts as virtuous is shaped by society as a whole. Unless I decide to live as a hermit, I cannot just make up for myself what clothes are respectable enough or what food is elaborate enough. I cannot decide alone what counts as a fair wage for a job or

THE VIRTUES OF THE 'UNDERGROWTH MOVEMENT' 243

an adequately heated workplace or an acceptable level of risk to health. Nor is it just up to me how far different virtues are recognised and prioritised, or what precise shape they take: for example, whether ecological damage counts as injustice. Such things are governed by the rules and conventions of whichever society, or sub-section of society, we find ourselves in. (This is not to say that virtues are simply relative, or that societies cannot be in need of reform, but simply to reiterate that different material and cultural conditions inevitably shape our precise understanding of particular virtues, while to demand higher standards than are currently accepted demands a prophetic insight and courage, not just ordinary decency.) For this reason, communities can be more or less virtuous *as a whole,* and not simply because they contain more or fewer virtuous members (Blum 1998).

Not only are the standards collectively set, but we need the support of others in our community to live up to our standards. We need practical support: you cannot use means of public transport or buy local vegetables if none are available. We also need moral support, the mutual encouragement that enables us to face the challenges of living within the limits of the planet and to resist the insidious social pressure that globalised consumerism imposes on our belief in our standards. Neither in theory nor in practice can we go it alone (cf. Atkins 2003).

Finally, we need communities because we are never simply virtuous. All of us are capable of failure, compromise or backsliding. Living with others helps us to be attentive to our weaknesses and temptations, to acknowledge our mistakes, and to pick ourselves up and begin again.

Alasdair MacIntyre, whose book *After Virtue* renewed the study of virtue within English-speaking philosophy, argued that every society will acknowledge a core of qualities related to the fundamentals of our shared human nature: the classical 'cardinal' virtues of courage, temperateness, justice and practical wisdom will be needed so long as human beings remain physically vulnerable, subject to feelings and emotions, social and free to make intelligent choices. He also showed, however, that virtue ethics is not a uniform tradition. Different cultures shape their ideas of virtue in different ways: compare the ideals of a Homeric warrior with those of a medieval abbess. Different contexts require different modalities of the core virtues, as well as different virtues to supplement them (MacIntyre 1981, especially ch. 14).

In our own age, then, we will need to develop an understanding and practice of the virtues that is shaped by ecological demands: a level of temperateness and justice in not using more than our fair share of the material goods, for example, or the courage to speak out against environmental abuses.

Hope from the Undergrowth

My third question arising from Mark Carney's lecture can offer hope for answering my second. For the 'mass of grassroots initiatives' that I mentioned grow out of communities of different kinds, which provide the soil, as it were, in which virtues might be nurtured. I was referring to a global phenomenon of the last couple of decades, as yet without an official name, which I have nicknamed 'the Undergrowth Movement'. Paul Hawken, whose book *Blessed Unrest* documented literally thousands of the projects that constitute this, described it in the book's subtitle as 'the largest movement in the world' (Hawken 2007).[9] It consists of a vast number of organisations that link together local communities, the voluntary sector, schools and universities, charities, and ethically minded (including not-for-profit) businesses, often working closely with local government. These are characterised by their goals, in that they are responding to social and ecological concerns; by an element of gratuity, in that labour is given either freely or on generous terms; by their small or medium size and local connections; and by their interest in building good personal and communal relationships.

Few of us nowadays can (or would want to) live in the all-encompassing kind of communities that Wendell Berry describes in reflecting on traditional agriculture (1987, pp. 179–192), in which the material economy, social life and spiritual commitments are inseparably intertwined, with almost no distinction between neighbours and friends. Very many of us, however, regret the enormous loss of neighbourly and community spirit that has resulted from a combination of reasons, including the motor car, electronic entertainment, contemporary patterns of work, fragile families and the design of modern towns. Insofar as genuine communities, bonded not least by personal friendships, come into existence through the committed engagement with shared and enduring projects, our towns and cities are no longer likely places for fostering a strong community spirit. The

Undergrowth Movement, however, with its emphasis on cooperation and relationships in the pursuit of shared ethical goals, has provided many people with the experience of participating in and helping to build a real community, often, though not always, explicitly linked to a geographical home. Such communities, in turn, provide the seedbeds for nurturing the kind of virtues that might sustain not only our financial sector, but also our business, engineering, agriculture, healthcare and education.

Descriptions of projects that contribute to the Undergrowth Movement do not in fact tend to focus on the virtues of the people involved, but rather they take them for granted. As Wendell Berry pointed out:

> When the virtues are rightly practised in the Great Economy, we do not call them virtues, we call them good farming, good forestry, good carpentry, good husbandry, good weaving and sewing, good home-making, good parenthood good neighbourhood, and so on.
>
> (1987, p. 74)

If you do ask the questions, though – whether traditional farmers or Undergrowth activists, for example, need to be patient, honest or coura-geous – the answers are clear. In these areas, successful people are good people, certainly not flawless, but good in essential, and quite ordinary ways. They are each embracing the challenge of adapting the traditional repertoire of virtues, as it were, to meet the needs of their own day (Atkins 2008; Deane-Drummond 2017, ch. 7).

Undergrowth projects require, for instance, the wisdom, imagination, fairness, openness and creativity to combine and integrate a variety of important goals; the determination, moderation and temperateness to live more lightly on the earth; the simplicity, thoughtfulness and inner freedom to reject a competitive understanding of goods when a cooperative one is possible; the compassion, kindness and humility to honour and encourage the capabilities of every member of a group or community; the reliability, generosity and persistence to act as one of the stable lynchpins on which every group relies; the patience and attentiveness to facilitate the difficult conversations and consultations essential to shaping each activity; the quiet selflessness of the washers-up, envelope-stuffers and lift-givers who do the unnoticed jobs that support every voluntary venture; the honesty and truthfulness to speak out about urgent issues and to gain the trust of one's colleagues; the humour, cheerfulness and hope that encourage everyone to keep going, however gloomy the bigger picture might appear.

The Undergrowth Movement might also help us to learn to be more discerning about our use of technology. To quote Pope Francis again:

> Liberation from the dominant technocratic paradigm does in fact happen sometimes, for example, when cooperatives of small producers adopt less polluting means of production, and opt for a non-consumerist model of life, recreation and community.
>
> (2015, 112)

In fact, the Movement has been heavily facilitated by the use of IT, often to create its groups and sustain and inform their activities. At the same time, its broad values tend to encourage its participants to be more sparing and intentional in their overall use of virtual communication, while the often local nature of the groups helps to reduce dependence on large-scale machines and infrastructure. Specifically, its focus on community and relationships gives it a basis for developing sound criteria for assessing the genuine value, as well as the dangers, of different uses of technology.

Furthermore, the Undergrowth Movement is characterised by ways of thinking that offer a healthy counter-balance to some of the weaknesses of the Technocratic Paradigm. Like technocracy, Undergrowth projects define their goals, but these are only ethical, not financial. Money is clearly a tool, never a competing, let alone primary, end. The ethical focus means that Undergrowth thinkers are less likely to fail to notice the natures of the things and people that they affect. Such attentiveness is reinforced by the local nature of most projects: when a group of residents comes together to build a community centre, they are unlikely to risk polluting the drinking water. The work of integrating one's personal moral vision is incorporated, at least implicitly, into every act of practical judgement.

Moreover, the emphasis on personal networks and good relationships fosters practices of respect for collaborators and other stakeholders: Undergrowth projects typically value learning and understanding, consultation and listening. Superb examples of the way such listening can be built into the fabric of projects are provided, for example, by the Transition Towns movement, or by the projects described by Hilary Cottam in her book *Radical Help* (2018). Relatedly, the Undergrowth Movement usually

THE VIRTUES OF THE 'UNDERGROWTH MOVEMENT' 247

both depends on and creates distributed rather than centralised, pyramidal, forms of authority: its analogue is perhaps a set of solar panels rather than a power station. Each group has its own team of leaders, while the style of leadership is usually egalitarian, with every member encouraged to play an important role in the group as a whole.

The Technocratic Paradigm, rooted in scientific methodology and large-scale industrial practices, focuses on providing solutions to individual problems. However, we are more aware than ever that, to quote a favourite phrase of *Laudato Si'*, 'everything is interconnected', in complex networks of mutually interacting systems (the philosopher Mark Taylor (2014, pp. 249–254) calls these Emerging Complex Adaptive Networks or ECANS).[10] This is true even of our ethical goals. Thirty years ago, for example, the goals of 'justice and peace' and 'the environment' often seemed to be in competition; nowadays Greenpeace takes it for granted that it must listen to poor local communities, while aid workers assume that ecological care is a priority. This realisation cuts across the political divide: on the political left, for instance, Naomi Klein (2015) shows how political corruption and injustice are accompanied by political bullying of local communities and the destruction of the water and land on which they depend, while on the political right, Steve Hilton (2015) provides an integrated exploration of innovative ideas in politics, schooling, health, food, business, social inequality and deprivation, childhood, architecture and nature.

Undergrowth projects regularly turn the theory of interconnectedness into practice. When, for example, I recently helped prepare a grant application to support local people in growing their own food, and we came to the checklist of the benefits of the project, one of my colleagues remarked, 'It ticks all the boxes' – mental health, physical health, reduced GHG emissions, community building, waste reduction and environmental education.[11] Rob Hopkins, founder of Transition Towns, provides a wealth of examples of such integration in his recent book *What Is to What If*. One of my favourites is the Playing Out scheme for closing off streets to allow children to play, which not only fosters their own physical and mental health and imaginations, and temporarily at least provides a relief from polluted air and petrol emissions, but has also created unexpected bonds of friendship among adults living in the area (2019, 15–19).

Whereas the Technological Paradigm tends to focus on projects as if they were unconnected, the Undergrowth Movement, influenced by the belief that the different elements of healthy individual and collective human lives are interrelated, is protected against the extreme inconsistency that our current British political approach to the environment has shown. For it assumes that actions that cause large-scale damage to our natural environment are unlikely to be good for our children's health, or, ultimately, our economy. This consideration helps to explain the remarkable fact that although it consists of a mass of independent groups right across the globe, its aims and activities are remarkably congruent. Naturally there will be some healthy disagreements within and among such groups, but broadly speaking groups that care about the climate, the countryside, animal welfare, biodiversity, social justice, mental and physical well-being, local communities, beauty and art are all pulling in the same direction.

In a society characterised by increasing conflict and distrust, The Undergrowth Movement alone will not create World Peace. However, its groups do build real peace from the bottom up, in the only way one can do that, by fostering communities. They bring together in common projects people of different political views and different backgrounds; they extend existing communities, based on churches or clubs, by reaching out to others; they want to listen to everyone's viewpoint and make use of everyone's talents. They aim to turn neighbours into friends. Moreover, because of their awareness of the trans-local, even global dimensions of their focus, they tend to have peaceful attitudes towards and practical connections with others across the world.

Again, the Undergrowth Movement cannot directly restore trust in our national politicians: it has tended in fact to build its relationships with local and municipal governments, where and insofar as these are allowed to be effective, or to bypass politics altogether. At the same time, the face-to-face activities of the Undergrowth provide schools of trust, as it were, as people learn how to be trusted and trustworthy, how to place trust and how to discern when trust should be cautious or withheld.

Finally, the communities created and strengthened by Undergrowth activities provide people with the kind of moral and practical support they need to be able to embrace freely the big changes in their personal lifestyles so urgently demanded as a response to the ecological crisis. Without such voluntary support, on a wide scale, and grounded in effective communal attitudes, no peaceful government will be able to encourage, let alone enforce, such changes.

The question of size

My fourth question prompted by Mark Carney's lecture was: 'What is the appropriate size and scale for each different kind of economic activity, in its own geographical and social context?' This question was powerfully posed, of course, by E. F. Schumacher in *Small Is Beautiful*, but has sadly been largely neglected since then. Our current economic system makes it unlikely that an organisation might deliberately remain smaller than serves the common good of society. On the other hand, it might become too big for this purpose in a variety of ways. By contrast with the care that small organisations will spontaneously give to their locality, a large distance between decision-makers and the people and places they affect often blinds the former to the consequences of their decisions. Where decisions need to be sensitive to the particularities of local ecology or society, large organisations are less likely to respond appropriately.[12] They usually depend on supply chains, including physical networks such as pipelines, that are energy-intensive. They will also tend to be lacking in rich personal relationships and unresponsive to the needs of individual employees or stakeholders; they are unwieldy, tending to inflexibility and inertia, often bound by long-term financial and material commitments that are not easy to reverse; they stand (often seek) to gain from monopolies of power and from undue political influence; their size means that if they collapse they may cause huge collateral damage. Consequently, a society relying on very large organisations to provide any essential service (not only banking) is unlikely to be resilient in response to crises.

Big companies do not hold a monopoly on bad behaviour, but their bad behaviour is more dangerous. Moreover, they are more likely to be tempted to behave selfishly and negligently, partly for the reasons I have suggested, and also for the more basic reason that, as our analysis of the Technocratic Paradigm suggests, power corrupts. Any serious thinking about the social changes we need, must, therefore, attend to the question of size.

A related principle of Catholic Social Teaching is subsidiarity, which can be defined as the principle 'according to which decisions and activities that naturally belong at a lower level should not be taken to a higher level' (O'Collins and Farrugia 1991, p. 230). The traditional definition assumes a relatively simple society in which families make up districts and districts towns, towns are part of regions, which are part of countries, which are part of continents and then of the whole globe. Any decision should be made by the smallest possible group capable of making that decision effectively and fairly. However, today's society further involves a complex web of different groups, made possible by modern transport and communications, as the Undergrowth Movement itself illustrates. As well as the idea of 'levels', which does not work for commercial, community or voluntary groups, we need to think also of distributed and interconnected forms of autonomy (within constraints themselves set by the common good). Within these networks, groups need to be free to find their appropriate size, rather than being pushed to grow bigger.[13]Swedish has a word which English perhaps needs to borrow: *lagom*, meaning 'just enough and not too much'. We need to attend to what counts as 'enough and not too much' in many areas of our society, not least the sizes of our collaborative endeavours, whether these are political structures, commercial organisations, settlements, schools, hospitals or voluntary activities.[14] The criteria should be human as much as environmental, with financial considerations relevant only, once again, insofar as money is a useful tool. Here again, though, we cannot rely on the methods of technocracy: checklists or algorithms cannot do our thinking for us, for we are dealing with fine matters of judgement about specific, concrete, complex, organically evolving, places and groups of people. Wendell Berry (1987, pp. 162–178), for example, ponders the question in relation to a family farm, integrating into his judgement the questions of human well-being, ecological flourishing and productive success. Interestingly, our most recent wave of technological innovation, specifically communications technology and alternative energy, provide us with new possibilities for distributed rather than centralised choices. Consequently, for example, the question of whether or not the provision of solar power can safely be left to a small number of very large companies, or whether it is wiser to take advantage of the opportunity of providing a huge number of local communities with a power supply that each owns, should not be left lazily to the result of commercial power-struggles, but squarely faced as a set of political decisions that call for wisdom and good sense.

Such considerations lead us to the questions of what government and political leadership might look like in a society that fosters and encourages the type of small- and middle-sized initiatives that, I have been arguing, will be central to any successful transition to a renewed society. The Undergrowth Movement shows us that we do not need to start from

THE VIRTUES OF THE 'UNDERGROWTH MOVEMENT' 251

scratch. What politics needs to do is first of all to notice the social movement that is already there, and then to link, support and coordinate its groups and projects, and enable them to grow and multiply exponentially. We need a national political system, as well as an ethical culture, that can foster and encourage both the Undergrowth Movement and effective local and regional politics, along with effective interaction among them.

To take such a politics of enablement with full seriousness would require a change in our attitudes, even perhaps in our language, more profound than we might realise. I suggest that we should even rethink the metaphors that come to our lips so easily when thinking of leadership: 'up' and 'down', 'higher' and 'lower'. E. F. Schumacher, in *Good Work*, a book less well known than *Small Is Beautiful* but equally visionary and important for our own time, drew a contrast with two pictures of leadership in a large company. The first was a

> Christmas tree, with the star at the top and all sorts of nuts underneath, more or less nourishing nuts. That is a monolithic organization... one normally looks to the star at the top for initiative, because all the rest are executors of the policy.

The second was

> a chap at a funfair, who in one hand holds hundreds of strings, and at the end of each string a balloon. Each balloon has its own buoyancy, a nice round thing. Of course you need someone to hold it all together, but it is not a star at the top, it is a man underneath and each balloon has its own buoyancy. Each balloon is somehow a limited thing, and thus in a manner of speaking, the more the merrier.
>
> (1979, p. 70)

Schumacher was writing of a single company; to picture a whole society animated by Undergrowth values, we might reimagine his balloon seller, now selling balloons that can intersect, separate and reintersect like bobbing 3-D Venn diagrams. Such an image of society has the intriguing and welcome additional consequence of forcing us to rethink our assumptions about who is important in society. Michael Sandel (2020) has recently argued in theory, and Covid-19 has reminded us forcefully in practice, that there is an urgent need in our divided society to return to ordinary workers the respect and dignity that is their due. Only when power and authority are properly distributed, so that each person is enabled to see the irreplaceable value of his or her contribution to the common good, will we be able to leave behind the sterile and demeaning language of 'winners' and 'losers', 'success' and 'failure', as if all of life were a football league. Other political and social tensions would also be eased: if being 'at the top' (or rather, holding the strings at the bottom) were not particularly important, it would matter much less how many women, or black people, or other kinds of apparently disadvantaged people, are there.

The real work is done by the balloons, which bob around not in competition, but in glorious complementarity. There is no need for a constant anxious sorting of social worth, as everyone is needed in a different way – just as it makes no sense to rank the contributions of the myriad different creatures that contribute to the ecology of a healthy piece of woodland. It may or may not be a coincidence that women play a very significant role in the Undergrowth Movement, from prophets like Greta Thunberg and scholars like Kate Raworth, to the prime ministers of small countries modelling new possibilities like Katrín Jakobsdóttir, to the millions of hard-working lasses who are the mainstay of the majority of voluntary groups. Whatever reasons there may be for this, one consequence at least is that if we consider the Undergrowth to be where most of the important work is being done, there is no question about the influence and impact of women in the world today.

Governing for transition

What would be the tasks of a 'Government for Transition' towards such a society, apart from the basics of ensuring a framework within which citizens are free to act – physical security, honest laws appropriately enforced, a fair and effective system of taxation and finance, and an uncorrupted, able and conscientious civil service and local governments?

The first task, I suggest, is to notice what not to do, and what activities not to encourage. Dave Goulson draws a timely lesson from the healthy maintenance of lawns: 'less is definitely more'. He comments wryly: 'There are many other areas of life in which I would advocate doing less …. Sadly it is hard to make money out of doing less, and it is people getting rich that drives political decisions' (Goulson 2019, p. 27). An obvious example:

THE VIRTUES OF THE 'UNDERGROWTH MOVEMENT' 253

before a government focuses on rewilding and tree-planting, it needs to outlaw all destruction of ancient forest or long-standing wildflower meadows for the purposes of construction (and certainly avoid commissioning or encouraging such construction).

Secondly, government for Transition will need to take note of the good things that are already happening, and ensure that nothing that public bodies do is hampering or harming these. This may sound obvious, but we have numerous examples of such hampering, including various forms of bureaucracy that deter volunteers and many small projects that have collapsed because of the untimely withdrawal of subsidies. These suggest that this basic, unassuming task of noticing is not to be taken for granted.

Thirdly, national governments will need to enable the coordination of the work of local authorities, ethically minded businesses, not-for-profits and charities, churches, community groups and volunteers, which may involve protective regulation, the safeguarding of communications, favourable financial regulations, or possibly the provision of appropriate grants or expertise.

This leads onto the fourth role of government, to support, facilitate the replication of and supplement the relatively unplanned projects and activities of the Undergrowth Movement. This is an area where there ought to be healthy debate as to how far, where, when and at what level and on what time scale, government intervention or initiative is required. Here, it is urgent that we in Britain move beyond our usual polarisation between right and left. What is essential is that decisions about the active role of government in supplementing local authorities and civil society are shaped by appropriate criteria. An intervention should not be chosen for party political or for financial reasons. The question that needs to be asked is, 'Is this important for enabling groups within society to safeguard and foster the common good?' In answering that question, we cannot afford to ignore important insights from any part of the political spectrum. Again take a simple example: Marcus Rashford has been praised for his courageous campaign to provide school meals for hungry children. A Scottish friend of mine, on the other hand, brought up with the independent family values of a traditional farming community, was shocked by the plan to give free meals to all schoolchildren on the grounds that feeding children is the role of parents. The choice between Rashford and my Scottish friend is not one of principle, but of practice.

In emergencies, the state does need to step in to ensure that parents are able to feed their children. A wise state, however, will try to ensure that supportive structures in the longer terms can set parents free to feed their own children with independence and security.[15] In short, I am arguing that law and politics should not function as a jelly-mould, shaping in detail the lives of a flaccid, passive, mass, but as a trellis, in which a small number of strong struts, firmly fixed together and with space between them, enables a luxuriant plant to grow freely between, around and over it. The job of government is to enable us to live our lives, not to live them for us; the job of the more comprehensive sorts of government is to enable the more local sorts to do their job, not to do it for them.

Virtues of political leadership

What type of leaders would such a national government need? I am not asking what they would do, but what sort of character they should have. For just as ordinary people can only consistently commit themselves to greener and fairer lifestyles by exercising the relevant kind of virtues, so good leaders need the virtues appropriate to their task. Although an opportunistic press can be quick to encourage us to blame politicians for specific failings, of act or omission, in fact we have very little lively or detailed public conversation about the personal qualities we would wish our leaders to possess, or how we might nurture and identify leaders of such a kind. Elections tend to be marked by attacks on the integrity of rival candidates rather than by calm and judicious discernment of their strengths, making use of a rich moral vocabulary.

Several factors, not least our adversarial electoral and parliamentary systems, make it difficult to elect political leaders on the basis of their personal virtues. One necessary condition for this, however, is possible to provide: a discussion of what the desirable virtues might be, for a society seeking a radical transition to a more sustainable way of living.

Political leaders will need, for example, the courage to make bold changes to ensure that our financial system is fit for purpose, to hold businesses accountable for the collateral damage they cause, and to ban or tax damaging products to allow alternatives to the commercial space to develop. They will need to act urgently, with great determination and decisiveness. They will need to be energetic and inspiring, to carry a democratic populace with them on a demanding, perhaps self-sacrificial, path of reform. In short, Government for Transition will demand a set of qualities we might label 'heroic'.

At the same time, however, it will call for a contrasting range of gentler virtues, which will be equally crucial. The boldness to act will need to be balanced by the courage to refrain from acting when appropriate and the modesty that enables others to act. Determination, decisiveness and good judgement must go hand in hand with attentive listening, in openness to the creativity and imagination of others. Charisma will have to be complemented by humility in recognising that the most important work will be done – indeed, *is already being done* – on the ground, that the most important gifts are those of 'ordinary' individuals. An inspiring public persona will need to be combined with integrity in a simple lifestyle that will witness to the common good that the leader professes. The urgent desire to tackle problems will need to be integrated with a humble and tolerant recognition that solutions cannot be fixed from the centre, that many projects are already in place (cf. Hawken 2007, 2017) and must not be damaged by interfering control, that attempts to 'scale up' existing initiatives will only succeed if the existing participants are listened to,[16] that the mistakes and false starts inevitable in an innovative system under pressure are opportunities for learning rather than blame. For neither people in society nor creatures in their ecosystems are machines: we cannot press a button to solve our problems, and we cannot be certain of the outcomes of our collective actions, however wisely and generously we engage in them. The hardest but most essential virtues will be patience, hope and trust.

Or perhaps not quite the most essential. The way to the truth, wrote St Augustine in his *Letter* 118, is 'first humility, second humility, third humility'. It is appropriate for our reflections that *humilitas* is derived from *humus*, meaning 'soil'. For if leaders are to focus on the common good and not on their own or their party's fortunes, to welcome with open arms the initiatives and abilities of others, to see themselves as facilitators and enablers not controllers, to be more concerned that someone else can continue their initiatives than that they receive the credit for them, then such leaders will need to be steeped in humility, preceding, accompanying and following, as Augustine put it, every one of their thoughts and actions.[17]

Much of what our leaders will have to do and be will contrast sharply with much recent political behaviour. In place of economic goals that pander to and inflame our feelings and emotions, they will need to encourage us to educate our desires. Instead of indulging the polarised rhetoric of right and left, they will need to embrace creativity and freedom as well as social solidarity, a conservative desire to preserve all that is best in our human traditions with a liberal openness to new possibilities. Rather than succumbing to ever greater speed and superficiality, driven by the fuel and IT giants, they will need to sink themselves into slow and profound thinking. Rejecting the incoherence of relativism and individualism, or the inconsistency of show and spin, they will need a deep integrity of both character and moral vision. Rejecting a political culture of self-promotion, they will need to be firmly rooted in the soil of humility.

Leaders with such a combination of demanding and contrasting qualities are rarely found and all too easily undermined. Like strong trees, they cannot grow in isolation, but will need to be nurtured and supported by a society that fosters, acknowledges, appreciates and encourages their qualities.

Conclusion

In order to meet the multiple challenges ahead of us, we will need new models of society, of politics and of leadership. Where a medieval monk may have spoken of the king as a 'shepherd', our ministers might aspire to become 'gardeners'. At any rate, this new vision of society will be unashamedly ethical, and will need leaders who unashamedly strive to live lives shaped by the virtues. Although leadership will be needed at every level of society, in every size and type of community, from the family outwards, political leaders at the regional, national and international levels will need to possess a challengingly varied combination of virtues.

Personal virtues grow in the soil of virtuous communities – families, schools, circles of friends, neighbourhoods, workplaces, churches and other religious groups, clubs and voluntary organisations. The Undergrowth Movement provides a rich ecosystem for nurturing potential leaders of our Transition Society,[18] as well as suitable examples of the flora and fauna needed to populate it. At a time when it might be easy to despair, here are major reasons for hope. So many of the solutions we need are already being used, so many of the activities we need are already under way, so many of the people we need are already available. Moreover, it is an extraordinary gift that so many different projects, rooted in so many different places and cultures, are converging on compatible, even congruent, goals. This makes sense once we realise that such projects are based, explicitly or implicitly, on a truthful and perceptive understanding of how human beings truly flourish, as persons in relationship with one another, and that our true flourishing, unlike the distorted image of success promoted by a technocratic and profit-driven society, is also in broad outline harmonious with the well-being of the natural world on which we depend. Our planet is neither a random collection of atoms nor a mass of material to be exploited, but a living, breathing, biological home, a patterned network into which we human beings are able to fit, so long as we honour its limits, and our own.[19]

Notes

1 Pope Francis's *Let Us Dream*, which I read after completing this article, shares and develops several of its themes (Francis 2020).
2 One might add 'and traditional communities', but that is a further story (cf. Klein 2015).
3 For a brilliant secular exploration of one effect of this paradigm, see Taylor (2014).
4 I leave it to the reader to ponder whether the non-inclusive language of the original reflects a society which is likely to be too little reflective about the uses of power.
5 Cf. Dunn (2019), pp. 178–183.
6 Berners Lee (2019), for example, in a moderate and hopeful analysis, highlights essential changes in eating and personal travel.
7 https://www.huffpost.com/entry/robert-swan-antarctica_b_1315047?guc-counter=1.
8 Developments in AI and robotics make this question all the more urgent. It is vital that we learn to make decisions about when to use these by considering the importance of safe and fulfilling work in human lives, rather than on the grounds of profit or convenience.
9 For further examples and discussion, as well as Hawken, see also Hopkins (2019), Cottam (2018), Klein (2015), and websites such as those of *The Guardian* Cities, the Wellbeing Economy Alliance and Democracy Collaborative. Murray (2009) was a shrewd early voice of analysis.
10 For a systems analysis of the benefits of a not-for-profit economy, see Hinton (2020).
11 Cf. Goulson (2019), pp. 234–242 on the multiple benefits, not least economic, of allotments.

12 Cf. Taylor (2021a) on the significance of distance for ethical business decisions.

13 Dutch political thinking, shaped by Christian Democracy under the influence of both Catholic Social Teaching and the Dutch Calvinist vision of Abraham Kuyper, emphasises the importance of the *Middenveld*, or 'middle field', 'a "vast network ... of communities of all kinds, ideologies and sizes" between individuals and the state' (Townsend 2015, quoting Fogarty 1995, p. 37).

14 Cf. Dietz and O'Neill (2013)

15 In more scholarly vein, contrast the argument of Roger Scruton (2012), a convinced Conservative, showing where state regulation has favoured big business over local, and more environmentally respectful, enterprises, with those of Mazzucato (2019), arguing for a greater recognition of the economic value of publicly funded initiatives. If we think carefully and patiently, we do not need to make a simple choice between their two sets of important evidence and insights.

16 Cottam (2018), pp. 249-251, offers a warning here.

17 Sandel (2020), pp. 81–85, describes in embarrassing detail the way in which US presidential candidates feel the need to boast about their college records, even to the point of misrepresentation. Note how Katrín Jakobsdóttir ensured that the introduction to Iceland of an economy based on well-being was agreed across the political parties in order to protect its future: https://www.bbc.co.uk/news/av/uk-politics-51928882.

18 Cf. Gregory and Atkins (2021).

19 I am grateful to several friends for responses to an earlier draft of this chapter, in particular to Edward Hadas, whose penetrating comments have greatly helped in reshaping this version.

Bibliography

Aquinas, T. (2005), *Disputed Questions on the Virtues*, (edd. E.M. Atkins and T. Williams). Cambridge: Cambridge UP.

Atkins, E.M. (2003), 'Temperateness, Justice and Chocolate,' *Priests and People*, October 2003; online at jerichotree.com/2015/08/10/living-simply-the-contemporary-relevance-of-the-virtue-of-temperance/.

Atkins, E.M. (2008), 'Passenger Pigeons and Polar Bears: The Ethics of Global Warming,' online at https://www.thinkingfaith.org/articles/20080128_1.htm.

Berners Lee, M. (2019), *There is No Planet B: A Handbook for the Make or Break Years*. Cambridge: Cambridge UP.

Berry, W. (1987), 'Two Economies', *Home Economics*. Berkeley: Counterpoint.

THE VIRTUES OF THE 'UNDERGROWTH MOVEMENT' 259

Blum, L. (1998), 'Community and Virtue', chapter 14 of R. Crisp, (ed.) *How Should One Live? Essays on the Virtues*. Oxford: Oxford UP.

Carney, M. (2020), Reith Lecture 2020: 'From Climate Change to Real Prosperity' online at https://www.bbc.co.uk/sounds/play/mooqkms.

Cottam, H. (2018), *Radical Help: How We Can Remake the Relationships between Us and Revolutionise the Welfare State*. London: Virago.

Deane-Drummond, C. (2017), *A Primer in Ecotheology: Theology for a Fragile Earth*. Eugene: Cascade Books.

Dunn, J. (2019), *Setting the People Free: The Story of Democracy*. Princeton: Princeton UP (2nd edition).

Dietz, R. and O'Neill, D. (2013), *Enough is Enough: Building a Sustainable Economy in a World of Finite Resources*. Oxford: Routledge.

Fogarty, M. (1995), *Phoenix or Cheshire Cat? Christian Democracy Past, Present… and Future?* Ware: Christian Democrat Press.

Francis (Pope Francis) (2015), *Laudato Si': On Care for Our Common Home*, online at www.vatican.va/content/francesco/en/encyclicals/documents/papa-francesco_20150524_enciclica-laudato-si.html.

Francis (Pope Francis) (2020), *Let Us Dream: The Path to a Better Future*. London: Simon & Schuster.

Goulson, D. (2019), *The Garden Jungle: or Gardening to Save the Planet*. London: Vintage.

Gregory, A.J. and Atkins, J.P. (2021), 'Green Shoots: Emergent Systemic Leadership and Critical Systems Practice,' in Taylor (2021b).

Guardini, R. (1998), *The End of The Modern World*. Wilmington: ISI Books.

Hawken, P., (ed.) (2017), *Drawdown: The Most Comprehensive Plan Ever Proposed to Reverse Global Warming*. New York: Penguin.

Hawken, P. (2007), *Blessed Unrest: How the Largest Movement in the World Came into Being and Why No One Saw It Coming*. New York: Viking.

Hilton, S. (2015), *More Human: Designing a World where People Come First*. London: W.H. Allen.

Hinton, J. (2020), Schumacher Lecture 'The Potential of the Not-for-Profit Economy,' online at https//www.youtube.com/watch?v=EMtpZ4EyNuM.

Hopkins, R. (2019), *What Is to What If: Unleashing the Power of Imagination to Create the Future we Want*. London: Chelsea Green Publishing.

Klein, N. (2015), *This Changes Everything*. UK: Penguin 2015.

MacIntyre, A. (1981), *After Virtue: A Study in Moral Theory*. London: Duckworth.

Mazzucato, M. (2019), *The Value of Everything: Making and Taking in the Global Economy*. London: Penguin.

Murray, R. (2009), *Danger and Opportunity: Crisis and the New Social Economy*. London: Nesta.

O'Collins, G., S.J. and Farrugia, E.G., S.J. (1991), *A Concise Dictionary of Theology*. Edinburgh: T & T Clark.

Ratzinger, J. (Pope Benedict XVI) (2002), *Truth and Tolerance: Christian Belief and World Religions*. San Francisco: Ignatius.

Raworthy, K. (2017), *Doughnut Economics*. London: Penguin Random House.

Sacks, J. (2020), *Morality: Restoring the Common Good in Divided Times*. London: Hodder & Stoughton.

Sandel, M. (2020), *The Tyranny of Merit*. London: Penguin Random House.

Sayer, A. (2016), *Why we Can't Afford the Rich*. Bristol: Polity Press.

Taylor, A. (2021a), 'Stewardship and Strategy in Turbulent Times,' in Taylor (2021b).

Taylor, A. (ed.) (2021b), *Rethinking Leadership for a Green World*. Oxford: Routledge.

Taylor, M.C. (2014), *Speed Limits: Where Time Went and Why we Have So Little Left*. New Haven and London: Yale UP.

Townsend, N. (2015), *Blue Labour + Red Tory = Christian Democracy?* in Ethics in Brief Series. Cambridge: Kirby Laing Institute for Christian Ethics.

12

THE 'INTERESTING' CASE OF EU COMMISSION LEADERSHIP AND THE EMISSION TRADING SCHEME

Vanessa Oakes and Adam Bronstone

Like a sports car that can go from 0 to 100 miles an hour in 10 seconds flat, so too did it appear that the European Union, and primarily the EU Commission, found religion when it came to developing a 'green' footprint before Kyoto. The development of the Commission as a friend and not a foe of environmental policy is a study in leadership – of taking advantage of an opportunity not for a greater sense of mission, but because it was, and remains, the right thing to do. The interesting case of Commission leadership and the establishment, development, maintenance, expansion of success of the Emissions Trading Scheme is, clearly, interesting.

Europe's Green New Deal

In 2019 the European Union launched its 'Green New Deal'. In an announcement that took place on 11 December 2019, Ursula von der Leyen, the president of the European Commission, committed the EU to achieving a climate-neutral economy by 2050. The goal of the EU is to leave no citizen

DOI: 10.4324/9781003190820-15

of the EU behind as the organisations seek to 'reconcile the economy with our planet' and 'to make it work for our people'. The president continued by stating that she is 'convinced that the old growth model based on fossil fuels and pollution is out of date and out of touch with our planet' (Smyth, 2019).

The Green New Deal has several sub-goals, which include the objective of a climate-neutral continent by 2050, a re-imagining of the economy to one that is 'circular', where the manufacturing of products in a sustainable manner is a key ingredient, as well as funds for the renovation of existing buildings, a commitment to biodiversity, a farm-to-fork strategy, clean transportation, funds for innovation in clean technology and an external relations component to this commitment.

The main points in the Commission plan are:

1. **'Climate-neutral' Europe**. This is the overarching objective of the European Green Deal. The EU will aim to reach net-zero greenhouse gas emissions by 2050, a goal that will be enshrined in a 'climate law' to be presented in March 2020.

   That means updating the EU's climate ambition for 2030, with a 50–55% cut in greenhouse gas emissions to replace the current 40% objective. The 55% figure will be subject to a cost–benefit analysis.

   The Commission wants to leave no stone unturned and plans to review every EU law and regulation in order to align them with the new climate goals. This will start with the Renewable Energy Directive and the Energy Efficiency Directive, but also the Emissions Trading Directive and the Effort Sharing Regulation, as well as the infamous LULUCF directive dealing with land use change. Proposals there will be submitted as part of a package in March 2021.

   A plan for 'smart sector integration', bringing together the electricity, gas and heating sectors closer together 'in one system', will be presented in 2020. This will come with a new initiative to harness 'the enormous potential' of offshore wind, officials said.

2. **Circular economy**. A new circular economy action plan will be tabled in March 2020, as part of a broader EU industrial strategy. It will include a sustainable product policy with 'prescriptions on how we make things' in order to use fewer materials, and ensure products can be reused and recycled. Carbon-intensive industries like steel, cement

and textiles, will also focus the attention under the new circular economy plan. One key objective is to prepare for 'clean steelmaking' using hydrogen by 2030, an EU official said. 'Why 2030? Because if you want clean industry in 2050, 2030 is the last investment cycle', he said. New legislation will also be presented in 2020 to make batteries reusable and recyclable.

3. **Building renovation**. This is meant to be one of the flagship programmes of the Green Deal. The key objective there is to 'at least double or even triple' the renovation rate of buildings, which currently stands at around 1%.

4. **Zero-pollution**. Whether in air, soil or water, the objective is to reach a 'pollution-free environment' by 2050. New initiatives there include a chemical strategy for a 'toxic-free environment'.

5. **Ecosystems and biodiversity**. A new biodiversity strategy will be presented in March 2020, in the run-up to a UN biodiversity summit taking place in China in October. 'Europe wants to lead by example with new measures to address the main drivers of biodiversity loss', an EU official said. That includes measures to tackle soil and water pollution as well as a new forest strategy. 'We need more trees in Europe', the official said, both in cities and in the countryside. New labelling rules will be tabled to promote deforestation-free agricultural products.

6. **Farm to fork strategy**. To be tabled in Spring 2020, the new strategy will aim for a 'green and healthier agriculture' system. This includes plans to 'significantly reduce the use of chemical pesticides, fertilisers and antibiotics', an EU official said. New national strategic plans due to be submitted next year by member-states under the Common Agricultural Policy will be scrutinised to see whether they are aligned with the objectives of the Green Deal.

7. **Transport**. One year after the EU agreed new CO2 emission standards for cars, the automotive sector is once again in the Commission's firing line. The current objective is to reach 95gCO2/km by 2021. Now, 'we need to work towards zero', sometime in the 2030s, an EU official said.

Electric vehicles will be further encouraged with an objective of deploying 1 million public charging points across Europe by 2025. 'Every family in Europe needs to be able to drive their electric car without having to worry about the next charging station', the official explained.

'Sustainable alternative fuels' – biofuels and hydrogen – will be promoted in aviation, shipping and heavy-duty road transport where electrification is currently not possible.

8. **Money**. To 'leave no-one behind', the Commission proposes a 'Just Transition Mechanism' to help regions most heavily dependent on fossil fuels. 'We have the ambition to mobilise €100 billion precisely targeted to the most vulnerable regions and sectors', said von der Leyen as she presented the Green Deal on Wednesday.

The proposed €100bn instrument has three legs:

- A just transition fund that will mobilise resources from the EU's regional policy budget;
- The 'InvestEU' programme, with money coming from the European Investment Bank;
- EIB funding coming from the EU bank's own capital.

Every euro spent from the fund could be complemented by two or three euros coming from the region. EU's state aid guidelines will be reviewed in that context so that national governments are able to directly support investments in clean energy, with blessing from the Commission's powerful competition directorate.

Regions will also be offered technical assistance in order to help them 'absorb' the funds while respecting the EU's strict spending rules.

However, any state aid would have to be vetted by the Commission as part of new regional transition plans submitted beforehand to Brussels.

9. **R&D and innovation**. With a proposed budget of €100bn over the next seven years (2021–2027), the Horizon Europe research and innovation programme will also contribute to the Green Deal. 35% of the EU's research funding will be set aside for climate-friendly technologies under an agreement struck earlier this year. And a series of EU research 'moonshots' will focus chiefly on environmental objectives.

10. **External relations**. Finally, EU diplomatic efforts will be mobilised in support of the Green Deal. One measure likely to attract attention – and controversy – is a proposal for a carbon border tax. As Europe

increases its climate ambitions, 'we expect the rest of the world to play its role too', an EU official explained. But if not, Europe is 'not going to be naïve', and will protect its industry against unfair competition, he added. To lead by example, the EU Commission itself will aim for climate neutrality by 2030 (European Union, 2021).

The European Union Emissions Trading Scheme (ETS)

During the announcement of the Green New Deal, the president also mentioned that existing directives would be subject to a review, including the Renewable Energy Directive, the Energy Efficiency Directive and the long-standing Emissions Trading Directive, which assisted in the establishment of the European Trading Scheme (ETS). The ETS began in 2005 as the first large greenhouse gas emissions trading scheme, with the goal of reducing emissions throughout the EU member-states, as a pillar of the EU's energy policy.

In brief, under the 'cap and trade' principle, a maximum (cap) is set on the total amount of greenhouse gases that can be emitted by all participating installations. EU Allowances for emissions are then auctioned off or allocated for free and can subsequently be traded. Installations must monitor and report their CO_2 emissions, ensuring they hand in enough allowances to the authorities to cover their emissions. If emission exceeds what is permitted by its allowances, an installation must purchase allowances from others. Conversely, if an installation has performed well at reducing its emissions, it can sell its leftover credits. This ability to sell credits allows the system to find the most cost-effective ways of reducing emissions without significant government intervention (European Union, EU ETS Manual, 2021).

The scheme has been divided into several 'trading periods'. The first ETS trading period lasted three years, from January 2005 to December 2007 and it is well-known that this phase, since this was the first trading scheme of its kind, was considered a 'learning phase'. The second trading period ran from January 2008 until December 2012, coinciding with the first commitment period of the Kyoto Protocol. The third trading period began in January 2013 and will span until December 2020. Finally, Phase 4, the phase of this program which is taking place at the time of the writing of this work, was revised in 2018 to enable the ETS program to match the emission targets of the EU as agreed in the Paris Agreement. The revised plan includes a focus on:

> Strengthening the EU ETS as an investment driver by increasing the pace of annual reductions in allowances to 2.2% as of 2021 and reinforcing the Market Stability Reserve (the mechanism established by the EU in 2015 to reduce the surplus of emission allowances in the carbon market and to improve the EU ETS's resilience to future shocks).

Continuing the free allocation of allowances as a safeguard for the international competitiveness of industrial sectors at risk of carbon leakage, while ensuring that the rules for determining free allocation are focused and reflect technological progress.

Helping industry and the power sector to meet the innovation and investment challenges of the low-carbon transition via several low-carbon funding mechanisms (see European Union, 'Revisions', 2021).

At present...

As of 2020, ETS operates in all EU countries plus Iceland, Liechtenstein and Norway and limits emissions from more than 11,000 heavy energy-using installations (power stations and industrial plants) and airlines operating between these countries. The scheme covers around 40% of the EU's greenhouse gas emissions. Further, the EU Emissions Trading System has proven to be an effective tool in driving emissions reductions cost-effectively. Emissions from installations covered by the ETS declined by about 35% between 2005 and 2019. The introduction of the Market Stability Reserve in 2019 has, also, led to a higher and more robust carbon price, which helped to ensure a year-on-year total emissions reduction of 9% in 2019, with a reduction of 14.9% in electricity and heat production and a 1.9% reduction in industry. Finally, the EU ETS is also inspiring the development of emissions trading in other countries and regions. The EU aims to link the EU ETS with other compatible systems (European Union, ETS, 2021b).

Criticisms and concerns

There is no doubt that along with the introduction of the ETS, has come criticisms of the plan from both environmentalists and the business community. These complaints concerned the presence of an over-allocation of credits, windfall profits for companies who used these credits, price volatility and, in general, an inability to meet stated goals. The response, as noted above, has been that the first phase of the ETS was a learning one, and perfection was never expected, and there was also an inevitable learning curve in the corporate world, and this learning curve lends itself to the lack of success in the reduction of emissions in relation to initial goals.

A possibly much more important criticism has come from the environmental community. In 2009, the World Wildlife Fund asserted that there was no indication that the ETS had influenced longer-term investment decisions. In a co-edited paper of the same year, a like-minded argument was posited insofar that, when examining the responses from the EU's Community Innovation Survey, changes in corporate thinking with respect to energy efficiency and reducing the environmental impact of manufacturing processes was ranked the lowest in the area of innovation motivation. Having said this, in a survey of research conducted in this area of research in 2013 (four years after the WWF comment), it was concluded by the authors of the study that there has been 'some impact ... on investment and innovation', but that this impact has been and will continue to be dependent on the stringency of the scheme – the more stringent the scheme, the greater the need to invest in innovation (Laing, 2014). The rationale for even looking at this aspect of the ETS is because a key objective of the scheme, alongside that of lowering carbon emissions, was to impact

> decision-making regarding low-carbon technologies. Along with driving short-term switching between fuel types, by setting a price on carbon, the intention is to drive innovation in new low-carbon technologies, incentivise additional investment in low[1]carbon assets, and reduce investment in carbon-intensive products and processes'.
>
> (Ibid.)

At the time of the writing of this piece, at least one expert is of the belief that innovation will increase for two reasons. The first reason is that the price of carbon trading has increased significantly from where it began at the outset of the program, and this increase will make inefficient plants too costly to maintain. The second reason being is that, finally, there are substantial funds being set aside for industrial innovation (see the details of the Green New Deal), which will encourage companies under the umbrella of the

ETS to innovate (Personal Interview, 2021). Finally, and in hand with these developments, a 2020 study estimated that the EU ETS had reduced CO_2 emissions by more than 1 billion tonnes between 2008 and 2016 or 3.8% of total EU-wide emissions (EU, Progress made in cutting emissions, 2021).

Leadership, leadership and leadership

This piece, however, as is the entire edited work, is about leadership, and in particular, leadership as it relates to green issues. This piece, while one could become 'bogged down' in the very details of the ETS with respect to carbon emission amounts overall, and per industry, and which country is doing better than other EU member-states, is not about the scheme itself, per se. This piece is focused on when did the EU become interested in green issues; when did the EU become interested in leading in the area of green issues; why did the EU become interested in acting as a global leader; what are the implications for this leadership; and, finally, what does all of the above tell us with respect to leadership and green policy.

The Single European Market

The role of the European Union in environmental policy predates the establishment of the ETS by decades, with the agreement to establish a Single European Market (SEM) in 1987. By understanding that climate-related issues impacted the whole of the EU, Jos Delbeke comments that 'it is not surprising that decisions on environmental policy were pushed to the European level ... [since] pollution often extends beyond borders' (p. 9). Delbeke gives examples of discharges into the Rhine, Meuse and Danube rivers may impact several EU member-states, and the same is true of acid rain caused by coal-fired power stations in Britain damaging forests in Scandinavian countries. Further, with competition becoming European-wide because of the SEM, it was deemed 'better that the EU adopt rules to protect the environment at European level, thereby minimizing the risk of distortions of competition with the EU's internal market' (ibid., p. 10). With these comments, Delbeke gives us insight into the twin pillars of EU-level environment policy – one being environmental/societal, and the other being economic. These two pillars will remain prevalent throughout this discussion.

Next phase of policy

In 1992, the EU Commission proposed the creation of a combined carbon and energy tax, as the next step in European-wide climate policy. This proposal failed, not because of its merits, but instead because of issues related to sovereignty, and how much power EU-level institutions should have on issues such as this, as compared to the individual member-states.

In light of this failure, the idea of an emission cap came to the forefront because of the introduction of this idea by the United States in international settings by way of the Kyoto negotiations process, and the inclusion of sulphur and other emission controls into the Kyoto Protocol itself. This elevation of climate issues to the international level, for Debekle, made the leadership of the EU realise that 'setting a limit on the total amount of emissions is truly an environmental benefit' (ibid., p. 10). This hesitancy on the part of the EU to more than dip its collective toes in the environmental policy water is not a new comment. Other scholars tracking EU environmental actions have at times characterised the EU as a 'fiend' when it came to emissions trading (see Damro and Mendez, 2012), especially because it took years and years for the EU to adopt a carbon tax strategy and then, it was less than two years' worth of time from the starting point of conversations about a trading scheme to the implementation of the same scheme. Nonetheless, what is apparent is the presence of the twin pillars of the rationale for this approach. In 2001, the then EC Commissioner for the Environment, Margot Wallström, commented that the rationale for EU-wide action (in comparison to member-state action) was to reduce emissions, and do so in a 'cost effective' manner (Wettestad, p. 1). This economic imperative is echoed by much earlier comments by the EC Commissioner for the Environment, Bjerregaard, who stated in 1998 that 'we (the EU) have to get involved in emissions trading [because] we cannot let others dictate the rules' (ibid., p. 3). Nonetheless, environmental groups have asserted that 'the EU emissions trading scheme looks set to be one of the most far-reaching and radical environmental policies for many years' (ibid., p. 2). Finally, and most important for the purposes of this conversation, Wettestand is the extremely strong role that the EU Commission has played throughout this time period in the development, implementation and maintenance of the trading scheme. It is this 'conundrum', as Wettestad calls it, that we will focus the balance of the energy of this chapter.

The European Commission and environmental leadership

It is well-known that, amongst the four primary institutions of the European Union, that the only entity that has the authority to initiate legislation is the Commission. This, of course, is of interest given the non-democratic nature of the Commission which is, to be honest, the bureaucracy of the European Union, in comparison to the European parliament, whose members are elected through democratic voting and the Council, which is where the heads of state of the member-states sit and make overall policy decisions. Nonetheless, as remarked above, attempts at policies such as a carbon tax failed at the EU level because of member-state concerns of a loss of sovereignty in this area of policy. If this was true, and there is no reason to doubt these reports, then how did the Commission manage to take control of a policy area that led to a substantial directive, in an area where such power had not been granted in the past?

Reasons for leading

Wettestad will contend that the 'strong entrepreneurial role of the Commission' may explain much with respect to the ability of the Commission to take ownership of this issue and therefore act quickly and decisively (ibid., p. 2). The question is why did, in the area of environmental policy, the Commission show such strong leadership?

Jos Delbeke, a senior Commission figure during this time period in the area of the environment, contends that there was an interest by the Commission to fill the gaps in the area of environmental policy that remained because of the what was and was not mentioned in the Treaty of Rome, the founding document of the now European Union. The Treaty of Rome accounted for coal and steel, in part because at the time coal and steel were the dominant materials of the day and were the then materials of war. The rationale for the Treaty in the 1950s was to ensure that war between European countries would be too costly, and one way of making that so was to supra-nationalise the production of coal and steel. In truth, coal and steel were perceived not in an environmental, but rather war-related manner. The Treaty of Maastricht was a significant upgrade on the Treaty of Rome and, as one example, included elements of environmental policy. The door for the Commission to be engaged in the initiation of environmental proposals was for the first time, since 1958, open.

THE 'INTERESTING' CASE OF THE EU COMMISSION 271

However, there was a caveat to this role, which was a key reason why the initial idea of a carbon tax failed. Financial matters within the EU are, at the level of the Council of Ministers, only agreed to on the basis of unanimity. Delbeke comments that it was on this basis that an alternative, which was designed to not be, and not even be seen, as a tax, was initiated (Delbeke, 2020). Even with the need for only a qualified majority, the process was not straightforward. As noted above, the EU was considered a 'foe' rather than a 'friend' on environmental issues, and the lack of desire to see an American-like sulphur cap-and-trade scheme included in the text of the Kyoto Protocols is an example of this assertion. However, and with great irony, the sulphur scheme never became part of an international agreement because Kyoto was never ratified by the United States (the US Senate was never going to agree to a perceived loss of sovereignty and thus the agreement was never voted on for ratification). With a 'hole' apparent, the EU agreed, and fairly quickly, to the alternative, that being the ETS, for several reasons. A first was that this was not a tax, and thus unanimity was not required from the Council of Ministers. Second, the directive allowed for member-state flexibility, which decreased the ability of member-states to complain about their loss of sovereignty. Third, while agreement was required amongst the member-states, the reductions were required of companies and not countries. Finally, and again as mentioned above, the EU leadership saw an opportunity to lead and set the rules of the cap-and-trade 'game' globally instead of having to follow. By leading, EU companies could, potentially, be always at an advantage in comparison to their competitors from other markets.

Do the above explanations fully make sense of the Commission's so-called 'extraordinary behavior' in the area of environmental policy? Or should we also add in that the president of the EC at that time, Jacque Delors, appeared to want to position himself as important as the heads of the member-states themselves and saw this, finally, as an opening that could not be missed? (Delors, 1990).

In speaking with and listening to former EC Commission staff involvement in the development of the ETS program, and with respect to the 'extraordinary' of the Commission, it would appear that these officials never saw their work as being anything but doing the so-called 'nuts and bolts' of the regular work of the Commission, and especially in light of three developments during that time period. The first development was that the Single European Market was still in its developing stage, and primarily as a commercial market. The signature components of the SEM were, at that time, the four freedoms of capital, goods, money persons and to establish and provide services. These freedoms had not yet been fully developed, and standards across the entirety of the EU were required in many areas of policy so that these freedoms could not only exist, but also allow these opportunities to take place for the citizens of the EU. A second development was, and as it related then to the standardisation of policy, that there were national emissions markets being created in countries such as Denmark and the United Kingdom. This process has begun, but in a sporadic and uneven manner. A third development was the Kyoto Protocol, and in two areas of the document. The first was the inclusion within the agreement of a sulphur emissions market process by the United States, as mentioned above. A second new initiative was included in Article 17, which allows countries that have emission units to spare to sell this excess capacity to countries that are over their targets. An emissions market was being introduced, and for EC Commission staff, a 'door' has been opened with respect to this issue that they could take positive advantage of for the benefit of the environment, if done properly and across the EU so that a standard was present and no country (or company) would be able to cheat and have an unfair advantage. These officials were not there to create a policy that would lead to some higher degree of political union or serve as the next Monnet or Schumann. They acted in what they saw was a logical manner within the context of environmental policy, given the current European and international political happenings and what would be the most efficient way to deliver this policy, especially in light of the lack of agreement among member-states on the ill-fated carbon tax.

There is one wrinkle to this story of the Commission doing the work that it was meant to do – to create a level playing field between member-states and actors within these member-states so that the Single European Market, as conceived, could be fully operational and to the benefit of every actor within the European Union. The wrinkle, and also alluded before, was the leadership of Jacque Delors. Delors, as the then EC President, had ambitions for 'Europe' and the EC Commission, given its authority to initiate legislation and, possibly, the at the time weakness of other institutions such as the European Parliament. These ambitions were no secret, as Delors spoke and wrote about these ambitions on a regular basis (Delors, 1990). While not having the same grand thoughts, Commission officials did intimate that their work was inspired by Delors and his vision for the Commission and the European Union. However, the same officials did revert back to the belief that, at the end, and with respect to the ETS program, that they were plugging a hole that required plugging and doing the 'nuts and bolts' detailed work that Commission staff was expected to do on a daily basis in the area of environmental policy, and every other area of policy that fell under the umbrella of the Commission.

Finally, one might say that the ETS program was, as a microcosm of the work taking place on environmental policy at the Commission was extraordinary in that this work was a break from past environmental work of the Commission, but *not* extraordinary in that the Commission staff were trying to do what they were there to do – fully implement the wishes of the council by filling the holes of the new internal market, so as to make the European Union a single market with a level playing field so that the four freedoms could be exercises by the citizens of the EU and simultaneously reduce carbon emissions in both the short and long term.

Leadership and the ETS

It would be useful at this juncture, before assessing the nature of the leadership of the EC Commission in the area of environmental policy (and in specific the ETS program), to reflect on 'leadership' as a quality and what is found in the literature on this subject.

If we look to recognised definitions of leadership in the context of international regime analysis, we find a number of authors who have commented on the 'modes' and 'styles' of leadership required to achieve results in a supranational organisation such as the European Union. Young (1991) prefers to focus on individuals who make a difference 'who endeavour to solve or circumvent the collective action problems that plague the efforts of parties seeking to reap joint gains in processes of institutional bargaining'. Underdal (1994) widens this definition to include institutions, defining it as an 'asymmetrical relationship of influence, where one actor guides or directs the behaviour of others towards a certain goal over a certain period of time'. Underdal (1994) further developed this definition by identifying four main qualifications: (1) that it is 'a relationship between leader and followers'; (2) that it is seen as 'associated with collective pursuit of some common or joint purpose'. Underdal (1994) also implies here that leaders are to exert 'positive influence'; (3) leadership cannot be forced or cooperation coerced, there must be 'a platform of shared values, interests and beliefs; and (4) finally, for a relationship to qualify as leadership 'it must be a fairly consistent pattern of interaction extending throughout a period of time'. Through examining the design, development and implementation of the ETS, most of these requirements are evident in some way, as this section will go on to show.

In their work on the relationship between leadership and cooperation in international climate change mitigation policy, Saul and Seidel (2011) compare the models of leadership identified by influential researchers of their time, which could contribute to the successful development and implementation of new legislative policy; predominantly the work of Young (1989, 1991), Underdal (1991, 1994) and Malnes (1995) are examined. These authors all recognise that leadership is characterised by specific intentions (outcomes) and specific means (method of achieving the outcome). The effective leader intends to contribute to the solving of the problem himself, and intends for others to participate in solving it too. On the topic of 'means', Saul and Seidel (2011) identify five 'leadership modes' which portray different leadership behaviours; these 'modes' call on the work of Young (1989, 1991), Underdal (1991, 1994) and Malnes (1995). The 'modes' will be used as a general structure for the remainder of this section, to examine the literature in respect of the likelihood that these leadership modes were employed in the design, development, and bringing-to-life of the ETS. See Table 12.1.

Saul and Seidel (2011) identify 'unilateral leadership' as a prominent leadership mode and suggest that it concerns the extent to which a leader sets a good example in solving collective problems. They recognise that

Table 12.1 Leadership modes in the account of Saul and Seidel (2011), Young (1991), Underdal (1994) and Malnes (1995)

Saul and Seidel (2011)	Young (1991)	Underdal (1994)	Malnes (1995)
Unilateral	–	Unilateral	Directional
Structural	Structural	Coercive	Threats and offers
Problem-solving	Entrepreneurial	Instrumental	Problem-solving
Intellectual	Intellectual	–	Directional
Institutional	–	–	–

this type of leader must formulate his own goals to solve the problem, demonstrating credibility in the process; he must 'elaborate and implement instruments (funding, technologies)' and finally, actually achieve the goals he sets out to. Underdal (1994) suggests that the main capability required for this leadership mode is a 'dominant position within the system in question'. Skodvin and Andresen (2006) argue that the EU satisfies the criterion for this type of leadership only in that it has been the most dominant player in the climate change negotiations, following the 1997 withdrawal of the United States from the Kyoto Protocol. They argue that this is the only way in which the European Union represents any leadership mode at all being 'predominantly based on self-interest, and therefore represents a (low cost) course of behaviour it is likely to have pursued anyway'. However, they strive to point out that whether a 'specific course of behaviour is categorised as leadership may be crucially dependant on when the assessment is made' and as Andresen and Agrawala (2002) are equally critical of the leadership of the EU just before and during the Kyoto negotiations, stating that

> while the EU has been a constant pusher in terms of negotiating positions and rhetoric, its leadership performance has been much less impressive. It may have served as a directional leader in pushing for numbers, but has been lacking in instrumental leadership.

The importance of instrumental leadership (or entrepreneurial leadership, Young 1991) here referring to the 'energy an actor brings to bear on the problem' Underdal (1994). Skodvin and Andresen (2006) identify that some leadership modes are primarily linked to states or other organisational entities, those whose structures support and facilitate cooperation, and whose capabilities cannot be held by individuals, but entrepreneurial leadership (or problem-solving leadership, Saul and Seidel, 2011, Malnes 1995) is a leadership mode primarily linked to individuals, even though the source of this leadership may be drawn from positional status, 'the individual's personal leadership capabilities seem to be a determinant of success' (Skodvin and Andresen, 2006).

The structural leadership mode identified by Saul and Seidel (2011) is characterised by the 'carrot and stick' approach. In the case of the ETS, this would only be relevant if the Commission had substantial power in themselves, to wield over member-states. Structural leadership is more likely to be wielded by other member-states upon each other through sanctions on those unwilling to cooperate or incentives and compensations (for instance, additional development aid) for those willing to cooperate. It is probably fair to rule out structural leadership as a mobilising driver for the ETS as the EC was not in a position to coerce or manipulate, rather to find reasons for member-states to choose to cooperate of their own accord.

The most identifiable leadership mode at play in this state of affairs is 'problem-solving' or 'entrepreneurial leadership', with a leader requiring effective negotiation skills, and the ability to mediate where conflict is apparent. Young (1991) defines an entrepreneurial leader as one who 'relies on negotiation skill to frame issues in ways that foster integrative bargaining' and Underdal (1994) also identifies that entrepreneurialism could relate to how the problem is framed 'one actor's guidance is accepted by others either because they become convinced about the (substantive) merits of the specific diagnosis he offers or the "cure" he prescribes'.

Following the successful adoption of the ETS scheme in 2003, the EC were quick to claim credit for their 'major innovation in environmental policy in Europe' (Wallström, European Commission, 2001a, cited in Wettestad, 2005). As previously identified, what was unusual about the development of this particular policy instrument was that initially the EU were resistant to the idea that emissions trading could be a viable option and secondly, that the turnaround from directive proposal to adoption was less than two years. Wettestad (2005) suggests that it is the strong entrepreneurial role played by the European Commission which may explain both of these factors. He also suggests that certain characteristics of ET systems; it's complexity and high uncertainty, may have provided the basis for the Commission to exert instrumental leadership (Underdal, 1994). The Commission was ideally located to learn from the systems that had gone before and ensure that theirs would be fit-for-purpose on a supranational level. The DG ENV, led by Josh Delbeke and others were able to 'sell' the emissions trading system to other DGs as a mechanism for 'reconciling EU economic and environmental goals' (Wettestad, 2005), creating strong internal coherence. The Commission also demonstrated entrepreneurship in the sequence of events – first proposing the emissions trading system in 2001, but postponing the most difficult discussion, about the level of national caps, to the follow-up process whilst bringing the discussion of the allocation method, likely to be a lot less contentious, to the fore in the initial stages. Latterly in the process, the pressure which the Commission found itself under to reach consensus amongst member-states, to retain its credibility as an effective policymaker, may have heightened the attention to speeding up the decision-making process.

In his work in determining the conditions for success in international cooperation, Moravcsik (1999) recognises that the Commission displays leadership behaviour informally, and that the lack of formal power leads them to use influence and persuasion to effect cooperation between member-states – referring to them as 'informal political entrepreneurs'. Cox (1996, cited in Moravcsik, 1999) stated that 'the quality of executive leadership may prove to be the most critical single determinant of the growth in scope and authority of international organisation' Moravcsik (1999) goes on to define the most important 'tool' of this type of leadership, being persuasion, consists of 'informal agenda-setting', mediation – intervening in interstate negotiations to propose new options or compromises and, finally, mobilisation of domestic social support so that agreements obtain democratic support through public channels. This final condition of the power of informal political entrepreneurs was not easily identifiable in the case of the development and implementation of the ETS, though strong support for the development of climate change policy could be found domestically, and could be harnessed as a means for achieving democratic agreement.

Another leadership mode suggested by Saul and Seidel (2011) which could explain the leadership role filled by the EC, 'intellectual leadership', identifies the need for the leader to employ cognitive abilities to solve a problem. In the case of the Commission as an organisation, this is related to the suggestions by Ellinas and Suleiman (2012), that the legitimacy of the Commission derives from its technical expertise in this case, in the realm of climate change policy, which member-states may not have the resources to develop. Delbeke and Vis (2015) recognise that in EU policy-making, there are often conflicting economic interests at stake, requiring a high level of both transparency and 'explicit analyses of costs and benefits to society' allowing decision-makers to take an evidence-based view. They also highlight the importance of 'active engagement with stakeholders', problem-solving leadership (Saul and Seidel, 2011), entrepreneurial leadership (Young, 1991), demonstrating that the employment of more than one leadership mode at the same time is both helpful in achieving cooperation, but imperative in achieving the required objectives.

The final leadership mode identified by Saul and Seidel (2011) as required in climate change mitigation policy is 'institutional leadership', a mode not previously recognised in the literature but one that is vital in enabling cooperation either through financial support or other support mechanisms, present only in the structure of the establishment that is the European Union, and its institutions. This role is most notable in the European Council (as suggested by Beach and Smeets, 2020) as 'control room' in the complex multilateral negotiations between many parties.

Leadership as a concept has always been difficult to pin down. It is usually the context in which the leadership is played out, the main players involved and the attitude to resolving or addressing a particular issue which can give the greatest clues about the type and effectiveness of the leadership behaviour at work. In the case of the EC and the implementation of the ETS, yes, there were enabling factors, such as the leadership from above who effectively gave 'permission' for a different approach, there were enabling factors in the member-states, such as those who were devising their own emissions trading programmes and those who were highly supportive and there was a compelling imperative by all involved to do something to tackle the problem of reducing emissions. All of these enabling factors moved things forward in some way but the EC, through their 'behind-the-scenes' leadership, were instrumental in pulling together the relevant strands, packaging them into something which member-states would accept and support and moved the EU a step further towards their Kyoto Protocol commitment.

Summary

What does the above examination of the EU's ETS program tell us, with respect to 'leadership in the area of environmental policy'? The authors of this paper would submit that one can take away several thoughts from the above research: these take-aways include:

On environmental issues like and dissimilar to other areas of policy — because there are interest groups both for and against such policies, leadership is required for decisive action to take place, as was seen because of the failure of the carbon tax proposal, which died on the altar of member-state sovereignty.

There will be external critics of such a policy, including business, academic and environmental. Again, this is also another reason why decisive leadership, by the one entity in the EU organisational structure that has the authority and power to lead, was so important in the move from proposal to implementation of ETS program.

It is common that environmental policy is agreed to for not always altruistic 'we should save the planet' reasons. For the leadership of the EU there were several reasons, including economic, trade-related, rule-setting and environmental ones. The first three do not invalidate the fact that the policy was established and carbon emission levels have and continue to decrease over time across the European Union.

The fact that the policy is not a complete success – that it took time to implement properly; that there were challenges along the way with the pricing; and that businesses still do not fully embrace 'green' issues in corporate policy as hoped for does not mitigate the success of the ETS program, from the fact of its implementation to its continued existence.

Leadership takes many forms. What we see within the context of the ETS program and the EC Commission is an organisation that, according to those who studied the EC and environmental policy historically, was not present with respect to environmental policy and being a leading entity in this policy area, and then became so over time within the European context and also globally.

Finally, this newfound leadership fits within the literature regarding 'leadership', as spoken above and, while there are people who have speculated why the EC acted in the way it did and when it did, we may not ever be completely sure as to the reasons. What one does know is that the EC acted in a way that has brought about a 'game changing' scheme with respect to carbon emissions that has reduced emissions throughout the EU and set the standard for such programs globally, in a way that no other country or entity had done previously or since the inception of the ETS.

Conclusion

The European Trading Scheme in carbon emissions is not perfect. It is, however, a scheme that has caused carbon emissions to be lowered and action taken beyond that of the European Union in the same area of environmental concern and stewardship. It is also a scheme that was borne out of EU member-state inaction, and when Commission staff saw an opportunity for an alternative plan, they seized the moment and created a program where none existed before, forged ahead, learned from their early steps and set a new international standard. It is evident that in this area of environmental policy, leadership by thinking creatively and boldly was clearly on display from those who consider themselves not the missionary thinking of political union, but by those who do the 'nuts and bolts' of Europe.

Bibliography

Andresen, S., and Agrawala, S. (2002), 'Leaders, Pushers and Laggards in the Making of Climate Regime', *Global Environmental Change* 12, pp.41–51.

Beach, D., and Smeets, S. (2020), 'New Institutionalist Leadership – How the New European Council-dominated Crisis Governance Paradoxically Strengthened the Role of EU Institutions', *Journal of European Integration* 42(6), pp.837–854.

Damro, C., and Mendez, P. (2012), Emissions Trading at Kyoto: From EU Resistance to Union Innovation', *Environmental Policy in the EU* 12(2), pp.271–294.

Delbeke J., and Vis, P. (2015), 'EU's Leadership in a Rapidly Changing World', in J. Delbeke, and P. Vis (Eds), *EU Climate Policy Explained*, Oxfordshire, Routledge.

Delbeke, J. (2020), 'Carbon Pricing History and Future: An Interview with Jos Delbeke, Environmental Insights, 2020.

Delors, J. (1990), 'Europe's Ambition's', *Foreign Policy*, No. 80, Autumn 1990.

Ellinas, A., and Suleiman, E. (2012), *The European Commission and Bureaucratic Autonomy*, Cambridge University Press, Cambridge.

European Union (2021), *EU ETS Handbook*, ets_handbook_en.pdf (europa. eu), 2021.

European Union (2021a), EU Climate Change and the Green New Deal, EU Climate Action and the European Green Deal | Climate Action, (europa .eu).

European Union (2021b), ETS (EU Emissions Trading System (EU ETS) Climate Action, (europa.eu)

European Union, 'Progress Made in Cutting Emissions', 2021 (Progress made in cutting emissions | Climate Action (ec.europa.eu)

European Union (2021), 'Revision for Phase 4 (2021–2030)'.

Laing, T. (2014), The Effects and Side-effects of the EU Emissions Trading Scheme, *Climate Change*, 2014.

Malnes, R. (1995), "'Leader' and 'Entrepreneur' in International Negotiations: A conceptual Analysis', *European Journal of International Relations* 1(1), pp.87–112.

Moravcsik, A. (1999), 'A New Statecraft? Supranational Entrepreneurs and International Cooperation', *International Organisation*, Spring 1999, 53(2), pp.267–306.

Saul, U., and Seidel, C. (2011), 'Does Leadership Promote Cooperation in Climate Change Mitigation Policy?', *Climate Policy* 11(2), pp.901–921.

Skodvin, T., and Andresen, S. (2006), 'Leadership Revisited', *Global Environmental Politics* 6(3), pp.9913–9927.

Smyth, P. (2019), "'EU's Green Deal a 'European man on the moon moment', says commission president', *The Irish Times*, December 11, 2019.

Underdal, A. (1994), 'Leadership Theory. Rediscovering the Arts of Management', in I. W. Zartman (Ed), *International Multilateral negotiations: Approaches to the Management of Complexity*, Jossey-Bass Publishers, San Francisco, pp.178–197.

Vis, Peter, Personal Interview, 2021.

Wettestad, J. (2005), 'The Making of the 2003 EU Emissions Trading Directive: An Ultra-Quick Process Due to Entrepreneurial Efficiency', *Global Environmental Politics* 5(1), pp. 1–23.

Young, O. R. (1991), 'Political Leadership and Regime Formation: On the Development of Institutions in International Society', *International Organization* 45(3), pp.281–308.

Young, O. R. (1989), 'The Politics of International Regime Formation: Managing Natural Resources and the Environment', *International Organization* 43(3), pp.349–375.

13

RESHAPING GREEN RETAIL SUPPLY CHAINS IN A NEW WORLD ORDER

*David B. Grant, Dan-Cristian Dabija
and Virva Tuomala*

Introduction

This chapter argues that all stakeholders in retail supply chains need to rethink their activities in the light of current economic, social, environmental and ecological subjects/approaches to provide better leadership. Overall, supply chain activities over the last four decades, from production through consumption, have dramatically changed and contributed to current developments and issues which have led to humankind being at a cusp in its relationship with the environment. Raising concerns across holistic and global supply chains, such as increasing pollution and waste and depletion of natural resources, suggest that a step-change and new way of thinking are required about how we engage with the planet, including in retail supply chains.

The neoclassical 'Chicago School of Economics', which included inter alia Friedrich Hayek, Frank Knight, Milton Friedman and Ronald Coase, encouraged libertarian, efficient or 'free market' economic models that have become manifested in global production and consumption supply

DOI: 10.4324/9781003190820-16

chains predicated on outsourcing and other techniques to produce and deliver at the lowest cost (Olsen, 2017). However, this model is increasingly coming under criticism for being not only economically but also environmentally unsustainable and is considered by some to be the progenitor of inappropriate human behaviour that led to the current situation and reactionary behaviour against it (Bello, 2002).

More abundant yet cheaper goods, over- or conspicuous consumption, issues of modern-day slavery in retail supply chains in Western economies and ever-increasing amounts of waste suggest we need to radically rethink and restructure these activities and imbed resultant solutions into the fabric of business and society so they stick, as well as address the UN's Sustainable Development Goals or SDGs (see https://sdgs.un.org/goals) and go beyond trends and fads that do not consider fundamental practices. For example, the 'up-and-coming' trend of the 'circular economy' is not new and is confusing in some situations, but symptomatic of rebranding initiatives in sustainability currently taking place. Concepts of reducing, reusing and recycling products, together with alternative methods for disposal, have been around since the 1970s and some good as well as poor practices are well-entrenched. However, apparent ignorance about them unfortunately implies there is little intergenerational knowledge being passed on and/ or absorbed, such that society must relearn the same lessons (Grant et al., 2017a).

We argue in this chapter that firms and consumers, in concert with other relevant stakeholders, need to address retail production and consumption behaviour to contribute to efforts to improve sustainability, through three extended examples suggested by our research. The first example argues food retailers have abrogated their responsibilities to provide access to all consumers/citizens through their store networks. As a result, despite more food being produced from mechanisation of farming, over 800 million persons worldwide go hungry, and some sectors in society, including the developed West, have insufficient and secure access to food in what are termed food deserts.

The second example is of e-commerce and online retailing platforms that are supplanting traditional in-store retailing across the globe. The new platforms are more costly, encourage poor operational and managerial practices in fulfilment and return centres, and have a negative impact on retailer costs due to free delivery and returns and on the natural environment due to increased movements that generate emissions and use resources. However, new retail models have been implemented in this 'fast and disposable' consumption world, where retailers have moved from traditional locations in city centres to malls, near business centres and are also relying on a diversified 'glocal and to-go assortment' driven by 'big data' and 'analytics', especially in online retailing.

The final and third example is a failure by retailers to properly acknowledge that younger generations of consumers, who are becoming a larger segment of the market each passing year, may genuinely not be interested in embracing massive consumption patterns like previous generations. Generations Y (or Millennials) and Z are nowadays more sustainability oriented and prefer green and environmentally friendly products as well as also favouring online retail modes. Thus, ensuring a retail strategy to meet these social consumption needs is a must for retailers (Dabija and Bejan, 2018, Dabija et al., 2018).

These three examples are not exhaustive of all impacting retailing and other aspects of sustainability. However, they are ones with which the authors are most familiar based on our extant research regarding important retail sustainability issues. We examine these three in concert with other state-of-the-art changes/developments in the context of possible de-consumption, de-production and de-globalisation, and propose alternatives which do not necessarily suggest economic retrenchment but more economic redeployment that will provide opportunities for producers and consumers in an economic fashion. We first consider some current issues affecting retailing and potential solutions.

Some current issues in retailing

Current issues in retailing are not new in themselves but have become exacerbated by exogenous, external events at the turn of this millennium's third decade, such as the coronavirus or Covid-19 pandemic and the UK's exit from the European Union, commonly known as Brexit. There has been much debate over the last decade as to whether physical retail stores, commonly referred to as 'brick and mortar' stores, will exist in 50 years or whether all retailing activity will take place online (Caro et al., 2019). Further, many cities in North America and Europe have seen a decline in city centre or 'high street' retailing.

There were around 40,000 retail stores vacant across the UK in 2010 which prompted the UK Government to appoint retail consultant Mary Portas to lead a review into the future of the UK's high (main) streets. The Government subsequently provided £2.3 million to fund 27 Portas Pilot Schemes to enable local councils, residents, retailers and other businesses to try out new ideas in local high streets to meet local circumstances (DCLG, 2013). However, some criticised the Portas Review as a celebrity gimmick as well as its contention that high streets must shift their focus away from retail to community activities (Pagano, 2013).

Bill Grimsey, former chief executive at the UK supermarket chain Iceland, conducted an independent review due to his frustrations with the Government over the Portas Review and Pilot Schemes, and pronounced the 'high street as most people know it is dead'. Grimsey's review concluded retail should be part of a total 'high street mix' and provided 31 recommendations that support the report's belief that, going forward, there will

> be far fewer shops and technology will completely redesign the way we see and use our local high street [... and] we expect it to develop around multipurpose community hubs ... education, housing, leisure, arts and health will play a much bigger role.
>
> (Mesure, 2013: 49)

Both reviews missed the point that the retail domain has been affected due to stemming from slow economic growth, changes in consumer expectations and behaviour due to demographics and lifestyle/life stages, the growth of e-commerce and online retailing, issues of sustainability, green propensity/inclination of younger consumer generations (Dabija et al., 2018) and a general lack of innovation. As a result, traditional, physical retail stores were no longer competitive with other mode choices and it was predicted that 50,000 shops and 400,000 jobs would disappear in the UK (Pagano, 2013).

However, others believed traditional retailing would survive, albeit in a modified format, with new offerings to provide a different and more holistic shopping experience (Sharma, 2014) as retail remains a key contributor for revitalising weak European economies (Dickinson, 2014). We argue that has not been the case and there is a lack of retail leadership that has seen these issues remain and increase their adverse effects on the sector. We will now highlight these effects in turn.

Economic growth has been slow for the past 40 years, exacerbated by the 2008–2010 financial crisis and the current coronavirus pandemic. World output was projected to be −4.4 per cent in 2020 and recovering to 5.2 per cent in 2021 but led by emerging markets at 6.0 per cent as opposed to advanced economies at 3.9 per cent (IMF, 2020). Retail sales have fallen leading to massive numbers of store and shopping mall closures across the advanced economies, net 6,001 UK shops in 2020, decreased retailer market values, with many brand names disappearing altogether as 'apex predator' retailers such as Amazon, Alibaba, Walmart and JD.com rise to the fore (Stephens, 2020).

Further, real incomes have fallen some USD 47 trillion over the last 40 years for the bottom 90 per cent of the population, reducing spending power (Price and Edwards, 2020) and global purchasing power is shifting from advanced economies to emerging markets. The UK Office of National Statistics notes consumer confidence is also down 20 per cent down from a 2016 baseline of 100, and consumers have adopted habits and behaviours to enhance well-being across three dimensions: physical (health), emotional and financial – pursuing money-saving measures and spending is for necessity and not discretionary (Danziger, 2020).

Depending on the year of birth and the period when they come of age, six consumer generations have been identified: the Silent or the people of the Great Depression (born between 1925 and 1945), Baby Boomers born after World War II (1946–1964), Generation X (1965–1979), Millennials or Generation Y (1980–1994), Generation Z (1995–2012) and now Generation Alpha (born after 2012). However, there has also been a significant demographic shift as the Millennials and Gen Z segments are starting to outpace the Silent, Baby Boomers and Generation X segments (Fry, 2020). The Gen Alpha segment is not yet mature enough to be counted as a legitimate market segment.

Hence, Millennials and Gen Z will be the significant target market segments going forward in the next decades until mid-century for retailers (Deloitte, 2020). Further, their needs and ways of 'shopping' are different to the previous three generations who are in less consumptive life stages and hence retail growth for them is limited, save for lifestyle services such as travel and healthcare (Popa et al., 2019).

Retail supply chain business models, predicated on annual growth and traditional in-store formats, will have to change their product and service offerings and attendant value propositions, as well as their distribution and supply chain networks, to reflect these changing economic and consumer needs. As a result, both private and public sector retailers will have to develop innovative new supply chain management (SCM) strategies for product and service 'delivery' to meet such needs, particularly in an increasingly online space (Abrudan et al., 2020).

For example, the Finnish National Police Board (FNPB) developed an online passport renewal service, i.e. a retail public service, based on an outsourcing model that is vertically integrated and includes photographers and printers as suppliers. The applicant or 'customer' completes an online form and pays the requisite fee, visits a photographer who electronically sends a photograph to FNPB, and then waits to receive a code from FNPB to retrieve the passport from an FNPB office or a subcontractor, such as R-Kioski convenience stores (Grant et al., 2017b).

Retailing has a major impact on global supply chains through increased global sourcing, outsourcing and deeper supplier relationships, more use of technology, lean and agile supply chain processes, and a one-way flow in the supply chain which have also been detrimental from a sustainability perspective. Reverse logistics or product recovery, emissions of CO_2 gases, use or misuse of fuel and other natural resources, pollution, and increased levels of waste from production and packaging are just some of these detriments in retail supply chains.

From a retail logistics perspective major, emissions are an important and visible problem with different transport modes having different effects: road freight has the highest emissions, with vans being worse than HGVs with 360 g/t-km of CO versus 138 g/t-km, respectively (Grant, 2012). Direct effects on economic sustainability of retailers include reductions in transport, loading/unloading efficiencies and a need to reschedule deliveries (Grant et al., 2017a). However, there are also indirect or external social and environmental sustainability effects include reduction of air quality, increased congestion and noise, potential damage to the architectural heritage of historic city centres and decreased safety for pedestrians (McKinnon et al., 2015).

Retailers need to improve their environmental performance through considering collaborative transportation initiatives to share capacity (Hingley et al., 2011), including one example undertaken in 2010 by United Biscuits and Nestlè, i.e. 'coopetiton' where competitors work together to solve mutual problems and achieve mutually beneficial solutions (Rafi-Ul-Shan et al., 2020). Retailers also need to consider other collaborative distribution initiatives, both horizontally and vertically, to achieve more operational and environmental efficient solutions for product storage and movement, such as urban consolidation centres or UCCs which have developed in the last half decade (Grandval et al., 2019).

Sustainability in this sector is therefore becoming increasingly important and needs to form part of a retailer's strategy. However, retailers can only really influence their own internal operations directly, and can only indirectly influence over raw material producers, suppliers, and manufacturers further upstream in their supply chains, i.e. closer to production. To effect better upstream control retailers should utilise appropriate frameworks or standards, such as the International Standards Organization or ISO 14000 series, to properly map and monitor their strategic sustainability efforts (Grant and Shaw, 2019). Such efforts are not only directed at ecological and economic sustainability, but should also be focused on societal sustainability to address issues of poor working conditions, akin to modern-day slavery, that are prevalent in some retails sectors such as fashion (Fernie and Grant, 2019, Grant et al., 2017b).

Finally, retailers' influence over consumers is still limited and more needs to be done to ensure consumers are cognisant of sustainability issues and practice what they believe. Retailers must liaise more with consumers to raise awareness of environmental issues. For example, Finnish fashion consumers believe lack of supply chain transparency is an issue for Finnish retailers. But, while they are aware of the sector's social issues and the negative impact their consumption behaviour has, price and availability remain primary factors affecting purchase decisions (Blechingberg-Kilpi and Grant, 2020).

Generationally, retailers who have a sustainability orientation and exhibit environmentally friendly behaviour may better meet the needs of Millennials and Gen Z and generate their loyalty. That is, good retailer practices in relation to the environment will see consumers more likely to trust the retailer as well as recommend their offers, brands and products to others (Dabija et al., 2018, Dabija and Băbuț, 2019). Regardless of these issues, the need to eat is one that never goes away, and we now discuss our first extended example of retail food access and security to enable that for all.

Leading to provide food retail access and security

Cities worldwide face challenges in planning and managing their resources to meet the needs of inhabitants (Lynch et al., 2013). As opportunities for livelihood become scarce in rural areas, people flock to urban centres in search of employment and increased quality of life. Urbanisation happens at such a pace that it is impossible for planners to keep up, placing poverty and urbanisation among the biggest development challenges of the 21st century (Frayne et al., 2014). Urban food insecurity is one of the most serious consequences of the prevalent rates of urbanisation and poverty. As over half of the global population currently resides in cities and the figure is expected to hit over two-thirds by 2050 (United Nations, 2015), urban issues including food insecurity in cities should top leadership and development agendas.

The FAO (2009) considers food security for all people to include having access to sufficient, safe and nutritious food to maintain a healthy and active life. Even though this widely accepted view of food security refers specifically to access, it is also about ensuring availability of food largely through increased production that garners attention in policy (Tuomala, 2020). This results from a persisting rural bias in food security issues, downplaying urban dwellers' nutritional challenges due to seemingly ample availability of food in urban markets. However, the access factor is particularly important here as food may be physically available, but spatial and financial constraints may prevent many urban residents from accessing it (Battersby and Crush, 2014). Thus, urban food security is overshadowed by other urban challenges such as unemployment, overcrowding and pollution, and underdeveloped infrastructure. In urban environments, food insecurity is usually experienced on a smaller scale, i.e. neighbourhood or even household scale, which adds to the 'invisible' nature of the urban food crisis.

There have been two notable food price spikes in the last decade, 2007–2008 and 2010–2011, which have had a significant effect on global poverty and food security. Urban populations, both wealthy and poor, are net food buyers, i.e. they mostly do not produce their own food. However, the price of food is only one aspect of its accessibility. The underlying political, economic and historical factors that frame food security debates have been downplayed in the discourse but are vital in fully understanding the crisis and its potential solutions (Myers and Sbicca, 2015).

Urban environments cannot be considered as merely physical spaces, but are rather a nexus of social, environmental and economic activities brought together by a myriad of people from all social strata of society, i.e. the triple bottom line of sustainability (Grant et al., 2017a). As a result, various factors are at play in urban settings that lead to food insecurity and other developments of inequality. A useful notion for conceptualising urban food insecurity is a food desert. Food deserts are areas where fresh and healthy food at affordable prices is either difficult or impossible to obtain and its discourse started in the UK in the mid-1990s (Myers and Sbicca, 2015).

The term was first developed to describe linkages between social exclusion, health issues and the lack of access to a healthy diet. Most studies on urban food deserts have been done in developed nations such as the UK and US, but the concept is becoming increasingly relevant in emerging economies as well. Battersby and Crush (2014) argue that while a food desert is a useful concept for spatialising food insecurity, but it fails to grasp the complexity of the foodscapes many urban poor, especially in a developing context, face. It is not uncommon for a poor urbanite to work far from their place of residence, meaning that a lot of their household expenditure is done in transit, as food retail outlets are much more likely to be located around transport hubs and business districts than in poorer communities. However, the food desert is a useful lens for conceptualising socio-economic and environmental factors that underlie urban food insecurity.

Urban residents may not be statistically considered poor, but there is an inherent contradiction when it comes to urban informality. A United Nations report on urbanisation (2015) estimates that 870 million people reside in urban informal settlements, or slums, which amounts to approximately one-third of all urban residents in developing nations. Informal settlements are characterised by precarious dwelling structures, lack of access to services, overcrowding and inadequate water and sanitation facilities. Since infrastructure is one of the most visible ways to 'measure' development, the prevalence of slums leaves many cities wanting in this respect. Further, the shortcomings of urban infrastructure and its inability to meet rapid urbanisation patterns of many developing countries contributes to the environmental context of urban poverty, which goes further than measuring mere income (Tuomala, 2020).

Informality is at the heart of urban poverty, encompassing habitat, employment, and nourishment. Informal settlements have been traditionally treated as by-products of modernisation, where rural migrants are forced to initially dwell before being integrated into urban society as their wealth increases (Tuomala, 2020). However, this view is heavily criticised due to the questionable practical and historical evidence of wealth trickling down as societies develop (Fox, 2014).

While slums represent the physical manifestation of informality and urban poverty, the informal economy plays just as relevant a role in the urban landscape. Study of this phenomenon encompasses several fields of research and focuses on its size and composition, drivers, causes and linkages between several areas of development. There are many definitions of the informal economy, but most of them include functioning outside of government regulation due to inefficient enforcement as well as not paying taxes (Elbahnasawy et al., 2016).

Urban dwellers, poor and wealthy, are predominantly dependent on the market for their nourishment, hence the global food supply chain is a relevant concept in the study of urban food insecurity. The retail market for food has transformed in the last two decades in several significant ways. The most relevant in terms of urban populations are the global level shifts in retail dynamics towards multinational companies (MNCs) and the increasing integration of supply chains that comes with it. MNCs are usually based in developed or advanced markets and see developing countries as new business opportunities and outlets, especially in the wake of globalisation-friendly policies put in place in the 1990s (Tuomala, 2020). There are, however, substantial challenges in the performance of operations as well as network designs affecting urban poor markets.

Lorentz et al. (2013) utilise the framework of geography, resources and institutions or GRI, not to be confused with the sustainability Global Reporting Initiative, to review how market characteristics affect supply chain functions and overall business success. The geographical attributes of a country may bring significant difficulties to logistics operations due to factors like topography, landlocked status and population density. Isolation from major trade routes and especially from seaports have been acknowledged as causes for food insecurity. The levels of infrastructure in a country or city are also a major player in isolating an area from the global market, often resulting from restricted availability or allocation of resources.

Other resource related challenges are the level of competence in the local labour force, issues with currency and interest rates and general lack of capital for SCM related activities. Institutional characteristics also contribute to the potential difficulties of entering a new market or in the isolation of it from global trade. Economic and political barriers are often more potent than physical ones in hampering participation in global trade. The institutions that uphold these barriers often control many SCM related activities such as international trade and transport infrastructure, as well as contribute to the overall business and national culture (Lorentz et al., 2013).

Lorentz et al.'s (2013) GRI framework is a useful tool for discussing the role SCM plays in urban food insecurity, because it considers underlying SCM factors that have considerable effect on activities in developing and otherwise challenging markets. Additionally, the food supply chain is extremely complex and dynamic, relevant to all and under constant scrutiny from consumers and industry alike (Beske et al., 2014). Considerations for the sustainability of the food supply chain have emerged from the scrutiny as negative environmental and social impacts of the food industry come to the attention of the public.

The classic triple bottom line sustainability factors of economic, social and environmental factors are encompassed in food research (Grant et al., 2017a). There is substantial literature that explores the environmental effects of food distribution, however social aspects of sustainability have been investigated less both in food retail SCM as well as sustainable SCM (Yawar and Seuring, 2017). While urban food insecurity has elements of all three aspects of sustainability, its social effects are the most far reaching and complex, encompassing health as well as, e.g. questions of race and class. Touboulic and Walker (2015) call for an increasingly holistic approach to sustainable SCM research, focusing on all three sustainability aspects, rather than focusing on just one. The incorporation of external stakeholder pressure, as opposed to incentives based purely on profitability, also indicates that sustainable SCM literature is widening its focus.

While sources of urban food insecurity are impossible to pinpoint to any single cause, one theme evident throughout the discourse is urban poverty. It is also a conceptually appropriate lens to synthesise urban food insecurity issues, despite sources of urban poverty being convoluted, context dependent and immeasurable. There are two different avenues to tackle urban food insecurity. The first is an inclusive supply chain, which is a top-down approach and a more refined version of the current MNC spearheaded perspective. The second one would harness current practices of food insecure urbanites and investigate how those could be utilised to achieve more equal and comprehensive food systems. The approaches overlap in many ways but are pertinent to initially explore separately.

Silvestre (2015) suggests that supply chains evolve through a learning process, and sustainability within a supply chain becomes relevant towards the end of that process. The external environment as well as institutional presence are key factors in the learning process, tying Silvestre's argument in with Lorentz et al.'s (2013) GRI framework. The challenging environments of emerging economies and their lack of institutional strength has contributed to the difficulties in establishing sustainable supply chains in such markets (Silvestre, 2015). A top-down approach needs to pay specific attention to this learning process, and particular dynamics involved. That also may include more collaborative or 'coopetitive' relationships (Hingley et al., 2011, Rafi-Ul-Shan et al., 2020) or hierarchical distribution between MNCs and local or micro-retailers (Hingley, 2005).

Authors in the SCM field have called for sustainable supply chain management practices to become more holistic and include social issues along with environmental and economic concerns (e.g. Touboulic and Walker, 2015, Grant et al., 2017a, Yawar and Seuring, 2017). As well, the predominantly Western and MNC perspectives on sustainability ignore the many nuances in cities of different geographical and cultural contexts, especially in the case of urban food insecurity (Tuomala, 2020). The challenges presented in the external environment and lack of institutional strength suggested by Silvestre (2015) are likewise observed from a Western perspective.

Thus, the relevance of knowing the different types of market dynamics needs to be incorporated into the evolution of retail supply chains. The spread of international supermarket chains and its effect on food security in many cities worldwide is a perfect example of this. If supply chain designs were originally more inclusive, in for example its location choices or being culturally sensitive, then their effects on food insecurity could be a positive one rather than an exacerbating issue.

Using the urban food desert concept as a lens also sheds some light on the complicated circumstances that can lead to food insecurity in certain areas. The neighbourhoods classified as food deserts, especially in developed countries such as the US or UK, are usually low income and inhabited by ethnic minorities. This speaks to classist and racist discrimination in the locations of food retail outlets. The exodus of supermarkets in favour of larger locations in the suburbs, unreachable without a private vehicle, has been justified by claims of profitability, leaving inner city low-income residents with no access to healthy and nutritional food such fresh fruit and vegetable produce (Battersby and Crush, 2014, Myers and Sbicca, 2015).

As racial and cultural aspects play a large role in the formation of food deserts, retail supply chains cannot therefore remain non-inclusive. These types of issues are present in cities across the world and would therefore benefit from a fresh approach (Battersby and Crush, 2014). Inclusiveness is a relevant theme in harnessing current coping mechanisms of the urban poor into policies and urban planning. An inclusive approach should emphasise bottom-up initiatives whereby marginalised communities can partake in decisions that concern their everyday lives and rights. In terms of food security this would give local or micro-retailers a better framework within which to do business (Hingley, 2005).

A more open approach to urban planning, where currently marginalised citizens are included in the process, could significantly improve the landscape of micro-retailers in the food sector. Consumers would benefit from a more reliable source of food, as vendors often need to switch locations due to checks from authorities, as well as health and safety standards resulting from, e.g. improved sanitation facilities (Tuomala, 2020).

It may be premature to suggest online food retailing as a solution for these contexts as it still does not play a large part in Europe. For example, Tesco touted double digit online food retailing growth in the mid-noughties. However, all their retailing activities were growing at a similar amount and as a result their online percentage of sales was consistent at around 3–4 per cent per year (Grant et al., 2006). Further, Grant et al. (2014) found that, while France and Germany were Europe's largest retail food markets, with annual sales over Euro 208 billion and Euro 190 billion, respectively, their online food retailing market shares hovered around 2.5 per cent and 0.06 per cent, respectively, compared to 3.8 per cent in the UK. This was surprising for Germany and inhibitors to a deeper market penetration included high delivery costs, limited geographical coverage, the influence of discounters and quality assurance of fresh products. There are also other issues in e-commerce and online, some of which were introduced in the current retail issues section, and the next section's extended example examines additional challenges for sustainable e-commerce retailing.

Leading to develop less costly, fairer and more sustainable e-commerce retailing

Online retailing has grown significantly since the mid-1990s and there has been much debate as to whether physical retail stores, commonly referred to as 'bricks and mortar' will exist in 50 years, or whether all retailing activity will take place online. One reason for the growth in online retailing is increased access and connectivity to the Internet, which is the primary vehicle for online activity. Such growth has increased during 2020 due to the coronavirus pandemic, but it is not known how much of that increase will be sustained after the IT subsides. Europe was the world leader with an estimated 82 per cent of households having Internet connectivity and access in 2018, followed by Russia and Eastern Europe at 75.9 per cent, the Americas at 70.9 per cent, Asia at 53.2 per cent and the Arab states at 51.7 per cent (Statista, 2019a).

Online retail sales have been growing almost exponentially every year since the early 2000s. Total worldwide retail sales were estimated to US $24.9 trillion in 2018 (Statista, 2019b) with e-commerce sales comprising $2.8 trillion or just over 11 per cent of that total (Statista, 2019c). The top countries in online retail sales in 2018 were estimated to be China at US $1.56 trillion, the US ($482 billion), the UK ($132 billion), Japan ($123 billion), Germany ($83 billion), France ($53 billion), Republic of Korea ($51 billion) and Canada ($40 billion).

The changing face of retail offers both opportunities and problems for the retail SCM sector, with many commentators forecasting that 25 per cent of retail could eventually be conducted online. In Europe, the UK currently leads the way, with online penetration of 20 per cent, and consumer expectations for increasingly prompt deliveries. Mainland Europe, however, shops online for only 8 per cent of its retail requirements; typically, the tipping point that triggers a significant drive for needing more distribution space is the 10 per cent level (Fernie and Grant, 2019).

As discussed in the current retailing issues section, many cities in North America and Europe have seen a decline in city centre or 'high street' retailing with quite a few well-known fashion and apparel, household and/

or lifestyle retailers going into administration or liquidation. Physical or 'brick and mortar' retail stores are thus having difficulty competing with online retailing or 'click and order' due to the changes noted previously in consumer preference, choice and behaviour towards online retailing from economic, lifestyle, demographic and other factors. However, while physical store retailing has its challenges, Morgan (2018) offers two scenarios regarding their survival. One is that they will survive due to technology such as artificial intelligence (AI) and augmented and virtual reality (AR, VR), allowing retailers to become more anticipatory about consumers' needs, size and preferences. The other is that they will survive due to an innate human need to physically touch items and try clothing on before purchase and the social aspect of shopping as consumers crave human and social interaction, which might come from talking with an in-store sales associate or meeting with a friend.

Morgan (2018) thus speculates that larger big-box stores will migrate online and smaller, niche stores will dominate traditional physical retail spaces while surviving retail stores will move towards a more experiential approach, more like showrooms that allow consumers to touch and feel the products and then have them delivered to their homes straight from a warehouse. Such experiential stores have existed for some time with Vans, Ikea and Apple having success with that format. However, in the end, Morgan believes retail will evolve to a blend of these two ideas, i.e. more integration between the physical retail and e-commerce spaces. That will have an impact on the design and implementation of retail logistical systems.

The term 'omnichannel' has come into use in the last ten years for the online retail phenomenon, which means that a consumer's entire online shopping experience, i.e. both buying and receiving their goods, is seamlessly and consistently integrated across all channels of interaction, including in-store digital media, including computers, mobiles and tablets, social media, catalogues and call centres (Fernie and Grant, 2019). Retailers will have to select the optimum distribution channel to succeed financially with online fulfilment, whether it is by consumers ordering in-store and the retailer delivering to home or consumers ordering online and the retailer or third-party logistics (3PL) service provider fulfilling from any store or online fulfilment centre (OFC) location. Each option has a different cost structure that retailers need to understand.

In the US, the ARC Advisory Group and *DC Velocity* magazine conducted a study of 177 retail executives regarding their efforts for omnichannel fulfilment (Cooke, 2013). What emerged from the study was evidence of a wide gap in the cost accounting capabilities. While most respondents could pinpoint costs associated with various activities at an OFC, few had a clear picture of the corresponding costs for store fulfilment.

For example, 78 per cent of respondents said they knew the cost of picking individual items by stock-keeping unit (SKU) or product class in their OFC. However, only 38 per cent could pin down the corresponding costs for the back room of a store and only 29 per cent said they understood the expenses associated with picking individual items in the front of the store. Additionally, 70 per cent said they could break out their transportation costs by SKU or product class for deliveries from an OFC but, only 57 per cent had that same level of understanding for shipments from a store (Cooke, 2013).

As for how retailers are filling their online orders, the study found that stores are playing a significant and growing role. Thirty-five per cent of retailers fill online orders from in-store stock and 56 per cent of those retail respondents who are not currently filling online orders from in-store stock plan to begin doing so within the next few years. While retailers may be shifting more of their e-commerce fulfilment activities to the stores, it is not clear if they have the proper groundwork in place, particularly where inventory accuracy is concerned. Today, cycle count accuracy levels at distribution centres (DCs) and OFCS that use warehouse management systems (WMS) software in conjunction with automatic identification technology exceeds 99 per cent (Grant, 2012).

Thus, for retailers to succeed in omnichannel distribution they will have to adopt many established upstream distribution practices within their in-store operations. Retailers will not fare well if they rely solely on buffer inventory in their stores and long lead-times for customer delivery. Transformations in store operations will be necessary to ensure that retailers' ability to profitably compete in an environment where consumers are becoming ever more demanding.

The issue here is that a lack of understanding of supply chain efficiency and logistics metrics and data means that the value and profitability equations are proving almost impossible to determine, while systems are busy moving goods and materials rapidly around in real time. One of the challenges is that many retailers do not know if the various channels they are using are making money and do not understand the 'cost to serve' consumers who want free delivery and free returns (Grant et al., 2017c).

Online consumers who continue to insist on a no-pay model which does not reflect true, actual costs to serve suggests retailers need to inform and educate consumers on these issues to enable them to develop a different mentality towards them and their various impacts, with the subsequent result being behavioural change. Retailers must therefore liaise more with consumers to raise awareness of costs to prevent both bad retail practices and consumer behaviour related to operations, e.g. over consumption on 'Black Friday' and 'showrooming' by examining goods in-store and then buying cheaper online.

Setting up an online service also requires a high initial investment but takes off rather slowly and may cannibalise other channels. Competition in the online environment also may decrease prices and affect margins or prompt channel conflict. As a result, it remains unclear whether the online channel itself provides strong performance and whether this performance contributes to the overall performance of the retailer or its third-party logistics partners, especially parcel carriers. Products delivery in urban areas with exceptional distribution process for both in-store and e-commerce intensities high levels of traffic which in turn have different impacts. Thus, retailers need to properly embrace technology as an enabler to assist with this 'choreography' of online retail supply chains (Grant, 2012).

One example of innovative value addition for online food consumers is the use of big data and analytical techniques by Mega Image, part of the Ahold Delhaize group who established themselves in the Romanian marketplace in 2019 (Peterse, 2019). They offer the usual loyalty card for use in-store at either a Mega Image supermarket or their chain's Shop & Go neighbourhood convenience stores and have also provided online ordering including home delivery for orders over 250 RON or about Euro 50. However, they are also uniquely offering personalised offers including discounts resulting from previous purchase information either online or from point-of-sale scanners in store.

All this comes into sharp focus when considering the needs of the two largest and growing consumer segments, Millennials and Generation Z, and our final extended example for that comprises the next section.

Leading to recognise and embrace different generations' retail needs

The third millennium has brought forth some new concerns among people and society in general, such as protection of the environment, the adoption of environmentally friendly behaviour, sustainable consumption of products manufactured according to sustainable principles, the purchase of sustainable or green products, a preference for companies and organisations abiding by the principles of sustainability, reuse, recycling, selective waste collection, etc. Retailers have rapidly understood these new trends in society and consumers' new needs and expectations, and have increasingly come up with healthy, functional, organic and fair-trade alternatives. Therefore, sustainable thinking has become more visibly incorporated into retail marketing strategies.

In an era of rapid technological advancement in which globalisation has eliminated physical borders between consumers and products, retail stores make use of the most up-to-date and effective customer relationship strategies. These strategies have developed considerably during this millennium due to the advancement of technology fostering the emergence of omnichannel retail. This new context has had a strong bearing not only on retailers, who were compelled to adapt their offerings and communication to the new reality, but also on consumer attitudes and behaviour (Verhoef et al., 2015).

Each consumer generation exhibits specific characteristics, attitudes, preferences and behaviour depending on the events that marked its existence and mankind's achievements it witnessed. The values shared by a generation determine its behaviour, which is a key element that sets one generation apart from the others. Marketers approach generational segments differently and focusing on specific needs according to their respective lifestyles, life stages and ways of thinking. Thus, a proper understanding of behaviour in consumer generations is a real challenge for the retailers that make great efforts to meet their expectations as much as possible and increase their satisfaction.

Retailers' development and implementation of market strategies and omnichannel strategies is accepted differently across consumers. The attitudes, preferences, expectations, interests and motivations of a generational cohort change as people age and from events that define their lives, i.e.

conflicts, social upheavals, need to work from an early age, etc. (Dabija et al., 2018). Thus, it is imperative for retailers and marketers to know, understand and develop strategies suited for each consumer segment because such strategies bring forth positioning benefits for retail brands and fulfilment modes.

Further, an increasing dominance of younger generation target segments introduced in the current retailing issues section, specifically Millennials and Gen Z, are inclined to use primarily e-commerce and omnichannel retail modes, which provides even more challenges for retailers (Grant et al., 2017c). A fundamental trait of Millennials and Generation Z, hereinafter referred to as 'YoungGens', is their early and frequent exposure to technology, which has implications for their cognitive, emotional and social development as individuals, consumers and professionals.

YoungGens have also grown up in a favourable period of economic prosperity (until recently) and in a context of innovation and rapid change. They have witnessed a turbulent development of communication technologies and social networking technology in a global and massively connected world. YoungGens were born into an environment dominated by innovation and rapid change; living almost symbiotically with different forms of personal technology, e.g. computers, tablets, smartphones, etc. as 'digital natives'. They are also highly educated, mostly being e-learners, very environmentally conscious and active (Popa et al., 2019).

Multiculturally and sexually tolerant, they are tech-savvy and always connected and they rely on technology for many purposes, including entertainment and interaction with other people. YoungGens also rely on themselves and possess a sense of independence and perfect autonomy; desirous of making their own choices, customising information received; possessing curiosity and doubt, a spirit of collaboration, a need for speed, entertainment, innovation.

They are also concerned with self-image and rely very much on social networking; use social media and applications for mobile devices to obtain information about new products or offers before or during visiting traditional or online stores; will compare other consumers' opinions from online forums, etc. (Dabija and Grant, 2016).

Alongside, YoungGens are commonly used to an increased availability of customised products and personalised services. They want to have control of their decision-making processes based on information received from multiple sources. Thus, empowered and well-informed YoungGens want to be present everywhere with any media; they are 'omniconsumers', shopping across channels to maximise their utility and increase their satisfaction and contentment. Therefore, managers and researchers need to understand expectations of YoungGens for their online shopping experience, and the implications for retail logistics and fulfilment (Grant et al., 2017c).

YoungGens look for information and carry out their online shopping relying on a variety of sources and multiple responses were allowed. It appears that search engines such as Google, Yahoo or MSN are the preferred tool used for online shopping (75 per cent), even more than e-stores/ web stores of retailers (54 per cent) and, surprisingly, more than buying platforms such as eBay or Amazon (45 per cent) or manufacturers' e-stores (44 per cent). Price comparison platforms such as Kelkoo are not very popular in terms of use among respondents (35 per cent) (Grant et al., 2017c). From these results, it is crucial for retailers to appear in the top-ranking websites according to search engines in order to be visible in the world of online shopping at the eyes of YoungGens.

The main motivation for YoungGens' shopping online is the possibility to shop anytime, day or night (78 per cent), together with the opportunity to have products delivered at home (77 per cent), and to avoid dealing with salespeople (77 per cent) (Grant et al., 2017c). Thus, it also seems that YoungGens are not willing to tolerate traditional inconveniences of in-store shopping (e.g. crowds, queues), and thus companies should make online shopping accessible and 'convenient for this category of customers as they may not wish to come to stores at all.

When it comes to the requirements for online fulfilment, established by Xing and Grant's (2006) e-fulfilment model, YoungGens confirm their clear preference for convenience (71 per cent), intended as ease to move within and find the desired product on the website followed by the possibility to return products (64 per cent) when easy and convenient return policies and conditions are offered. Timeliness, intended as a reasonable amount of time necessary to buy a product, represents another relevant item (59 per cent), followed by cost (58 per cent), in terms of the total product price as well as payment terms. The latter quite surprisingly is not ranked among the most relevant requirements for YoungGens.

As far as YoungGens' preferred delivery options are concerned, home delivery via courier is the most preferred (72 per cent), followed by home deliveries arranged by retailers with their own van/lorry (56 per cent). It is interesting to note YoungGens do not attribute very high importance to the click and collect option (41 per cent) or postal services (36 per cent) (Grant et al., 2017c). Consistent with their expectations for online fulfilment, low levels of preference are attributed to those delivery options that entail collection locations different from the ones to where they placed their order. Again, consistent with their convenience preference, YoungGens highly value the possibility to reschedule (53 per cent) and redirect (55 per cent) deliveries when required. It appears YoungGens perceive couriers as the most qualified actors to offer prompt deliveries and they express a clear preference for delivery options that, besides being convenient, are simple and easy to manage to suit their potentially changing needs.

YoungGens do not return products in a very frequent fashion; 64 per cent return products only once in ten orders, 19 per cent in 3 of 10 orders, 6 per cent every other order and 5 per cent almost never. YoungGens will return products when they are different from those ordered (78 per cent each), or if they receive a wrong product, it is defective or if the quality is poor (73 per cent). Thus, YoungGens appear not to be casually buying to try and return and seem focused in obtaining what they need in their buying activities, casual buyers and returners, but it is evident that they want correct, complete and accurate products (Grant et al., 2017c).

When YoungGens need to return a product, they are consistent with their inclination for convenience, they favour having a carrier picking up the products they need to return at their address, free of charge (74 per cent) (while they have an opposite attitude if they have to pay for this return service, 34 per cent). Alternatively, they will also accept to drop the product at a physical store of the retailers (59 per cent) or to a collection and drop-off point, if free of charge (58 per cent). However, if the return at a collection and drop-off point entails a payment, the YoungGens' level of preference drastically falls (27 per cent). In line with their desire to keep the process simple, similar to delivery services, YoungGens prefer not to deal with intermediaries or third parties when arranging a return (33 per cent) as 71 per cent want to have a direct contact with the retailers (Grant et al., 2017c).

Retailers will need to better understand all consumer needs in this changing environment, but especially YoungGens, i.e. 'what they really, really want' as demand from them is quite different to the Silent, Baby Boomers and Generation X segments (Dabija and Grant, 2016, Deloitte,

2020). YoungGens are a real challenge for retailers because they are non-conformist and independent in the decision-making process, are relatively self-sufficient, hard to place in behaviour patterns, assume high risks and break traditional norms and values.

Supported by their values and beliefs, these segments are interested in quality products, services and experiences and, despite paying a fair price relative to quality, i.e. respecting the price–value relationship, but are nevertheless cost-conscious (Deloitte, 2020). As a result, retailers should be providing tailored offerings for YoungGens in terms of products, promotion and place, especially online versus traditional in-store retail online shopping experience to allow them to be satisfied at the outset with purchases. Further, retailers who have a sustainability orientation and exhibit environmentally friendly behaviour may better meet the YoungGens needs and generate loyalty.

Conclusions

There is an array of challenges facing the retail sector at this point in history. These challenges are vast and complex, but also provide opportunities for retailers to demonstrate sustainable leadership to generate competitive advantage over competitors, add value to the consumer experience, become more efficient and effective in their operations, and address the three triple bottom line sustainability elements. It is difficult to synthesise all these challenges and opportunities in one book chapter, especially as they are exacerbated by external pressures at a macro level, such as the global economy, changing political structures and health pandemics. However, based on our own research, observations and examples provided above, we believe that retailers can do so in four ways through organisational and strategic adaptation as follows:

1. Adapting to a loss of consumerism from the Silent, Baby Boomer and Generation X market segments by focusing on succeeding Millennial and Gen Z segments who are now surpassing the earlier segments in terms of size;
2. Adapting to the corresponding rise in technology to provide different online shopping experiences for sourcing, browsing, payment and fulfilment;

3. Adapting to increased online activity due to the coronavirus pandemic encouraging people to buy online, during the coronavirus pandemic and afterwards, through better forecasting and operational decision-making while ensuring such activity is sustainable;
4. Adapting to strategically address ongoing fundamental societal problems across the globe such as food access and security or modern-day slavery in retail supply chains at producer, distribution and retail levels in developing nations to demonstrate their commitment to sustainable retailing across all three triple bottom line elements.

Retailers' current postures and activities are unsustainable and thus, using an old aphorism, they need to 'adapt or die' in this dynamically changing world. We thus conclude with a call for retailers to develop or incorporate smart, responsible and accountable leadership across the entire sector to make retailing a leader in sustainable operations and consumption.

References

Abrudan, I.N., Dabija, D.-C. and Grant, D.B. (2020) Omni-channel retailing strategy and research agenda. In: Sroka, W. (ed.) *Perspectives on Consumer Behaviour: Theoretical Aspects and Practical Applications*, pp. 261–280, Cham CH: Springer International.

Battersby, J. and Crush, J. (2014) Africa's urban food deserts. *Urban Forum*, 25, pp. 143–151, https://doi.org/10.1007/s12132-014-9225-5.

Bello, Waldon (2002). *Deglobalization: Ideas for a New World Economy*, London: Zed Books Ltd.

Beske, P., Land, A. and Seuring, S. (2014) Sustainable supply chain management practices and dynamic capabilities in the food industry: A critical analysis of the literature. *International Journal of Production Economics*, 152, pp. 131–143, https://doi.org/10.1016/j.ijpe.2013.12.026.

Blechingberg-Kilpi, P. and Grant, D.B. (2020) Corporate and social responsibility perspectives of Finnish fashion retailers and consumers. In: Idowu, S.O. and Sitnikov, C. (eds.) *Essential Issues in Corporate Social Responsibility: New Insights and Recent Issues*, pp. 55–71, Cham CH: Springer International.

Caro, F., Kök, A.G. and Martínez-de-Albéniz, V. (2019) The future of retail operations. *Manufacturing & Service Operations Management*, 22 (1), pp. 47–58. https://doi.org/10.1287/msom.2019.0824.

Cooke, J.A. (2013) Retail stores can't handle omnichannel fulfillment on their own. *CSCMP's Supply Chain Quarterly*, https://www.supplychainquarterly.com/articles/755-retail-stores-can-t-handle-omnichannel-fulfillment-on-their-own [Accessed 27 December 2020].

Dabija, D.-C. and Grant, D.B. (2016) Investigating shopping experience and fulfilment in omnichannel retailing: A proposed comparative study in Romania and UK of generation Y consumers. *Proceedings of the 21st Annual Logistics Research Network (LRN) Conference*, Hull UK, September.

Dabija, D.-C. and Bejan, B.M. (2018) Green DIY Store Choice among socially responsible consumer generations. *International Journal of Corporate Social Responsibility*, 3 (13), pp. 1–12. https://doi.org/10.1186/s40991-018-0037-0.

Dabija, D.-C., Bejan, B.M. and Grant, D.B. (2018) The impact of consumer green behaviour on green loyalty among retail formats: A Romanian case study. *Moravian Geographical Reports*, 26 (3), pp. 173–185, http://dx.doi.org/10.2478/mgr-2018-0014.

Dabija, D.-C. and Băbuț, R. (2019). Enhancing apparel store patronage through retailers' attributes and sustainability. A generational approach. *Sustainability*, 11 (17), Article 4532. https://doi.org/10.3390/su11174532.

Danziger, P.N. (2020) Consumer spending tanked in second quarter. What the trends mean for retailers. *Forbes*, 4th August, https://www.forbes.com/sites/pamdanziger/2020/08/02/consumer-spending-tanked-in-second-quarter-what-the-trends-mean-for-retailers/.

DCLG (2013) *The Future of High Streets: Progress since the Portas Review*, July, London: Department for Communities and Local Government.

Deloitte (2020) The Deloitte global Millennial survey 2020. *Deloitte*, https://www2.deloitte.com/global/en/pages/about-deloitte/articles/millennialsurvey.html.

Dickinson, H. (2014) Retail can drive UK economy forward. *Raconteur Future of Retail Supplement in The Times*, 24th June, p. 15.

Elbahnasawy, N.G., Ellis, M.A. and Adom, A.D. (2016) Political instability and the informal economy. *World Development*, 85, pp. 31–42, https://doi.org/10.1016/j.worlddev.2016.04.009.

Fernie, J. and Grant, D.B. (2019) *Fashion Logistics*. 2nd ed. London: Kogan Page.

FAO (2009) *Declaration of the World Summit on Food Security WSFS 2009/2*, Food and Agriculture Organization of the United Nations, 16th–18th November, Rome.

Fox, S. (2014) The political economy of slums: Theory and evidence from Sub-Saharan Africa. *World Development*, 54, pp. 191–203, https://doi.org/10.1016/j.worlddev.2013.08.005.

Frayne, B., Crush, J. and McLachlan, M. (2014) Urbanization, nutrition and development in Southern African cities. *Food Security*, 6, pp. 101–112. https://doi.org/10.1007/s12571-013-0325-1.

Fry, R. (2020) Millennials overtake Baby Boomers as America's largest generation. *Pew Research*, https://www.pewresearch.org/fact-tank/2020/04/28/millennials-overtake-baby-boomers-as-americas-largest-generation/.

Grandval, S., Nimtrakool, K. and Grant, D.B. (2019) Factors of adoption governing the emergence of urban consolidation centres. *Supply Chain Forum: An International Journal*, 20 (4), pp. 247–256, https://doi.org/10.1080/16258312.2019.1631713.

Grant, D.B. (2012) *Logistics Management*, Harlow UK: Pearson Education Limited.

Grant, D.B., Kotzab, H. and Xing, Y. (2006) Success@tesco.com: Erfolg im online-lebensmittelhandel oder 'Wie macht das der Tesco?' In: Schnedlitz, P., Buber, R., Reutterer, T., Schuh, A. and Teller C. (eds.) *Innovationen In Marketing Und Handel*, pp. 203–213, Vienna: Linde.

Grant, D.B., Fernie, J. and Schulz, B. (2014) Enablers and barriers in German online food retailing. *Supply Chain Forum: An International Journal*, 15 (3), pp. 4–11, https://doi.org/10.1080/16258312.2014.11517346.

Grant, D.B., Trautrims, A. and Wong, C.Y. (2017a) *Sustainable Logistics and Supply Chain Management*. 2nd ed. London: Kogan Page.

Grant, D.B., Bask, A. and Kovács, G. (2017b) Service failure and recovery in public sector digital services. *Proceedings of the 24th International European Operations Management Association (EurOMA) Conference*, Heriot-Watt University UK, July.

Grant, D.B., Dabija, D.-C., Colicchia, C., Creazza, A., Philipp, B., Spens, K. and Băbuţ, R. (2017c). Expectations of Millennial consumers regarding online shopping and fulfilment. *Proceedings of the 22nd Annual Logistics Research Network (LRN) Conference*, Southampton Solent University UK, September.

Grant, D.B. and Shaw, S. (2019) Environmental or sustainable supply chain performance measurement standards and certifications. In: Sarkis,

J. (ed.) *Handbook on the Sustainable Supply Chain*, pp. 357–376, Northampton MA: Edward Elgar Publishing.

Hingley, M.K. (2005) Power imbalance in UK agri-food supply channels: Learning to live with the supermarkets? *Journal of Marketing Management*, 21, pp. 63–88, https://doi.org/10.1362/0267257053166758.

Hingley, M., Lindgreen, A., Grant, D.B. and Kane, C. (2011) Using fourth party logistics management to improve horizontal collaboration among grocery retailers. *Supply Chain Management: An International Journal*, 16 (5), pp. 316–327, https://doi.org/10.1108/13598541111155839.

IMF (2020) *World Economic Outlook*. International Monetary Fund, October, https://www.imf.org/en/Publications/WEO/Issues/2020/09/30/world-economic-outlook-october-2020.

Lorentz, H., Kittipanya-Ngam, P. and Singh Srai, J. (2013) Emerging market characteristics and supply network adjustments in internationalising food supply chains. *International Journal of Production Economics*, 145 (1), pp. 220–232, https://doi.org/10.1016/j.ijpe.2013.04.038.

Lynch, K., Maconachie, R., Binns, T., Tengbe, P. and Bangura, K. (2013) Meeting the urban challenge? Urban agriculture and food security in post-conflict Freetown, Sierra Leone. *Applied Geography*, 36, pp. 31–39, https://doi.org/10.1016/j.apgeog.2012.06.007.

McKinnon, A., Browne, M., Piecyk, M. and Whiteing, A. (eds.) (2015) *Green Logistics*. 3rd ed. London: Kogan Page.

Mesure, S. (2013) The high street of the future is like nothing we know. *The Independent on Sunday*, 1st September, pp. 10–11.

Morgan, B. (2018) Will there be a physical retail store in 10–20 years? *Forbes.com*, https://www.forbes.com/sites/blakemorgan/2018/10/15/will-there-be-a-physical-retail-store-in-10-20-years/#57e3aa1b723f.

Myers, J.S. and Sbicca, J. (2015) Bridging good food and good jobs: From secession to confrontation within alternative food movement politics. *Geoforum*, 61, pp. 17–26, https://doi.org/10.1016/j.geoforum.2015.02.003.

Olsen, N. (2017) From choice to welfare: The concept of the consumer in the Chicago School of Economics. *Modern Intellectual History*, 14 (2), pp. 507–535. https://doi.org/10.1017/S1479244431616000202.

Pagano, M. (2013) Look to the past for high street's future. *The Independent on Sunday*, 23rd June, p. 74.

Peterse, R. (2019) Mega Image takes over regional supermarket chain in Romania. *Fresh Plaza*, 15 March, https://www.freshplaza.com/article/9083003/mega-image-takes-over-regional-supermarket-chain-in-romania/.

Popa, I.D., Dabija, D.-C. and Grant, D.B. (2019) Exploring omnichannel retailing differences and preferences among consumer generations. In: Văduva, S. et al, (eds.) *Applied Ethics for Entrepreneurial Success: Recommendations for the Developing World*, pp. 129–146, Cham CH: Springer International.

Price, C.C. and Edwards, K.A. (2020) Trends in income from 1975 to 2018. RAND Corporation, https://www.rand.org/pubs/working_papers/WRA516-1.html.

Rafi-Ul-Shan, P.M., Grant, D.B. and Perry, P. (2020) Are fashion supply chains capable of coopetition? An exploratory study in the UK. *International Journal of Logistics: Research and Applications*, https://doi.org/10.1080/13675567.2020.1784118.

Sharma, R. (2014) Physical stores won't go away, but they must change to keep customers. *The Wall Street Journal Europe*, 28th–30th November, p. 11.

Silvestre, B.S. (2015) Sustainable supply chain management in emerging economies: Environmental turbulence, institutional voids and sustainability trajectories. *International Journal of Production Economics*, 167, pp. 156–169, https://doi.org/10.1016/j.ijpe.2015.05.025.

Statista (2019a) Percentage of households with internet access worldwide in 2018, by region. *Statista*, http://www.statista.com/statistics/249830/households-with-internet-access-worldwide-by-region/.

Statista (2019b) Total retail sales worldwide from 2015 to 2020 (in trillion U.S. dollars). *Statista*, https://www.statista.com/statistics/443522/global-retail-sales/.

Statista (2019c) Retail e-commerce sales worldwide from 2014 to 2021 (in billion U.S. dollars). *Statista*, https://www.statista.com/statistics/379046/worldwide-retail-e-commerce-sales/.

Stephens, D. (2020) Opinion: How to survive the future of retail. *Business of Fashion*, 28th July, https://www.businessoffashion.com/search?q=future%20of%20retail%20doug%20stephens%20ama%E2%80%A6.

Touboulic, A. and Walker, H. (2015) Theories in sustainable supply chain management: A structured literature review. *International Journal of Physical Distribution & Logistics Management*, 45 (1/2), pp. 16–42, https://doi.org/10.1108/IJPDLM-05-2013-0106.

Tuomala, V. (2020) Towards inclusive urban food supply chains. In: E. Aktas and M. Bourlakis (eds.) *Food Supply Chains in Cities: Modern tools for circularity and sustainability*, pp. 1–32, Cham CH: Springer International.

United Nations (2015) *World Urbanization Prospects: The 2014 Revision*, New York: United Nations Department of Economic and Social Affairs, Population Division.

Verhoef, P.C., Kannan, P.K. and Inman, J.J. (2015) From multi-channel retailing to omni-channel retailing. Introduction to the special issue on multi-channel retailing. *Journal of Retailing*, 21 (2), pp. 174–181, https://doi.org /10.1016/j.jretai.2015.02.005.

Xing, Y. and Grant, D.B. (2006) Developing a framework for measuring physical distribution service quality of multi-channel and 'pure player' internet retailers. *International Journal of Retail & Distribution Management*, 34 (4/5), pp. 278–289, https://doi.org/10.1108/09590550610660233.

Yawar, S.A. and Seuring, S. (2017) Management of social issues in supply chains: A literature review exploring social issues, actions and performance outcomes. *Journal of Business Ethics*, 141 (3), pp. 621–643, https://doi.org /10.1007/s10551-015-2719-9.

14

CLIMATE RISK AND ADAPTATION IN WALES

LEADERSHIP FOR FUTURE GENERATIONS?

Alan Netherwood and Andrew Flynn

Introduction

Alongside the greater prominence given to sustainability challenges is an increasing awareness of the scale of the societal and economic changes that will be needed to tackle them. More than ever, there is a need for sustainability leadership from public and private sectors and civil society to help guide the transition to less carbon-intensive and more socially just societies. In the narratives on environmental governance, there is increasing attention being given to the transformative role of the private sector and to reporting on business success stories. In this chapter, we wish to redress the balance by first focusing on the way in which sustainability leadership is being addressed in the public sector. The public sector is a key actor in moves to promote sustainability and is often looked to lead on sustainability measures. These might be policy ideas, rules, more rigorous enforcement of environmental regulations or governance initiatives such as partnership working. Second, we adopt a more critical perspective on leadership by drawing attention to challenges rather than achievements. In fact, studying

DOI: 10.4324/9781003190820-17

failure may be more important at the present time because the making and delivery of policy is beset by challenges rather than achievements (except at an abstract or aspirational level). The better we understand why things may not work as intended the more we may be able to improve them in the future. Third, we bring together analytical and normative perspectives. Based upon our interpretation of the challenges for public sector sustainability leadership we suggest a set of normative measures that could help to invigorate sustainability leadership in the public sector.

In this chapter, we concentrate on the challenges of public sector sustainability leadership in Wales, one of the UK nations. Wales is a good case study, where lessons can be drawn that are much more widely applicable because it has become widely recognised as an innovator in legislation for sustainable development. The achievements and challenges of Wales provide opportunities for other countries to learn from. In its most recent piece of sustainability legislation, the Well-being of Future Generations Act 2015, Wales has sought to further develop its ideas on sustainability. The Act and its implications are discussed further below. Our examination of sustainability leadership in Wales, focuses on one of the problematic features of the climate change debate, namely, how to deal with the impacts of climate change on communities. Here, the Well-being of Future Generations Act provides a particularly helpful analytical lens because leaders must develop ideas for both current and future generations and at different spatial scales (national, regional and local). So, the legislation should help to bring to the fore climate change and climate change adaptation. As we argue, though, this has so far not been the case. Better understanding why climate change adaptation is marginalised offers important insights into the difficulties faced by public sector sustainability leaders.

Our analysis and interpretation of sustainability in Wales draws upon our involvement in both sustainable development and climate adaptation debates at a national and local level in Wales since 2002. We have participated in professional, consultancy and academic work. This has provided access to key actors and organisations. For example, we have contributed to collaborative and commissioned work with the UK Climate Change Committee, Welsh Government, local authorities, public agencies and communities. There have also been discussions with the Welsh Local Government Association and Future Generations Commissioner. In 2020, the authors were commissioned to provide recommendations on a regional

North Wales response to the Climate Emergency. This gathered information on climate mitigation at strategic, organisational, operational and community-based levels in the region. We have used a variety of sources of data, including participant observation, active participation, interviews with politicians and key officials and representatives of key stakeholder groups and analysis of key documents to provide well-evidenced examples of sustainability leadership in practice.

The chapter is organised as follows. First we examine ideas on sustainability leadership and how they help our understanding of what happens in the public sector. We argue that too often the literature fails to fully appreciate the governance context in which public sector leaders operate and so the rest of the section briefly explains the Well-being of Future Generations Act. The next section further develops ideas on governance and pays particular attention to climate change and climate change adaptation debates in Wales. We also analyse the reasons why adaptation debates have a much lower profile than those related to mitigation, especially where the latter can be linked to competitive opportunities arising from a shift to a low-carbon economy. Next, we examine a series of opportunities for leadership interventions. We follow this by describing key leadership characteristics and how they operate in practice. The final section draws the chapter to a close and concludes that public sector leadership may need to be rejuvenated by rethinking how governance operates.

Leadership and governance

In this section we first analyse sustainability leadership and especially what it means for the public sector, and second, we place leadership in the context of environmental governance in Wales. Our argument here is that too often the literature on leadership fails to fully appreciate the governance context in which individuals and their organisations operate. As a result, analysis and normative thinking tends to be too generic.

Sustainability leadership

In thinking about leadership on climate adaptation and risk in Wales, it is important to examine the burgeoning and increasingly diverse literature on sustainability leadership. We focus on what the literature tells us about

CLIMATE RISK AND ADAPTATION IN WALES   313

approaches to sustainability leadership training; promotion of leadership; and leadership in public administration. Too often approaches fail to factor in the governance context in which leaders and their organisations operate. Governance draws our attention to the relationships between government and government bodies, businesses and citizens. All three sets of actors have interests in climate adaptation and risks. Sometimes those interests will be shared but other times not. To engage citizens and businesses, leaders may address climate risks in more abstract ways because that can build consensus, but be more wary of focusing on places, communities and timeframes as this may arouse controversies.

Leadership training in sustainability typically covers many themes that would also be found in more mainstream leadership programmes, such as network-building, systems thinking and project-based learning, while also focusing on issues of environmental performance and social justice (Shriberg and MacDonald 2013). Perhaps, not surprisingly, leadership training seems to be more focused on ideals to be found in the private sector, where much innovative work on sustainability practices is taking place. Unfortunately, though, one consequence is the marginalisation of the role of the public sector, because in many places government and allied bodies are important actors in shaping sustainability and that includes building climate resilience.

Promotion of sustainability leadership within organisations is another key theme of the literature. For example, Galpin and Whittington (2012) argue that leadership is concerned with an intra-organisational dynamic to engage a workforce in sustainability practices. More ambitiously, Ferdig (2007) claims that sustainability leadership applies to anyone who takes responsibility for understanding and acting on sustainability challenges, even if they do not hold a formal leadership position. Such bottom-up activity conceives of sustainability leaders as persuaders as they can convince others that there is an alternative, better way, for organisations to work, innovate and to help deliver more sustainable activities. In the context of climate risk and resilience it is the absence of leaders as persuaders that is notable, as we shall see later in the chapter. While it is important to draw attention to actors' agency on climate impacts, it is also important to recognise the context in which these actors operate: do leaders or potential leaders feel enabled or constrained to highlight climate risks, the sufficiency of current approaches, or are they able to highlight the gaps in policy and delivery?

Others advocate a more 'top-down' approach to sustainability leadership. For example, edie (2021) provide an annual update on corporate sustainability leadership. This is leadership as target and agenda setting and assumes that those who set targets and agendas are a) setting meaningful ones, and b) have the capacity to be able to deliver on them. A fascinating picture emerges of a business-led sustainability agenda in which efforts are being made to internalise negative impacts and mainstream environmental management. In the case of climate risk, negative impacts will be internalised (whether they like it or not) by communities, the local economies that provide them with work, the infrastructure that provides services and mobility and landscapes that provide recreation and a home for nature. For leaders in the public sector, there is, therefore, a different challenge to those working in the private sector, for they need to be able to communicate how cascading, structural and existential risks for communities arising because of climate change may or may not be dealt with.

There is increasing recognition of the important part that local government leaders can play in promoting sustainability (Wang et al., 2014; Niu et al., 2018). Like their private sector counterparts, sustainability leaders in the public sector can mobilise resources to support favoured activities and bring together what might otherwise have been rather disparate functions in a more integrated framework (Wang et al., 2014; Zeemering 2018) so that planning processes explicitly recognise sustainability or climate change adaptation as a public policy goal. In practice, efforts to integrate services will depend in part on the priority accorded to climate change. Homsy (2018) argues that public sector leaders focus on climate change for three main reasons. First, local leaders reframe climate change action to save money and attract economic development, second, leaders have a commitment to environmental protection and third, citizens support climate change actions (see also Niu et al., 2018, for similar findings). While Homsy's argument is persuasive for climate mitigation, in the UK at least, leaders have yet to monetise climate risks in the face of many competing financial agendas. So, while there is a good understanding of budgets for infrastructure developments, which will be impacted by climate change, there is less concern with those climate change adaptation costs. As we show below, in Wales, despite widespread recognition of a climate emergency and policy and legislative duties on sustainable development climate risks and adaptation struggle for the attention of leaders.

The work of Niu et al. (2018) and Homsy (2018) are important as they draw attention to the way in which issues are framed to generate action and the critical role of governance – or as they would term it, the situational context – as providing the setting within which formal and informal leaders operate. The next sections of the chapter focus specifically on how climate risk and adaptation are being addressed in Wales and what this tells us about leadership approaches, within strategic, organisational, operational and community-based contexts.

Governance in Wales

Climate change and sustainable development have been major policy challenges for many countries. In Wales, the venture was given a further twist under the Government of Wales Act 1998, as this created a devolved legislative body and required the new organisation to promote sustainable development in all its work. The use of legislation to enshrine sustainability in practice has been a reoccurring theme for Welsh Government. The most recent legislation has been the Well-being of Future Generations Act (WBFGA) 2015. Davidson (2020), an ex-Cabinet Minister, provides a unique insight into the legislation. The Act provides the opportunity for leaders in Welsh Government and public bodies to help frame their activity around well-being to deal with climate risk and adaptation. Public bodies and Welsh Ministers are now required to adopt and use a sustainable development principle[1] in their governance and operations; reframe their work around seven national well-being goals, linked to the UN Sustainable Development Goals;[2] work together in 19 local partnerships called Public Services Boards (PSBs) who produce well-being plans; and regularly report on progress to the Wales Audit Office, with support from Future Generations Commissioner and Office (OFGC). The legislation provides Wales with a revised governance structure for public bodies to focus on well-being and future generations but, as we explain below, it has not proved to be straightforward to use the Act to tackle the complex challenge of climate risk and adaptation.

Future generations and climate change policy in Wales

Climate modelling and risk assessments (UK Committee on Climate Change 2017) highlight that Wales can expect more frequent and severe incidents of extreme weather in the future. Risks include more frequent prolonged summer heatwaves; an increase in winter rain and snow; less rain in summer, but more intense downpours; wetter winters; and an increase of water flows in rivers. Sea level rise of over one metre will also present Welsh communities with greater risk from river and coastal flooding. The likely impact of these changes on communities will be complex and spatially variable. The evidence suggests that leaders need to plan for a range of interconnected challenges including thinking about infrastructure – our roads, bridges and railways to keep them working; plan for changes to soils, food production and farming; manage water to have enough during droughts and deal with too much during flooding; plan utilities to ensure energy, water, communications and IT 'kit' can cope; manage landscapes to ensure ecosystem resilience and reduce fire risk and protect coastal communities and let some of them go (Welsh Government 2019).

A national leadership vacuum on climate change adaptation in Wales

Climate change policy in Wales is influenced by both UK legislation, the UK Climate Change Act (2008) and Wales' own WBFGA (2015). The Climate Change Act requires Welsh Government to report its own approach to climate adaptation to the UK Climate Committee (UKCCC) through a devolved climate adaptation plan. This is informed and refreshed every five years by a UK Climate Risk Assessment (CCRA).

As we have noted in previous work (Flynn et al., 2016), Welsh Government has not exercised the powers available from the UK Climate Change Act to compel public authorities to report on their plans for climate adaptation. Since the passage of the WBFGA there has been no Wales Climate Change Commission or Committee in Wales or grouping to develop multi-stakeholder action or discourse on adaptation.

Prosperity for all: A Climate Conscious Wales (Welsh Government 2019) is Welsh Government's response to CCRA2 (2017). It focuses internally on the government's own responsibilities to address dealing with risks to people; communities; buildings; water supplies; land management practices; ecosystems; agriculture and lists their research priorities.[3] While relevant delivery partners are identified, this is a plan for government and not partner organisations. In terms of accountability, the Welsh Government's actions are scrutinised by the Climate Change Subcommittee on Climate Change of the Welsh Senedd (Parliament), with no other mechanism for external scrutiny. The plan suggests an External Stakeholder Forum for knowledge exchange and to advise on Welsh Government's programme of work, but government has been slow to deliver on a Forum.

An unintended consequence of framing climate change through the WBFGA (2015) has been its marginalisation. Climate change is only referred to twice: the first time in the context of a 'Prosperous Wales' aiming for a low-carbon society; the second time in the context of a 'Resilient Wales' referring to the role of ecosystems to adapt to climate change. Work examining Public Services Boards in Wales, and their constituent organisations, found that climate adaptation had had very little profile in well-being assessments, well-being plans or organisational plans resulting from the Act. There is also little evidence to show that the Future Generations Commissioner or their Office had addressed climate risk or adaptation in their work since 2016 (Netherwood and Flynn 2020). The prioritisation and marginalisation of environmental issues is well-recognised (Kurze and Lenschow 2018), and the well-being approach draws attention to carbon mitigation (a low-carbon society) but underplays adaptation. With a limited institutional base for climate change discussions in Wales, suggestions for advancing climate adaptation are easily ignored.

In contrast, plans for climate mitigation have a high political and strategic profile. Wales's national strategy for decarbonisation Prosperity for All: Low-Carbon Wales (Welsh Government 2019) contains 76 policies and 24 interventions to achieve a Low-Carbon Wales by 2050 and beyond. A key focus for the public sector in Wales is to become carbon-neutral by 2030 and Wales to become net zero by 2050. Most interventions are for Welsh Government to either deliver or stimulate decarbonisation across areas of influence, providing leadership on this issue, but significantly they also detail multi-stakeholder activity in partnership with public, private and third sector bodies. The activities can be broken down into four categories:

1. Organisational mechanisms that promote decarbonisation;
2. Ensuring decarbonisation is delivered through policy and funding mechanisms;
3. Stimulating operational activity which enables decarbonisation;
4. Activities which build capacity to respond to decarbonisation in different groups of people and communities of interest.

It is notable that debate, policy and legislation have developed rapidly on decarbonisation since the publication in 2019 of Low-Carbon Wales. The Welsh Government has produced a specific Low-Carbon Delivery Plan 2 (2020) designed to engage stakeholders from power, transport, industry, land use, agriculture, buildings and waste sectors, and the public sector to develop more collaborative working arrangements. Decarbonisation has also been a feature of the work of the Future Generations Commissioner and Office. In July 2020, Ministers established a taskforce to ensure that climate mitigation is at the heart of post-Covid-19 recovery planning in Wales. In February 2021, Ministers laid regulations in the Senedd, which will formally commit Wales, for the first time, to legally binding targets to deliver the goal of net-zero emissions. The carbon reduction agenda, in contrast to adaptation, has had powerful political and administrative leadership, strategic buy-in and legislation to further drive change.

Decarbonisation fits well with a neoliberal governance agenda that promotes resource efficiency and promises economic benefits. Low-carbon policies bring together governments and businesses (though high energy-using businesses and those wedded to fossil fuels are likely to remain outside this consensus). For both government and businesses, efforts to promote a low-carbon economy show an intent to engage with a high-profile issue that matters to the public and consumers. Decarbonisation attracts political and business leadership.

Climate change adaptation, meanwhile, is lower profile and problematic as it is less easy to bring together businesses and governments. In part this is because political and administrative leaders perceive climate adaptation in Wales as a single-issue problem – that of managing increased flood risk in the future – that can be dealt with for the most part by well-managed bureaucratic arrangements. The institutional and policy response to flooding is well-organised and multi-level in Wales. Climate projections are considered in forward planning in management for shorelines, coasts and river catchments and development. Welsh Government's Flood and Coastal Erosion Risk Management Strategy (2020) is designed to develop collaborative action to manage increasing risks by using natural systems to reduce negative impacts of climate change. This sets the overall policy framework for Local Flood Management Strategies delivered through Natural Resources Wales and local authorities. A national Flood Management Committee provides institutional leadership on this issue. Here climate change adaptation is framed to become the management of flood risk (Devitt and O'Neill 2017) rather than a political issue about resource distribution and social justice.

Reconceptualising flood risks needs to recognise that it is not a single issue but rather the challenge of managing a series of interacting risks at a local level. Climate adaptation because of its complexity, with a need to plan for cumulative, long-term and multi-faceted impacts on communities is a problem for leaders. The nature of these impacts does not lend itself to a single area of responsibility and raises difficult questions of sufficiency of current planning for the future, requiring collaborative approaches to risk assessment and management that challenge current approaches to inter-agency working.

While the Wales Green Recovery Action Plan (2020) (Natural Resources Wales 2020) focuses on nature-based activities to restore and enhance eco-systems services and habitats, which implicitly enhance climate resilience, most of the Plan focuses on a decarbonisation agenda; greenspace; active travel; housing; sustainable tourism, resource use and skills development. Beyond one reference to coastal risk from sea level rise the Plan contains no reference to climate risks from CCRA. Specific strategic activity related to climate adaptation is not part of the green recovery discourse in Wales.

Preparations for the third UK Climate Change Risk Assessment (CCRA3) (due to be published by the UK Climate Change Committee in 2022) (Climate Change Commission) have shown first, that current systems, plans, strategies and investments in Wales will not, in their current form, be sufficient to manage the scale of the risks presented by climate change in Wales, and more effective ways are needed for integrating climate risks into forward plans across multiple sectors. Second, that measures are still needed to improve the evidence base to show the impact of climate change on different communities, landscapes, and infrastructure. Third, that more needed to be done to understand and explore the management of key risks through different adaptation pathways. Fourth, that much stronger collaboration between governments, local authorities, public bodies, the third sector and communities is needed to plan for individual and cascading climate risks.

A key feature of the analysis for CCRA3 was the plethora of plans and strategies for different places in Wales, for example, river basin planning, regeneration, community development, health and biodiversity that are unconnected to each other, and which do not recognise the interconnected nature of climate impacts, or in many cases, climate risk as a relevant issue. Another feature was the variety for institutional arrangements to address different policy challenges at local, regional and national level that focused primarily on opportunities for decarbonisation rather than climate risks. Based on this evidence, climate risk and adaptation continue to have very limited profile in public policy in Wales.

So, for leaders, the national policy agenda for post-Covid-19 recovery – which, of course, they have helped to develop – presents them with little incentive to steer their organisations into the difficult, complex and controversial area of managing climate risk and adapting current approaches to policy delivery. Not surprisingly, local leaders are sensitive to national agendas. It is, therefore, understandable that currently there are no local climate adaptation plans from local government in Wales, an absence of climate risk management and adaptation in the corporate or operational plans of public bodies, limited partnership work between public bodies on adaptation and a lack of community level discussion on future climate risk. Nevertheless, as we show below, there are activities emerging that seek to tackle climate risk.

Local leadership on climate risk

In this subsection we explore some of the locally led climate risk projects that have been undertaken. Climate Ready Gwent was a project run in 2018 with five Public Services Boards (PSBs)[4] in the Gwent area of South East Wales. This involved engaging local public bodies and communities to understand local perspectives of climate change and priorities for forward planning in nine different localities and contexts – involving your people, the elderly, a coastal village upland farmers, town councillors, a World Heritage Site, local government and environmental bodies. This produced case studies and a report with a detailed business case for forward action. A key finding was the ability for multiple partners and the community to think about a locality's future and understand how different climate impacts from severe weather can play out, and the challenges for local leaders to respond and plan forward. Community leaders, including town councillors, were engaged in the project. However, there is little evidence that PSBs have used the evidence to develop climate adaptation options or engage political or partnership leaders on this issue. This is an example of public bodies commissioning evidence to support their thinking on the issue of climate risk, without establishing ways of using the evidence to engage and embolden leaders to act.

Another project for the Climate Emergency for the four North Wales PSBs and the North Wales Regional Leadership Board gathered information on climate mitigation at a strategic, organisational, operational and community-based levels in the region, undertook a gap analysis and recommended new enhanced governance arrangements to tackle the climate emergency, involving leaders. The analysis provided detail for a three-year regional plan focused on net zero, land management to sequester carbon and climate adaptation. This is an example of a project where political and executive leaders were involved from the outset and were able to identify their own roles in climate leadership. A workshop in February 2020 identified key characteristics needed by leaders to drive the climate change agenda:

- Leaders should create the conditions for others to increase the scale and ambition of regional activity on climate change and to introduce high-level governance, finance and management;
- Leaders should change the way their organisations approach climate change – to make climate change mitigation and adaptation a central part of the function of their organisations – given its potential impact on the region and community well-being;
- Leaders should act as both an advocate and provocateur to challenge colleagues and partners on climate mitigation and climate resilience;
- Leaders should intervene at the highest level to change activity to support climate change response, not just to be reported to;
- Leaders should intervene to help to connect and manage the diversity of interests and responses to climate change.

This example illustrates that local leaders could appreciate the shift in strategy and practice that is required to systematically tackle climate adaptation. To make ideas meaningful for participants, the project highlighted the potential choices that arose for leaders and partner organisations in tackling the climate emergency. Three options were outlined:

1. Do partners maintain a fragmented and incremental approach to climate adaptation? This would mean continuing to do good things to

address climate change but in an unconnected way, responding to different drivers, e.g. partners develop predominantly operational responses to climate change and move incrementally towards low/zero carbon while identifying communities at risk from climate impacts, without adaptation planning. This is the situation now in North Wales. It is not treating climate change as an emergency, but as an operational issue, that will be dealt with incrementally within current systems.

2. Do partners develop an integrated approach? This is where there is some partnership work to address climate change, creating some efficiencies and improvement of organisational and partnership action, e.g. partners introduce climate change as a consideration in reports, develop shared evidence, coordinate aspects of their climate planning and implement some joint demonstration projects. North Wales partners are working towards this type of approach, however the scale and pace of activity to address climate change is modest. This is a situation where North Wales PSBs treat climate change, not as an emergency, but as another issue to be addressed over time from a long list of shared policy challenges.

3. Do partners pursue a transformative approach? This is where organisations work together to coordinate, manage, influence, collaborate and implement to shift the scale and pace of work on both climate mitigation and adaptation, e.g. new approaches to storing carbon in land assets; new infrastructure for low-carbon vehicles; influencing and winning government funding streams for addressing climate change; creating the conditions for others to contribute to mitigation and adaptation; coordinating activity to influence drivers at cross border, and at a Wales and UK level. This is treating climate change as a strategic, existential issue, fundamental to the future well-being of the region.

While, of course, many leaders will be sympathetic to the third option of promoting a transformative approach, in practice change is likely to be more modest, as the case below illustrates.

Political, partnership and organisational leaders were involved in a Climate Resilience Pilot in a small coastal town and port, Fishguard and Goodwick, undertaken for Pembrokeshire PSB during 2020. This project identified climate adaptation priorities in the community by engaging with public bodies, businesses, community groups and residents on current plans, gaps and locally based risks. A Climate Resilience Plan has been produced. Of note were potential impacts on road transport infrastructure; landscape scale risks, both inland and coastal; essential infrastructure utilities, energy, communication, water; and the sufficiency of current planning for future. The Plan identified five priorities which can build resilience through agencies, authorities and the community working together. These included exploring climate risks and assessing the future costs and benefits of climate change. Local political, community and business leaders were able to discuss their own roles in a series of one-to-one discussions and virtual workshops and showed a willingness, particularly in the case of Lower Fishguard, to open up debate about adaptation options for the small port and the trunk road which are at serious threat from coastal inundation. A detailed plan has been developed for a multi-agency task group to take this forward. Engaging Cabinet members, CEOs of both the Council and National Park as well as councillors has been a feature of this Pilot. However, at the same time, plans developed independently of the Pilot project, for post-Covid-19 recovery and regeneration over the next decade, have not included managing climate risk. The disconnection between thinking in the Pilot project and plan development raises important questions about the level of ambition of leaders for climate adaptation, their appetite to address climate risk and integrate this across the full range of their responsibilities.

These examples illustrate that the leadership of PSBs in Wales are beginning to explore climate adaptation at the pilot level. Leaders are able to think creatively but these pilot projects make little demand upon leaders for delivery. Without national strategic guidance and funding drivers or accountability mechanisms to their communities to drive climate adaptation, then local leadership, like that at the national level, is found to be wanting.

The example of Fairbourne in Gwynedd, in North Wales, shows what happens when leaders are forced to address climate risk and adaptation as a result of sea level rise and coastal change (Gwynedd Consultancy 2019). This is one of the first communities in the UK whose long-term sustainability is compromised as result of climate change. Climate modelling in the 2010s suggested that as a result of rising sea levels much of the village would be below normal high tide levels within the next 50 years and that there would be a need to relocate the population elsewhere. Property blight, financial losses, a decline in mental health, loss of community facilities and loss of tourism are all significant impacts which are currently being managed through a multi-sector partnership. There is a planned approach to the decommissioning of the village, including a resettlement plan for residents, and partners are investigating 'equity release' for adaptive use and identifying funding needs. While local political and organisational leaders and Welsh Government Ministers have been involved in discussions for the last decade, the overall financial implications of planned relocation are still to be considered alongside the financial impacts on communities in the area. This is the type of detailed planning that leaders will be increasingly involved in. There are many other cases of villages such as Fairbourne already identified as 'at risk' from climate impacts in Wales (Gwynedd Consultancy 2019).

Leadership for climate change

In this section we first examine a series of opportunities for interventions that seek to draw in external expertise and establish greater legitimacy for actions so as to create an agenda for change that leaders can both draw on and contribute to. We follow this by describing key leadership characteristics and how they operate in practice.

Leadership interventions for climate change

We believe that leadership interventions on climate adaptation are complex and will require actions that go beyond the production of a strategy or plan, declaration of a climate emergency, or providing examples of where the organisation is already doing well. There are several mechanisms that are often used by leaders to establish activity on policy. Here we examine those often used in Wales and in other parts of the UK:

- **A commitment, declaration, charter or covenant** [a written agreement usually formal to do (or not to do) something]. In Wales, 16 of 22 Welsh local authorities and Welsh Government itself had declared climate emergencies by March 2021 (Climate Emergency UK 2021). (Climate Change Commitments had also been declared by all 22 councils in

2008 via the Welsh Local Government Association): In the past, Welsh Government had encouraged organisations in all sectors to make commitments as part of a Sustainable Development Charter prior to the WBFGA. The EU has a covenant of Mayors for climate change and energy (of which there are no Welsh signatories). We suggest that these are often political or organisational statements of intent that may result in public bodies illustrating what they are already doing, but often do not drive change.

- **An alliance or coalition** [an arrangement for combined action to influence policy] is often developed by civil society or bodies outside the government policy arena. Wales has a Sustainable Development Alliance, a third sector body, and has Stop Climate Chaos and Fuel Poverty coalitions which collectively represents the views of thousands of members in Wales. These bodies seek to influence Welsh Government policy.
- **A taskforce** [a unit especially organised for a specific task over an agreed period]. Examples include the UK Federation of Small Businesses Task Force on Climate-related Financial Disclosures (TCFD) and the UK Local Government Association, which has recently proposed setting up a national taskforce with Whitehall departments to tackle climate change and coordinate policies to deliver net-zero carbon emissions by 2030. A taskforce may be set up to measure the potential for land carbon sequestration on publicly owned land or coordinating approaches to agricultural emissions within the farming and food and drink supply industries. These are often short-term arrangements which build a business case for change in policy or delivery.
- **A steering committee, advisory group or commission** [a group of people who are chosen to direct the way something is dealt with]. These bodies generally provide guidance on strategy, policy, choosing priorities, budgets, resources, coordinating and managing the general course of activity. Steering Groups are often made up of a combination of authority and public body elected members and staff, academic, third sector, government and community partners. In Wales, these have been established to support collaborative work on regional investment, waste and social value. Individual bodies also often establish steering groups to manage crosscutting issues such as equalities, Welsh language or sustainability. Leeds has a well-established Climate Commission chaired by University and Council with members being drawn from key organisations and groups

from across the city. Their work focuses on low-carbon development, climate resilience and public engagement and communications. Bristol City Council have an advisory committee on climate change (Bristol online). Devon Council have established a Climate Change Response Group with 25 organisations from across sectors including health, university, utility and district council partners (Devon Climate Emergency).

- **A citizens assembly** is a well-established mechanism in government which helps to gather ideas, reflect on important policy matters, develop policies, explore public views and engage public bodies and industry in dialogue about policy and response. For example, there is a House of Commons Citizen Assembly for 'A Path to Net Zero' (Climate Assembly) which is advising six select committees how the UK can reduce greenhouse gas emissions to net zero by 2050. Citizen assemblies have also been established during 2020 in response to climate emergency declarations, including Bristol, Oxford Newham, Leeds, Brent, Camden and Cambridge. These arrangements are in their early stages but being used to inform high-level strategy and key actors.

Leadership capabilities for climate risk and adaptation: the Belfast Climate Commissioner

The recruitment process for the Belfast Climate Commissioner provides insights into how one public sector body, Belfast City Council, perceived the core competencies required of a Commissioner post (Belfast City Council 2021). This provides us with insights into what the public sector regards as important leadership skills.

Belfast, in Northern Ireland, is a partner in the 100 Resilient Cities global partnership and has a well-established Belfast Resilience Strategy which focuses on the challenges to the city's infrastructure, development and growth. The Resilience Plan sets out 30 programmes of work, to deliver an 'inclusive, net zero emission, climate resilient economy in a generation'. Specific responsibilities for the new Commissioner were co-chairing a Resilience and Sustainability Board for the city region; being responsible for a multi-party political working group on the climate crisis; leading stakeholder relationship management across the city; and building and sustaining industry partnerships. The post was seen by BCC as a change management role which would impact on the work of the Council and partnerships;

commissioning research to support delivery of climate mitigation and adaptation. To achieve these objectives, Belfast City Council sought a person able to demonstrate generic management skills: able to develop and deliver policy; lead organisational change; broker collaborative relationships; deal with resistance; show political sensitivity; be able to exercise financial planning and budgetary control; deliver cross-cutting projects and have analytical and problem-solving skills. Surprisingly, there was no specific requirement to show previous specific knowledge of climate change as part of the core competencies for the leadership role. This suggests that the Commissioner's role would be to deliver on an established agenda of climate resilience rather than develop independent thinking in this area.

The core competencies required of the Belfast Climate Commissioner vividly highlight a tension: between management skills and a commitment to climate change. The core competencies would certainly help in the delivery of climate risk and adaptation. As others have pointed out, though, personal engagement with climate change can also be an important part of leadership.

Leadership and personal engagement

Personal engagement of leaders on climate change is a central part of the agenda of the global Climate Coaching Alliance (CCA). This was set up in late 2019 to bring together coaches, coaching psychologists, coaching supervisors, facilitators, and other leadership professionals to share practice. The aim of many of these coaches is to enable leaders to step into their role to address the climate emergency. The alliance has 700 members across six continents. In Spring 2021 an online workshop was devoted to the relationship between climate risk and leadership in Wales (Netherwood and Nash 2021). Exercises were carried out – taking coaches through four leadership scenarios: the loss of a coastal community; organisational change; establishing a citizen's jury; and financing climate risk management. From a leadership coaching perspective, the following challenges were identified:

- To enable the leaders to explore their own fears and uncertainties; lack of knowledge; dealing with uncertainty; and addressing the belief that climate change is too big an issue, that it can 'overwhelm' leaders. Individually and collectively these issues can discourage leaders from engaging with climate change;

- To enable leaders to explore opportunities, such as reconnecting leaders with their motivation for public service; enabling them to focus on their legacy; supporting them to manage their own uncertainties; exploring their approaches to delegating responsibilities; developing leaders' skills in conflict management; and connecting leaders to their accountability to future generations and their own convictions for addressing the issue;
- Enable the leader to explore and understand their personal beliefs, assumptions, areas of discomfort and 'pain' to better understand the effect of their own behaviour in managing climate risks, helping them to take what they perceive as 'risks' to address the issue.

While leadership will need generic senior competencies, as in the Belfast example, confronting climate change will also likely require personal competencies, especially a commitment to want to tackle climate change.

Climate risk and intra- and inter-generational challenges

An important part of the challenge for leaders in their thinking and action on climate is how to deal with current and future generations. For local leaders, thinking of what climate change might mean for current and future generations has a spatial aspect. This is because much public sector work is focused on service delivery, and service delivery matters for communities. So, whereas at higher levels of governance climate change risks may be more abstract, at the more local level they will have meaning. Local leaders need to be able to distinguish between different groups of people living in different periods of time to enable them to explore trade-offs and compromises which are fundamental to long-term planning.

The following categories describe one way in which leaders might differentiate between the needs of different generations of people living in their area, where a generation is a group of individuals born and living at the same time:

- **Inter-generational needs** – between current and future generations;
- **Trans-generational needs** – beyond current generations – for future generations;
- **Multi-generational needs** – focusing on outcomes for multiple generations;

- **Intra-generational needs** – focusing on outcomes within a current generation;

Addressing **inter-generational needs** might be exemplified by actions which deliberately maintain a soil resource upon which current agriculture and future agriculture might be reliant. This recognises that current levels of soil exploitation cannot continue. This specifically recognises that our approach to growth needs to tackle things now to benefit people now and in the future. Such action enables existing and future generations to access healthy soil to grow food. This activity is mutually beneficial to both groups of people.

A stable climate is an example of **trans-generational need** where current generations need to reduce their emissions and adapt to climate change, incurring 'costs' and making challenging choices now about growth and development to maintain well-being for future generations. This recognises that we need to make decisions that we may not benefit from now, so that future generations can maintain their well-being.

Multi-generational needs can be addressed through activity which supports multiple generations of people living in a locality, as a by-product of addressing the needs of current generations. For example, investing in green infrastructure can benefit current generations but longer-term benefits may be even more significant for generations to come.

Intra-generational needs can be addressed through activity which focuses on the present; for example, developing a day care centre next to a school to encourage support within current generations. The centre may or may not be there for future generations.

Within Welsh governance well-being is a central theme and is the lens through which climate change strategies are viewed. As we have argued above, climate change adaptation has been marginalised. The WBFGA should be an opportunity to boost interest in climate change adaptation but, again, as we have seen, that has not happened. It is, therefore, worthwhile briefly exploring why leaders, who have a responsibility to think about future generations under the WBFGA, find it so difficult to do so. A better grasp of the challenges that leaders face in thinking about future generations will also help to understand why climate change adaptation efforts are frequently stifled because this too demands analysis over longer time horizons.

Work on the well-being planning process, a core part of the WBFGA, has found that it is not significantly lengthening time horizons of public service planning or representing the needs of future generations (Netherwood and Flynn 2020). A key part of the governance that has been designed to safeguard the interests of future generations is not achieving its purpose of a long-term focus or exploring inter-generational equity. Meaningful insight into long-term outcomes for future generations is limited amongst stakeholders involved in well-being planning. Despite key actors' best efforts, well-being planning, to date, presents us with a weak concept of long-term well-being for future generations and indicates that unborn generations are yet to find a voice in this area of Welsh public policy. Much of the policy thinking on future generations includes implicit assumptions that benefits to future generations will accrue as a by-product of activity focused on current generations, without defining how this might impact positively (or negatively) on generations to come.

There are several reasons why the aspirations of the WBFGA are being stifled. One is that the various tools to consider the long term have not generated meaningful analysis and insight into long-term outcomes. A second factor is that the accountability framework which has developed around the Act is also failing as it does not specifically address the needs of future generations. The Wales Audit Office, Scrutiny Committees and the Future Generations Commissioner's activity seem to be focused on the *process* of delivering the legislative requirements of the Act rather than the *content* of well-being plans or the potential long-term *outcomes* of well-being planning.

Wallace (2019) too has argued that public bodies' response to the WBFGA is focused on process and performance management, short-term outcomes and delivery, with limited discourse on social progress over the long term. As a result, planning is focused on more joined-up service delivery for current generations rather than focusing on specific outcomes for future generations in the place that they will live. Well-being planning is reinforcing the 'presentism' described by Thompson (2010) and the Oxford Martin Commission (2013) in doing little to challenge models of short-term institutional governance, policy and behaviour. In other words, despite legislation enabling leaders at national and local levels to think longer-term, they continue to reproduce well-established management repertoires – the activities that are valued in training and job specifications – such as more integrated service delivery. To move the debate on there needs to be a shift in governance that can give future generations a greater voice in public policy, and that voice should include climate change adaptation (see Conclusions below).

While we have drawn attention to the limitations of governance, institutional and policy reform within public sector partnerships as a result of the WBFGA, we recognise that change often takes longer to achieve than its advocates would have hoped. Our findings are applicable to a much wider audience that is grappling with the challenges of how to better meet the needs of future generations and planning for the long term. Our work shows that establishing statutory obligations, new governance procedures and a Commissioner is no guarantee that future generations will be better represented by public services. Institutional reform and new mechanisms only provide the potential to reframe public service delivery, and as long as this remains the case, a climate change adaptation agenda will remain marginalised.

It is, therefore, imperative that leaders in Wales feel empowered, that they perceive that they have the resources, capacity and commitment, to make positive changes to policy development and delivery over shorter and extended time horizons. In the subsection below we briefly outline ideas that might help.

Approaches to strategic leadership for climate risk and adaptation

With much attention being focused on climate mitigation, one easy route forward is to look at how the topic is presented and to apply similar thinking to climate change adaptation. A reframing of the climate change adaptation agenda may raise its profile. One example that could be drawn upon is from the Welsh Parliament (Senedd) that commissioned research in 2019 (NAW 2019) to explore what characteristics are needed on a national level to drive forward climate mitigation activity. Applying the ideas to climate risk and adaptation would combine strategic, financial, communication and engagement activity which involves communities but also politicises the issue of climate risks. It could do this by:

- Developing multi-partner regional and local adaptation plans that enhance, coordinate and scrutinise current approaches to adaptation;

- Budgeting for climate risks, from the increased number and impact of severe weather and flooding events and building in resilience to infrastructural investment;
- Communicating the merit of adaptation now to reduce risk later through front-loaded actions to minimise risks to the economy, environment, society and the infrastructure it relies on;
- Engaging civil society on the impacts that communities are likely to experience and their role in building resilience with public bodies and agencies;
- Establishing political understanding of the complexity of climate risks and the scale of response required;
- Ensuring approaches to growth factor in climate risks and adaptation pathways under different scenarios.

Meanwhile, the work of OECD (Corfee et al., 2009) provides insights into the way in which leaders can develop multi-level governance approaches to deal with the complexity of risks and response to climate change. While the original work focused primarily on climate mitigation, its lessons can be applied to climate risk adaptation. We have taken the core characteristics of effective governance for climate change identified by OECD and adapted these to the types of activity which leaders might use to drive climate adaptation across Wales.

- **Integration of climate adaptation activity** needs to be both vertical (hierarchical) and horizontal (across sectors) connecting key actors, institutions and similar initiatives. In Wales this might mean strategic, organisational and operational climate adaptation is addressed within the public sector alongside engagement with industrial partners, utilities and third sector to help to identify opportunities to work together;
- **Common institutional foundation and knowledge base** so that organisations all have common purpose and evidence to inform their actions. In Wales this might mean that leaders instigate common approaches and requirements to climate adaptation within PSBs, public bodies and local authorities;
- **Public bodies have multiple roles that need to be recognised by leaders** so that public bodies are *facilitators* between actors through local partnerships and programmes of work; they provide *direct services*

CLIMATE RISK AND ADAPTATION IN WALES 333

in response to climate impacts, for example, emergency response and health services; are *investors* in infrastructure which needs to be climate resilient; are *place makers* managing the growth and development of communities; which will be impacted by climate change; *decision-makers* that do or do not consider climate risks in multiple decisions affecting the future of communities; and *regulators* through the planning system;

- **Cooperation across boundaries** because leadership on climate change deals with institutional change; spatial differences; develops tools to support change; and provides resources for change across political boundaries;
- **Scaling to achieve influence and change** because credibility and authority is enhanced where organisations work together to influence policy, innovate and address barriers. Leaders in Wales should seek to influence Welsh Government to ensure fiscal mechanisms, performance frameworks and investment strategies are adequate to support climate risk management and adaptation.

The Centre for Alternative Technology in Zero Carbon Britain – Rising to the challenge of the Climate Emergency (2020) also provide a useful frame to think about how leaders might influence change in relation to climate mitigation. Again, the thinking can usefully be applied to climate change adaptation. Public sector leaders might seek to influence:

- *Upwards*: influencing government in relation to strategy, funding, performance frameworks and reporting;
- *Downwards*: influencing activity within their own organisation, including service business and financial planning;
- *Sideways*: would mean influencing the focus of regional and local partnerships to identify specific adaptation options for communities and investment priorities;
- *Inwards*: influencing the activity of staff within their own organisations to recognise climate risks and adaptation in their own roles;

To this we could add

- *Outwards*: to the communities that public bodies serve, increasing understanding local perspectives on climate risks and identifying local assets (natural, economic and social) to address climate adaptation.

While many of these ideas are helpful insights to encourage improvements in leadership, they are revisions within existing systems of governance. These reforms will not challenge existing governance arrangements but rather seek to make them work more effectively; in this case paying more attention to climate change adaptation. As our analysis of intra- and inter-generational tensions showed, however, governance in Wales struggles to engage with long-term thinking. This flaw is not conducive to developing leadership on climate change adaptation. In our Conclusions below, we reflect on these twin challenges – how to develop longer-term analyses and how best to raise the political profile of climate change adaptation – and argue that a more deliberative style of governance should be pursued.

Conclusions

In this chapter we have argued that the WBFGA is not significantly lengthening time horizons of public service planning or representing the needs of future generations. It presents us with a weak concept of long-term well-being for future generations and indicates that unborn generations are yet to find a voice in Welsh public policy. We believe, on the basis of our work on climate adaptation explored in this chapter, that current policy development around climate risks is reinforcing the 'presentism' described by Thompson (2010) and the Oxford Martin Commission (2013) and doing little to challenge models of short-term institutional governance, policy and behaviour. Our work shows that establishing statutory obligations, new governance procedures and a Commissioner is no guarantee that future generations will be better represented by public services, or that climate risks will be treated as a priority. Institutional reform and new mechanisms only provide the potential to reframe public service delivery.

The absence of a Climate Commission or Committee in Wales to drive policy and accountability, with no requirements on public bodies to report on climate adaptation, means that the onus for change will need to come from the public bodies and communities that will be impacted by climate risks. The leadership vacuum will need to be filled by local leaders who can understand the specific risks to their local communities rather than the current approach of local authorities declaring climate emergencies, and only focusing on climate mitigation. How can leaders begin to understand

CLIMATE RISK AND ADAPTATION IN WALES 335

the complexity of climate change risks, listen to their communities and promote the interests of future generations?

We suggest that as a first step, that leaders should take a more rigorous and deliberative approach to distinguishing between the risks of climate change to different groups of people living in different periods of time. We think this is essential to enable them to explore trade-offs and compromises between generations which are fundamental to long-term planning (see also Jacobs (2016) and Boston (2017)).

The categories shown in Figure 14.1 describe how leaders might differentiate between the needs of different generations of people living in their area in relation to climate risk and adaptation, and how they could adopt a more deliberative approach to thinking about future generations' needs.

Based on our understanding of current practice highlighted in this chapter, leaders' approaches to climate risk in Wales are often driven by concerns of future flooding from an intra-generational perspective through emergency response, and, through a multi-generational frame through statutory requirements for current flood risk management planning. We suggest that leaders will increasingly need to work with others within inter-generational and trans-generational frames to identify solutions to climate risks, rather than adopting a reductionist approach to climate change through flood risk management and further emissions reduction.

Our findings indicate that longer-term planning for the types of interconnected risks highlighted in CCRA3, and those highlighted by the various examples discussed, will need a more deliberative approach to consider the relationships between decisions made now, the specific impact of these on future generations, and the sufficiency of current planning to provide future generations with the means to maintain their well-being. To help in this, leaders could:

- Establish more effective methods of *representation* of the needs of future generations to challenge and inform institutional agendas. For example, leaders working with independent 'place'-focused citizens juries or citizens assemblies, with leaders providing advocacy on behalf of future generations to establish dialogue and representation of their needs in relation to climate risk;
- Develop an understanding of how *approaches to development* in communities might play out within and between generations under climate change

DELIBERATIVE

inter-generational needs:
this might be exemplified by actions which deliberately maintain a soil resource, upon which current agriculture and future agriculture might be reliant. This recognises that current levels of soil exploitation cannot continue and that climate risks related to soil loss and soil productivity need to be addressed and managed. Such action enables existing and future generations to access healthy soil to grow food. Leadership on this issue is mutually beneficial to both current and future generations. This involves a deliberate focus on the needs of future generations.

trans-generational needs
exemplified where current generations need to reduce their emissions and adapt to climate change, incurring 'costs' and making challenging choices now about growth and development in order to maintain well-being for future generations. This recognises that we need to make decisions that we may not benefit from now, so that future generations can maintain their well-being. Leadership on this issue is mutually beneficial to both current and future generations. This involves a deliberate focus on the needs of future generations.

multi-generational needs
can be addressed through activity which supports multiple generations of people living in a locality, as a by-product of addressing the needs of current generations. For example, investing in green infrastructure can benefit current generations but longer-term benefits may be even more significant for generations to come through carbon sequestration and flood risk management. Benefits to future generations are unintentional and undefined.

intra-generational needs
can be addressed through activity which focuses on the present, for example, developing an emergency response plan for a town which repeatedly floods or wildfires, ensuring the elderly residents are supported by less vulnerable residents. The ability of future generations to cope with increased flooding and wildfires are not considered by leaders. Future generations needs are discounted to address more immediate concerns.

UNINTENTIONAL/DISCOUNTED

Figure 14.1 Deliberative approach to future generations and climate risk.

scenarios. This could be based on trans-generational and inter-generational focus on particular places. Leaders could utilise this approach to develop long-term plans which truly focus on the distinctive needs of future generations impacted by climate change;

- Define specific long-term outcomes for future citizens as part of public policy and service and place planning in relation to climate change. Leaders need to be guiding their own organisations and others to define outcomes and adaptation for communities at existential risk from climate impacts.

We have argued in this chapter that it is not enough for leaders to identify climate risk as an issue to be tackled, but that it is essential for leaders to use their experience to manage change in the way that communities develop, in the way that public services are provided and the way in which partners collaborate to manage climate risks in coming decades. Despite legislation, climate risk assessments, strategy, policy and improved evidence, the Welsh public sector is not planning for climate risks to the communities they serve. Even though they have legislation which compels them to think about the interests of future generations over the long term.

In this chapter we have examined the absence of drivers for leaders in Wales to engage with climate risk and the complexity, wide variety and urgency of risks identified by CCRA3, which leaders will need to contend with. We have drawn on examples of emerging multi-partner climate risk and adaptation and the roles of leaders within them, identifying different ways for leaders to approach climate change strategically, organisationally, operationally, in the community and partnerships. We have also provided some thoughts on the leadership capabilities that are required to address climate risk and adaptation and offered a way in which leaders can think about climate risks to future generations.

Leaders in Wales, and elsewhere, will need to adapt their ways of working to address climate risk: becoming more analytical and critical where forward planning is not sufficient to deal with projected climate risks across economic, social and environmental systems; more open to engaging with communities who are threatened by climate impacts; more systemic in their thinking about cascading climate risks; and finally, self-critical in their thinking about how their professional capabilities and qualities can be used and developed to address a changing climate. In other words, leadership needs to become more deliberative to engage with climate risk fully.

Notes

1 The sustainable development principle is described as five ways of working: (1) looking to the long-term so that we do not compromise the ability of future generations to meet their own needs; (2) taking an integrated approach so that public bodies look at all the well-being goals in deciding on

their well-being objectives; (3) involving a diversity of the population in the decisions that affect them; (4) working with others in a collaborative way to find shared sustainable solutions; and (5) understanding the root causes of issues to prevent them from occurring.

2 A prosperous Wales; A resilient Wales; A healthier Wales; A more equal Wales; A Wales of cohesive communities; A Wales of vibrant culture and Welsh language; A globally responsible Wales

3 **Strategic**: Communication; Policy & Business Planning UK Research Programmes; International **Adaptive Nature & The Rural Economy**; Land – carbon storage & sequestration; Woodlands; Non –native Species; Forestry & Agriculture – Flood & Drought; Climate Smart Agriculture Framework; CSC Agriculture Programme; Land Management Programme **Protecting Our Coasts And Seas**; Coastal Zone Resilience; Marine Ecosystems **Staying Healthy** Increased temperature; Fuel Poverty – Warm Homes; Health & Social Care – risks; Air Quality Policy; Vector Borne Pathogens **Safe Homes & Places**; Planning System; Design of Homes & Buildings; Flood Protection; Community Adaptation; Regional Public Services Boards **Caring For Historic Environment** HECC Adaptation Plan; Understanding Risks; Awareness & Guidance **Successful Business**; Sectoral risk UK research; Business Adaptation Support **Resilient Infrastructure & Transport** Transport Infrastructure; interdependent infrastructure risks Bridges & Pipelines.

4 Public Services Boards are formal partnerships involving local authorities, health boards, Natural Resources Wales, Police and Fire and Rescue Authority among others. They are required to develop collaborative local well-being plans, informed by well-being assessments. This is in response to their legal duties under the Well-being of Future Generations Act (Wales) 2015.

Bibliography

Belfast City Council: Climate Commissioner: Candidate Brief via AS Associates (January 2021).

Boston, J. and Berman, E., (2017) *Governing for the future: Designing democratic institutions for a better tomorrow*. Bingley: Emerald.

Bristol online https://www.bristolonecity.com/bringing-a-wealth-of-expertise -to-bristols-net-zero-2030-ambition/ Accessed 30 March 2021.

Climate Assembly https://www.climateassembly.uk/about/ Accessed 30 March 2021.

Climate Change Commission (2021) *Evidence for the third UK Climate Change Risk Assessment Summary for Wales: Principal Author: Dr. A Netherwood.*

Climate Coaching Alliance https://www.climatecoachingalliance.org/ Accessed 30 March 2021.

Climate Emergency UK (2021) https://www.climateemergency.uk/wales/ Accessed 30 March 2021.

Corfee-Morlot, J., Kamal-Chaoui, L., Donovan, M.G., Cochran, I., Robert, A. and Teasdale, P.J. (2009) Cities, Climate Change and Multilevel Governance.

Davidson, J. (2020) *#futuregen: Lessons from a Small Country*. London: Chelsea Green Publishing Co.

Devitt, C. and O'Neill, E. (2017) The framing of two major flood episodes in the Irish print news media: Implications for societal adaptation to living with flood risk. *Public Understanding of Science*, 26(7), pp. 872–888.

Devon Climate Emergency https://www.devonclimateemergency.org.uk/ governance/devon-climate-emergency-response-group/ Accessed 30 March 2021.

edie (2021) *The 2021 Sustainable Business Leadership Report*. https://www.edie .net/downloads/The-2021-Sustainable-Business-Leadership-Report/537

Ferdig, M.A. (2007) Sustainability leadership: Co-creating a sustainable future. *Journal of Change Management*, 7(1), pp. 25–35.

Flynn, A., Kythreotis, A.P. and Netherwood, A. (2016) Climate change adaptation in Wales: Much Ado about nothing? *The Environmental Scientist*, 25(3), pp. 32–39

Galpin, T. and Whittington, J.L. (2012) Sustainability leadership: From strategy to results. *Journal of Business Strategy*, 33(4), pp. 40–48.

Gwynedd Consultancy (2019) Fairbourne Framework for the Future.

Homsy, G.C. (2018) Unlikely pioneers: Creative climate change policymaking in smaller US cities. *Journal of Environmental Studies and Sciences*, 8(2), pp. 121–131.

Jacobs, A.M. (2016) Policy making for the long term in advanced democracies. *Annual Review of Political Science*, 19, pp. 433–454.

Kurze, K. and Lenschow, A. (2018) Horizontal policy coherence starts with problem definition: Unpacking the EU integrated energy-climate approach. *Environmental Policy and Governance*, 28(5), pp.329–338.

Natural Resources Wales (2020) *Green Recovery: Priorities for Action Report*, 3 December 2020.

NAW (2019) *Addressing the Climate Policy Gap in Wales Research Briefing July 2019 Dr Filippos Proedrou from the University of South Wales.*

Netherwood, A., Flynn, A. and Lang, M. (2017) *Well-Being Assessments in Wales: Overview Report: A report commissioned by the Office of the Future Generations Commissioner.*

Netherwood, A. and Flynn, A. (2020) A shift in governance, policy, and delivery for future generations? Well-being Planning in Wales. Discussion Paper, School of Geography & Planning, Cardiff University, July 2020.

Netherwood, A. and Nash, T. (2021) The coaching effect: Helping public leaders act on climate change. Online workshop. https://www.climate coachingalliance.org/event/training-or-workshop-the-coaching-effect -helping-public-leaders-act-on-climate-change/

Niu, X., Wang, X. and Xiao, H. (2018) What motivates environmental leadership behaviour—an empirical analysis in Taiwan. *Journal of Asian Public Policy*, 11(2), pp. 173–187.

Oxford Martin Commission (for Future Generations) (2013) *Now for the Long-Term.*

Shriberg, M. and MacDonald, L. (2013) Sustainability leadership programs: Emerging goals, methods & best practices. *Journal of Sustainability Education*, 5(1), pp. 1–21.

Thompson, D.F. (2010) Representing future generations: Political presentism and democratic trusteeship. *Critical Review of International Social and Political Philosophy*, 13(1), pp. 17–37.

UK Committee on Climate Change Wales Summary (2017) https://www.theccc .org.uk/uk-climate-change-risk-assessment-2017/national-summaries/ wales/

UK Government (2008) *Climate Change Act 2008.*

Wallace, J. (2019) *Wellbeing and Devolution: Reframing the Role of Government in Scotland, Wales and Northern Ireland.* Chapter 4 Well-being as Sustainable Development. Cham, Switzerland: Palgrave McMillan.

Wang, X., Van Wart, M. and Lebredo, N. (2014) Sustainability leadership in a local government context: The administrator's role in the process. *Public Performance & Management Review*, 37(3), pp. 339–364.

Welsh Government (2019) *Prosperity for Wales: A Climate Conscious Wales.* https://gov.wales/prosperity-all-climate-conscious-wales

Zeemering, E.S. (2018) Sustainability management, strategy and reform in local government. *Public Management Review*, 20(1), pp. 136–153.

Part IV

FURTHER READING

15

BIBLIOMETRIC ANALYSIS OF MANAGEMENT AND LEADERSHIP IN THE SUSTAINABILITY AGENDA

Dr Ashish Dwivedi

Introduction

According to Akmal, Podgorodnichenko, Greatbanks and Everett (2018, p. 333),

> 'Bibliometric analysis is part of scientometrics developed to measure scientific performance based on output' ... Within a research community, bibliometric analysis is used to measure and map research communications as well as to quantitatively showcase the development of a field of knowledge, typically based on the number of publications and citations.

This book chapter aims to better understand how the discipline of management and leadership in the sustainability agenda has grown. The focus on the use of bibliometric techniques was to provide indications on the growth and development of research published on management and leadership in the sustainability agenda.

DOI: 10.4324/9781003190820-19

A research design was created wherein journal articles were identified so as to provide dependable and comprehensive information about research published on management and leadership in the sustainability agenda. Figure 15.1 shows the key steps that were involved in creating and analyse research published on management and leadership in the sustainability agenda via bibliometric techniques. The book chapter is structured as follows.

First, a brief overview of the development of management and leadership in the sustainability agenda published is provided. This is followed by

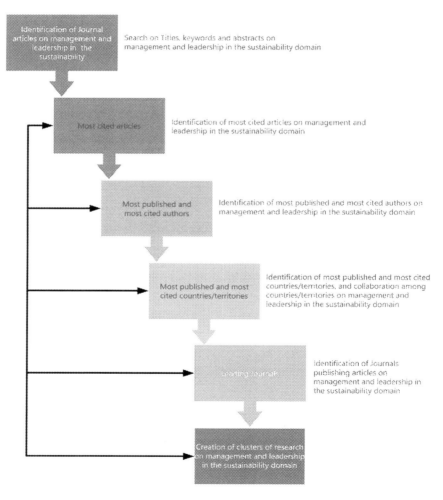

Figure 15.1 Key steps about the application of bibliometric techniques.

a description of the methods employed in the study. Then we present the results of the analysis of the management and leadership in the sustainability agenda published. In this section, we present also the most published authors and the most influential book chapters on management and leadership in the sustainability agenda published. Finally, in the conclusions, we discuss the future trajectories of research on management and leadership in the sustainability agenda published and provide some insights into the possible future development of discourse in this field.

Results

Figure 15.2 traces the evolution of research on management and leadership within the broader sustainability domain. The first recorded journal article on management and leadership within the broader sustainability domain was in 1998, and since then the interest in management and leadership within the broader sustainability domain has had exponential growth, particularly after 2006.

One possible interpretation for this exponential rise could be the broad level of interest by international organizations such as the United Nations – Millennium Development Goals and later Sustainable Development Goals

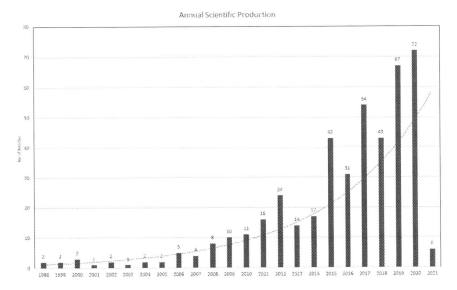

Figure 15.2 Annual scientific production.

– and the simultaneous impact of the environmental agenda on sustainability and a broader level of interest in climate change and sustainability agenda in the context of the exponential human population growth.

Figure 15.3 shows the average citation of an article per year. The peak citation of articles on MTS was in 2005, followed by 2021. However, it is pertinent to note that the average citation of an article per year had fallen in 2015 to two below 2006 levels. An analysis shows that every peak in average article citation per year is followed by a sharp fall. However, an average trendline analysis shows that the average citation of an article per year is rising, indicating sustained interest in management and leadership within the broader sustainability domain.

Figure 15.4 shows the various publication outlets that publish journal articles on the theme of management and leadership within the broader sustainability domain. As expected, the journal publication titled *Sustainability* is the largest source of articles on management and leadership within the broader sustainability domain, followed by the *Journal of Cleaner Production* and the *Journal of Business Ethics*. It is noteworthy to see that the difference between the *Journal of Cleaner Production* which is ranked second, and the journal *Sustainability*, is more than 50%, thus making *Sustainability* the leading

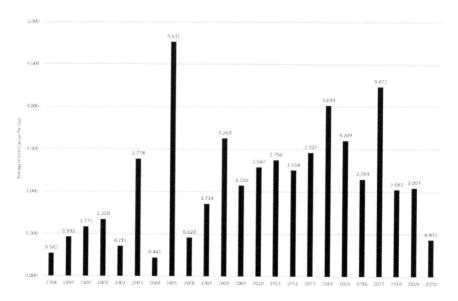

Figure 15.3 Average article citation per year.

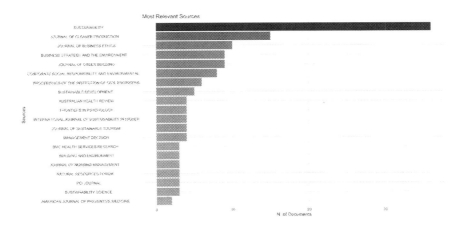

Figure 15.4 Most relevant sources.

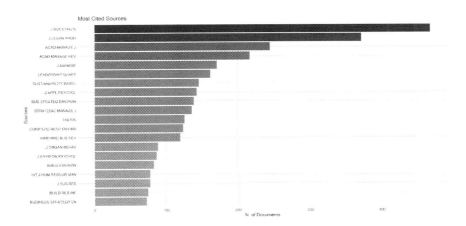

Figure 15.5 Most local cited sources.

relevant publication outlet for research on management and leadership within the broader sustainability domain.

However, if one is focused on citations, which is a broad level of indicator of how readers who published research on management and leadership within the broader sustainability domain find various publication outlets useful in terms of journal articles, the *Journal of Business Ethics* comes at the top (Figure 15.5). There is also a substantial difference between the publication outlets featured in Figure 15.4, which refer to journals publishing research on management and leadership within the broader sustainability domain in terms of output, and Figure 15.5, which refers to journals being cited by academics on management and leadership within the broader sustainability domain. Several leading journals such as the *Academy of Management*, *Academy of Management Review*, *Journal of Management*, *Harvard Business Review* are all very highly regarded cited journals that do not appear in Figure 15.4. In a sense, this reflects the trade-off between producing disciplinary research and publishing on the transdisciplinary matter without extensive empirical support. This difference also highlights that readers would have to carefully look at journal articles that are highly cited on a specific area of leadership on sustainability issues or on management challenges concerning sustainability issues to be aware of theoretical propositions proposed and empirically tested on management and leadership within the broader sustainability domain. However, if readers are keen to be aware of current possibilities on management and leadership within the broader sustainability domain, readers may find it more useful to look at journal outlets featured in Figure 15.4.

Figure 15.6 details the most productive authors in terms of the number of publications. The difference in productivity can be largely attributed to the focus of individual researchers, their approach towards research (empirical research or theoretical research), their publication strategy for disseminating their research, which in some cases may result in a single piece of research which is substantial empirical data being published in several publications.

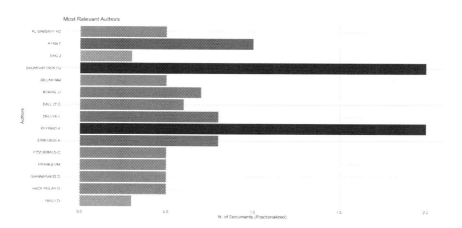

Figure 15.6 Most relevant authors.

Figure 15.7 provides an alternative perspective, wherein author productivity is not seen as the key criteria; rather, the citations received by an author are considered as a whole. The advantage of this approach is that one can identify authors who are producing work on management and leadership within the broader sustainability domain which is highly cited, in comparison to the work shown by the colleagues in Figure 15.6. A careful examination of authors who appear in Figure 15.6 and Figure 15.7 shows that there is a substantial difference between the names of authors who appear in both lists. There are only a couple of authors who are appearing in both these lists, and, as such, it would be fair to say that these are the authors who could be regarded as being significant authors in the discipline of management and leadership within the broader sustainability domain if one adopts a synergistic outlook encompassing productivity and academic relevance as judged by their peers.

Figure 15.8 shows the productivity of top authors over an extended time period. As shown in Figure 15.8, on the right-hand side of the figure there are two circles, which relate to the number of times an article is cited and the number of articles published by individual authors. With regard to interpreting these two circles, it should be noted that the significance is linked to the size of the circle. This implies that the larger the circle size, the more number of articles have been published by individual authors in a particular year. The years are shown on the x-axis. Another significant point is to identify the colouring of the circle. Circles that have a darker shade indicate that

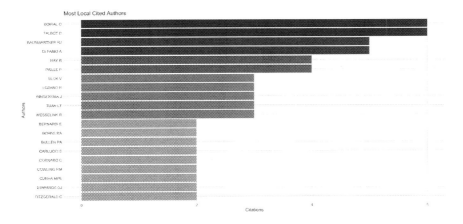

Figure 15.7 Most local cited authors.

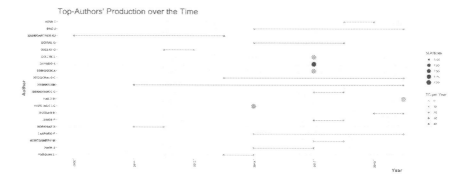

Figure 15.8 Top authors production over time.

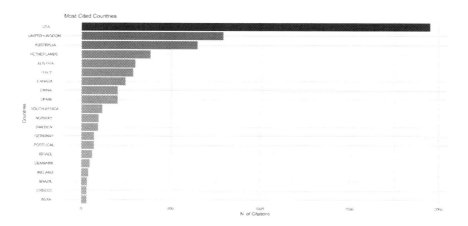

Figure 15.9 Most cited countries.

their citation count is higher – this implies that extremely dark-shaded circles are receiving very high citation counts per year, in comparison to those circles which have a very light shade. Another possible way of interpreting Figure 15.8 is to examine the distance between circles on a straight line for each author. If there is a very great distance between any two circles on a straight line, it implies that a specific author has had a gap between publishing articles on management and leadership within the broader sustainability domain. For example: Franks had published his first article in 2011, which was highly cited, and the next article was published in 2020.

Figure 15.9 shows the most cited countries of authors or publishing research in management and leadership within the broader sustainability domain. The USA stands out as providing leading cutting-edge research, which is being referenced by researchers globally on management and leadership within the broader sustainability domain. The USA is closely followed by the United Kingdom and Australia.

In a sense, this helps us to identify the critical mass of countries that are producing research that is regarded to be significant, as measured in terms of citations by their peers.

Figure 15.10 provides a breakup of collaboration between authors from different countries. If we look at the USA – which produces the most amount of research on management and leadership within the broader sustainability domain – we can see that only a small component of that research is based upon collaboration with colleagues outside their own country (i.e. USA). The vast majority of the research produced by USA-based colleagues constitutes collaboration with colleagues based in the USA only. In-contrast, there is a significantly smaller amount of research that is produced in collaboration with colleagues based in different countries.

This situation is radically reversed for a country like Norway, wherein the vast majority of research is produced with colleagues based in other countries. Part of the difference can also be attributed to size, but this does not hold true if one looks at South Africa, Brazil and India, which, despite being significantly geographically larger countries, and having a greater number of universities and academics, tend to produce research with colleagues based in their own countries.

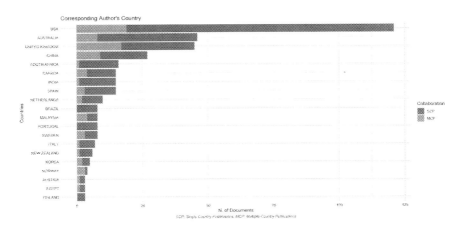

Figure 15.10 Most relevant countries.

An exception to this is China, which among other developing countries that figure in Figure 15.10 tends to have, in comparison to other developing countries, a higher percentage of collaboration with colleagues based in other countries.

Figure 15.11 shows the affiliation of authors who are publishing research in management and leadership within the broader sustainability domain. To a certain extent, it could be argued that the institutions which are shown in Figure 15.11 have priorities to support research in management and leadership within the broader sustainability domain. This is their account of institutions trying to build up critical mass in specific areas of research as part of the long-term strategy.

The only institution which stands out from this list, which does not figure in Figure 15.9 or Figure 15.10, is King Abdul Aziz University, based in Saudi Arabia. It could be argued that the amount of funding that is available to King Abdul Aziz University has enabled it to have a limited number of researchers who are producing research specific to management and leadership within the broader sustainability domain substantially higher in comparison to other countries on account of the funding available to researchers based at King Abdul Aziz University.

This finding also demonstrates the importance of funding for research in management and leadership within the broader sustainability domain.

Figure 15.12 shows the most cited articles published in management and leadership within the broader sustainability domain. The most cited

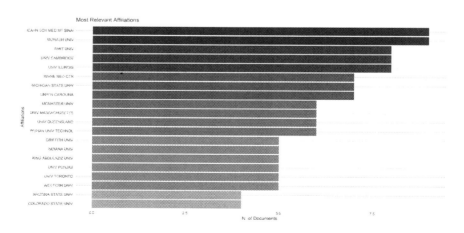

Figure 15.11 Most relevant affiliations.

BIBLIOMETRIC ANALYSIS OF LEADERSHIP

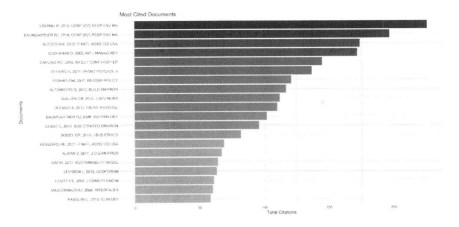

Figure 15.12 Most cited articles.

articles based on total citations is by Lozano (2015) with over 200 citations, followed by Baumgartner (2014). It is interesting to note that two of the most cited articles are not in traditionally high-ranked journals. If one looks at the rest of the articles, which are highly cited, it is observed that the rest of the highly cited articles are from several different disciplines, including management, healthcare, construction, psychology and development – thereby indicating that management and leadership within the broader sustainability domain is a multidisciplinary field of research.

Conclusion, limitations and future research

The results of the bibliometric study can help prospective authors and readers to acquire a general outlook of research on management and leadership within the broader sustainability domain. Given the importance of management and leadership within the broader sustainability domain, it is important to recognise which journals are the most relevant, which authors are regarded as influential leaders and which publications are the most cited. The results of the bibliometric study have identified the most relevant and influential journals, authors and papers on management and leadership within the broader sustainability domain, to enable prospective authors and readers to understand trends in authorship and content. Identification of the most relevant and influential journals, authors and papers on management and leadership within the broader sustainability domain can help prospective authors and readers to develop a better understanding of existing challenges on management and leadership within the context of sustainability. To conclude, this research contributes to knowledge by identifying the relevancy and productivity of the main authors, including the most cited authors and papers in the field of management and leadership within the broader sustainability domain.

References

Akmal, A., Podgorodnichenko, N., Greatbanks, R., & Everett, A. M. 2018. Bibliometric analysis of production planning and control (1990–2016). Production Planning & Control, 29(4): 333–351.

Dataset of 456 papers used for Bibliometric analysis

Abdallah, M., & El-Rayes, K. 2016. Multiobjective optimization model for maximizing sustainability of existing buildings. *Journal of Management in Engineering*, 32(4): 13.

Abdul-Aziz, A. R., & Ofori, G. 2012. Genesis of Malaysia's policy relating to sustainability of the built environment. *Open House International*, 37(4): 39–49.

Abiodun, A. A. 2012. Trends in the global space arena – Impact on Africa and Africa's response. *Space Policy*, 28(4): 283–290.

Abrampah, N. M., Montgomery, M., Bailer, A., Ndivo, F., Gasasira, A., Cooper, C., Frescas, R., Gordon, B., & Syed, S. B. 2017. Improving water, sanitation and hygiene in health-care facilities, Liberia. *Bulletin of the World Health Organization*, 95(7): 526–530.

Affolderbach, J., O'Neill, K., & Preller, B. 2019. Global-local tensions in urban green neighbourhoods: A policy mobilities approach to discursive change in Freiburg, Vancouver and Luxembourg. *Geografiska Annaler Series B-Human Geography*, 101(4): 271–290.

Afionis, S., & Stringer, L. C. 2012. European union leadership in biofuels regulation: Europe as a normative power? *Journal of Cleaner Production*, 32: 114–123.

Ahmed, M., Sun, Z. H., Raza, S. A., Qureshi, M. A., & Yousufi, S. Q. 2020. Impact of CSR and environmental triggers on employee green behavior: The mediating effect of employee well-being. *Corporate Social Responsibility and Environmental Management*, 27(5): 2225–2239.

Ahn, Y. H., Kwon, H., Pearce, A. R., & Wells, J. G. 2009. The systematic course development process: Building a course in sustainable construction for Students in the USA. *Journal of Green Building*, 4(1): 169–182.

Ajayi, S. O., Oyedele, L. O., & Dauda, J. A. 2019. Dynamic relationship between embodied and operational impacts of buildings: An evaluation of sustainable design appraisal tools. *World Journal of Science Technology and Sustainable Development*, 16(2): 70–81.

Akhanova, G., Nadeem, A., Kim, J. R., & Azhar, S. 2019. A framework of building sustainability assessment system for the commercial buildings in Kazakhstan. *Sustainability*, 11(17): 24.

Ali, S. S., Kaur, R., Persis, D. J., Saha, R., Pattusamy, M., & Sreedharan, V. R. 2020. Early Access Article. Developing a hybrid evaluation approach for the low carbon performance on sustainable manufacturing environment. *Annals of Operations Research*, 1–33.

Alkhani, R. 2020. Understanding private-sector engagement in sustainable urban development and delivering the climate agenda in Northwestern Europe-A case study of London and Copenhagen. *Sustainability*, 12(20): 35.

Allchin, B., Goodyear, M., O'Hanlon, B., & Weimand, B. M. 2020. Leadership perspectives on key elements influencing implementing a family-focused intervention in mental health services. *Journal of Psychiatric and Mental Health Nursing*, 27(5): 616–627.

Al-Shaiba, A., Al-Ghamdi, S. G., & Koc, M. 2020. Measuring efficiency levels in Qatari organizations and causes of inefficiencies. *International Journal of Engineering Business Management*, 12: 18.

Alsharif, M. A., Peters, M. D., & Dixon, T. J. 2020. Designing and implementing effective campus sustainability in Saudi Arabian Universities: An assessment of drivers and barriers in a rational choice theoretical context. *Sustainability*, 12(12): 23.

Altahat, S. M., & Atan, T. 2018. Role of healthy work environments in sustainability of goal achievement; ethical leadership, intention to sabotage and psychological capital in Jordanian Universities. *Sustainability*, 10(10): 15.

Altomonte, S., & Schiavon, S. 2013. Occupant satisfaction in LEED and non-LEED certified buildings. *Building and Environment*, 68: 66–76.

Alwan, Z., Jones, P., & Holgate, P. 2017. Strategic sustainable development in the UK construction industry, through the framework for strategic sustainable development, using building information modelling. *Journal of Cleaner Production*, 140: 349–358.

Al-Youbi, A. O., Al-Hayani, A., Rizwan, A., & Choudhry, H. 2020. Implications of COVID-19 on the labor market of Saudi Arabia: The role of universities for a sustainable workforce. *Sustainability*, 12(17): 13.

Amini, M., Zhang, B., & Chang, S. 2018. Selecting building designs with consideration of sustainability and resiliency. *Journal of Architectural Engineering*, 24(1): 11.

Amoozad Mahdiraji, H., Turskis, Z., Jafarnejad, A., & Rezayar, A. 2019. Non-cooperative two-echelon supply chains with a focus on social responsibility. *Technological and Economic Development of Economy*, 25(6): 1162–1187.

Ancker, S., & Rechel, B. 2015. HIV/AIDS policy-making in Kyrgyzstan: A stakeholder analysis. *Health Policy and Planning*, 30(1): 8–18.

Anderson, E., Bakir, A., & Wickens, E. 2015. Rural tourism development in Connemara, Ireland. *Tourism Planning & Development*, 12(1): 73–86.

Andrews, D. R., No, S., Powell, K. K., Rey, M. P., & Yigletu, A. 2016. Historically black colleges and universities' institutional survival and sustainability: A view from the HBCU business deans' perspective. *Journal of Black Studies*, 47(2): 150–168.

Anning, H. 2009. Case study: Bond university mirvac school of sustainable development building, Gold Coast, Australia. *Journal of Green Building*, 4(4): 39–54.

Arnette, A., & Brewer, B. 2017. The influence of strategy and concurrent engineering on design for procurement. *International Journal of Logistics Management*, 28(2): 531–554.

Arruda, N. D., Hino, M. C., & Beuter, B. P. 2019. Including SDGs in the education of globally responsible leaders. *International Journal of Sustainability in Higher Education*, 20(5): 856–870.

Arsanti, T. A., Sugiarto, A., Pasharibu, Y., & Wijayanto, P. 2021. Pro-environment behavior at the workplace: Role of leadership and motivation. *Quality-Access to Success*, 22(180): 126–130.

Aryanasl, A., Ghodousi, J., Arjmandi, R., & Mansouri, N. 2017. Components of sustainability considerations in management of petrochemical industries. *Environmental Monitoring and Assessment*, 189(6): 10.

Aslanyan, G., Molodtsov, S., & Iakobtchouk, V. 2005. Monitoring the sustainability of Russia's energy development. *Natural Resources Forum*, 29(4): 334–342.

Atkociuniene, V., Vaznoniene, G., & Pakeltiene, R. 2015. Aim of the development of rural social infrastructure: A sustainable community. *Transformations in Business & Economics*, 14(2A): 509–528.

Bakri, N., & Abbas, S. 2020. The role of transformational leadership in promoting sustainability among property development companies in Malaysia. *International Journal of Organizational Leadership*, 9(3): 123–137.

Balint, T. S., & Freeman, A. 2017. Designing the design at JPL'S innovation foundary. *Acta Astronautica*, 137: 182–191.

Banker, R. D., Mashruwala, R., & Tripathy, A. 2014. Does a differentiation strategy lead to more sustainable financial performance than a cost leadership strategy? *Management Decision*, 52(5): 872–896.

Bantha, T., & Nayak, U. 2020. The relation of workplace spirituality with employees' innovative work behaviour: The mediating role of psychological empowerment. *Journal of Indian Business Research*, 13.

Bao, J., Rodriguez, D. C., Paina, L., Ozawa, S., & Bennett, S. 2015. Monitoring and evaluating the transition of large-scale programs in global health. *Global Health-Science and Practice*, 3(4): 591–605.

Barnard, Z., & Van der Merwe, D. 2016. Innovative management for organizational sustainability in higher education. *International Journal of Sustainability in Higher Education*, 17(2): 208–227.

Barrick, K. A. 2010. Protecting the geyser basins of yellowstone national park: Toward a new national policy for a vulnerable environmental resource. *Environmental Management*, 45(1): 192–202.

Bastian, N. D. 2011. Optimizing army sustainability at fort bragg: A case study connecting life-cycle cost analysis with leadership in energy and environmental design for existing buildings. *Emj-Engineering Management Journal*, 23(2): 42–54.

Baumgartner, R. J. 2009. Organizational culture and leadership: Preconditions for the development of a sustainable corporation. *Sustainable Development*, 17(2): 102–113.

Baumgartner, R. J. 2014. Managing corporate sustainability and CSR: A conceptual framework combining values, strategies and instruments contributing to sustainable development. *Corporate Social Responsibility and Environmental Management*, 21(5): 258–271.

Bawa, K., & Balachander, G. 2016. Sustainability science at ATREE: Exhilaration, bumps, and speed-breakers when rubber meets the road. *Current Opinion in Environmental Sustainability*, 19: 144–152.

Becker, S. L., & Reusser, D. E. 2016. Disasters as opportunities for social change: Using the multi-level perspective to consider the barriers to disaster-related transitions. *International Journal of Disaster Risk Reduction*, 18: 75–88.

Belwalkar, S., Vohra, V., & Pandey, A. 2018. The relationship between workplace spirituality, job satisfaction and organizational citizenship behaviors – An empirical study. *Social Responsibility Journal*, 14(2): 410–430.

Benoliel, P., & Schechter, C. 2017. Promoting the school learning processes: Principals as learning boundary spanners. *International Journal of Educational Management*, 31(7): 878–894.

Berardi, A., Mistry, J., Tschirhart, C., Bignante, E., Davis, O., Haynes, L., Benjamin, R., Albert, G., Xavier, R., Jafferally, D., & de Ville, G. 2015. Applying the system viability framework for cross-scalar governance of nested social-ecological systems in the Guiana Shield, South America. *Ecology and Society*, 20(3): 16.

Berardo, R., Olivier, T., & Lavers, A. 2015. Focusing events and changes in ecologies of policy games: Evidence from the parana river delta. *Review of Policy Research*, 32(4): 443–464.

Bergh, A. M., Allanson, E., & Pattinson, R. C. 2015. What is needed for taking emergency obstetric and neonatal programmes to scale? *Best Practice & Research Clinical Obstetrics & Gynaecology*, 29(8): 1017–1027.

Bernardi, E., Carlucci, S., Cornaro, C., & Bohne, R. A. 2017. An analysis of the most adopted rating systems for assessing the environmental impact of buildings. *Sustainability*, 9(7): 27.

Bhatnagar, J., & Aggarwal, P. 2020. Meaningful work as a mediator between perceived organizational support for environment and employee eco-initiatives, psychological capital and alienation. *Employee Relations*, 42(6): 1487–1511.

Bhupendra, K. V., & Sangle, S. 2017. What drives successful implementation of product stewardship strategy? The role of absorptive capability. *Corporate Social Responsibility and Environmental Management*, 24(3): 186–198.

Bobea, L. 2012. The emergence of the democratic citizen security policy in the Dominican Republic. *Policing & Society*, 22(1): 57–75.

Boddy, C. R., Ladyshewsky, R. K., & Galvin, P. 2010. The influence of corporate psychopaths on corporate social responsibility and organizational commitment to employees. *Journal of Business Ethics*, 97(1): 1–19.

Boiral, O., Raineri, N., & Talbot, D. 2018. Managers' citizenship behaviors for the environment: A developmental perspective. *Journal of Business Ethics*, 149(2): 395–409.

Boiral, O., Talbot, D., & Paille, P. 2015. Leading by example: A model of organizational citizenship behavior for the environment. *Business Strategy and the Environment*, 24(6): 532–550.

Booker, C., Turbutt, A., & Fox, R. 2016. Model of care for a changing healthcare system: Are there foundational pillars for design? *Australian Health Review*, 40(2): 136–140.

Boschmann, E. E., & Gabriel, J. N. 2013. Urban sustainability and the LEED rating system: Case studies on the role of regional characteristics and adaptive reuse in green building in Denver and Boulder, Colorado. *Geographical Journal*, 179(3): 221–233.

Bosire, S. M. 2017. Selected factors that influence successful strategic planning in South African higher education. *Independent Journal of Teaching and Learning*, 12(2): 6–25.

Bowles, W., Boetto, H., Jones, P., & McKinnon, J. 2018. Is social work really greening? Exploring the place of sustainability and environment in social work codes of ethics. *International Social Work*, 61(4): 503–517.

Brandrud, A. S., Schreiner, A., Hjortdahl, P., Helljesen, G. S., Nyen, B., & Nelson, E. C. 2011. Three success factors for continual improvement in healthcare: An analysis of the reports of improvement team members. *Bmj Quality & Safety*, 20(3): 251–259.

Breslin, D. A., & Wang, Y. L. 2004. Climate change, national security, arid naval ship design. *Naval Engineers Journal*, 116(1): 27–40.

Bridges, A. 2016. The role of institutions in sustainable urban governance. *Natural Resources Forum*, 40(4): 169–179.

Brilliant, E. L. 2015. Constancy and change in the women's funding network: International horizons and core values. *Foundation Review*, 7(4): 110–+.

Brunstein, J., Sambiase, M. F., & Brunnquell, C. 2018. An assessment of critical reflection in management education for sustainability: A proposal on content and form of shared value rationality. *Sustainability*, 10(6): 25.

Brunton, M., Cook, C., Walker, L., Clendon, J., & Atefi, N. 2020. Home and away: A national mixed-methods questionnaire survey of host and migrant Registered Nurses in New Zealand. *Collegian*, 27(2): 164–173.

Buchanan, D., Fitzgerald, L., Ketley, D., Gollop, R., Jones, J. L., Lamont, S. S., Neath, A., & Whitby, E. 2005. No going back: A review of the literature on sustaining organizational change. *International Journal of Management Reviews*, 7(3): 189–205.

Buckeridge, J. 2014. Environmental ethics: An overview, assessing the place of bioscientists in society, supplemented with selected Australian perspectives. *Integrative Zoology*, 9(1): 14–23.

Buil-Fabrega, M., Alonso-Almeida, M. D., & Bagur-Femenias, L. 2017. Individual dynamic managerial capabilities: Influence over environmental and social commitment under a gender perspective. *Journal of Cleaner Production*, 151: 371–379.

Bukhari, S., Said, H., & Nor, F. M. 2020. Conceptual Understanding of Sustainability Among Academic Administrators of Pakistan Public Universities. *Qualitative Report*, 25(1): 28–59.

Burke, N. M., Chomitz, V. R., Rioles, N. A., Winslow, S. P., Brukilacchio, L. B., & Baker, J. C. 2009. The path to active living physical activity through community design in Somerville, Massachusetts. *American Journal of Preventive Medicine*, 37(6 Supplement 2): S386–S394.

Buscaj, E., Hall, T., Montgomery, L., Fernald, D. H., King, J., Deaner, N., & Dickinson, W. P. 2016. Practice facilitation for PCMH implementation in residency practices. *Family Medicine*, 48(10): 795–800.

Bussin, M. H. R., Mohamed-Padayachee, K., & Serumaga-Zake, P. 2019. A total rewards framework for the attraction of Generation Y employees born 1981–2000 in South Africa. *Sa Journal of Human Resource Management*, 17: 14.

Buttazzoni, A. N., Coen, S. E., & Gilliland, J. A. 2018. Supporting active school travel: A qualitative analysis of implementing a regional safe routes to school program. *Social Science & Medicine*, 212: 181–190.

Butzer, K. W. 2012. Collapse, environment, and society. *Proceedings of the National Academy of Sciences of the United States of America*, 109(10): 3632–3639.

Buykx, P., Humphreys, J. S., Tham, R., Kinsman, L., Wakerman, J., Asaid, A., & Tuohey, K. 2012. How do small rural primary health care services sustain themselves in a constantly changing health system environment? *Bmc Health Services Research*, 12: 7.

Caperchione, C., Mummery, W. K., & Duncan, M. 2011. Investigating the relationship between leader behaviours and group cohesion within women's walking groups. *Journal of Science and Medicine in Sport*, 14(4): 325–330.

Capezuti, E. A., Briccoli, B., & Boltz, M. P. 2013. Nurses improving the care of healthsystem elders: Creating a sustainable business model to improve care of hospitalized older adults. *Journal of the American Geriatrics Society*, 61(8): 1387–1393.

Carling, P. C., Parry, M. M., Rupp, M. E., Po, J. L., Dick, B., Von Beheren, S., & Healthcare Environmental Hygiene Study Group. 2008. Improving cleaning of the environment surrounding patients in 36 acute care hospitals. *Infection Control and Hospital Epidemiology*, 29(11): 1035–1041.

Carvalho, C. L., & da Costa, S. R. R. 2020. Organizational management: Proposal of an evaluation method from the perspective of the organizational entropy concepT. *Sistemas & Gestao*, 15(3): 277–293.

Celikyay, M., & Adiguzel, Z. 2019. Analysis of product innovation performances in terms of competitive strategies of companies in production sector under the influence of technology orientation. *International Journal of Organizational Leadership*, 8(3): 43–59.

Chagunda, M. G. G., Mwangwela, A., Mumba, C., Dos Anjos, F., Kawonga, B. S., Hopkins, R., & Chiwona-Kartun, L. 2016. Assessing and managing intensification in smallholder dairy systems for food and nutrition security in Sub-Saharan Africa. *Regional Environmental Change*, 16(8): 2257–2267.

Chambers, M., & Muecke, M. 2010. Biobased products and the leed (R) rating system. *Journal of Green Building*, 5(4): 91–107.

Chang, C. Y., & Besel, K. 2020. Cultivating next generation of healthcare leaders in Havana: Barriers and recommendation for succession planning. *International Journal of Healthcare Management*, 1–9.

Chen, J. K. C. 2020. Perspective on the influence of leadership on job satisfaction and lower employee turnover in the mineral industry. *Sustainability*, 12(14): 16.

Chu, K. W. 2016. Leading knowledge management in a secondary school. *Journal of Knowledge Management*, 20(5): 1104–1147.

Cicmil, S., Lindgren, M., & Packendorff, J. 2016. The project (management) discourse and its consequences: On vulnerability and unsustainability in project-based work. *New Technology Work and Employment*, 31(1): 58–76.

Cidell, J. 2009. Building green: The emerging geography of LEED-certified buildings and professionals. *Professional Geographer*, 61(2): 200–215.

Cinderby, S., Haq, G., Cambridge, H., & Lock, K. 2016. Building community resilience: Can everyone enjoy a good life? *Local Environment*, 21(10): 1252–1270.

Cochrane, L., & Cundill, G. 2018. Enabling collaborative synthesis in multi-partner programmes. *Development in Practice*, 28(7): 922–931.

Collins, J., Huggins, C. E., Porter, J., & Palermo, C. 2017. Factors influencing hospital foodservice staff's capacity to deliver a nutrition intervention. *Nutrition & Dietetics*, 74(2): 129–137.

Cop, S., Olorunsola, V. O., & Alola, U. V. 2021. Achieving environmental sustainability through green transformational leadership policy: Can green team resilience help? *Business Strategy and the Environment*, 30(1): 671–682.

Cottafava, D., Cavaglia, G., & Corazza, L. 2019. Education of sustainable development goals through students' active engagement A transformative learning experience. *Sustainability Accounting Management and Policy Journal*, 10(3): 521–544.

Cowan, D. M., Dopart, P., Ferracini, T., Sahmel, J., Merryman, K., Gaffney, S., & Paustenbach, D. J. 2010. A cross-sectional analysis of reported corporate environmental sustainability practices. *Regulatory Toxicology and Pharmacology*, 58(3): 524–538.

Crossman, J. 2011. Environmental and spiritual leadership: Tracing the synergies from an organizational perspective. *Journal of Business Ethics*, 103(4): 553–565.

Curaj, A., Paunica, M., Popa, A., Holeab, C., & Jora, O. D. 2020. Sustainability through directed change in the visionary university: From predicting to producing the future. *Amfiteatru Economic*, 22(55): 905–919.

Curran, G. 2015. Political modernisation for ecologically sustainable development in Australia. *Australasian Journal of Environmental Management*, 22(1): 7–20.

da Fonseca, L. 2015. ISO 14001:2015: An improved tool for sustainability. *Journal of Industrial Engineering and Management-Jiem*, 8(1): 37–50.

Dalati, S., Raudeliuniene, J., & Davidaviciene, V. 2017. Sustainable leadership, organizational trust on job satisfaction: Empirical evidence from higher education institutions in Syria. *Business Management and Education*, 15(1): 14–27.

Dall'O, G., Galante, A., Sanna, N., & Miller, K. 2013. On the integration of leadership in energy and environmental design (LEED)(R) ND protocol with the energy planning and management tools in italy: Strengths and weaknesses. *Energies*, 6(11): 5990–6015.

Dall'O, G., Speccher, A., & Bruni, E. 2012. The green energy audit, a new procedure for the sustainable auditing of existing buildings integrated with the LEED protocols. *Sustainable Cities and Society*, 3: 54–65.

Davidson, C. I., Hendrickson, C. T., & Matthews, H. S. 2007. Sustainable engineering: A sequence of courses at Carnegie Mellon. *International Journal of Engineering Education*, 23(2): 287–293.

Dawar, G., & Singh, S. 2020. How can small and medium enterprises effectively implement corporate social responsibility?: An Indian perspective. *Global Business Review*, 1–29.

De Wolf, C., Yang, F., Cox, D., Charlson, A., Hattan, A. S., & Ochsendorf, J. 2016. Material quantities and embodied carbon dioxide in structures. *Proceedings of the Institution of Civil Engineers-Engineering Sustainability*, 169(4): 150–161.

Del Brio, J. A., Junquera, B., & Ordiz, M. 2008. Human resources in advanced environmental approaches – a case analysis. *International Journal of Production Research*, 46(21): 6029–6053.

Dellve, L., & Eriksson, A. 2017. Health-promoting managerial work: A theoretical framework for a leadership program that supports knowledge and capability to craft sustainable work practices in daily practice and during organizational change. *Societies*, 7(2): 18.

Deschamps, E., & Franklin, M. 2020. Great Western railway electrification, UK: Collectively delivering a sustainability strategy. *Proceedings of the Institution of Civil Engineers-Civil Engineering*, 173(6): 5–10.

Desmond, S. 2016. Implementing climate change mitigation in health services: The importance of context. *Journal of Health Services Research & Policy*, 21(4): 257–262.

Di Fabio, A. 2017. Positive healthy organizations: Promoting well-being, meaningfulness, and sustainability in organizations. *Frontiers in Psychology*, 8: 6.

Di Fabio, A. 2017. The psychology of sustainability and sustainable development for well-being in organizations. *Frontiers in Psychology*, 8: 7.

Di Nauta, P., Iannuzzi, E., Milone, M., & Nigro, C. 2020. The impact of the sustainability principles on the strategic planning and reporting of universities. An exploratory study on a qualified italian sample. *Sustainability*, 12(18): 21.

Diaz-Sarachaga, J. M., Jato-Espino, D., & Castro-Fresno, D. 2018. Evaluation of LEED for neighbourhood development and envision rating frameworks for their implementation in Poorer Countries. *Sustainability*, 10(2): 16.

Dimmock, K., & Musa, G. 2015. Scuba diving tourism system: A framework for collaborative management and sustainability. *Marine Policy*, 54: 52–58.

Dixon, D., & Carlson, B. 2009. Introducing sustainable choices into suburbs: The path from auto-choked roads to walkable streets in Atlanta's Druid Hills. *Journal of Green Building*, 4(3): 21–43.

Dodds, R., & Walsh, P. R. 2019. Assessing the factors that influence waste generation and diversion at Canadian festivals. *Current Issues in Tourism*, 22(19): 2348–2352.

Dominguez-Escrig, E., Mallen-Broch, F. F., Lapiedra-Alcami, R., & Chiva-Gomez, R. 2019. The influence of leaders' stewardship behavior on innovation success: The mediating effect of radical innovation. *Journal of Business Ethics*, 159(3): 849–862.

Donghwan, G., Yong, K. H., & Hyoungsub, K. 2015. LEED, its efficacy in regional context: Finding a relationship between regional measurements and urban temperature. *Energy and Buildings*, 86: 687–691.

Donnelly, S., Dinesh, D., Dew, K., & Stubbe, M. 2019. The handover room: A qualitative enquiry into the experience of morning clinical handover for acute medical teams. *Internal Medicine Journal*, 49(5): 607–614.

Downer, A., Shapoval, A., Vysotska, O., Yuryeva, I., & Bairachna, T. 2018. US e-learning course adaptation to the Ukrainian context: Lessons learned and way forward. *BMC Medical Education*, 18: 10.

DuBose, J. R. 2000. Sustainability and performance at interface, Inc. *Interfaces*, 30(3): 190–201.

Duff, A. J., Zedler, P. H., Barzen, J. A., & Knuteson, D. L. 2017. The capacity-building stewardship model: Assessment of an agricultural network as a mechanism for improving regional agroecosystem sustainability. *Ecology and Society*, 22(1): 10.

Eide, A. E., Saether, E. A., & Aspelund, A. 2020. An investigation of leaders' motivation, intellectual leadership, and sustainability strategy in relation to Norwegian manufacturers' performance. *Journal of Cleaner Production*, 254: 12.

El Achi, N., Papamichail, A., Rizk, A., Lindsay, H., Menassa, M., Abdul-Khalek, R. A., Ekzayez, A., Dewachi, O., & Patel, P. 2019. A conceptual framework for capacity strengthening of health research in conflict: The case of the Middle East and North Africa region. *Globalization and Health*, 15(1): 15.

El Hajj, M. C., Abou Moussa, R., & Chidiac, M. 2017. Environmental sustainability out of the loop in Lebanese universities. *Journal of International Education in Business*, 10(1): 49–67.

Ely, L. T. 2015. Nurse-managed clinics: Barriers and benefits toward financial sustainability when integrating primary care and mental health. *Nursing Economics*, 33(4): 193–202.

Erkan, T. E., & Can, G. F. 2014. Selecting the best warehouse data collecting system by using ahp and fahp methods. *Tehnicki Vjesnik-Technical Gazette*, 21(1): 87–93.

Ertuna, B., Karatas-Ozkan, M., & Yamak, S. 2019. Diffusion of sustainability and CSR discourse in hospitality industry Dynamics of local context. *International Journal of Contemporary Hospitality Management*, 31(6): 2564–2581.

Escott, H., Beavis, S., & Reeves, A. 2015. Incentives and constraints to Indigenous engagement in water management. *Land Use Policy*, 49: 382–393.

Espinoza, O., Buehlmann, U., & Smith, B. 2012. Forest certification and green building standards: Overview and use in the U.S. hardwood industry. *Journal of Cleaner Production*, 33: 30–41.

Evashwick, C., & Ory, M. 2003. Organizational characteristics of successful innovative health care programs sustained over time. *Family & Community Health*, 26(3): 177–193.

Everett, L. Q., & Sitterding, M. C. 2011. Transformational leadership required to design and sustain evidence-based practice: A system exemplar. *Western Journal of Nursing Research*, 33(3): 398–426.

Fahmy, M., Ibrahim, Y., Hanafi, E., & Barakat, M. 2018. Would LEED-UHI greenery and high albedo strategies mitigate climate change at neighborhood scale in Cairo, Egypt? *Building Simulation*, 11(6): 1273–1288.

Faling, M., & Biesbroek, R. 2019. Cross-boundary policy entrepreneurship for climate-smart agriculture in Kenya. *Policy Sciences*, 52(4): 525–547.

Farreny, R., Oliver-Sola, J., Montlleo, M., Escriba, E., Gabarrell, X., & Rieradevall, J. 2011. Transition towards sustainable cities: Opportunities, constraints, and strategies in planning. A neighbourhood ecodesign case study in Barcelona. *Environment and Planning a-Economy and Space*, 43(5): 1118–1134.

Fatoki, O. 2019. Hotel employees' pro-environmental behaviour: Effect of leadership behaviour, institutional support and workplace spirituality. *Sustainability*, 11(15): 15.

Fenner, R. A., & Ryce, T. 2008. A comparative analysis of two building rating systems. Part 2: Case study. *Proceedings of the Institution of Civil Engineers-Engineering Sustainability*, 161(1): 65–70.

Flatman, J., & Doeser, J. 2010. The international management of marine aggregates and its relation to maritime archaeology. *Historic Environment-Policy & Practice*, 1(2): 160–184.

Fonseca, I., Paco, A., & Figueiredo, V. 2021. Nonprofit organisations, management and marketing strategies for survival: The case of philharmonic bands. *International Journal of Nonprofit and Voluntary Sector Marketing*, 26(1): 13.

Franks, D. M., Boger, D. V., Cote, C. M., & Mulligan, D. R. 2011. Sustainable development principles for the disposal of mining and mineral processing wastes. *Resources Policy*, 36(2): 114–122.

Franks, D. M., Ngonze, C., Pakoun, L., & Hailu, D. 2020. Voices of artisanal and small-scale mining, visions of the future: Report from the International Conference on Artisanal and Small-scale Mining and Quarrying. *Extractive Industries and Society-an International Journal*, 7(2): 505–511.

Fraundorfer, M. 2017. The role of cities in shaping transnational law in climate governance. *Global Policy*, 8(1): 23–31.

Fujita, N., Nagai, M., Diouf, I. S. N., Shimizu, T., & Tamura, T. 2016. The role of a network of human resources for health managers in supporting leadership for health systems strengthening in Francophone African Countries. *Health Systems & Reform*, 2(3): 254–264.

Gabaldon-Estevan, D., Criado, E., & Monfort, E. 2014. The green factor in European manufacturing: A case study of the Spanish ceramic tile industry. *Journal of Cleaner Production*, 70: 242–250.

Gabler, C. B., Panagopoulos, N., Vlachos, P. A., & Rapp, A. 2017. Developing an environmentally sustainable business plan: An international B2B case study. *Corporate Social Responsibility and Environmental Management*, 24(4): 261–272.

Gadakari, T., Hadjri, K., & Mushatat, S. 2017. Relationship between building intelligence and sustainability. *Proceedings of the Institution of Civil Engineers-Engineering Sustainability*, 170(6): 294–307.

Ganann, R., Peacock, S., Garnett, A., Northwood, M., Hyde, A., Bookey-Bassett, S., Kennedy, L., Markle-Reid, M., Ploeg, J., & Valaitis, R. 2019. Capacity development among academic trainees in community-based primary health care research: The aging, community and health research unit experience. *Primary Health Care Research and Development*, 20: 4.

Gao, T. T., Ding, X. N., Chai, J. X., Zhang, Z., Zhang, H., Kong, Y. X., & Mei, S. L. 2017. The influence of resilience on mental health: The role of general well-being. *International Journal of Nursing Practice*, 23(3): 7.

Garaway, C. J., Arthur, R. I., Chamsingh, B., Homekingkeo, P., Lorenzen, K., Saengvilaikham, B., & Sidavong, K. 2006. A social science perspective on stock enhancement outcomes: Lessons learned from inland fisheries in southern Lao PDR. *Fisheries Research*, 80(1): 37–45.

Gaspar, F., & Leal, F. 2020. A methodology for applying the shop floor management method for sustaining lean manufacturing tools and philosophies: A study of an automotive company in Brazil. *International Journal of Lean Six Sigma*, 11(6): 1233–1252.

Gauthier, J., & Wooldridge, B. 2012. Influences on sustainable innovation adoption: Evidence from leadership in energy and environmental design. *Business Strategy and the Environment*, 21(2): 98–110.

Gavrikova, E., Volkova, I., & Burda, Y. 2020. Strategic aspects of asset management: An overview of current research. *Sustainability*, 12(15): 29.

Geall, S., & Ely, A. 2018. Narratives and pathways towards an ecological civilization in Contemporary China. *China Quarterly*, 236: 1175–1196.

Giannarakis, G., Konteos, G., Sariannidis, N., & Chaitidis, G. 2017. The relation between voluntary carbon disclosure and environmental performance The case of S&P 500. *International Journal of Law and Management*, 59(6): 784–803.

Giannarakis, G., Zafeiriou, E., Arabatzis, G., & Partalidou, X. 2018. Determinants of corporate climate change disclosure for european firms. *Corporate Social Responsibility and Environmental Management*, 25(3): 281–294.

Gigol, T. 2020. Influence of authentic leadership on unethical pro -organizational behavior; the intermediate role of work engagement. *Sustainability*, 12(3): 14.

Gilinsky, A., Newton, S. K., Atkin, T. S., Santini, C., Cavicchi, A., Casas, A. R., & Huertas, R. 2015. Perceived efficacy of sustainability strategies in the US, Italian, and Spanish wine industries A comparative study. *International Journal of Wine Business Research*, 27(3): 164–181.

Glass, C., Cook, A., & Ingersoll, A. R. 2016. Do women leaders promote sustainability? Analyzing the effect of corporate governance composition on environmental performance. *Business Strategy and the Environment*, 25(7): 495–511.

Goby, V. P., & Nickerson, C. 2012. Introducing ethics and corporate social responsibility at undergraduate level in the United Arab Emirates: An experiential exercise on website communication. *Journal of Business Ethics*, 107(2): 103–109.

Goh, C. S., Jack, L., & Bajracharya, A. 2020. Qualitative study of sustainability policies and guidelines in the built environment. *Journal of Legal Affairs and Dispute Resolution in Engineering and Construction*, 12(2): 7.

Goldman, D., Pe'er, S., & Yavetz, B. 2017. Environmental literacy of youth movement members – is environmentalism a component of their social activism? *Environmental Education Research*, 23(4): 486–514.

Gomes, O., & Gubareva, M. 2020. Complex systems in economics and where to find them. *Journal of Systems Science & Complexity*, 1–25.

Gomez, W. A., Aranda-Camacho, Y., & Fuentes, J. C. B. 2020. Analytical model to assess the functionality of small farmers' organizations. *Economia Agraria Y Recursos Naturales*, 20(1): 7–35.

Goodfellow-Smith, M. E., Rogers, C. D. F., & Tight, M. R. 2020. Infrastructure value maximisation: Overcoming the infrastructure valley of death. *Infrastructure Asset Management*, 7(2): 95–102.

Goodman, D. S. G. 2004. Qinghai and the emergence of the west: Nationalities, communal interaction and national integration. *China Quarterly*, 178: 379–399.

Gorgenyi-Hegyes, E., & Fekete-Farkas, M. 2019. Internal CSR as a strategic management tool in reduction of labour shortages. *Polish Journal of Management Studies*, 19(2): 167–181.

Gorsevski, E. W. 2012. Wangari maathai's emplaced rhetoric: Greening global peacebuilding. *Environmental Communication-a Journal of Nature and Culture*, 6(3): 290–307.

Green, J. M. H., Cranston, G. R., Sutherland, W. J., Tranter, H. R., Bell, S. J., Benton, T. G., Blixt, E., Bowe, C., Broadley, S., Brown, A., Brown, C., Burns, N., Butler, D., Collins, H., Crowley, H., DeKoszmovszky, J., Firbank, L. G., Fulford, B., Gardner, T. A., Hails, R. S., Halvorson, S., Jack, M., Kerrison, B., Koh, L. S. C., Lang, S. C., McKenzie, E. J., Monsivais, P., O'Riordan, T., Osborn, J., Oswald, S., Thomas, E. P., Raffaelli, D., Reyers, B., Srai, J. S., Strassburg, B. B. N., Webster, D., Welters, R., Whiteman, G., Wilsdon, J., & Vira, B. 2017. Research priorities for managing the impacts and dependencies of business upon food, energy, water and the environment. *Sustainability Science*, 12(2): 319–331.

Hack-Polay, D., Rahman, M., Billah, M. M., & Al-Sabbahy, H. Z. 2020. Big data analytics and sustainable textile manufacturing Decision-making about the applications of biotechnologies in developing countries. *Management Decision*, 58(8): 1699–1714.

Hack-Polay, D., Rahman, M., Billah, M. M., & Al-Sabbahy, H. Z. 2020. Big data analytics and sustainable textile manufacturing Decision-making about the applications of biotechnologies in developing countries. *Management Decision*, 1–16.

Haggman-Laitila, A., & Rekola, L. 2014. Factors influencing partnerships between higher education and healthcare. *Nurse Education Today*, 34(10): 1290–1297.

Hailu, D., Hordofa, D. F., Endalew, H. A., Mutua, D. K., Bekele, W., Bonilla, M., Celiker, M. Y., Challinor, J., Dotan, A., Habashy, C., Kumar, P. N., Rodriguez-Galindo, C., Wali, R. M., Weitzman, S., Broas, J., Korones, D. N., Alexander, T. B., & Shad, A. T. 2020. Training pediatric hematologist/oncologists for capacity building in Ethiopia. *Pediatric Blood & Cancer*, 67(12): 7.

Haines, H. M., Baker, J., & Marshall, D. 2015. Continuity of midwifery care for rural women through caseload group practice: Delivering for almost 20 years. *Australian Journal of Rural Health*, 23(6): 339–345.

Hakansson, M., Holden, R. J., Eriksson, A., & Dellve, L. 2017. Managerial practices that support lean and socially sustainable working conditions. *Nordic Journal of Working Life Studies*, 7(3): 63–84.

Hall, J. A., Fusch, P. I., & Booker, J. M. 2019. Tribal gaming leader strategies toward a sustainable future. *Qualitative Report*, 24(4): 887–905.

Hamadamin, H. H., & Atan, T. 2019. The impact of strategic human resource management practices on competitive advantage sustainability: The mediation of human capital development and employee commitment. *Sustainability*, 11(20): 19.

Hammond, G. P. 1998. Alternative energy strategies for the United Kingdom revisited – Market competition and sustainability. *Technological Forecasting and Social Change*, 59(2): 131–151.

Han, Z. Y., Wang, Q., & Yan, X. 2019. How responsible leadership motivates employees to engage in organizational citizenship behavior for the environment: A double-mediation model. *Sustainability*, 11(3): 13.

Hannan, T. J., Bart, S., Sharp, C., Fassett, M. J., & Fassett, R. G. 2010. The sustainability of Medical Morning Handover Reporting: Adherence in a regional hospital. *Australian Health Review*, 34(3): 325–327.

Hay, R. 2010. The relevance of ecocentrism, personal development and transformational leadership to sustainability and identity. *Sustainable Development*, 18(3): 163–171.

Hazem, N., Abdelraouf, M., Fahim, I. S., & El-Omari, S. 2020. A novel green rating system for existing buildings. *Sustainability*, 12(17): 15.

Heikkinen, S., Lamsa, A. M., & Niemisto, C. 2020. Work-family practices and complexity of their usage: A discourse analysis towards socially responsible human resource management. *Journal of Business Ethics*, 1–17.

Hermans, J., Slabbinck, H., Vanderstraeten, J., Brassey, J., Dejardin, M., Ramdani, D., & van Witteloostuijn, A. 2017. The power paradox: Implicit and explicit power motives, and the importance attached to prosocial organizational goals in SMEs. *Sustainability*, 9(11): 26.

Hilts, L., Howard, M., Price, D., Risdon, C., Agarwal, G., & Childs, A. 2013. Helping primary care teams emerge through a quality improvement program. *Family Practice*, 30(2): 204–211.

Hoffman, S. J., Rosenfield, D., Gilbert, J. H. V., & Oandasan, I. F. 2008. Student leadership in interprofessional education: Benefits, challenges and implications for educators, researchers and policymakers. *Medical Education*, 42(7): 654–661.

Holcombe, R. F., Evangelista, M., & Cartwright, F. 2016. Delivery of quality oncology care in a large, urban practice: A primer. *Journal of Oncology Practice*, 12(10): 892.

Holdsworth, S., Thomas, I., Wong, P., Sandri, O., Boulet, M., Chester, A., & McLaughlin, P. 2019. Graduate attribute for minimising environmental harm – Assessing effectiveness in the graduates' workplaces. *Journal of Cleaner Production*, 211: 396–407.

Hollander, R. 2015. ESD, federalism and intergovernmental relations in Australia. *Australasian Journal of Environmental Management*, 22(1): 21–32.

Homsy, G. C. 2018. Unlikely pioneers: Creative climate change policymaking in smaller U.S. cities. *Journal of Environmental Studies and Sciences*, 8(2): 121–131.

Horan, D. 2019. A new approach to partnerships for SDG transformations. *Sustainability*, 11(18): 22.

Horlings, I., & Padt, F. 2013. Leadership for sustainable regional development in rural areas: Bridging personal and institutional aspects. *Sustainable Development*, 21(6): 413–424.

Horlings, L. G. 2015. The inner dimension of sustainability: Personal and cultural values. *Current Opinion in Environmental Sustainability*, 14: 163–169.

Horlings, L. G. 2015. Values in place: A value-oriented approach toward sustainable place-shaping. *Regional Studies Regional Science*, 2(1): 257–274.

Horne, J. 2016. Water policy responses to drought in the MDB, Australia. *Water Policy*, 18: 28–51.

Houghton, A. 2011. Health impact assessments a tool for designing climate change resilience into green building and planning projects. *Journal of Green Building*, 6(2): 66–87.

Hristov, D., & Zehrer, A. 2019. Does distributed leadership have a place in destination management organisations? A policy-makers perspective. *Current Issues in Tourism*, 22(9): 1095–1115.

Hulcombe, J., Sturgess, J., Souvlis, T., & Fitzgerald, C. 2014. An approach to building research capacity for health practitioners in a public health environment: An organisational perspective. *Australian Health Review*, 38(3): 252–258.

Hunt, S. R., Probst, J. C., Haddock, K. S., Moran, R., Baker, S. L., Anderson, R. A., & Corazzini, K. 2012. Registered nurse retention strategies in nursing homes: A two-factor perspective. *Health Care Management Review*, 37(3): 246–256.

Hussain, K., Abbas, Z., Gulzar, S., Jibril, A. B., & Hussain, A. 2020. Examining the impact of abusive supervision on employees' psychological wellbeing and turnover intention: The mediating role of intrinsic motivation. *Cogent Business & Management*, 7(1): 21.

Hussain, K., He, Z., Ahmad, N., Iqbal, M., & Mumtaz, S. M. T. 2019. Green, lean, Six Sigma barriers at a glance: A case from the construction sector of Pakistan. *Building and Environment*, 161: 16.

Hussaini, A., Pulido, C. L., Basu, S., & Ranjit, N. 2018. Designing place-based interventions for sustainability and replicability: The case of go! Austin/ VAMOS! Austin. *Frontiers in Public Health*, 6: 8.

Idris, A., See, D., & Coughlan, P. 2018. Employee empowerment and job satisfaction in urban Malaysia Connecting the dots with context and organizational change management. *Journal of Organizational Change Management*, 31(3): 697–711.

Ikegbu, E. A. 2017. Harmonious complementarity in leadership: A necessary tool for environment and sustainability. *European Journal of Sustainable Development*, 6(3): 141–154.

Innes, J. E., & Booher, D. E. 1999. Metropolitan development as a complex system: A new approach to sustainability. *Economic Development Quarterly*, 13(2): 141–156.

Isa, R., Emuze, F., Das, D., & Awuzie, B. O. 2018. Modeling a transformational route to infrastructure sustainability in South Africa. *Built Environment Project and Asset Management*, 8(2): 147–159.

Isbell, M., & Lee, A. 2006. Charlotte-Mecklenburg successfully integrates field operations by managing individual and organizational strengths. *Journal American Water Works Association*, 98(9): 85–+.

Ishaq, M. I. 2020. Multidimensional green brand equity: A cross-cultural scale development and validation study. *International Journal of Market Research*, 1–16.

Islam, T., Khan, M. M., Ahmed, I., & Mahmood, K. 2020. Promoting in-role and extra-role green behavior through ethical leadership: Mediating role of green HRM and moderating role of individual green values. *International Journal of Manpower*, 1–22.

Ismail, N. A. M., Welch, C., & Xu, M. 2015. Towards a sustainable quality of university research: Knowledge sharing. *Knowledge Management Research & Practice*, 13(2): 168–177.

James, S. W., Friel, S., Lawrence, M. A., Hoek, A. C., & Pearson, D. 2018. Inter-sectoral action to support healthy and environmentally sustainable food behaviours: A study of sectoral knowledge, governance and implementation opportunities. *Sustainability Science*, 13(2): 465–477.

Jangland, E., & Gunningberg, L. 2017. Improving patient participation in a challenging context: A 2-year evaluation study of an implementation project. *Journal of Nursing Management*, 25(4): 266–275.

Jelinek, R. 2017. A permaculture primer: Using eco-theory to promote knowledge acquisition, dissemination and use in the sales organization. *Industrial Marketing Management*, 65: 206–216.

Jeon, S. H., Park, M., Choi, K., & Kim, M. K. 2018. An ethical leadership program for nursing unit managers. *Nurse Education Today*, 62: 30–35.

Jiang, M. Q., Wang, H. Y., & Li, M. Z. 2019. Linking empowering leadership and organizational citizenship behavior toward environment: The role of psychological ownership and future time perspective. *Frontiers in Psychology*, 10: 13.

Jones, L., & Wong, W. 2016. More than just a green building developing green strategies at the Chinese University of Hong Kong Library. *Library Management*, 37(6–7): 373–384.

Kamal, A. H., Anderson, W. G., Boss, R. D., Brody, A. A., Campbell, T. C., Creutzfeldt, C. J., Hurd, C. J., Kinderman, A. L., Lindenberger, E. C., & Reinke, L. F. 2016. The cambia sojourns scholars leadership program: Project summaries from the inaugural scholar cohort. *Journal of Palliative Medicine*, 19(6): 591–600.

Kang, Q. 2020. Library directors' concerns and attitudes towards going green and sustainability in China: An unexplored area. *Journal of Librarianship and Information Science*, 52(2): 382–398.

Karakhan, A. A., & Gambatese, J. A. 2017. Identification, quantification, and classification of potential safety risk for sustainable construction in the United States. *Journal of Construction Engineering and Management*, 143(7): 10.

Kasonde, M., & Steele, P. 2017. The people factor: An analysis of the human resources landscape for immunization supply chain management. *Vaccine*, 35(17): 2134–2140.

Kenward, R. E., Whittingham, M. J., Arampatzis, S., Manos, B. D., Hahn, T., Terry, A., Simoncini, R., Alcorn, J., Bastian, O., Donlan, M., Elowe, K., Franzen, F., Karacsonyi, Z., Larsson, M., Manou, D., Navodaru, I., Papadopoulou, O., Papathanasiou, J., von Raggamby, A., Sharp, R. J. A., Soderqvist, T., Soutukorva, A., Vavrova, L., Aebischer, N. J., Leader-Williams, N., & Rutz, C. 2011. Identifying governance strategies that effectively support ecosystem services, resource sustainability, and biodiversity. *Proceedings of the National Academy of Sciences of the United States of America*, 108(13): 5308–5312.

Khan, M. A. S., Du, J. G., Ali, M., Saleem, S., & Usman, M. 2019. Interrelations between ethical leadership, green psychological climate, and organizational environmental citizenship behavior: A moderated mediation model. *Frontiers in Psychology*, 10: 12.

Kieu, T. K., & Singer, J. 2020. Youth organizations' promotion of education for sustainable development competencies: A case study. *European Journal of Sustainable Development*, 9(4): 376–394.

Kim, W., & Park, J. 2017. Examining structural relationships between work engagement, organizational procedural justice, knowledge sharing, and innovative work behavior for sustainable organizations. *Sustainability*, 9(2): 16.

Kim, W. G., McGinley, S., Choi, H. M., & Agmapisarn, C. 2020. Hotels' environmental leadership and employees' organizational citizenship behavior. *International Journal of Hospitality Management*, 87: 12.

Kirchhoff, C. J., & Watson, P. L. 2019. Are wastewater systems adapting to climate change? *Journal of the American Water Resources Association*, 55(4): 869–880.

Kirsh, S. R., Lawrence, R. H., & Aron, D. C. 2008. Tailoring an intervention to the context and system redesign related to the intervention: A case study of implementing shared medical appointments for diabetes. *Implementation Science*, 3: 15.

Kleinman, G., Kuei, C. H., & Lee, P. C. 2017. Using formal concept analysis to examine water disclosure in corporate social responsibility reports. *Corporate Social Responsibility and Environmental Management*, 24(4): 341–356.

Koh, S. Y., Ong, T. S., & Samuel, A. B. 2017. The impacts of physical, psychological, and environmental factors on employees job satisfaction among public accounting professionals in Malaysia. *Asia-Pacific Management Accounting Journal*, 12(2): 129–156.

Kooskora, M., & Cundiff, K. 2019. The development towards corporate sustainability in a transitional economy, case estonia. *Journal of East European Management Studies*, 203–221.

Korkmaz, S., & Singh, A. 2012. Impact of team characteristics in learning sustainable built environment practices. *Journal of Professional Issues in Engineering Education and Practice*, 138(4): 289–295.

Kosamu, I. B. M. 2014. Conditions for sustainability of the elephant marsh fishery in Malawi. *Sustainability*, 6(7): 4010–4027.

Kurtboke, D. I. 2016. Applied microbiology and biotechnology teaching tailored towards regional needs and graduate employment. *Microbiology Australia*, 37(2): 69–72.

Laing, D., & Kean, W. F. 2011. The greening of healthcare: Fabrics used in health care facilities. *Journal of Green Building*, 6(4): 45–64.

Lambriex-Schmitz, P., van der Klink, M. R., Beausaert, S., Bijker, M., & Segers, M. 2020. When innovation in education works: Stimulating teachers' innovative work behaviour. *International Journal of Training and Development*, 24(2): 118–134.

Larsson, J., & Holmberg, J. 2018. Learning while creating value for sustainability transitions: The case of Challenge Lab at Chalmers University of Technology. *Journal of Cleaner Production*, 172: 4411–4420.

Lasrado, F., Arif, M., & Rizvi, A. 2015. Employee suggestion scheme sustainability excellence model and linking organizational learning Cases in United Arab Emirates. *International Journal of Organizational Analysis*, 23(3): 425–455.

Lasrado, F., & Zakaria, N. 2020. Go green! Exploring the organizational factors that influence self-initiated green behavior in the United Arab Emirates. *Asia Pacific Journal of Management*, 37(3): 823–850.

Lau, K. H. 2012. Demand management in downstream wholesale and retail distribution: A case study. *Supply Chain Management-an International Journal*, 17(6): 638–654.

Lauderdale, J. W. 1999. What is the pharmaceutical industry doing, and what does the pharmaceutical industry want from animal science departments? *Journal of Animal Science*, 77(2): 367–371.

Lavoie, A., Lee, J., Sparks, K., Hoseth, G., & Wise, S. 2019. Engaging with women's knowledge in bristol bay fisheries through oral history and participatory ethnography. *Fisheries*, 44(7): 331–337.

Lee, S. H. N., Ha-Brookshire, J., & Chow, P. S. 2018. The moral responsibility of corporate sustainability as perceived by fashion retail employees: A USA-China cross-cultural comparison study. *Business Strategy and the Environment*, 27(8): 1462–1475.

Lee, Y. S. 2011. Lighting quality and acoustic quality in leed-certified buildings using occupant evaluation. *Journal of Green Building*, 6(2): 139–155.

Leffers, J., Levy, R. M., Nicholas, P. K., & Sweeney, C. F. 2017. Mandate for the nursing profession to address climate change through nursing education. *Journal of Nursing Scholarship*, 49(6): 679–687.

Legros, S., Massoud, R., & Urroz, O. 2002. The Chilean legacies in health care quality. *International Journal for Quality in Health Care*, 14 Supplement 1: 83–88.

Lehmann, S. 2011. Optimizing urban material flows and waste streams in urban development through principles of zero waste and sustainable consumption. *Sustainability*, 3(1): 155–183.

Lei, H. S., Lai, C. F., & Chen, C. C. 2018. How does project supervisor maintain sustainability of project members? A study from leadership perspective. *Sustainability*, 10(8): 14.

Lenka, P., & Kar, S. 2021. Role of ethical leaders in sustainable business: An aristotelian virtue ethics perspective. *Problemy Ekorozwoju*, 16(1): 201–207.

Levidow, L. 2013. EU criteria for sustainable biofuels: Accounting for carbon, depoliticising plunder. *Geoforum*, 44: 211–223.

Levitt, R. E. 2007. CEM research for the next 50 years: Maximizing economic, environmental, and societal value of the built environment. *Journal of Construction Engineering and Management*, 133(9): 619–628.

Li, J., Zhao, F. Q., Chen, S. L., Jiang, W. X., Liu, T., & Shi, S. P. 2017. Gender diversity on boards and firms' environmental policy. *Business Strategy and the Environment*, 26(3): 306–315.

Li, Y. N., Ye, F., Dai, J., Zhao, X. D., & Sheu, C. W. 2019. The adoption of green practices by Chinese firms: Assessing the determinants and effects of top management championship. *International Journal of Operations & Production Management*, 39(4): 550–572.

Liang, W., Li, T., Lu, L., Kim, J., & Na, S. 2020. Influence of implicit followership cognitive differences on innovation behavior: An empirical analysis in China. *Sustainability*, 12(12): 15.

Liang, X., Xiu, L., Wu, S. B., & Zhang, S. J. 2017. In search of sustainable legitimacy of private firms in China. *Chinese Management Studies*, 11(3): 555–578.

Licen, S., & Jedlicka, S. R. 2020. Sustainable development principles in US sport management graduate programs. *Sport Education and Society*, 1–14.

Lillie, E., O'Donohoe, L., Shamambo, N., Bould, D., Ismailova, F., & Kinnear, J. 2015. Peer training and co-learning in global health care. *Clinical Teacher*, 12(3): 193–196.

Lin, S., Albarhami, B., Mayoral, S., & Piacenza, J. 2020. Understanding the effects of capturing climate and occupancy trends during concept-stage sustainable building design. *Journal of Solar Energy Engineering-Transactions of the Asme*, 142(6): 11.

Liu, Y. H., Chen, S., Gao, J. T., Zhang, Y., Booher, K., Ding, X. F., Shu, W., Du, J., Bao, J., Hafner, R., Hamilton, C. D., & Li, L. 2020. The China tuberculosis clinical trials consortium network: A model for international TB clinical trials capacity building. *Infectious Diseases of Poverty*, 9(1): 7.

Lloyd, S., Low, S., Win, S. L., Fitzgerald, G., Cliff, C., & Collie, J. 2018. The Ingredients for Innovation: Impacts for practice and the education of health service managers. *Asia Pacific Journal of Health Management*, 13(2): 15–23.

Lopez-Bonilla, L. M., Reyes-Rodriguez, M. D., & Lopez-Bonilla, J. M. 2020. Golf tourism and sustainability: Content analysis and directions for future research. *Sustainability*, 12(9): 18.

Lopez-Gamero, M. D., Zaragoza-Saez, P., Claver-Cortes, E., & Molina-Azorin, J. F. 2011. Sustainable Development and Intangibles: Building sustainable intellectual capital. *Business Strategy and the Environment*, 20(1): 18–37.

Love, P. E. D., Niedzweicki, M., Bullen, P. A., & Edwards, D. J. 2012. Achieving the green building council of Australia's world leadership rating in an office building in Perth. *Journal of Construction Engineering and Management-Asce*, 138(5): 652–660.

Lozano, R. 2015. A holistic perspective on corporate sustainability drivers. *Corporate Social Responsibility and Environmental Management*, 22(1): 32–44.

Lu, X. M., Zhu, W. Z., & Tsai, F. S. 2019. Social responsibility toward the employees and career development sustainability during manufacturing transformation in China. *Sustainability*, 11(17): 17.

Lueg, R., Pedersen, M. M., & Clemmensen, S. N. 2015. The role of corporate sustainability in a low-cost business model – A case study in the scandinavian fashion industry. *Business Strategy and the Environment*, 24(5): 344–359.

Lukersmith, S., & Burgess-Limerick, R. 2013. The perceived importance and the presence of creative potential in the health professional's work environment. *Ergonomics*, 56(6): 922–934.

Luu, T. T. 2019. Green human resource practices and organizational citizenship behavior for the environment: The roles of collective green crafting and environmentally specific servant leadership. *Journal of Sustainable Tourism*, 27(8): 1167–1196.

Maboya, M., & McKay, T. 2019. The financial sustainability challenges facing the South African non-profit sector. *Td-the Journal for Transdisciplinary Research in Southern Africa*, 15(1): 10.

Macris, L. I., & Sam, M. P. 2014. Belief, doubt, and legitimacy in a performance system: National sport organization perspectives. *Journal of Sport Management*, 28(5): 529–550.

Mah, D. N. Y., & Hills, P. 2012. Collaborative governance for sustainable development: Wind resource assessment in Xinjiang and Guangdong Provinces, China. *Sustainable Development*, 20(2): 85–97.

Majukwa, D., Fan, S. S. K., & Dwyer, R. J. 2020. Impact of sustainability strategies on small- and medium-sized enterprises in Zimbabwe. *World Journal of Entrepreneurship Management and Sustainable Development*, 16(2): 149–163.

Marjanovic, N., Jovanovic, V., Ratknic, T., & Paunkovic, D. 2019. The role of leadership in natural resource conservation and sustainable development – A case study of local self-government of eastern serbia. *Ekonomika Poljoprivreda-Economics of Agriculture*, 66(3): 889–903.

Martin, E. G., & Begany, G. M. 2017. Opening government health data to the public: Benefits, challenges, and lessons learned from early innovators. *Journal of the American Medical Informatics Association*, 24(2): 345–351.

Martinez, F. 2019. On the role of faith in sustainability management: A conceptual model and research agenda. *Journal of Business Ethics*, 155(3): 787–807.

Marzouk, M., Abdelhamid, M., & Elsheikh, M. 2013. Selecting sustainable building materials using system dynamics and ant colony optimization. *Journal of Environmental Engineering and Landscape Management*, 21(4): 237–247.

Maslennikova, I., & Foley, D. 2000. Xerox's approach to sustainability. *Interfaces*, 30(3): 226–233.

Matinaro, V., & Liu, Y. 2017. Towards increased innovativeness and sustainability through organizational culture: A case study of a Finnish construction business. *Journal of Cleaner Production*, 142: 3184–3193.

Mazumdar, M., Poeran, J. V., Ferket, B. S., Zubizarreta, N., Agarwal, P., Gorbenko, K., Craven, C. K., Zhong, X. B., Moskowitz, A. J., Gelijns, A. C., & Reich, D. L. 2020. Developing an institute for health care delivery science: Successes, challenges, and solutions in the first five years. *Health Care Management Science*, 1–10.

Mc Morran, R., Scott, A. J., & Price, M. F. 2014. Reconstructing sustainability; participant experiences of community land tenure in North West Scotland. *Journal of Rural Studies*, 33: 20–31.

McBride, L. J., Fitzgerald, C., Costello, C., & Perkins, K. 2020. Allied health pre-entry student clinical placement capacity: Can it be sustained? *Australian Health Review*, 44(1): 39–46.

McCourt, C., Rance, S., Rayment, J., & Sandall, J. 2018. Organising safe and sustainable care in alongside midwifery units: Findings from an organisational ethnographic study. *Midwifery*, 65: 26–34.

McGehee, N. G., Knollenberg, W., & Komorowski, A. 2015. The central role of leadership in rural tourism development: A theoretical framework and case studies. *Journal of Sustainable Tourism*, 23(8–9): 1277–1297.

McMillan, S. G., & Binns, T. 2011. Environmental education and learning communities: The case of Kaikorai Stream, Dunedin, New Zealand. *New Zealand Geographer*, 67(3): 199–212.

Mehalik, M. M., Gould, C., & Edwards, B. 2007. Making major retail establishments sustainable: The case of the mall at robinson. *Journal of Green Building*, 2(4): 14–22.

Mellado, F., Wong, P. F., Amano, K., Johnson, C., & Lou, E. C. W. 2020. Digitisation of existing buildings to support building assessment schemes: Viability of automated sustainability-led design scan-to-BIM process. *Architectural Engineering and Design Management*, 16(2): 84–99.

Mellner, C., Niemi, M., Pollanen, E., & Osika, W. 2020. Enhancing social and individual sustainability in urban co-living. *International Journal of Housing Markets and Analysis*, 1–16.

Metaxas, I. N., Chatzoglou, P. D., & Koulouriotis, D. E. 2019. Proposing a new modus operandi for sustainable business excellence: The case of Greek hospitality industry. *Total Quality Management & Business Excellence*, 30(5–6): 499–524.

Metcalf, L., & Benn, S. 2012. The corporation is ailing social technology: Creating a 'fit for purpose' design for sustainability. *Journal of Business Ethics*, 111(2): 195–210.

Miller, L., Dorsey, J., & Jacobs, K. 2012. The importance of ergonomics to sustainability throughout a building's life cycle. *Work-a Journal of Prevention Assessment & Rehabilitation*, 41(Supplement 1): 2129–2132.

Miralles-Quiros, M. D., Miralles-Quiros, J. L., & Arraiano, I. G. 2017. Sustainable development, sustainability leadership and firm valuation: Differences across Europe. *Business Strategy and the Environment*, 26(7): 1014–1028.

Misso, M. L., Ilic, D., Haines, T. P., Hutchinson, A. M., East, C. E., & Teede, H. J. 2016. Development, implementation and evaluation of a clinical research engagement and leadership capacity building program in a large Australian health care service. *Bmc Medical Education*, 16: 9.

Mitra, D. L. 2009. The role of intermediary organizations in sustaining student voice initiatives. *Teachers College Record*, 111(7): 1834–1869.

Moffat, A., & Auer, A. 2006. Corporate environmental innovation (CEI): A government initiative to support corporate sustainability leadership. *Journal of Cleaner Production*, 14(6–7): 589–600.

Montgomery, M., & Vaughan, M. 2018. Ma Kahana ka 'Ike: Lessons for community-based fisheries management. *Sustainability*, 10(10): 16.

Moodle, V. R. 2019. Towards a culture of quality assurance in optometric education in sub-Saharan Africa. *African Vision and Eye Health Journal*, 78(1): 8.

Morland, K. B. 2010. An evaluation of a neighborhood-level intervention to a local food environment. *American Journal of Preventive Medicine*, 39(6): E31–E38.

Moullin, J. C., Ehrhart, M. G., & Aarons, G. A. 2018. The role of leadership in organizational implementation and sustainment in service agencies. *Research on Social Work Practice*, 28(5): 558–567.

Munene, L. N. 2019. Reducing carbon emissions: Strathmore University contributions towards sustainable development in Kenya. *African Journal of Business Ethics*, 13(1): 1–11.

Murphy, S. 2020. Science education success in a rural australian school: Practices and arrangements contributing to high senior science enrolments and achievement in an isolated rural school. *Research in Science Education*, 1–13.

Murray, F. 2013. The changing winds of atmospheric environment policy. *Environmental Science & Policy*, 29: 115–123.

Mustamil, N., & Najam, U. 2020. The impact of servant leadership on follower turnover intentions: Mediating role of resilience. *Asian Journal of Business and Accounting*, 13(2): 125–145.

Nagle, D. S., & Vidon, E. S. 2020. Purchasing protection: Outdoor companies and the authentication of technology use in nature-based tourism. *Journal of Sustainable Tourism*, 1–17.

Nasser, G. 2008. One of the first schools in the United States to be LEED certified – Riverside High School, Greer, SC. *PCI Journal*, 53(1): 144–152.

Ndaba, T., Taylor, M., & Mabaso, M. 2020. Establishing a community advisory group (CAG) for partnership defined quality (PDQ) towards improving primary health care in a peri-urban setting in KwaZulu-Natal, South Africa. *Bmc Health Services Research*, 20(1): 7.

Nguyen, T. H., Toroghi, S. H., & Jacobs, F. 2016. Automated green building rating system for building designs. *Journal of Architectural Engineering*, 22(4): 10.

Nilan, P., & Wibawanto, G. R. 2015. "Becoming" an environmentalist in Indonesia. *Geoforum*, 62: 61–69.

Nomura, K., & Abe, O. 2010. Higher education for sustainable development in Japan: Policy and progress. *International Journal of Sustainability in Higher Education*, 11(2): 120–129.

Nowoswiat, A., Slusarek, J., Zuchowski, R., & Pudelko, B. 2018. The impact of noise in the environment on the acoustic assessment of green houses. *International Journal of Acoustics and Vibration*, 23(3): 392–401.

Nzimande, Z., & Chauke, H. 2012. Sustainability through responsible environmental mining. *Journal of the Southern African Institute of Mining and Metallurgy*, 112(2): 135–139.

Oates, D., & Sullivan, K. T. 2012. Postoccupancy energy consumption survey of Arizona's LEED new construction population. *Journal of Construction Engineering and Management-ASCE*, 138(6): 742–750.

Obata, S. H., Agostinho, F., Almeida, C., & Giannetti, B. F. 2019. LEED certification as booster for sustainable buildings: Insights for a Brazilian context. *Resources Conservation and Recycling*, 145: 170–178.

O'Donnell, D., She, E. N., McCarthy, M., Thornton, S., Doran, T., Smith, F., O'Brien, B., Milton, J., Savin, B., Donnellan, A., Callan, E., McAuliffe, E., Gray, S., Carey, T., Boyle, N., O'Brien, M., Patton, A., Bailey, J., O'Shea, D., & Marie, T. C. 2019. Enabling public, patient and practitioner involvement in co-designing frailty pathways in the acute care setting. *Bmc Health Services Research*, 19(1): 11.

Okello, M. M., Seno, S. K. O., & Nthiga, R. W. 2009. Reconciling people's livelihoods and environmental conservation in the rural landscapes in Kenya: Opportunities and challenges in the Amboseli landscapes. *Natural Resources Forum*, 33(2): 123–133.

Olender, L., Capitulo, K., & Nelson, J. 2020. The impact of interprofessional shared governance and a caring professional practice model on staff's self-report of caring, workplace engagement, and workplace empowerment over time. *Journal of Nursing Administration*, 50(1): 52–58.

Olinzock, M. A., Landis, A. E., Saunders, C. L., Collinge, W. O., Jones, A. K., Schaefer, L. A., & Bilec, M. M. 2015. Life cycle assessment use in the North American building community: Summary of findings from a 2011/2012 survey. *International Journal of Life Cycle Assessment*, 20(3): 318–331.

Opoku, D. G. J., Agyekum, K., & Ayarkwa, J. 2020. Drivers of environmental sustainability of construction projects: A thematic analysis of verbatim comments from built environment consultants. *International Journal of Construction Management*, 1–9.

Orr, J., Ibell, T., Evernden, M., & Darby, A. 2015. Day one sustainability. *European Journal of Engineering Education*, 40(3): 285–296.

Owusu-Agyeman, Y. 2020. Formation of a sustainable development ecosystem for Ghanaian universities. *International Review of Education*, 1–30.

Painter-Morland, M., Sabet, E., Molthan-Hill, P., Goworek, H., & de Leeuw, S. 2016. Beyond the curriculum: Integrating sustainability into business schools. *Journal of Business Ethics*, 139(4): 737–754.

Pandey, P. C. 2015. Business as a force for good: Action and leadership through and beyond post 2015 agenda. *Asian Biotechnology and Development Review*, 17(2): 69–84.

Papajohn, D., Brinker, C., & El Asmar, M. 2017. MARS: Metaframework for assessing ratings of sustainability for buildings and infrastructure. *Journal of Management in Engineering*, 33(1): 21.

Parand, A., Dopson, S., & Vincent, C. 2013. The role of chief executive officers in a quality improvement initiative: A qualitative study. *Bmj Open*, 3(1): 13.

Parsons, M. L., & Cornett, P. A. 2011. Sustaining the pivotal organizational outcome: Magnet recognition. *Journal of Nursing Management*, 19(2): 277–286.

Pasquini, L., & Shearing, C. 2014. Municipalities, politics, and climate change: An example of the process of institutionalizing an environmental agenda within local government. *Journal of Environment & Development*, 23(2): 271–296.

Pasquini, L., Ziervogel, G., Cowling, R. M., & Shearing, C. 2015. What enables local governments to mainstream climate change adaptation? Lessons learned from two municipal case studies in the Western Cape, South Africa. *Climate and Development*, 7(1): 60–70.

Patro, C. S. 2020. An evaluation of employees' competence towards the development of a learning organization. *International Journal of Knowledge Management*, 16(4): 26–41.

Paul, R., McCutcheon, S. P., Zenios, S. A., Tregarthen, J. P., & Denend, L. T. 2014. Sustaining pressure ulcer best practices in a high-volume cardiac care environment how one hospital reduced the incidence of hospital-acquired pressure ulcers to zero. *American Journal of Nursing*, 114(8): 34–44.

Pearse, B. L., Rickard, C. M., Keogh, S., & Fung, Y. L. 2019. A retrospective explanatory case study of the implementation of a bleeding management quality initiative, in an Australian cardiac surgery unit. *Australian Critical Care*, 32(2): 92–99.

Pearson, C. E., Butler, A. J., & Murray, Y. P. 2018. Understanding veterinary leadership in practice. *Veterinary Record*, 182(16): 460–+.

Pelt, C. E., Anderson, M. B., Erickson, J. A., Gililland, J. M., & Peters, C. L. 2018. Adding value to total joint arthroplasty care in an academic environment: The utah experience. *Journal of Arthroplasty*, 33(6): 1636–1640.

Perenyi, A., Selvarajah, C., Tanas, J., Tuckova, Z., Odrowaz-Coates, A., Toth-Bozo, B., & Minarova, M. 2020. Exploring ethical business in central Europe: Leaders' values and perspectives on good practices. *Sustainability*, 12(2): 30.

BIBLIOMETRIC ANALYSIS OF LEADERSHIP   383

Perez-Gomez, H. R., & Ramos-Zuniga, R. 2012. Medical education and its impact on public health. Perspectives and challenges. *Cirugia Y Cirujanos*, 80(2): 188–194.

Peterlin, J., Dimovski, V., Tvaronaviciene, M., Grah, B., & Kaklauskas, A. 2018. The strategic process of developing social aspects of sustainability through the vision reflection in business education. *Technological and Economic Development of Economy*, 24(4): 1718–1736.

Pham, H., & Kim, S. Y. 2019. The effects of sustainable practices and managers' leadership competences on sustainability performance of construction firms. *Sustainable Production and Consumption*, 20: 1–14.

Phillips, S., Thai, V. V., & Halim, Z. 2019. Airline value chain capabilities and CSR performance: The connection between CSR leadership and CSR culture with CSR performance, customer satisfaction and financial performance. *Asian Journal of Shipping and Logistics*, 35(1): 30–40.

Pitman, S. D., & Daniels, C. B. 2020. Understanding how nature works: Five pathways towards a more ecologically literate world – A perspective. *Austral Ecology*, 45(5): 510–519.

Pittman, J., Cohee, A., Storey, S., LaMothe, J., Gilbert, J., Bakoyannis, G., Ofner, S., & Newhouse, R. 2019. A multisite health system survey to assess organizational context to support evidence-based practice. *Worldviews on Evidence-Based Nursing*, 16(4): 271–280.

Pitts, S. B. J., Graham, J., Mojica, A., Stewart, L., Walter, M., Schille, C., McGinty, J., Pearsall, M., Whitt, O., Mihas, P., Bradley, A., & Simon, C. 2016. Implementing healthier foodservice guidelines in hospital and federal worksite cafeterias: Barriers, facilitators and keys to success. *Journal of Human Nutrition and Dietetics*, 29(6): 677–686.

Pla-Julian, I., & Guevara, S. 2020. Mainstreaming gender and sustainability jointly: A case study from a local government in Spain. *Local Environment*, 25(3): 14.

Plaut, J. 1998. Industry environmental processes: Beyond compliance. *Technology in Society*, 20(4): 469–479.

Portes, L. H., Machado, C. V., Turci, S. R. B., Figueiredo, V. C., Cavalcante, T. M., & Silva, V. 2018. Tobacco control policies in Brazil: A 30-year assessment. *Ciencia & Saude Coletiva*, 23(6): 1837–1848.

Prabhu, C. J., Mehta, M., & Srivastava, A. P. 2020. A new model of practical spiritual intelligence for the leadership development of human capital in Indian Universities. *Journal of Applied Research in Higher Education*, 12(5): 957–973.

Prasad, D. S., Pradhan, R. P., Gaurav, K., Chatterjee, P. P., Kaur, I., Dash, S., & Nayak, S. 2018. Analysing the critical success factors for implementation of sustainable supply chain management: An Indian case study. *Decision*, 45(1): 3–25.

Prusaczyk, B., Mixon, A. S., & Kripalani, S. 2020. Implementation and sustainability of a pharmacy-led, hospital-wide bedside medication delivery program: A qualitative process evaluation using RE-AIM. *Frontiers in Public Health*, 7: 9.

Purnomo, A. B. 2020. A Model of interreligious eco-theological leadership to care for the earth in the indonesian context. *European Journal of Science and Theology*, 16(4): 15–25.

Quayle, B., Sciulli, N., & Wilson-Evered, E. 2020. Accountable to who, to whom, for what and how? Unpacking accountability in local government response to climate change. *Australasian Accounting Business and Finance Journal*, 14(3): 19.

Quazi, H. A. 2001. Sustainable development: Integrating environmental issues into strategic planning. *Industrial Management & Data Systems*, 101(1–2): 64–70.

Quinn, M., Kowalski-Dobson, T., & Lachance, L. 2018. Defining and measuring sustainability in the food & fitness initiative. *Health Promotion Practice*, 19: 78S–91S.

Ramachandaran, S. D., Krauss, S. E., Hamzah, A., & Idris, K. 2017. Effectiveness of the use of spiritual intelligence in women academic leadership practice. *International Journal of Educational Management*, 31(2): 160–178.

Rambakus, Z., Hoque, M., & Proches, C. N. G. 2020. Evaluating the extent of intrapreneurship in a sugar producing company in KwaZulu-Natal, South Africa. *Cogent Business & Management*, 7(1): 19.

Rand, C. M., Concannon, C., Wallace-Brodeur, R., Davis, W., Albertin, C. S., Humiston, S. G., & Szilagyi, P. G. 2020. Identifying strategies to reduce missed opportunities for HPV vaccination in primary care: A qualitative study of positive deviants. *Clinical Pediatrics*, 59(12): 1058–1068.

Rego, A., Cunha, M. P. E., & Polonia, D. 2017. Corporate sustainability: A view from the top. *Journal of Business Ethics*, 143(1): 133–157.

Retzaff, R. C. 2009. The use of LEED in planning and development regulation an exploratory analysis. *Journal of Planning Education and Research*, 29(1): 67–77.

Ribeiro, S. M., Bogus, C. M., & Watanabe, H. A. W. 2015. Agroecological urban agriculture from the perspective of health promotion. *Saude E Sociedade*, 24(2): 730–743.

Richardson, J., Clarke, D., Grose, J., & Warwick, P. 2019. A cohort study of sustainability education in nursing. *International Journal of Sustainability in Higher Education*, 20(4): 747–760.

Rikkerink, M., Verbeeten, H., Simons, R. J., & Ritzen, H. 2016. A new model of educational innovation: Exploring the nexus of organizational learning, distributed leadership, and digital technologies. *Journal of Educational Change*, 17(2): 223–249.

Ristimaki, M., & Junnila, S. 2015. Sustainable urban development calls for responsibility through life cycle management. *Sustainability*, 7(9): 12539–12563.

Rivera, A., Gelcich, S., Garcia-Florez, L., & Acuna, J. L. 2019. Social attributes can drive or deter the sustainability of bottom-up management systems. *Science of the Total Environment*, 690: 760–767.

Robu, V., Cismasu, I. D., & Petcu, A. M. 2019. The assessment of the quality of leadership as a resource for sustainable development. *Quality-Access to Success*, 20: 491–496.

Rodriguez-Garcia, M., Orero-Blat, M., & Palacios-Marques, D. 2020. Challenges in the business model of low-cost airlines: Ryanair case study. *International Journal of Enterprise Information Systems*, 16(3): 64–77.

Rohe, J., Schluter, A., & Ferse, S. C. A. 2018. A gender lens on women's harvesting activities and interactions with local marine governance in a South Pacific fishing community. *Maritime Studies*, 17(2): 155–162.

Rolander, B., Jonker, D., Winkel, J., Sandsjo, L., Balogh, I., Svensson, E., & Ekberg, K. 2013. Working conditions, health and productivity among dentists in Swedish public dental care – a prospective study during a 5-year period of rationalisation. *Ergonomics*, 56(9): 1376–1386.

Roos, J. 2017. Practical wisdom: Making and teaching the governance case for sustainability. *Journal of Cleaner Production*, 140: 117–124.

Rosenkrantz, A. B., Lawson, K., Ally, R., Chen, D., Donno, F., Rittberg, S., Rodriguez, J., & Recht, M. P. 2015. Focused process improvement events:

Sustainability of impact on process and performance in an academic radiology department. *Journal of the American College of Radiology*, 12(1): 75–81.

Ross, C., Woo, M., & Wang, F. R. 2016. Megaregions and regional sustainability. *International Journal of Urban Sciences*, 20(3): 299–317.

Ryan-Fogarty, Y., O'Regan, B., & Moles, R. 2016. Greening healthcare: Systematic implementation of environmental programmes in a university teaching hospital. *Journal of Cleaner Production*, 126: 248–259.

Sabella, A. R., & Eid, N. L. 2016. A strategic perspective of social enterprise sustainability. *Journal of General Management*, 41(4): 71–89.

Sajwani, A., & Nielsen, Y. 2017. The application of the environmental management system at the aluminum industry in UAE. *International Journal of Geomate*, 12(30): 1–10.

Sanchez, R. G., Florez-Parra, J. M., Lopez-Perez, M. V., & Lopez-Hernandez, A. M. 2020. Corporate governance and disclosure of information on corporate social responsibility: An analysis of the top 200 universities in the Shanghai Ranking. *Sustainability*, 12(4): 22.

Sanhudo, L. P. N., & Martins, J. 2018. Building information modelling for an automated building sustainability assessment. *Civil Engineering and Environmental Systems*, 35(1–4): 99–116.

Saraiva, T. S., de Almeida, M., & Braganca, L. 2019. Adaptation of the SBTool for sustainability assessment of high school buildings in Portugal-SAHSB(PT). *Applied Sciences-Basel*, 9(13): 15.

Sarvet, B. D., Ravech, M., & Straus, J. H. 2017. Massachusetts child psychiatry access project 2.0 A case study in child psychiatry access program redesign. *Child and Adolescent Psychiatric Clinics of North America*, 26(4): 647.

Savaya, R., Spiro, S., & Elran-Barak, R. 2008. Sustainability of social programs a comparative case study analysis. *American Journal of Evaluation*, 29(4): 478–493.

Savita, J. T., Bharat, V. D., Avinash, B. B., & Meeta, N. J. 2020. An approach to the evaluation of program outcomes and consideration of activities beyond curriculum for improvement of program outcome attainment. *Indian Journal of Pharmaceutical Education and Research*, 54(4): 896–904.

Schmidt, C. 2014. Foreword by the federal minister of food and agriculture christian schmidt. *Berichte Uber Landwirtschaft*, 43.

Schmitz, C. L., Matyok, T., Sloan, L. M., & James, C. 2012. The relationship between social work and environmental sustainability: Implications for interdisciplinary practice. *International Journal of Social Welfare*, 21(3): 278–286.

Schneider, B. S., Menzel, N., Clark, M., York, N., Candela, L., & Xu, Y. 2009. Nursing's leadership in positioning human health at the core of urban sustainability. *Nursing Outlook*, 57(5): 281–288.

Scholz, R. W., Yarime, M., & Shiroyama, H. 2018. Global leadership for social design: Theoretical and educational perspectives. *Sustainability Science*, 13(2): 447–464.

Schuler, R. S. 2015. The 5-C framework for managing talent. *Organizational Dynamics*, 44(1): 47.

Schuster, D. B. 2015. International telecommunication union-150 years of history: Adaptation to change and the opportunity for reform. *IEEE Communications Magazine*, 53: 10–15.

Segovia-Perez, M., Laguna-Sanchez, P., & de la Fuente-Cabrero, C. 2019. Education for sustainable leadership: Fostering women's empowerment at the university level. *Sustainability*, 11(20): 14.

Selden, S. C., & Sowa, J. E. 2015. Voluntary turnover in nonprofit human service organizations: The impact of high performance work practices. *Human Service Organizations Management Leadership & Governance*, 39(3): 182–207.

Setyahadi, R. R., & Narsa, I. M. 2020. Corporate Governance and Sustainability in Indonesia. *Journal of Asian Finance Economics and Business*, 7(12): 885–894.

Sewpersadh, N. S. 2019. An examination of CEO power with board vigilance as a catalyst for firm growth in South Africa. *Measuring Business Excellence*, 23(4): 377–395.

Shah, A. K., Yu, J. T., Sukamani, D., & Kusi, M. 2020. How green transformational leadership influences sustainability? Mediating effects of green creativity and green procurement. *Risus-Journal on Innovation and Sustainability*, 11(4): 69–87.

Shen, W. X., Tang, W. Z., Siripanan, A., Lei, Z., Duffield, C. F., & Hui, F. K. P. 2018. Understanding the green technical capabilities and barriers to green buildings in developing countries: A case study of Thailand. *Sustainability*, 10(10): 17.

Shikweni, S., Schurink, W., & van Wyk, R. 2019. Talent management in the South African construction industry. *Sa Journal of Human Resource Management*, 17: 12.

Shinbrot, X. A., Wilkins, K., Gretzel, U., & Bowser, G. 2019. Unlocking women's sustainability leadership potential: Perceptions of contributions and challenges for women in sustainable development. *World Development*, 119: 120–132.

Siew, R. Y. J. 2018. Green township index: Malaysia's sustainable township rating tool. *Proceedings of the Institution of Civil Engineers-Engineering Sustainability*, 171(4): 169–177.

Silimperi, D. R., Franco, L. M., Van Zanten, T. V., & Macaulay, C. 2002. A framework for institutionalizing quality assurance. *International Journal for Quality in Health Care*, 14(Supplement 1): 67–73.

Silliman, S. E., Hamlin, C., Crane, P. E., & Boukari, M. 2008. International collaborations and incorporating the social sciences in research in hydrology and hydrology engineering. *Journal of Hydrologic Engineering*, 13(1): 13–19.

Silva, M. F., Malheiro, B., Guedes, P., Duarte, A., & Ferreira, P. 2018. Collaborative learning with sustainability-driven projects: A summary of the EPS@ISEP programme. *International Journal of Engineering Pedagogy*, 8(4): 106–130.

Silvestri, A., & Veltri, S. 2020. Exploring the relationships between corporate social responsibility, leadership, and sustainable entrepreneurship theories: A conceptual framework. *Corporate Social Responsibility and Environmental Management*, 27(2): 585–594.

Singh, A., Syal, M., Korkmaz, S., & Grady, S. 2011. Costs and benefits of IEQ Improvements in LEED office buildings. *Journal of Infrastructure Systems*, 17(2): 86–94.

Singh, P. 2019. Lean in healthcare organization: An opportunity for environmental sustainability. *Benchmarking-an International Journal*, 26(1): 205–220.

Singh, S., & Mittal, S. 2019. Analysis of drivers of CSR practices' implementation among family firms in India A stakeholder's perspective. *International Journal of Organizational Analysis*, 27(4): 947–971.

Singleton, J. A., Lau, E. T. L., & Nissen, L. M. 2018. Waiter, there is a drug in my soup – using Leximancer((R)) to explore antecedents to pro-environmental behaviours in the hospital pharmacy workplace. *International Journal of Pharmacy Practice*, 26(4): 341–350.

Smith, G. A., & Stevenson, R. B. 2017. Sustaining education for sustainability in turbulent times. *Journal of Environmental Education*, 48(2): 79–95.

Smith, J. M. 2020. Surgeon coaching: Why and how. *Journal of Pediatric Orthopaedics*, 40(Supplement 1): S33–S37.

Smith, W. 2020. The leadership role of teachers and environment club coordinators in promoting ecocentrism in secondary schools: Teachers as exemplars of environmental education. *Australian Journal of Environmental Education*, 36(1): 63–80.

Snyder, S. 2000. North Korea's challenge of regime survival: Internal problems and implications for the future. *Pacific Affairs*, 73(4): 517–+.

Song, W. H., Wang, G. Z., & Ma, X. F. 2020. Environmental innovation practices and green product innovation performance: A perspective from organizational climate. *Sustainable Development*, 28(1): 224–234.

Spencer, R. A., Joshi, N., Branje, K., McIsaac, J. L. D., Cawley, J., Rehman, L., Kirk, S. F. L., & Stone, M. 2019. Educator perceptions on the benefits and challenges of loose parts play in the outdoor environments of childcare centres. *Aims Public Health*, 6(4): 461–476.

Spoelstra, S. L., Schueller, M., & Sikorskii, A. 2019. Testing an implementation strategy bundle on adoption and sustainability of evidence to optimize physical function in community-dwelling disabled and older adults in a Medicaid waiver: A multi-site pragmatic hybrid type III protocol. *Implementation Science*, 14: 13.

Storms, K., Simundza, D., Morgan, E., & Miller, S. 2019. Developing a resilience tool for higher education institutions: A must-have in campus master planning. *Journal of Green Building*, 14(1): 187–197.

Strauss, K., Lepoutre, J., & Wood, G. 2017. Fifty shades of green: How microfoundations of sustainability dynamic capabilities vary across organizational contexts. *Journal of Organizational Behavior*, 38(9): 1338–1355.

Sun, Z., Jai, K., & Zhao, L. 2019. Corporate social responsibility and sustainability of local community: A case study of the transnational project in China-Pakistan economic corridor. *Sustainability*, 11(22): 18.

Swaffield, S. 2014. Sustainability practices in New Zealand agricultural landscapes under an open market policy regime. *Landscape Research*, 39(2): 190–204.

Tan, B., Pan, S. L., & Zuo, M. Y. 2015. Harnessing collective IT resources for sustainability: Insights from the green leadership strategy of China mobile. *Journal of the Association for Information Science and Technology*, 66(4): 818–838.

Tandon, A., & Nair, U. K. 2020. Understanding and managing learning in social enterprises: The role of implicit organizational boundaries. *Nonprofit Management & Leadership*, 31(2): 259–286.

Tang, J. Y., Tang, L. W., Li, Y., & Hu, Z. Y. 2020. Measuring eco-efficiency and its convergence: Empirical analysis from China. *Energy Efficiency*, 13(6): 1075–1087.

Thomas, A. U., Fried, G. P., Johnson, P., & Stilwell, B. J. 2010. Sharing best practices through online communities of practice: A case study. *Human Resources for Health*, 8: 8.

Throop, W., & Mayberry, M. 2017. Leadership for the Sustainability Transition. *Business and Society Review*, 122(2): 221–250.

Tingley, D. D., Cooper, S., & Cullen, J. 2017. Understanding and overcoming the barriers to structural steel reuse, a UK perspective. *Journal of Cleaner Production*, 148: 642–652.

Tiwari, V., & Thakur, S. 2020. Environment sustainability through sustainability innovations. *Environment Development and Sustainability*, 1–25.

Tomsic, N., Bojnec, S., & Simcic, B. 2015. Corporate sustainability and economic performance in small and medium sized enterprises. *Journal of Cleaner Production*, 108: 603–612.

Trebilcock, M. 2019. The puzzle of Canadian exceptionalism in contemporary immigration policy "Canada could be the first post-national state. There is no core identity, no mainstream in Canada." Prime Minister Justin Trudeau New York Times Magazine, November 10, 2015. *Journal of International Migration and Integration*, 20(3): 823–849.

Tsai, Y. S., Poquet, O., Gasevic, D., Dawson, S., & Pardo, A. 2019. Complexity leadership in learning analytics: Drivers, challenges and opportunities. *British Journal of Educational Technology*, 50(6): 2839–2854.

Tsymbal, L., & Aslanzade, R. 2020. Supply chain management from a social responsibility perspective. *Bulletin of the National Academy of Sciences of the Republic of Kazakhstan*, 3: 160–168.

Tuan, L. T. 2018. Activating tourists' citizenship behavior for the environment: The roles of CSR and frontline employees' citizenship behavior for the environment. *Journal of Sustainable Tourism*, 26(7): 1178–1203.

Umar, T. 2020. An integrated sustainability-management approach for universities. *Proceedings of the Institution of Civil Engineers-Engineering Sustainability*, 173(7): 344–355.

Usheva, M., & Danchova, M. V. 2019. Contemporary leadership in bulgarian economics. *Revista Inclusiones*, 6: 77–89.

Valdes, R. M. A., Burmaoglu, S., Tucci, V., Campos, L., Mattera, L., & Comendador, V. F. G. 2019. Flight path 2050 and ACARE goals for maintaining and extending industrial leadership in aviation: A map of the aviation technology space. *Sustainability*, 11(7): 24.

Vandersmissen, A., & Welburn, S. C. 2014. Current initiatives in one health: Consolidating the one health global network. *Revue Scientifique Et Technique-Office International Des Epizooties*, 33(2): 421–432.

VanGeem, M. 2006. Achieving sustainability with precast concrete. *PCI Journal*, 51(1): 42–+.

Vercher, N., Barlagne, C., Hewitt, R., Nijnik, M., & Esparcia, J. 2021. Whose narrative is it anyway? Narratives of social innovation in rural areas – A comparative analysis of community-led initiatives in Scotland and Spain. *Sociologia Ruralis*, 61(1): 163–189.

Verhoef, G., & Drotskie, A. 2015. Sustained in a competitive environment: Organizational capabilities and Sanlam, 1918–1945. *Management & Organizational History*, 10(3–4): 251–275.

Vieira, E., & Ferreira, J. 2020. What generic strategies do private fitness centres implement and what are their impacts on financial performance? *Sport Business and Management-an International Journal*, 10(3): 317–333.

Vijayanand, K., Kumar, J. A., Sathish, S., & Amarnath, D. J. 2015. Evaluation and Comparison of Utility Consumption for the Sustainable and Normal building. *Research Journal of Pharmaceutical Biological and Chemical Sciences*, 6(5): 1462–1466.

Viswanathan, M., Venugopal, S., Minefee, I., Guest, J. S., Marians, B. J., Bauza, V., Valentino, L., Kupaza, R., & Jones, M. 2016. A bottom-up approach to short-term immersion in subsistence marketplaces: Methodological and substantive lessons on poverty and the environment from Tanzania. *Organization & Environment*, 29(4): 438–460.

Viswanathan, S., & Radhakrishnan, B. 2018. A novel 'game design' methodology for STEM program. *International Journal of Game-Based Learning*, 8(4): 1–17.

Vogel, D. 2019. Promoting sustainable government regulation: What we can learn from California. *Organization & Environment*, 32(2): 145–158.

Wallen, G. R., Mitchell, S. A., Melnyk, B., Fineout-Overholt, E., Miller-Davis, C., Yates, J., & Hastings, C. 2010. Implementing evidence-based practice: Effectiveness of a structured multifaceted mentorship programme. *Journal of Advanced Nursing*, 66(12): 2761–2771.

Wamsler, C., Luederitz, C., & Brink, E. 2014. Local levers for change: Mainstreaming ecosystem-based adaptation into municipal planning to foster sustainability transitions. *Global Environmental Change-Human and Policy Dimensions*, 29: 189–201.

Wang, X. H., Xiao, H. Y., Chen, K., & Niu, X. J. 2020. Why administrative leaders take pro-environmental leadership actions: Evidence from an eco-compensation programme in China. *Environmental Policy and Governance*, 30(6): 385–398.

Wanyonyi, E. I., Gathungu, E. W., Bett, H. K., & Okello, D. O. 2020. Determinants of Porter's competitive strategy utilization among agro-dealers in Kenya. *Cogent Food & Agriculture*, 7(1): 16.

Watson, P., Gabriel, M., & Rooney, M. 2015. Get bill smart: A community-partnership approach to supporting low-income households to achieve home energy savings. *Indoor and Built Environment*, 24(7): 867–877.

Wesselink, R., Blok, V., & Ringersma, J. 2017. Pro-environmental behaviour in the workplace and the role of managers and organisation. *Journal of Cleaner Production*, 168: 1679–1687.

Wilson, L., Orff, S., Gerry, T., Shirley, B. R., Tabor, D., Caiazzo, K., & Rouleau, D. 2013. Evolution of an innovative role: The clinical nurse leader. *Journal of Nursing Management*, 21(1): 175–181.

Wofford, L., Wyman, D., & Starr, C. W. 2020. Do you have a naive forecasting model of the future? *Journal of Property Investment & Finance*, 38(4): 267–269.

Woo, E. J., & Kang, E. 2020. Environmental issues as an indispensable aspect of sustainable leadership. *Sustainability*, 12(17): 22.

Worden, K., Hazer, M., Pyke, C., & Trowbridge, M. 2020. Using LEED green rating systems to promote population health. *Building and Environment*, 172: 8.

Wysen, K. 2021. Listen and be ready to shift: How racial equity and community leadership launched "communities of opportunity". *Journal of Public Health Management and Practice*, 27(1): E48–E56.

Xing, Y. J., & Starik, M. 2017. Taoist leadership and employee green behaviour: A cultural and philosophical microfoundation of sustainability. *Journal of Organizational Behavior*, 38(9): 1302–1319.

Yahanpath, N., Pacheco, P., & Burns, E. A. 2018. Discussing a balanced scorecard for one local independent New Zealand church. *Journal of Management Spirituality & Religion*, 15(1): 1–19.

Yap, X. S., & Truffer, B. 2019. Shaping selection environments for industrial catch-up and sustainability transitions: A systemic perspective on endogenizing windows of opportunity. *Research Policy*, 48(4): 1030–1047.

Yiemwattana, S., & Charoenkit, S. 2019. Towards an engaging, inclusive and meaningful planning development of an urban park in Phitsanulok, Thailand. *Geographia Technica*, 14: 76–86.

Ying, M., Faraz, N. A., Ahmed, F., & Raza, A. 2020. How does servant leadership foster employees' voluntary green behavior? A sequential mediation model. *International Journal of Environmental Research and Public Health*, 17(5): 21.

Yoon, J., & Park, J. 2015. Comparative analysis of material criteria in neighborhood sustainability assessment tools and urban design guidelines: Cases of the UK, the US, Japan, and Korea. *Sustainability*, 7(11): 14450–14487.

York, L., Janet, L., & Lanasa, S. 2014. Go green, get healthy: An agencywide effort to reduce energy use and move the centers for disease control and prevention toward sustainability. *Journal of Energy Engineering*, 140(2): 7.

Young, J., & Osmani, M. 2013. Investigation into contractors' responsible sourcing implementation practice. *Proceedings of the Institution of Civil Engineers-Engineering Sustainability*, 166(6): 320–329.

Yu, V. F., & Ting, H. I. 2012. Financial development, investor protection, and corporate commitment to sustainability Evidence from the FTSE Global 500. *Management Decision*, 50(1–2): 130–146.

Zapka, J., Lemon, S. C., Estabrook, B. B., & Jolicoeur, D. G. 2007. Keeping a step ahead: Formative phase of a workplace intervention trial to prevent obesity. *Obesity*, 15 Supplement 1: 27S–36S.

Zellmer, W. A. 2012. The future of health-system pharmacy: Opportunities and challenges in practice model change. *Annals of Pharmacotherapy*, 46(4): S41–S45.

Zhang, Q. H., Chen, Y. Y., Tao, Y., Farid, T., & Ma, J. H. 2019. How consistent contributors inspire individuals to cooperate: The role of moral elevation and social value orientation. *Sustainability*, 11(7): 19.

Zhang, Y. P., Liu, W. H., Yan, Y. T., Porr, C., Zhang, Y., & Wei, H. H. 2019. Psychometric testing of the evidence-based practice nursing leadership scale and the work environment scale after cross-cultural adaptation in Mainland China. *Evaluation & the Health Professions*, 42(3): 328–343.

Zida, A., Lavis, J. N., Sewankambo, N. K., Kouyate, B., & Moat, K. 2017. The factors affecting the institutionalisation of two policy units in Burkina Faso's health system: A case study. *Health Research Policy and Systems*, 15: 15.

Zuniga-Teran, A. A., Orr, B. J., Gimblett, R. H., Chalfoun, N. V., Going, S. B., Guertin, D. P., & Marsh, S. E. 2016. Designing healthy communities: A walkability analysis of LEED-ND. *Frontiers of Architectural Research*, 5(4): 433–452.

Zuo, Q., & MaloneBeach, E. E. 2017. Assessing staff satisfaction with indoor environmental quality in assisted living facilities. *Journal of Interior Design*, 42(1): 67–84.

16

CONCLUSION

If the Covid-19 pandemic reveals nothing else, it is the interconnected and systemic nature of the challenges that the world faces. Of course, the pandemic is no more than a timely reminder of our status as a component part of the natural world rather than its master. As Shiva puts it, 'instead of being connected through biodiversity we become connected through disease' (Shiva 2020, p. 11). Societal-wide switches to digital communication in response to the pandemic have underscored both a desire to reconnect people and place (as seen in surging property prices for houses with gardens in the UK) and the impact of getting systems-level political leadership wrong. There is little doubt that the leadership of most developed countries (with notable exceptions such as New Zealand) failed to grasp the complex and emergent nature of Covid-19 or its systemic potential to disrupt health, economic and other services. We all now see that the power of information to connect with values and influence behaviour has an exponential character within networks such that it doesn't in a linear world. This book has sought to understand rising complexity in relationships between people,

DOI: 10.4324/9781003190820-20

environment and economics and to consider the key leadership challenges presented therein.

Going forward, it is clear that the key elements of any model leadership that is genuinely able to deliver both environmental and financial sustainability will need:

1. To be distributed within a network system that is based upon a culture of double loop learning (Argyris 1991) that rewards the exploration of problems; to know when to apply best practice and when to channel emergence.
2. To redefine innovation as focused upon not just doing more with less, but, through attention to feedback loops innovation is able to create value from doing less with less.
3. To be based upon developing resilience over robustness which is based upon understanding that financial gain is conditional upon environmental gain.
4. To be grounded in smaller scale, overlapping nested networks, where networks of networks create complex adaptive systems. Developing more of Kohr's (1957) mattress effect (where the loss of one spring does not cause the whole mattress to collapse) is key. This is the exact opposite of business models being developed by the tech giants right now.
5. To draw from Pioneers the sense of ethical agency in order to reconnect Prospectors with Settlers. Without this, the idea of developing resilience will fail. For it is Settlers that are rooted in place. They enjoy local networks and they value resilience over robustness. Pioneers combine both the agency and the sense of virtuous mission to develop such ideas into examples of leadership that we might have once called stewardship.

In short, leadership needs to become a systemic practice that takes place within locally specific but connected networks, that cherishes our partnership with nature and does so by requiring that rights to profit are genuinely conditional upon duties to care. This, of course, will not be easy, but as the consequences of not doing so pile up we both see few alternatives and are heartened by the emergence of enterprise models that are setting an example.

Systems and complexity

Cremene explained the systemic nature of environmental problems that are characterised by externalities that flow from feedback loops emerging from often hidden and unexpected network relationships. She demonstrates how linear responses to complex problems continue to fail as solutions to complex problems. Merali shows how, even when using ecosystems as metaphors, managers find it difficult to escape thinking in modularised ways, resulting in what Tett (2015) calls *The Silo Effect*. This is because, as Gregory and Atkins explain, authority (which is often mistaken for leadership) is fine in stable systems, but disruption and complexity require leadership which is adaptive and emergent. Both Cremene and Merali note that cascading effects in networks cause exponential consequences if we fail to act upon externalities with systemic feedback loops. Cremene, Gregory, Atkins and Merali all point to the urgent need for agency in addressing environmental problems. However, as we have seen from Rose and Dade, Settlers lack agency and are looking to authoritarian leaders to protect them from encroaching, unknown, destabilising forces. Prospectors are busy riding the opportunities of the moment. Whilst Pioneers have become disconnected from both and thus are unable to bridge the gap. Indeed, the implicit demand of youth protesters and organisations is for Pioneers to step forward. Putting politics aside, Gregory and Atkins have shown that if we cannot get Pioneers to engage then authoritarian solutions will fail to solve complex issues and the world will start to resemble the 1930s again.

Values and people

It is clear from the work of Rose and Dade that how we think about issues is highly dependent upon how they are framed and communicated. They showed how the convergence of technology and globalisation is leaving Settlers behind and, whilst Prospectors may be having the time of their lives, the increasing separation between lives is making it hard for Pioneers to bridge the gap. The example of Brexit, used by Rose and Dade, shows how stark this divide has become and why it matters so much. Collins and Zehndorfer have shown how both climate change deniers and reactionary politicians have grasped these new social divides that define us to develop and diffuse contrarian narratives that challenge established orthodoxies. They have done so by appealing to the basic values of Rose and Dade's Settlers, rather than engaging with established facts, evidence or models. As one member of Farage's UK Independence Party said to your editor prior to the Brexit vote:

> We want to talk about immigration, not freedom of movement. It's the same thing, but feels different.

Addressing environmental problems is, therefore, as much of a communication issue as it is a technical or behavioural problem. To some extent this has always been true and nowhere more so than in America. Crawford and Bronstone show the tensions between economics and environment that are so embodied in the idea of the West as an imagined place of wilderness that in contemporary politics it has become a metaphor for the boundary between the two. Music, literature, photography and film continue to shape questions of purpose, place and belonging as much as hard facts. The trouble is that those narratives are being increasingly played within tribal bubbles that are coming to resemble echo chambers. When we know that 'The best decisions result from constant social exploration' (Pentland 2013, p. 5). In recent memory families all watched the evening news which, in the UK at least, sought to inform and question without too much prejudice. Digital networks enable us to select the voices that we wish to hear, whilst computer algorithms increasingly select those voices that resonate for us. Thus, we have created a paradoxical situation in which access to knowledge has never been greater and yet sheer range of choice is creating such an overload that we are retreating back into our established prejudices. We are, in fact, fulfilling an Orwellian prophecy and enabling technology to imprison us within our own minds, thereby denying ourselves the motivational forces that might drive agency.

Ethics

Underlying both the ecological and socio-economic problems that we face are questions of place and belonging. These go beyond geography to extend to our place within the natural order of things. Since the enlightenment, Cartesian logic has enabled humankind to position itself as the conqueror of nature, with Bacon providing the tools to utilise science as our sword (Dobson 1995). Such an anthropocentric (human-centred) worldview is only possible by maintaining the illusion of people as separate from nature. Freed from our resource base we have twisted utilitarian logic to exploit the planet and most of its people for economic gain. Where in pre-modern times rights were contingent upon duties, as a cultural tie to nature, modernism has been defined by the removal of limits, scale and connection, in the search for growth and domination of nature.

It was writers such as Rachel Carson (1965) and James Lovelock (1979) that first pushed back against this linear anthropocentric view of the world, by reference to identifying its ecological consequences. Carson (1965) recorded the poisonous systemic consequences of the use of bio-chemical pesticides and herbicides in American agriculture, whilst Lovelock (1979, 1988) pioneered the use of computer modelling to hypothesise the hole in the ozone layer and later the greenhouse effect. He did this by correctly identifying the non-linear patterns of complex interaction that occur in ecological networks and by mapping patterns of emergence in the stratosphere. His conclusion that the earth should be seen as one living organism of incredible complexity (Lovelock 1979, 1988) that humans were assuming rights over without an understanding of the complex consequences was mostly ignored and he was for a long time marginalised (Lovelock 1990). Discovery that his predictions have been broadly borne out by evidence has, in more recent times, recast Lovelock's central idea that complexity requires far greater humility on the part of humankind (Lovelock 2007) back into the ethical spotlight.

Writers such as Naess (1973), Singer (1975), Eckersley (1992) and Curry (2011) have all argued that it is time to adopt a more ecocentric basis for organising human activities. As noted by both Taylor and Atkins, such a view cannot take place within current constructions of utilitarianism and, indeed, is far more likely to emerge from a re-examination of virtue ethics. In simple terms, it is time that we remembered that our rights are contingent upon our duties, that money is a means and not an end in itself and that the measure of life is what we sustain and not what we collect. It is a yearning for virtue over greed that is driving Extinction Rebellion and youth protests around the world. The challenge going forward is how to construct such an ethic in practice.

Systemic leadership in practice

Going forward, leadership requires, as Taylor notes, that we rediscover narratives that reconnect people and place, but which can travel as fables or metaphors to transcend place. In short, we need to re-inject life into the old ideas of stewardship such that they are fit for the digital age. For all the problems created by technology, its systemic and networked basis represents an opportunity to design resilience, purpose and virtue into our social systems. Taylor and Atkins provide contemporary examples of how combining such ideas with entrepreneurship is proving transformational. The examples provided demonstrate how systemic disintermediation is blurring the boundaries between commerce and community that injects purpose into the former and sustainability into the latter. Atkins uses the metaphor of a gardener to describe the role of leading through this period of transition as being less about doing and more about facilitating connections of care and responsibility. Schumacher (1993) has shown how smaller scale and distance between actions and outcomes is key for developing systemic resilience. Kohr (1957) calls this the mattress effect, where if one spring in the mattress fails the mattress is able to absorb the loss and resist. Both Atkins and Taylor agree that creating systems with shorter and more immediate feedback loops will be required to bring the consequences of leaders' actions home. In doing so we will need to find new ways to internalise existing externalities such that the innovation required is likely to give rise not only to new business models but perhaps to even whole new markets.

The Grant, Dabika, Tuomola, and Oakes and Bronstone chapters reveal that a new architecture for markets and new models for business that both seek to internalise existing externalities and provide greater social resilience are required and emerging. Grant, Dabija and Tuomola describe food deserts, fast disposable, car-centric retailers, the end of mass markets and the rise of green consumption by younger consumers who are pushing for that expression to become less oxymoronic. Traditional retailers are struggling to adapt whilst established online retailers are focused more on the fast and disposable than the green. This is very much a case where the end of the choice between market richness and reach (Evans and Wurster 1997) and the rise of the so-called long tail economy (Anderson 2006) is creating space for new models of business and demanding new models of

CONCLUSION   401

leadership that think beyond systemic costs and profits.[1] Whilst Oakes and Bronstone, in line with a growing number of writers (Ban and Patenaude 2019, Mazzucato 2018), show how the role of the state in both shaping markets and as an actor in its own right can, and increasingly is, providing innovative leadership to both internalise social and environmental costs and improve outcomes through regulatory incentives. Through an implicit recognition of the limits of free markets, Oakes and Bronstone show how renewed public sector engagement is not a rejection of markets so much as an embrace of systemic leadership that markets alone cannot provide.

Oakes and Bronstone, and Netherwood and Flynn reveal the importance and possibilities of internalising externalities. They do so by reminding us that transformational leadership is needed from public institutions. It is clear that public authorities in Wales are not likely to be alone in struggling to prepare for climate change and struggle to develop systemic resilience over traditional linear models of predictable robustness. Oakes and Bronstone show that the EU Emission Trading Scheme (EU ETS) is an example of leadership in a complex and systemic problem emerging from a very large bureaucracy. One that demonstrated an ability to embrace complex systems failure and construct market mechanisms, within a regulatory framework, to internalise environmental costs through entrepreneurial innovation. As such, EU ETS is a surprising yet powerful example of enabling entrepreneurship that has proved transformational. Despite initial problems, EU ETS works because regulatory legal structures and parameters of the market for emissions reductions creates positive feedback loops for those who innovate and negative feedback loops for those who don't. In short, bureaucratic leadership has unexpectedly provided systemic pressure to align the utilitarian search for profit with an ownership of responsibility that we might describe as more virtuous.

If we are serious about providing leadership that is genuinely sustainable it will require us to embrace a sense of stewardship that is rooted in a more ecocentric mode of living, such that success is defined by what we sustain and enrich and not by what we possess. Such words are easy, but practice will necessitate not just a nod to systems thinking, but a meaningful acceptance of our role as stewards within ecological networks. On the other hand, acceptance of complexity is likely to reward innovation and creativity far more than current models of organisation, which reduce millions of people to servants of linear systems just to survive. For us all to survive the ecocide we are committing, any model of leadership will need human creativity to flourish. Commercial success is increasingly going to be contingent upon the ability to use innovation to create new value from re-purposing today's externalities as sources of value to be internalised and/or developed into new business channels. It is for this reason we are hopeful in the examples we have highlighted in this book. The combination of the push from youth and from the pandemic indicate that we have reached a tipping point. One of the key lessons from the pandemic is the need for leadership to be more distributed, more local and more defined as useful to the extent that it provides social purpose. The emerging models of organisation highlighted here that are using digital technology to enrich community and ethical enterprises provide hope that we can adapt if we can connect a profound sense of questioning about means and purpose to a humility that has too long been absent from human affairs. In an expression that is often overused, yet perfectly captures our model, we might say that real leadership is about thinking global and acting local. The real danger to the world is not wickedness so much as utilitarian leadership based upon personal entitlement, ambition and greed for its own sake. We can do better than that.

Note

1 For more details of such models and examples of them, please see Taylor, A. and Bronstone, A. (2019), *People, Place & Global Order: Foundations of a Networked Political Economy*. London: Routledge.

References

Anderson, C. (2006) *The Long Tail: Why the Future of Business Is Selling Less of More*. New York: Hyperion.

Argyris, C. (1991) 'Teaching Smart People to Learn', *Harvard Business Review*, May – June.

Ban, C. & Patenaude, B. (2019) 'The Professional Politics of the Austerity Debate: A Comparative Field Analysis of the European Central Bank and the International Monetary Fund', *Public Administration*, Vol. 97, No. 3, 9, pp. 530–545.

Carson, R. (1965) *Silent Spring*. London: Penguin.

Curry, P. (2011) *Ecological Ethics: An Introduction* (2nd Edition). Cambridge, UK: Polity Press.

Dobson, A. (1995) *Green Political Thought* (2nd Edition). London: Routledge.

Eckersley, R. (1992) *Environmentalism and Political Theory: Toward an Ecocentric Approach*. London: UCL Press.

Evans, P. & Wurster, S. (1997) 'New Economics of Information', *Harvard Business Review*, Sept-October.

Kohr, L. (1957) *The Breakdown of Nations*. London: Routledge & Kegan Paul 1957.

Lovelock, J. (1979) *Gaia: A New Look at Life on Earth*. Oxford: Oxford University Press.

Lovelock, J. (1988) *The Ages of Gaia: A Biography of our Living Earth*. New York: Norton.

Lovelock, J. (1990) 'Stand up for Gaia' in *The Green Fuse*, edited by Button, J. London: Quartet Books.

Lovelock, J. (2007) *The Revenge of Gaia*. London: Penguin.

Mazzucato, M. (2018) *The Entrepreneurial State*. Harlow, UK: Penguin Books.

Naess, A. (1973) 'The Shallow and the Deep, Long-Range Ecology Movement. A Summary', *Inquiry*, Vol. 16, No. 1, pp. 95–100.

Pentland, A. (2013) 'Beyond the Echo Chamber'. *Harvard Business Review*, November 2013.

Schumacher, E. (1993) *Small is Beautiful: A Study of Economics as if People Mattered*. London: Vintage.

Shiva V. (2020) 'One planet: One health'. *Resurgence & Ecologist*, Issue 321, May/June.

Singer, P. (1975) *Animal Liberation*. New York: HarperCollins.

Tett, G. (2015) *The Silo Effect: The Peril of Expertise and the Promise of Breaking Down Barriers*. New York: Simon & Schuster.

INDEX

Page numbers in *italic* represent photos or figures, while page numbers in **bold** represent tables.

Abbey, E. 96, 101
Academy of Management 348
Academy of Management Review 348
acid rain 25–27
Acid Rain Peer Review Panel 26–27; and 'Climategate' 25
adaptation 155; and change 177–178; and the short-term 155–156
affluenza 223
Africa, rare earths in 219
After Virtue (MacIntyre) 243
Agrawala, S. 275
agriculture 75; *see also* regenerative agriculture
air pollution 2
Alibaba 220
alternative facts 131–134, 136
Amazon 18–19, 35n5, 219–220
Amazon region 197–198
American culture, music in 97
American Dream 94; *see also* United States
American lifestyle, consequences of 113
Amish people 241
Andresen, S. 275
Anthropocene age 40, 65, 92–93, 177
anthropocentrism 3, 215, 217

Arctic National Wildlife Refuge (ANWAR) 108, 122
Aristotle 214
Arthur, W. B. 219
article citation, on sustainability 346–347, 348–349, 350, 353
Atkins, Jonathan P. 6, 176–187, 397
Atkins, Sr Margaret 7, 235–258, 400
attitudes 41
audiences, involving 184–185
Audubon Society 102
Augustine 255
authoritarianism 397; and an anti-science agenda 125–126, 130–131, 136; and climate change denial 126; and immigration 64; and religion 128
authority 179; and issue-implementing 180; and leadership 176–177, 179, 187
authors, writing on sustainability 348–350

Baik, K. 180
balloons 251–252
Band Aid 221
Bangladesh 218, 220; sweatshops 221
Bannon, Steve 121
Bari, Judi 101

406 INDEX

Bascompte, A. L. 192–193
Basic Human Values model 45
Bass, B. M. 186
Battersby, J. 290
Baumgartner, R. 353
Beach, D. 278
behavioural complexity 157
Belfast (Northern Ireland) 326–327
Benedict XVI (Pope) 238, 240
Berry, Wendell 244–245, 250
bibliometric analysis 343, 353–354;
    results 345–349; technique application
    344, 345
Biden, Joe 112–113
'big data' 284
'big society' 225
big tobacco *see* tobacco industry
Big Yellow Taxi (Mitchell) 97
Billimoria, J. 74
biodiversity 193
Blessed Unrest (Hawken) 244
Boje, D. 15, 17–18
Boone, M. E. 217
Bormann, Herbert 25
Borzaga, C. 70–71
bottom-up leadership 313
Brexit 44, 58, 59, 60–64, 199, 221,
    397–398; and retail 284; *see also* United
    Kingdom
Brexit Warning blog 61–62
Bronstone, Adam 5, 7, 92–113, 227,
    261–280, 398, 401
Budget Bedlam 49, 50
Burns, J. M. 186
Bush, George H. 105–106
businesses: large corporation economic
    dominance 198–199; and Systemic
    Leadership 158
business interconnectedness 146
business models 170, 396; ecosystem
    models 190–191, 198; environmental
    impacts on 146; short-term *vs.* long-
    term thinking 148
'Butterfly Defect' 2

Cameron, David 225
'cap and trade' principle 7, 265–267,
    272, 276
capitalism 6–7; consumer capitalism
    199–200; rethinking 197–200
Caputo, Michael 132–133
carbon credits 74–75

carbon taxes and the EU 264–265, 269,
    271–272
Carney, Mark 197–198, 200, 205, 236–237,
    242, 244, 249
cars, electric cars 159–160
Carse, James P. 65–66
Carson, Rachel 104–105, 215, 399
Carter, Jimmy 26, 104
Catholic Climate Covenant 108–109
Catsimatidis, John 135
Catsimatidis, Margo 135
cause-effects views 3
Centre for Alternative Technology in Zero
    Carbon Britain 333
Chafetz, Josh 134
change 179–180; and adaptation 177–178;
    rates of 157–158; spreading across
    society 51, 53, 61–62; and Systems
    Leadership 158–159
change-makers, mantras of 63
change management 179
charismatic authority 134; and right-wing
    populism 126, 130, 132–134
'Chicago School of Economics' 282–283
children, arguments about 85
China 221, 352; mining in 219
Chouinard, Yvon 84–85
Christianity Today 130
Churchman, C. W. 178, 184
circular economies 262–263, 283
citizens assemblies 326
civil unrest, and Force value 57, 58
class structures 222
'Clean Air for All' campaign 2
clean industries, in the EU 262–263
clientelism 121, 135–136
climate change 2, 176–177; anthropogenic
    factors of 191; complexity of 177;
    historical recognition of 148–149;
    increased interest in 345–346; leadership
    interventions for 324–326; and natural
    disasters 108; and political lack of
    urgency 94, 177, 192, 195, 202–203,
    206, 235; and poverty 195; and social
    enterprises 71; statistics 191–192; *see also*
    global warming
climate change adaptation 318–319,
    331–334
climate change contrarians/skeptics 28,
    30, 35n7; attacks by 29, 33, 35n6;
    reaching out to 34; in the US 108–109,
    123–124

climate change denial: and big tobacco 4, 14, 22–23, 27; and charismatic authority 5, 126; and the GOP 108–109, 125–126; 'hoax' claims 28, 30; and information weaponisation 197; narrative creation by 19, 29; and religion 129; and right-wing populism 126–127; statistics 109; by the Trump administration 122–124, 126, 130; *see also* 'Climategate'

climate change planning, and Wales 8, 314–316, 319–322, 334, 336, 337

climate change research 8

Climate Coaching Alliance (CCA) 327

climate emergencies, declarations of 324–325

'Climategate' 14, 23–25, 29, 33, 34n2; and FOI requests 29, 31–32; and narratives 19, 23–24, 30–31, 33; and Phil Jones 23–24, 30, 36n12; *see also* 'tobacco strategy'

climate goals, and post-COVID-19 recovery 169–170

climate-neutral economies, and the EU 261–262

Climate Ready Gwent 320

Climate Research journal 30–31

climate science 30; and media broadcasters 33–34

Clinton, Bill 101, 106

Clinton administration 106–107

Coase, Ronald 282

cognitive bias, bypassing 149

Cognitive Congruence Framework (Merali) 195, 196, 205

collective intelligence 168–169

Collins, David 4, 13–36, 18, 397

Collins, H. 132, 135

communication flows 169

communities: support from 243; traditional agriculture 244; and the Undergrowth Movement 248

community energy enterprises 228

community enterprises 227–230

competition, and evolution 151

complex adaptive systems 6, 201, 203–204

complexity: and adaptation 155–156; managing 162

complex systems literacy 154–160, 170

connectivity 154

consequentialism 214, 401

conspicious consumption 283–284

conspiracies 197; and right-wing populism 126–127

constitutional maturity 134

consumer capitalism 199–200

consumer demands 222, 297–298; shifting 8, 288, 299; YoungGens 301–303; *see also* e-commerce

consumer generations 286, 299–300; *see also specific generations*

consumers: behaviours of 283; retail influence on 288, 298

convergence 217–221

conversations 168–169

Conway, E. 19–22, 27, 35n8

Conway, Kellyanne 132

Cook, Ken 124

cooperation 153, 225; and evolution 151; and games 151–152; at a global level 150; and punishment 152; and small businesses 225–226, 228; and the Undergrowth Movement 245

corporate enterprises, *vs.* social enterprises 70

corporate social responsibility (CSR) 191

corporate sustainability leadership 314

cost-benefit perspectives 150

Cottam, Hilary 246

counter-revolutions 44; Brexit as 59

courier services 301–302

Cousteau, Jacques 99

COVID-19 pandemic 2, 65, 146, 200, 217, 395, 402; and *Amazon* 35n5; anti-science agendas 123; border closures 223; death rates 134; and ecosystems perspectives 191; environmental impacts of 72; and job losses 72; negative impacts of 72, 395; and populist political leaders 121, 132; and retail 284; and the Trump administration 120–121, 123, 131, 133; vaccines 131

Cox, John 33

Crawford, Heather 5, 92–113, 398

creationism 128

creativity, encouragement of 168

Cremene, Ligia 6, 145–170, 397

Creswick, C. 1

Critical Systems Practice (CSP) 6, 183, 186–187

Critical Systems Thinking (CST) 183

Crush, J. 290

Crutzen, Paul 40

Csikszentmihalyi, Mihaly 165–166

408   INDEX

Cullis-Suzuki, Severn 181
Cultural Dynamics model 42, 44; groups in 45–48, 49–50, 52, 58, 60, 61, 62, 64–65; *see also* Values Modes
Cultural Dynamics VOCS 53, 55
Cultural Evolution (Inglehart) 44
culture wars 41
Curry, O. S. 151
Curry, P. 214, 399
custodianship 212–217, 224
Cynefin framework 166–167, 217
Czarniawska, B. 15

Dabija, Dan-Cristian 7–8, 282–304, 400
Dade, Pat 4–5, 40–67, 222, 397–398
Davidson, J. 315
death penalty support, and Brexit 61
decarbonisation focus, in Wales 317–318
deep greens 215
'deep state' 131–133
deforestation 77, 157, 202, 211–212, 253
deglobalisation 223
Delbeke, Jos 268–271, 276–277
Delors, Jacque 271–273
Democratic Party and the GOP 111
Denver, John 97
deontology 213
design thinking 168
deterministic systems 146, 156; *vs.* complex systems 156
developing countries, and large corporations 198–199
DeVos, Betsy 128
Diamond, Jared 1–3
Dickens, C. 24
digital communication 395
digital cooperatives 227
digital devices, environmental impacts of 219
digital markets 226
digital networks 225, 227–228; for sustainability 225
digitization 220
digtal network economy 220, 229
dilemma wizarding 165–166
Dionne, E. J. 110
direct action 102; environmental activism 101; *see also* eco-terrorism
Disney 97
Doomsday Clock 113
Duffy, Philip 125
Dust Bowl 95, 98–99

duty: Kant on 213; and leadership 6
Dwivedi, Dr Ashish 8, 343–354

Earth Day 96
Earth First! 100–102
Earth Liberation Front 100–101
Earth Song (Jackson) 97
Earth Summit in Rio de Janeiro (1992) 181
Eatwell, R. 130
echo chamber effects 398
Eckersley, R. 399
eco-centric ethics 98
ecocentrism, shift towards 3
eco-colonisation 218
ecological feedback loops 3–4
ecological resilience, *vs.* economic efficiency 3
e-commerce 212, 220, 222, 296; costs of 298; delivery options 301–302; and food 294–295, 298; and Generation Z 284, 287; omnichannel 296–297; rise of 8, 283–284, 295; and YoungGens 300–301; *see also* consumer demands; retail
economic efficiency, *vs.* ecological resilience 3
economic growth, statistics 286
economic values 197–198, 205
ecosystems: human impacts on 191–192, 194–195; interactions in 193–194; in management discourse 190–191, 397; motifs in 193; as networks 192–194
eco-terrorism 100–102
Ecuador 181
Eden, C. 185
Einstein, Albert 168
electric cars 159–160, 197, 263–264
The Electric Company 159
Ellinas, A. 277
Emerging Complex Adaptive Networks (ECANS) 247
emerging economies: and environmental awareness 85; and poverty reduction 75–76; and sustainability agendas 76, 86
Emerson, R. W. 95–96, 103, 111
emissions caps 269
emotional flexibility 164
employee-owned enterprises 225
employees: importance of 251–252; and organisation size 249; replacing 223
employment practices, *Amazon* 18, 35n5

energy lobbyists, and the Trump administration 124
entreprenurial leadership 277
environmental activism: *vs.* environmental leadership 73, 86; and Generation Z 83; and music 97
Environmental Children's Organization (ECO) 181
Environmental Defense fund 105
environmental leadership 69–70; defined 5, 72–73; *vs.* environmental activism 73, 86; and Generation Z 69–70; and millennials 69–70; non-governmental 99–100; qualities for 73–74; and sustainability 310; *see also* leadership; youth leadership and climate change
environmental problems, as externalities 147–148
environmental protection reversals 112; and the Trump administration 121–122
environmental racism, in the US 93–94
epic fails 159–160
ethical goals 247
ethics 214, 255, 398–399; and stewardship 213
EU Commission 261, 269, 271–273; climate neutrality 264–265; environmental leadership of 270; and leadership 273, **274**, 275–279; and money 264
EU Emission Trading System (EU ETS) 7, 265–268, 271–273, **274**, 275–280, 401
European Union (EU) 7; biodiversity strategies 263; carbon taxes 264–265, 271–272; circular economy 262–263; and climate-neutral economies 261–262; covenant of Mayors 325; Effort Sharing Regulation 262; Emissions Trading Directive 262, 265; Energy Efficiency Directive 262, 265; environmental interest in 268, 270–271, 279; farm to fork strategies 263; Green New Deal 261–264; Horizon Europe research and innovation programme 264; LULUCF directive 262; Market Stability Reserve 266; Renewable Energy Directive 262; transportation in 263–264; Treaty of Maastricht 270; Treaty of Rome 270; values split in 59
Evangelical Christians, and science denial 129
Evangelical Climate Initiative 110

Evans, R. 132, 135
Everett, L. Q. 343
externalities (social dilemmas) 147–148
Extinction Rebellion 197, 202
extinctions 191–192
Exxon 150

facilitation 167–168
failures 159–160; studying 310–311
"fake news" 197
families, and virtues 242
farm to fork strategies (EU) 263
fast fashion 220
Fauci, Dr Anthony 133
fear 92
feedback delays 169
feedback loops 6, 397; bio-physical ecosystems 191; in ecosystems 193–194; and the EU 7
Ferdig, M. A. 313
Finite and Infinite Games: A Vision of Life as Play and Possibility (Carse) 65–66
Finnish National Police Board (FNPB) 287
fisheries policy 43; in the US 95
Fishguard (Wales) 322–323
'flat' tradition 92
flooding forecasts, and Wales 316, 318–319, 323–324, 335
Flynn, Andrew 8, 310–338, 401
followers, Settler mode 47
food deserts 283, 290, 293–294
food insecurity 283; urban 289–290, 292, 294
food prices 289
food retailers 283, 400; and e-commerce 294–295, 298; supply chains 291, 294; sustainability 292; *see also* retail
food security 289
Force value 53–54, 55–57, 58
Ford 218
forest preservation, and eco-terrorism 101
fossil fuel industries, and the Trump administration 122
Francis (Pope) 238, 246
'free market' economic models 282–283
Freitas, Chris de 31
Friedman, Milton 282
future generations 336; failure to consider 330–331, 334

Gabriel, Y. 15, 17
Gaia 3

Galpin, T. 313
games, and cooperation 151–152
Game Theory 150–152
GDP 214, 240
Generation Z 69–70, 82–83, 284, 286, 288;
    see also YoungGens
Generativity theory 73
Genghis Khan 43
geography, resources and institutions
    framework (GRI) 291–292
Gibran, Kahlil 216
global financial crash (2008) 53
global interconnection 1–2; and local
    activities 156–157
globalisation 93, 212, 217–218, 224, 299
global issues, and cooperation 150
global networks, social costs of 7–8
global supply chains 199, 211–212, 217–218,
    282; food 291; and retail 287
global villages 222–223, 229
global warming: hearings into 106; *see also*
    climate change
Global Warming Policy Foundation
    31–32
God Bless the Grass (Seeger) 97
Golden Dreamers 46, 54, 58, 59, 62
Goldin, Ian 2
Goodhart, D. 222
Good Work (Schumacher) 251
GOP party/administrations 95, 105, 110;
    and climate change denial 108–109;
    and the Clinton administration
    106; controlled by Trump 127; and
    Democrats 111; industrial support for
    107; and religion 128–129; science
    rejection by 111, 121, 125; *see also specific
    people/administrations*; United States
Gore, Al 106–107, 110–111
Goulson, Dave 252
governance 313
government policies: need for 84; and
    political funding 95, 103, 112; and
    transitions 252–255
governments for transitions 252–255
Grant, David B. 7–8, 14–15, 282–304, 294,
    301, 400
grassroots initiatives 244
Great Society plan 104
greenhouse gas emissions: EU net-zero
    262; and retail 287; statistics 191–192;
    trading schemes 7, 265–268, 272, 276;
    and the US 5
GreenPeace 197, 247

green principles: investing in 197;
    promotion of 150–151
green thinking 215
Gregory, Amanda J. 6, 176–187, 397
Grimes, Tom 162
Grimsey, Bill 285
growth 239
growth models 200; and the Green New
    Deal (EU) 262
Gualinga, Helena 181
Gurov, D. 135–136
Guthrie, Woody 98–99, 215

Hamel, G. 218
Hamilton, L. C. 126
Hamlet (Shakespeare) 24
Hamm, Harold 124, 135
Hammer, G. 218
hand-washing 148
Handy, C. 225
Handy, Charles 1
Harvard Business Review 217, 221, 348
Hawken, Paul 244
Hayek, Friedrich 282
Heifetz, R. A. 177–179, 182, 185
Helfat, C. E. 78
Higgins, Les 44, 65
high streets 285, 295–296
Hildebrand, Jeffery 135
Hildebrand, Melinda 135
Hilton, Steve 247
homo economicus 150, 196
homo reciprocans 196
Homsy, G. C. 314–315
Hopkins, Rob 247
Horizon Europe research and innovation
    programme 264
hub companies 220–221, 286
Hulme, Mike 28
Hult Prize Foundation 77
human nature, and values 41
human relations school 224
humbleness 167–168
humility 255
Hurricane Katrina 95, 108
Hurricane Sandy 110–111
hydroxychloroquine 132
Hynes, H. Patricia 105

Iansiti, M. 219
identity, and Brexit 61
immigration, and authoritarianism 64
inclusiveness 294

INDEX   411

incomes, drops in 286
inconsistent decision-making 240
The Inconvenient Truth (Gore) 107
India 77–78, 181
Indigenous peoples, in the US 93–95, 112
individuals, in the *Cognitive Congruence Framework* 195, 196
industrial Age 235–237
industrialism 221, 224
Industrial Revolution 224, 235
informal leadership 277
informal settlements 291
'informal waste management' 77
information, weaponisation of 197
information age 149
Inglehart, Ron 42–45
Inhofe, James 24, 28
inner work 164
innovation 401–402
institutional leadership 278
instrumental leadership 276
integrative complexity 165
intellectual leadership 277
interconnectedness 190, 247, 395; neglect of 240
interdependence 161, 166–167; and social dilemmas 153–154
inter-generational needs 329, 336
Intergovernmental Panel on Climate Change (IPCC) 28; and 'Climategate' 25
internet connectivity 295
intra-generational needs 328–329, 335, 336
issue-creation 184
issue leaders 180

Jackson, M. C. 186–187
Jackson, Michael 97
Jakobsdóttir, Katrín 252
James, Oliver 3
Japan, whaling 102
Jaramillo, Dom 181
job losses, from COVID-19 72
Johnson, Lyndon 104
Jones, Phil 23–24, 29–31, 36n12
Journal of Business Ethics 346, 347
Journal of Cleaner Production 346, 347
Journal of Management 348
journals, boycotts of 30–31
Justice, Jim 135

Kaiman, J. 219
Kangujam, Licypriya 181
Kant, I. 213, 215

Kaufer, Katrin 147
Kaufmann, Eric 61
Kennedy, John F. 104
Kessler, Gladys 19
Kichwa Sarayaku 181
kindness 242
King Abdul Aziz University 352
Klau, M. 182–183
Klein, Naomi 247
Knight, Frank 282
knowledge economies 218
Kodak 160
Kohr, L. 217, 396, 400
Kollock, P. 147
Krouwel, W. 217
Kyoto Protocols 265, 269, 271–272, 275, 278

Lagarde, Christine 2
lagom 250
Lakhani, K. 219
Lamb, Hubert 28
land ethic 216
land ownership 43; and leadership 42; *see also* property rights
large corporations 198–200, 220, 286; and resilience 249
Latour, B. 34
lawn metaphor 252
Lawson, Lord 31–32
leaders: and complex systems 154; defined 47; good/bad 186; inter/intra-generational considerations 328–329, 335; issue leaders 180; personal engagement of 327–328; and self-criticalness 337
leadership 40, 71–72, 179, 278; and authority 176–177, 179, 187; charismatic authority as 5; common in Wales 324–326; contemporary understandings of 13, 32; education for 182–183, 313; environmental perspectives on 72; and the ETS 268, 273, **274**, 275–278; of the EU Commission 273, **274**, 275–279; and land ownership 42; metaphors of 251; modes of **274**, 275–276; in popular management books 16–17; requirements of 396; research into 351; and storytelling 13–14, 16; systems-based understanding of 177; and systems theory 183; virtues for 254–256; *see also* environmental leadership

INDEX

Leading from the Emerging Future: From Ego-system to Eco-system Economies (Scharmer & Kaufer) 147
learning 184–185
Lee, Mike 125
Leeds Climate Commission 325
Leopold, A. 216
Leopold, Aldo 98, 104
lifestyle changes 197, 241
Lincoln, Abraham 93
linear deterministic systems, reliance on 6
Linsky, M. 185
listening 164
Little, C. C. 20
Lofgren, Mike 131
long tail economy 400
Lorentz, H. 291–292
Lorraine, DeAnna 133
Louv, R. 92
Lovelock, James 1–3, 221, 399
Lowe, Ben 109
Lowe, P. 215
Lozano, R. 353
lung cancer 20–22

Macfarlane, R. 113
MacIntyre, Alasdair 243
Madoff, Bernard 150
'Make America Great Again' slogan 129
Malnes, R. **274**
managers: control of resources by 3; and sustainability strategies 71–72; and systems thinking 162
Mann, Mike 23, 28–31
markets: and globalisation 217–218; valuing by 197–198, 205, 221
Maslow Groups 45, 49, 51, 60
Maslow's hierarchy of needs 45, 48
Maslow Space 50
May, R. M. 194
Mazar, N. 150
McBurney, S. 221
McConnell, Mitch 107
McIntrye, Steve 28–29, 32
McKittrick, Ross 28–29
McLaughlin, John 132
Meadows, Donella 163
Meadows, Mark 131
media broadcasters: and climate science 33–34; and the Dakota Access Pipeline 94; political control of 94; and the tobacco industry 21

mental flexibility 164
Merali, Yasmin 6, 190–206, 397
Merchant Princes 224, 226, 228
'The Merchant Princes' (Kennedy) 212, 224
Messiah figures, Trump as 130
Midgley, G. 184
'Mike's *Nature* trick' 30
millennials 69–70, 284, 286, 288; *see also* YoungGens
Mintzberg, Henry 1
Miorita 216
misinformation campaigns 197
Mock COP 181–182
Modernization, Cultural Change and Democracy: The Human Development Sequence (Inglehart and Welzel) 43–44
money: and the EU Commission 264; focus on 240
'The Monkey Wrench Gang' 101
Monsell, Kristen 122
morality 163
Moravcsik, A. 277
Morgan, B. 296
motifs, in ecosystems 193
Muir, John 100, 104
multi-generational needs 329, 336
multinational corporations 198, 218, 220, 286, 291
music 97, 99, 215–216, 221

Naess, Arne 101–102, 399
narrative control, by right-wing populists 130–131
narratives: and 'Climategate' 19, 23–24; and counternarrative 19; growing interest in 14–15; and sensegiving 15–18; and sensemaking 15–18
National Wilderness Preservation System 105
natural disasters: and climate change 108; flooding forecasts 316, 318–319, 335; hurricanes 95, 108, 110, 113; wildfires 107, 113; *see also specific disasters*
Nature (Emerson) 95–96
Nature journal 120
Navarro, Peter 131
negative impacts, internalising 314
neoliberalism, and decarbonisation 318
Netherwood, Alan 8, 310–338, 401
network approaches 192–194, 203
network of networks 203

network organisation, and Complex Adaptive Systems 201–202, 203, 204
networks 250
net-zero greenhouse gas emissions, and the EU 262
New England Journal of Medicine 120, 123, 136
Nierenberg, Bill 26–27
Niu, X. 315
Nixon, Richard 96
Nixon administration 111
Nokia 160
non-governmental environmental leadership 99–103
Norquist, Grover 110
Norway 351
Nudge (Thaler & Sunstein) 149

Oakes, Vanessa 7, 261–280, 401
Obama administration 123, 134
Oikophilia 223, 225
O'Keeffe, N. 180
one-size-fits-all solutions 204–206
100 Resilient Cities global partnership 326
Operations Research profession 178
opinions 41
Oreskes, N. 19–22, 27, 35n8
organisational discourse studies 14–15
organisational health 169
organisational storytelling *see* storytelling
organisational strategy, and stakeholder engagement 82
organisations: interest in sustainability 345–346; and size 249; voices of 159
Ostrom, Elinor 205–206, 226
Ostrom, Vincent 226–227
outcome-oriented models of control 7
overlapping commons 226–227
Oxford Martin Commission (2013) 330, 334

palm oil 211–212
pandemics 2; *see also* COVID-19 pandemic
Paris Agreement (2015) 107, 113, 121, 197, 202
Paul, Rand 127–128
Pearce, F. 28–31, 33, 34n1, 36n12
peer groups, and virtues 242
peer review processes 31, 36n12
Pence, Mike 128
Penn State University 23
Penrose, E. 78
Pentland, Alex 169

Peters, Tom 15–16
Philipsen, Dirk 150
Phone Coop 227, 229
Pink, D. 224
Pioneer group 45–48, 49, 50, 59–60, 61, 62, 64–65, 225, 230, 396–397
pioneering 92
planned obsolescence 199
plastic credits 75, 79
plastic pollution 2
plastics 155
pleasure *vs.* pain 214
polarisation 241
political correctness 60–61, 62, 63
political leaders: distrust of 241, 248; role of 236; small/middle-size initiatives 250–251; virtues of 254–256
politics 240–241; inconsistency of 240; and science 111, 120, 125
pollution: air pollution 2; Bangladesh 220; Green New Deal (EU) 263; plastic pollution 2
polycentric commercial spaces 229
popular management themed texts 15–17
populist political leaders 126; and charisma 126, 130, 132–133; and COVID-19 121, 132; and denigration of science 5, 121, 135–136; *see also* right-wing populism
poverty: and climate change 195; and food security 289
poverty reduction: and emerging economies 75–76; and UNESCO 75
power relations: and large corporations 198–199; in systems thinking 184
Prahalad, C. K. 218
private sector, and leadership training 313
propaganda techniques, and the Trump administration 127
property rights 43; *see also* land ownership
Prospector group 45–48, 49, 50, 54, 59–60, 62, 64–65, 223, 397
Prosperity for all: A Climate Conscious Wales report 316–318
protests: Dakota Access Pipeline 94; and youths 176; *see also* school strikes
Pruitt, Scott 123–125, 136
public relations campaigns, *Amazon* 18–19
public sector, and sustainability leadership 310, 312, 401
punishment, and cooperation 152

414 INDEX

Quayle, James Danforth 105

Radical Help (Cottam) 246
Rainwater, K. 18
rare earths 219
Rashford, Marcus 253
Ratzinger, Joseph 238
Raworth, Kate 252
Reagan, Ronald 105
real estate 223
Redekop, B. W. 72
reducing, reusing, recycling 283
regenerative agriculture 75, 78–79
regulations 152
relationship enactments 195, 196
relationship scripts 195, 196
religion: and authoritarianism 128; and
    Donald Trump 129–130
religious environmental groups 111; *see also*
    Young Evangelists for Climate Action
    (YECA)
Resource-Based Views (RBV) 78, 86
retail 282–284, 303–304, 400; and
    collaboration 287–288; and
    globalisation 299; and global supply
    chains 287; omnichannel 296–297;
    order fulfilment 297, 302–303; physical
    stores 285, 295–296; shifting online
    284, 295–296; slowing of 286; *see also*
    consumer demands; e-commerce; food
    retailers
Revelle, Dr Roger 106
Richmond, Barry 162
right-wing populism 128; anti-science
    rhetoric 121, 125–126; and
    charismatic authority 126, 130,
    132–134; and climate change denial
    126, 128; common characteristics of
    126–127; as investment strategy
    135–136; and narrative control
    130–131; and religion 128; *see also*
    populist political leaders
Rittel, H. W. J. 178
Roach, A. A. 182–183
role modelling 164–165
Romania 218
Roosevelt, Theodore 95–97, 100, 104, 111
Rose, Chris 4, 40–67, 222, 225–226,
    229–230, 397–398
Rosling, Hans 43
Rubio, Marco 110

Russell, Muir 23
Ryan, A. 213

Sacks, Jonathan 241
Saito, K. 126
'*A Sand County Almanac*' (Leopold) 98
Sandel, Michael 251
Saul, U. **274**, 275, 277–278
Scharmer, Otto 147
school meals 253–254
schools, and plastics 84
school strikes 73, 93, 180; *see also* protests
Schumacher, E. F. 200, 249, 251, 400
Schwartz, Shalom 45, 50
science 20, 26; and politics 111, 120–121,
    123; and populist political leaders
    5, 121, 125, 135–136; and religion
    128–129
Science study 133
scientific leadership, perils of 33
Scruton, R. 216, 223, 225, 230
SDGs. *see* United Nations Sustainable
    Development Goals (SDGs)
sea level rises 108
Sea Shepherd 100, 102
Seeger, Pete 97
Seidel, C. **274**, 275, 277–278
self-awareness 163–164
self-concept 195, 196, 200
Send it On 97
Senge, Peter 159, 177, 179
sensegiving, and storytelling 15–18
sensemaking, and storytelling 15–18
Settler group 45–47, 49, 50, 54, 58, 59–60, 61,
    62, 64–65, 222, 225–226, 229, 396–397
Shaiiko, R. 213, 215
Shao, W. 126
Shiva, V. 217
Sierra Club 100, 102
Silent Revolution (Inglehart) 44
'Silent Spring' (Carson) 105
Silo Effect 397
Silvestre, B. S. 293
Simpson, Dan 162
Singer, Fred 26–28
Singer, Peter 214, 223, 399
Singh, Bharati 5, 69–86
Single European Market 272
Sixth Catastrophic Extinction 191
Skodvin, T. 275
slavery, modern-day 283

slums 290–291
small businesses, and cooperation 225–226, 228
Small Is Beautiful (Schumacher) 249, 251
Smeets, S. 278
Snowden, Dave 1, 217
The Social Conquest of Earth (Wilson) 40
social dilemmas 146–147, 153–154; externalities 147–148
social elastic 62, 63, 65
social enterprises 81, 85–86, 225; and climate change 71; defined 69–70, 80; social value *vs.* economic value 71, 197–198, 205; and stakeholder engagement 86
social impacts 81
socially defecting behaviours 149–150, 153
social networks 152–154
social norms 152–153; violations of 149–150
Social Physics (Pentland) 169
social signals, and women 169
social traps 155–156
social values 197–198, 205
society 242–243
socio-economic 200–201
soft HR model 224
soft systems methodology (SSM) 184
solar power 250
south–south cooperation 76
species declines 2
speciesism 223
Spicer, Sean 132
stakeholder engagement: and organisational strategy 82; and social enterprises 86; and sustainability strategies 82
Steidlmeier, P. 186
Stevens, R. 71
stewardship 212–217, 224–227, 401
Stocker, F. 82
storytelling: contemporary interests in 15; and leadership 13–14; organisational 16–17; and sensegiving 15–18; and sensemaking 15–18
Strategic Assumption Surfacing and Testing (SAST) 185–186
strategic linkages 79
subsidiarity 249–250
Suleiman, E. 277
Sunstein, C. 149

supply chains 249; food retailers 291, 294; global 199, 211–212, 217–218, 282; lack of understanding of 297–298; and retail 287; unsustainability of 7–8, 282
sustainability: articles production about 345; and human factors 95; importance of 146; leadership for 311–314; and local governments 314; sustainable development principle 337–338n1
sustainability agendas 81; and emerging economies 76, 86; *see also* Wales
Sustainability journal 346, 347
Suzuki, David 99
Swan, Robert 241
sweatshops 220–221; fires 218
systemic changes, need for 197
Systemic Leadership 145, 158–162, 170; and businesses 158; skills for 163–169; and systems thinking 158
systemic perception 160–161
systems 156
systems complexity 145; *vs.* deterministic systems 156
systems theory, and leadership 183
systems thinking 6, 157, 161–162, 166–167; and power relationships 184

tame problems 178
taskforces 325
Taylor, Andrew 1–9, 211–230, 400
technocratic paradigm 237–242, 247, 249
technological changes 218, 221
technological mindsets 236, 239–242
technology: gratitude for 241; and the Undergrowth Movement 246
Teece, D. J. 78–79
Tesco 294
Tett, G. 1–2, 397
Thaler, R. 149
Thomas Aquinas 242
Thompson, D. F. 330, 334
Thoreau, H. D. 95–96, 103
Thunberg, Greta 6, 93, 180–181, 252
Tillerson, Rex 124
Titanic metaphor 3
tobacco industry 19, 35n8; and climate change denial 4, 14, 22–23; funding scientific research 21, 36n11; lawsuits agains 19–20; and media broadcasters 21; *see also* 'tobacco strategy'

416 INDEX

'tobacco strategy' 14, 19–22, 31–33; and climate change 27; *see also* 'Climategate'
'tone at the top' 74
top-down structures 154, 239, 292–293
Torbert, B. 177
Touboulic, A. 292
trans-generational needs 329, 335, 336
Transition Towns Movement 7, 246–247
transportation, and retail 287
trickle-down models 198, 291
Triodos Bank 228–229
Triple Bottom Line 81–82, 86
Trump, Donald 4, 44, 58, 105, 107, 180, 221; anti-science agenda 125, 127; charismatic authority of 134–135; and constitutional maturity 134; on the 'deep state' 131; and Evangelical Christians 129–130; lies 133; and political correctness 62
Trump administration 105, 107; and alternative facts 132–134; anti-science agenda 125, 130–131, 136; attacks by 133; Bureau of Land Management 122–123; and the CDC 132–133; and climate change 103–104, 122; and climate change denial 122–123, 125–126, 130; and COVID-19 120–121, 123, 132–133; and creationist education policy 128; and environmental protections 121–122, 136; and the EPA 122, 124; Evangelical support for 128–129; and fossil fuel industries 122, 134, 136; Great American Outdoors Act (2020) 108; and inexperience 133; and propaganda techniques 127
truth 136, 255
Tullis, P. 211–212
Tuomala, Virva 7–8, 282–304, 400

Ulrich, W. 184
Underdal, A. 273, **274**, 275–276
Undergrowth Movement 7, 244–248, 250–253, 255
Undergrowth projects 245–247
Unilever 211–212
United Kingdom 60, 61; Centre for Alternative Technology in Zero Carbon Britain 333; Climate Change Act (2008) 316; climate change leadership interventions 324–326; Climate Change Risk Assessment (CCRA3)

319–320, 335; environmentalism 248; Environment Bill (2020) 84; and Generation Z 83; high streets 285; immigration in 64; and international dependence 223; lack of climate mitigation financing 314; non-governmental environmental leadership 99–100; Portas Pilot Schemes 285; retail in 285; statistics 286; *see also* Brexit; Wales
United Nations Conference on Trade and Development (UNCTAD) 76
United Nations Sustainable Development Goals (SDGs) 74, 81, 283, 315, 345–346
United States: and acid rain 25–27; Affordable Healthcare Act (Obamacare) 134; American Antiquities Act (1906) 95; and the Arctic National Wildlife Refuge 108, 122; Boone and Crockett Club 95; Bureau of Land Management 122–123; Capitol riots 58; Center for Disease Control and Prevention (CDC) 132–133; Clean Air Act 27, 105; Clean Power Plan 121, 124; climate-related inquiries in 23–24; and COVID-19 133–134; cultural icons in 5; Dakota Access Pipeline protests 94; Dawes General Allotment Act (1887) 93; education policy in 128; electric cars 159–160; emissions caps 269; Environmental Protection Agency (EPA) 24, 105, 112, 122, 124; environmental racism in 93–94; fisheries policy in 95; and the GOP 95, 105–111, 125, 127; Great American Outdoors Act (2020) 108, 113; and greenhouse gas emissions 5; Green New Deal 107, 110–111; Homestead Act (1862) 93, 95; indigenous peoples in 93–95, 112; Kyoto Protocols 271–272, 275; national monuments in 122; and Native Americans 93–95; New Deal 94, 98, 107; non-governmental environmental leadership 99–101, 103; Penn State University 23; property rights in 43; Racketeer Influenced and Corrupt Organizations (RICO) Act 19; religion 129; research in 351; Supreme Court 112; voting in 103; water rights in 93–94; water shortages 107; White House Council on Environmental Quality 27; wildfires in

107; *see also* American Dream; Trump administration; West (US)
universities 83
University of East Anglia (UEA) 23, 31–32; Climatic Research Unit (CRU) 14, 23, 33; hacking at 29; *see also* 'Climategate'
urban environments 290; informal settlements 291
urban food security 289–290, 292–294
urban infrastructure 290
urbanisation 289–290
urban planning 294
US Global Change Research Program 105–106
utilitarianism 214–215, 221, 402
utility: measuring 214; *vs.* virtue 216

vaccines, and COVID-19 131
values: changing 54; defining 41
'values bombing' 61–62
values conveyors 52–53
Values Maps 49
Values Modes 44, 51; Force value 53–54, 55–57, 58; groups in 45–48, 49–50, 52, 58, 60, 61, 62, 64–65; *see also* Cultural Dynamics model
vegetarianism 77–78
vehicles, as systems 156
Vickers, I. 69
virtue ethics 214–215, 243
virtues 242–245, 254–256
Vis, P. 277
von der Leyen, Ursula 261, 264
voting, in the US 103
VUCA world 157

Walden (Thoreau) 96
Wales 311, 401; climate change and leadership in 327–328, 331; climate change leadership interventions 324–326; and climate change planning 8, 314–316, 319–322, 334, 336, 337; Climate Change Risk Assessment (UK CCRA3) 319–320, 335; Climate Ready Gwent 320; Climate Resilience Pilot 322–323; decarbonisation focus 317–318; Fairbourne 323–324; Fishguard 322–323; Flood and Coastal Erosion Risk Management Strategy (2020) 318–319; and flooding forecasts 316, 318–319, 323–324, 335; government

311, 314–318, 331; Government of Wales Act (1998) 315; and local governments 314–315, 317, 320–322, 334–335, 338n4; *Prosperity for All* report 317–318; Sustainable Development Alliance 325; Wales Green Recovery Action Plan (2020) 319; Well-being of Future Generations Act (2015) 311, 315, 317, 329–331, 334; *see also* United Kingdom
Walker, H. 292
Wallström, Margot 269
Warren, Kelcy 135–136
wars, casualty rates of 43
waste, increasing amounts of 283
water rights, in the US 93–94
water shortages, in the US 107
Watson, Paul 102
Weber, Max 132–134
Welzel, Christian 43–44
West (US): attitudes towards 92–93; popularisation of 96–97; *see also* United States
Wettestad, J. 269–270, 276
whaling 102
What Is to What If (Hopkins) 247
What Makes People Tick: The Three Hidden Worlds of Settlers, Prospectors and Pioneers (Rose) 41
White-Cain, Paula 129–130
White House Council on Environmental Quality 27
Whitman, Christine Todd 130
Whittington, J. L. 313
wicked problems 178
wilderness: exploiting 93; Leopold on 98
wildfires, American West 107
Wilks, Dan 135
Wilks, Farris 135
Wilks, Jo Ann 135
Williams, R. 1
Wilson, E. O. 40, 42
The Winning of the West (Roosevelt) 95
women: and social signals 169; and the Undergrowth Movement 252
wood chopping 239
Worcester, Sir Robert 41
work, redefining 224–225
World Development Report: 'Mind, Society, and Behavior' report 149
World Values Survey 41–42
World Wildlife Fund 267

INDEX

Xing, Y. 301

Young, O. R. 273, **274**, 276
Young Evangelists for Climate Action
(YECA) 102, 109–112; *see also* religious
environmental groups
YoungGens 300–303; *see also* Generation Z;
millennials
youth leadership and climate change
6, 72–73, 75–83, 176; education for
182–183; and Evangelist religion
109–110; examples of 180–181; *see also*
environmental leadership
youths 402; as consumers 284; influence
of 85; and protests 176; and the SDGs
74; statistics on 74; *see also* school strikes

Zankina, E. 135–136
Zehndorfer, Elesa 4–5, 120–137, 397
zooming in/out 167

Printed in the United States
by Baker & Taylor Publisher Services